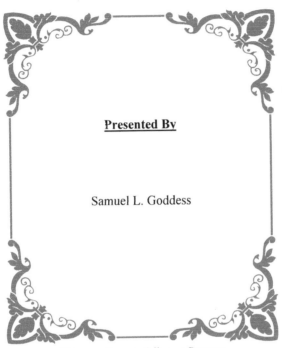

Presented By

Samuel L. Goddess

IRON MEN
WOODEN BOATS

The Epic Story of
American PT Boats
in World War II

Howard F. West

2005

EAGLE EDITIONS
AN IMPRINT OF HERITAGE BOOKS, INC.

Books, CDs, and more – Worldwide

For our listing of thousands of titles see our website
at
www.HeritageBooks.com

Published 2005 by
HERITAGE BOOKS, INC.
Publishing Division
65 East Main Street
Westminster, Maryland 21157-5026

International Standard Book Number: **0-7884-2537-4**

CONTENTS

LIST OF ILLUSTRATIONS

All photos Courtesy of WWII PT Boats Museum and Archives,
Germantown, Tennessee, USA, unless otherwise noted

PT base 17, Bobon Point, Samar, the Philippines 388

An S-boat, or *Schnellbooten*, Germany's motor torpedo boats 388

At the end of the Pacific war, the Japanese command of by-passed Halmahara Island surrendered formally to Allied commanders on nearby Morotai Island. .... facing 388

MAPS

INTRODUCTION

O ne of the more baffling things in naval history is the way in which a type of ship or weapon designed for one purpose turns out to be useless in that role but very valuable in another. For example, the original task of aircraft carriers, the basis of naval power today, was to provide an "air umbrella" for the fleet focused on the "Queen of the Sea," the battleship. During World War II, the aircraft carrier became *the* offensive weapon without peer, and battleships became mere protectors of the flattops or were used as bombardment ships supporting amphibious landings. Destroyers, originally intended as "torpedo-boat destroyers," with the demise of torpedo boats became *the* indispensable vessel, necessary to combat the threat posed by the submarine, and as fleet and convoy escorts. So it was with motor torpedo boats. Designed as a weapon system to attack enemy warships at night with torpedoes. Early in the war, at Guadalcanal, that function proved futile, when it was not suicidal.

However, it was quickly discovered that the PTs' guns provided a necessary counter to Japanese motorized barges (*daihatsus*), which in the Central Solomons and New Guinea, soon became the enemy's major surface craft delivering supplies and reinforcements to his island garrisons. In the end, armed with heavier guns providing increased fire-power, with radar added, PT boats became the ultimate "barge busters," as the role was termed by the PT crews. As a consequence, during the rest of the war the PTs' torpedoes became a sort of vermiform appendix for lack of employment. Indeed, more PT boats would be lost due to running aground while hunting enemy barges close to island shores than in any other activity; far more in fact, than were lost while making torpedo attacks on ships.

In addition to their major role of sinking barges, during World War II PTs were called upon to support amphibious landings, act as troops transports, to secretly land and pick up spies from hostile shores, and to land reconnaissance and raiding parties behind enemy lines. PT boats also served as ambulances for ground troops wounded in combat, as taxis for generals and admirals, as couriers, and on occasion as mine layers. In the European theater, the boats were also used to guard Allied ships against the threat of attacks by enemy motor torpedo boats; and in the Philippines toward the end of the war, to defend Allied shipping against attacks by small Japanese suicide boats. Altogether, not bad for a boat designed solely to attack ships with torpedoes.

For all of their accomplishments, as war clouds gathered over the Pacific in September 1941, PT boats were few and far between in the U.S. Navy, as were crews to man them. Indeed, the few PT boats available were still in the experimental stage when the Pacific War erupted.

That the U.S. Navy even had any PT boats was something of a miracle. By World War I there had been a proliferation of small, hit-and-run torpedo-armed boats. But it was the Italian Navy that led the world in their development. Powered by their excellent Isotta Fraschini engines, by the end of the war, the Italian Navy employed some 350 MAS boats, standing for Motoscafo Armato SVAN, after the yard in Venice that built them, and later, Motoscafo Anti-Sommergible (motor anti-submarine boats). Among their most notable accomplishments were the sinking of the Austrian cruiser *Wein* at Trieste on December 9, 1917, and the battleship *Szent Istvan* on June 8, 1918 in the Straits of Otranto.[1]

With the end of World War I, the Italian Navy continued to improve its motor torpedo boats, to train crews, and develop a doctrine for operations based on its wartime experience, followed closely by Germany. For the U.S. Navy, dominated by admirals favoring battleships, otherwise known as the "Big Gun Club," motor torpedo boats continued to be of no interest. In all fairness, it should be noted that for the navies of the day, battleships were considered the standard by which naval power was judged.

In 1936, scattered individuals within the U.S. Navy, aware of the technological advances being made in European navies in developments of motor torpedo boats, on their own initiative urged the American navy to consider use of such craft. In December, Rear Admiral Emory S. Land, Chief of the Navy's Bureau of Construction and Repair, submitted a note to Chief of Naval Operations, Admiral Leahy, drawing attention to the fact that much had occurred in the way of motor torpedo boat advances since the end of World War I: Admiral Land suggested the U.S. Navy consider use of motor torpedo boats as a defensive force protecting coastal regions, freeing larger warships for offensive operations on the high seas.[2]

Leahy passed the note on to the Secretary of the Navy Claud Swanson, who in turn, sent it to the Navy's General Board for consideration. The Board responded that while the use of such craft might be limited in peacetime in view of America's geographic location, "...future situations might occur under which it would be possible for such small craft to be used on directly offensive missions - as is no doubt contemplated in certain foreign navies." The Board proposed the initiation of a modest developmental program. On May 7, 1937, the Secretary of the navy endorsed the Board's recommendation.[3] There is reason to believe the Board reached its conclusion as the result of President Roosevelt's influence. As Assistant Secretary of the Navy during World War I, Roosevelt had become convinced of the value of such craft; the result was a Congressional appropriation of fifteen million dollars for the development of a suitable boat, to be spent at the discretion of the President. Finally, the U.S. Navy was committed to a force of motor torpedo boats. But the boats were still far from being a reality.

Shortly after the appropriation, the Navy sponsored a design contest for such craft; the significant specification called for a 70-foot boat armed with two 21-inch torpedoes, depth charges and antiaircraft guns, with a top speed of over 40 knots and a 550-mile cruising range. September 30, 1938 was the deadline for submission. By that date the Navy had thirty-seven proposals on hand, doubtless due to the fifteen-thousand-dollar prize going to the winning design. Five designs coming close to the required specifications were chosen; the Navy then asked for more detailed plans by November 7, 1938.

Seven months later, after studying the detailed plans submitted, the Navy announced contracts would [be] awarded to three winning private boat yards for construction of six experimental boats based on their respective designs. In addition, the Navy would build two 81-foot boats at the Philadelphia Navy Yard designed by its own Bureau of Ships. Appropriately, these first boats were numbered *1* through *8.*

By now, the service had adopted the term "Patrol Torpedo Boat" for its soon to be acquired craft, with each boat to be given a "PT" number, thus assuring forevermore that American motor torpedo boats would be called "PT boats."[4] Additionally, the Navy decided the boats would be formed into 12-boat squadrons, as opposed to the 6-boat-flotilla motor torpedo boat units common to European navies. By now, World War II, with Hitler the prime instigator, was a mere three months away.

At this point the American PT program took an historic turn: Assistant Secretary of the Navy Charles Edison, aware the experimental boats were at least a year away from completion, decided it would be wise to have a backup plan. He proposed obtaining a British MTB for purposes of comparison.

The Board agreed, stating "inasmuch as said design is known to be the result of several years' development, the General Board considers it highly advisable that such craft be obtained as a check on our own development."[5] With the approval of the President, and with five million dollars remaining of the original fifteen million, Edison put his own plan into motion.

As it would have been politically unwise for the U.S. government to purchase a boat from a foreign country, such action being virtually certain to prompt cries of protest from American boat builders and the organized unions, Edison approached Henry R. Sutphen, the executive vice president of the multi-division Electric Boat Company of Bayonne, New Jersey. In what today would seem unthinkable, he proposed that Sutphen travel to England aboard a liner at his own expense, with no written agreement. Once in England, Sutphen would evaluate Britain's various MTBs: the executive would purchase one, with his own money, and ship it back to the United States with an eye toward building the boat under license for the U.S. Navy. Sutphen accepted the proposal, sailing for England on February 10, 1939.

Arriving in England, Sutphen proceeded to duly examine the British MTBs. On the basis of speed and maneuverability, as well as its sleek lines and grace so pleasing to the eye, he selected the 70-footer built by the British Power Company.[6] As *PT 9*, the boat would be the "forerunner" of the Elco boats that equipped the majority of the American PT squadrons of World War II.

In September 1939, Sutphen returned to New York with the purchased boat secured on the deck of the SS *President Roosevelt*, along with three Rolls-Royce engines and the rights to manufacture the boat in the United States. Hitler's armies having invaded Poland, World War II was two days old.

Given the slow progress by the builders of the other experimental boats, Edison recommended the President spend the remaining five million dollars on as many duplicates of the British Power Boat as the money would cover. In fact, tests would reveal the 70-foot boat was unsatisfactory.

The duplicate 70-footers and *PT 9* were then handed over to the Royal Navy under lend lease agreements to be used in the Mediterranean. And with a new construction program on hand as part of a fifty million dollar appropriation, the Navy requested Elco add seven feet to the stern, bringing the overall length of the boat to seventy-seven feet. The Navy had decided that unlike the British boats fitted with two torpedoes, its PTs would be armed with four torpedoes, too much of a load for a 70-foot boat. The Navy ordered twenty-nine of them. It was the new 77-foot Elco boat soon to be built as an experiment, that with the outbreak of the Pacific war would end up as the first American PT to face combat.

Even as Elco was building its lengthened 77-foot PT, the Higgins Industries of New Orleans was preparing a 76-foot competitor. Andrew Higgins, owner of the Higgins Yard, using his own funds, was building the boat with the understanding that the Navy would purchase the craft if it proved satisfactory. Like the Elco, the Higgins boat was powered by three 1200-hp Packard engines.

At this point the Navy decided there was need for comparisons. In August 1941, the Navy began PT tests, evaluating such qualities as seakeeping, structural strength, and maximum sustained speed. Termed the "Plywood Derby" by newspapers, the tests included a 190-mile run that soon became a race. Starting at New London, Connecticut, the course ran around Block Island; out to and around the Fire Island Light Ship; around the Montauk Whistling Point Buoy, and finally back to New London.[7]

Another contender of note would be the Huckins Yacht Corporation of Jacksonville, Florida. Unlike other boats, Huckins's PT was powered by four Packard engines, two each in two separate engine rooms. Like Andrew Higgins's boat, the Huckins boat was built at the expense of the company with the same agreement.

By the conclusion of the tests, Elco's boats had demonstrated their superiority and proved to be the fastest boats; the Higgins did almost as well, with the added advantage of being able to turn tighter than the Elco. Least satisfactory was the Huckins. Its tendency to yaw excessively in a following sea was one flaw; and while in echelon formation, the boat would fall off the bow wave ahead causing the helmsman to lose control.

Based on the results, the Navy had decided there was need for boats between 75 and 82 feet in length: its PTs would carry additional ordnance along with the four torpedoes. The three companies were thus asked to submit designs for boats accordingly. After duly considering the designs submitted, contracts were let to the three builders; Elco was asked to build thirty-six boats of its 80-foot design; Higgins to build twenty-four of its 78-foot boat design, and Huckins, eight boats. All would be powered by Packard engines and would have to exceed 40 knots. It was now December 1941.

The first 80-foot Elco, *PT 103,* was laid down in January 1942, to be completed in May. At thirty-eight tons, it was five tons heavier than the 77-foot Elco. Although slightly slower than the 77-footer, it had the advantage of better sea-keeping qualities. Not only was the 80-footer a better riding boat, but also it could carry a greater warload, a factor that was to prove invaluable during World War II. It was this boat, operated by most South Pacific squadrons, that came to symbolize the American PT in action. From 1942 to 1945 when building ceased, Elco would build 326 80-foot PT boats.[8]

Not as well known as Elco, the 78-foot Higgins, the second major PT boat to equip the Navy's squadrons, also played a key role. Displaced thirty-five tons, sometimes termed a box with a point on one end by its detractors, Higgins PTs had a more spacious deck than the Elco or Huckins. But since the engine room occupied fully half the space below decks rather than the quarter of space on the Elco, the Higgins's crew's quarters were extremely cramped. Higgins would build 199 78-foot PT boats before the war's end halted construction. Of these, one hundred forty-six would serve in the U.S. Navy, the remainder in the navies of Britain and Russia.[9]

As a weapon system, the heart of a motor torpedo boat lay with its engines and torpedoes. With the engines, the U.S. Navy was lucky. For the Italian Navy's MAS boat it was the Isotta Fraschini, superior marinized aircraft engine; until Italy joined Germany in

World War II against Great Britain, the Italian engines had powered the British MTBs, since the British built Rolls-Royce was confined to use by the Royal Air Force. For the U.S., it was the Packard, the only high-performance marine engine available to the Navy.

That the Packard engine even existed was due largely to the efforts of Garfield Wood, a wealthy industrialist with a passion for racing. During the 1920s, Wood had realized that the marinization of aviation engines was the way to success in the sport of boat racing. He chose to develop the 750-hp Liberty aircraft engine designed by E.J. Hall of the Hall-Scott Company and J.G. Vincent of Packard Motor Company. During the 1920s and early 1930s, Wood's Packard powered boats reigned virtually supreme in competition for the prestigious British International Trophy. By 1928, Wood's hydroplanes, with 1,000-hp Packard engines, were capable of 90 knots. In 1933, driving *Miss America X* with four 1,600-hp supercharged Packard engines, Wood established the world speed record at 108.4 knots.[10]

This is not to say that Gar Wood lacked competition. One of his most formidable challengers was a British sportsman, Hubert Scott-Paine. As owner of Britain's Supermarine Aviation, Scott-Paine had built the 1922 winning aircraft of the world famous Schneider Trophy Race, going on from there to become a leading figure in the founding of British Airways.

By 1927 Scott-Paine had established the British Power Boat Company, ironically the same British Power Boat Company that a decade later would provide the U.S. Navy with its "pattern" boat, *PT 9,* the basis for the Elco PT boat.

In 1928, Scott-Paine was approached by the famous land-speed record holder, Sir Henry Seagrave, and asked to design and build a boat to beat Gar Wood and return the absolute water speed record to England. The result was *Miss England;* Scott-Paine arrived in America in 1928 with his 28-foot hydroplane to compete against Wood and his *Miss America VII.*

Due to complications, the Trophy race between the two boats never occurred, and Wood retained the Trophy against all competitors, culminating in the last race in 1933. That year, Scott-Paine returned to America for one more effort to reclaim the Trophy. Unfortunately, by that time, with Rolls-Royce Merlin engines allocated for RAF use, Scott-Paine's *Miss Britain III* was powered by a single 1,400-hp Napier Lion engine. This was not sufficient to equal *Miss America X*'s speed of 100 knots plus.

By this time, Wood had invested thousands of dollars of his own money along with the Packard Company in supercharging the engine. For the U.S. Navy, having failed to develop a high-speed marine engine for use in small craft, with the decision to build PT boats, Wood's engine proved to be virtually ready-made for the Navy. Modified for PT boats, the militarized 12-cylinder supercharged Packard engine was superior to all other available engines of this type in America. Providing 1200-hp, later increased to 1350 and, before the end of the war, to 1500-hp, Packard engines would power all U.S. PT boats. In the fall of 1940 the Packard Company established a training school for the Navy's engineer PT personnel at their plant in Detroit.[11]

Also, following the entry of the United States into World War II, Packard engines began to power Britain's MTBs, replacing the Napier-Lion engines on those boats; this resulted in a ten-knot speed increase, giving the MTBs a top speed of 40 knots plus. For PT boats operating in the South Pacific, where Japanese destroyers were capable of speeds in excess of 35 knots or more, the American PT boats would need all the speed the Packard engines could provide if they were to survive engagements with the enemy.

Unfortunately, a fact critics overlook, the armament for the PTs was not of the same quality as the engines. Designed as a weapon system centered on torpedoes, the sad fact is that the PTs' torpedoes as well as its torpedo launching system, were a disaster, rendering the PT a questionable weapon system in the role for which it was intended. Indeed, naval historians agree that American World War II torpedoes were the worst of all navies' torpedoes in the war, and the torpedo that armed the PT boats, the Mark VIII, was the worst and most flawed of all U.S. torpedoes. Designed and built in 1913 for destroyers, the Mark VIII torpedo had been in storage since then. These vintage missiles, twenty-one feet in length weighing 3050 pounds, were big and heavy, with a slow speed of 28 knots, and a relatively small three-hundred-pound warhead at a time when warships averaged 30 knots or more, and torpedo speeds averaged 35 knots plus with warheads of four hundred to five hundred pounds;[12] yet, in all fairness, they were the only torpedoes the Navy had to arm their PTs at the time.

Lest there be any doubt, tests carried out after the war began determined that 63 percent of the of the Mark VIII torpedoes were defective—some were duds, failing to detonate on impact—others prematured, that is exploded during the run and before reaching the target, revealing the presence of the PT to the enemy. Some torpedoes ran deeper than they were set, passing beneath the targeted ship, or worse, porpoised, and ran erratically, again revealing the presence of the PT to the ships' gunners.

Equally troublesome was the PTs' torpedo launching system. Carried in heavy welded steel tubes, the torpedoes were heavily greased before being inserted in the tube so as to assure a smooth ejection when fired via a black powder charge set off electrically by firing buttons located on the bridge, giving the skipper control of when the torpedoes were to be fired, and in what sequence. In the event of a malfunction, a torpedoman was posted by each torpedo tube with a wooden mallet to hit a manual percussion cap. In practice, however, during a night attack, the black powder frequently ignited in grease in the tube as the torpedo emerged, resulting in a brilliant red flash providing a target for the alert enemy ships' gunners. In addition, the torpedo left the tube theoretically at a velocity of forty feet a second, clearing the deck by some five feet plus. But sometimes, there were partial or complete torpedo misfires: in the case of a partial misfire the torpedo's tail fins might strike the deck causing an erratic run, a miss; or the torpedo could emerge partially from the tube to hang suspended while its engine made a "hot run." Although there was no danger of the warhead exploding, unless stopped within seconds the missile's engine could disintegrate, showering lethal pieces of steel across the deck.[13]

In mid-1943, the Navy provided the PTs with the new Mark XIII aerial torpedo. Although lighter in weight at 1,927 pounds, and slightly faster at 33.5 knots, sadly the new torpedo proved as trouble-prone as the discarded Mark VIII torpedo. Fortunately, owing to developments in the Pacific war, from mid-1943 to the end of the war, with enemy motorized barges their prime opponent, there was little need for the PTs' torpedoes as it was a rarity for the boats to encounter enemy ships among the islands of the South Pacific.

Intended primarily for antiaircraft defense, the twin-.50-caliber Browning machine guns on all PTs mounted in two turrets were hard-hitting weapons firing 300-400 rounds per minute, with armor-piercing and incendiary rounds, and with every fifth round a tracer, an orange ball helping the gunner zero in on his target. The guns were also useful against small craft and as anti-personnel weapons. Shortly after the war began, a 20-mm Oerlikon cannon was mounted aft on the PT's fantail. Firing at a rate of 450 rounds per minute, with a range of 5,500 yards, the new weapon gave the PTs the increased firepower they so sorely needed. Sixty rounds of high explosive and tracer shells were carried in a magazine. Thus armed, experience would show that a PT boat attacked by aircraft, considered its nemesis before the war, had a better than even chance of emerging the winner.

With the PTs tasked with sinking motorized barges, heavier guns were nonetheless necessary. Resourceful PT skippers in the Solomons and New Guinea soon acquired single-shot 37-mm cannon from local army units, mounting the weapons forward on the PT's bow. With a range of 8,875 yards with armor-piercing and tracer shells, the new addition proved highly effective as a weapon against barges and small enemy craft. With its proven value, the 37-mm cannon soon became a factory installation on new PTs.

Arguably, however, the PTs' most effective weapon against barges was the 40-mm Bofers cannon. Appearing on the boats in mid-1943, with rate of fire of 130 rounds per minute, the Bofers with its three-man-crew, a pointer, trainer and loader, had a range of 5,420 yards. With each round weighing on average two pounds, this weapon made the PT boats true "barge busters."[14]

By the latter part of the Pacific war, virtually every PT boat was armed with a Bofers cannon mounted aft; the 20-mm cannon initially fitted aft was moved to the foredeck for added firepower. By now, PT boats could be better termed gunboats carrying torpedoes. Added personnel necessary to man the guns increased crew size to generally two officers and fifteen men for a total of seventeen crewmen.

Under the pressure of events, even more weaponry was added: Normal PT armament included at least two depth charges for use against submarines; since PT boats lacked underwater detection gear, the 300-pound depth charges proved more valuable in discouraging pursuing enemy destroyers, as was sometimes the case.

Of particular value on PT boats in their new and varied role was an 81-mm mortar mounted on what was now an increasingly crowded foredeck. The mortar could be employed when approaching a suspected enemy position on islands where dense vegetation grew down to the water making the PT's guns less effective. Mortars were also useful in illuminating targets with flares, and against barges that stubbornly refused to sink under gunfire.

While not armament in the strict sense, any description of PT boats is incomplete without mentioning their smoke dispensers. Fitted with a standard Navy type smoke generator, a refillable tank was secured by an emergency release strap. PTs retreating under fire after an attack sometimes used the quick release strap, dropping the generator over the side while still emitting smoke to discourage or mislead pursuing enemy destroyers or blind enemy shore batteries. Later, Elco designed its own smoke generator, a non-refillable steel bottle resting on wooden blocks secured by two steel straps. A nozzle fitted on the end of a two-foot long pipe spewed a dense cloud composed of titanium tetrachloride. But the smoke had to be used with discretion so as not to provide a screen for the enemy rather than the PT, or used in a manner that hindered other vessels attempting to attack the enemy.

Mufflers were the second essential PT equipment rarely mentioned in articles concerning PTs. Indeed, when stalking the elusive enemy barges in the blackness of night along hostile shores, stealth was essential: Normally a PT's three aircraft type engines could be heard for miles on a tropical night. With the exhaust stacks fitted with butterfly valves, the PT's engineer could close the stacks, routing the exhaust gases down through the mufflers to emerge underwater, permitting the boat to glide silently along with the only sound the hiss of water along the hull. Standard procedure called for engines to be muffled as the PT slowed its approach to enemy-held shores where the boat would begin to hunt for enemy barges attempting to deliver supplies or reinforcements to the enemy garrisons ashore. However, with the mufflers engaged, care was necessary to not run the engines at too high an rpm to prevent damaging backpressure. In general, the maximum speed a PT could travel with mufflers engaged was around 12 knots.

One last item of note adding immeasurably to the PTs' effectiveness was radar. With radar sets on virtually all vessels today, it is hard to imagine that at the start of World War II, radar was just being installed on the U.S. Navy's heavy ships. For PT boats, there would be no radar until later. During the early months of the war, in the Philippines, no less than in the hard-fought Guadalcanal campaign and the first uncertain months in New Guinea, PT skippers depended solely on the eyes of their lookouts with binoculars to detect the enemy in the darkness. Not until mid-1943 would the PTs begin to receive radar, special sets designed for PT boats.

By the latter half of 1941, with the surprise attack on Pearl Harbor only months away, time was running out for the Navy with its PT program. With contracts let to three builders, it would be several months before the new boats were completed and delivered; more time would be needed to train crews and form new squadrons. As yet, no PT doctrine existed concerning tactical operations. Not until March 1942 would the Navy establish its PT training center at Melville, Rhode Island. All the Navy had were the twenty-nine 77-foot experimental PT boats provided by Elco. For the first time in its history, the U.S. Navy was about to find out just how effective its PTs were in actual combat.

By December 7, 1941, the Navy had formed its twenty-nine PTs into three squadrons. Squadron 1 with twelve boats was based at Pearl Harbor, commanded by Lt. Comdr. William C. Specht. Squadron 2 comprising eleven boats fitting out in the New York Navy Yard was due for shipment ten days later to Panama to augment the defense of the Canal, commanded by Lt. Comdr. Earl S. Caldwell. Squadron 3 with six boats was based at Luzon's Cavite Navy Yard on Manila Bay in the Philippines and was commanded by Lt. John D. Bulkeley; they arrived in the islands on September 28, 1941, barely a week prior to the attack on Pearl Harbor.[15] By the time the war ended, the U.S. Navy would employ PT boats in every theater of war, from Alaska to the Panama Frontier, from Pearl Harbor to the Philippines, and from the Mediterranean to the English Channel.

FIRST BLOOD

B anks of clouds clung to the peaks of the mountains east and west of Pearl Harbor. Below, the waters of the Harbor—originally named Wai Moni, "water of pearl"—reflected the brilliant blue of the sky above. In the distance a few civilian aircraft circled lazily; but the only military planes in the air were seven Navy PBYs on patrol many miles to the southwest. Aboard the seventy combat ships and twenty-four auxiliaries of the United States Pacific Fleet below, duty crewmen went about their routine chores; since it was Sunday and the nation was at peace, their duties were light. Most officers and men were deep in sleep following a Saturday night ashore in Honolulu, many nursing hangovers.

On this Sunday, December 7, 1941, few ships had steam enough to make a quick sortie in case of an emergency. Few guns were manned; the same applied to plotting rooms and ammunition storage compartments. Indeed, in accord with standard procedure, the ammunition itself was under lock and key, the keys in possession of the officer of the deck on each vessel. Ashore, the Army was equally off guard. Of the area's thirty-one antiaircraft defense batteries, only four were in position, and they could be discounted since their ammunition was stored in depots, unavailable for immediate use.[1] To Comdr. Mitsuo Fuchida, the leader of the Japanese air armada circling over the west coast of Oahu, it was apparent that surprise had been achieved: the time was 7:53 a.m.

At Pearl Harbor's submarine base, a short distance from Battleship Row, six PT boats of Squadron 1, numbers *20* through *25*, lay moored alongside a covered barge serving as a tender. Shortly before 8 a.m., a puzzled Ens. N.E. Ball, the squadron duty officer, gazing across Kuhua Island, noted numerous aircraft orbiting over the west coast of Oahu. At first, he thought the aircraft were part of the series of practice alerts that had been common during recent days. Suddenly, Ball's heart skipped a beat; he had glimpsed a Rising Sun on the wings of one aircraft. Almost immediately, a bomb exploded and a towering column of smoke rose from the harbor. Dashing into the nearby mess hall where a number of PT men were eating breakfast, Ens. Ball sounded the alarm, shouting, "We're under attack! Man the guns!"

For seconds, the men sat in frozen disbelief, then there was a mad scramble for the door. Even as they did so, two sets of twin .50-caliber machine guns began firing from one of the moored PTs: GM1/c Joy Van Zell de Jong and TM1/c George B. Huffman had been relaxing on the deck of *PT 23* when the planes swooped down. Scrambling into the boat's two turrets, the two men barely had time to charge their weapons before a low-flying Japanese torpedo plane appeared; the two opened fire, and watched as the riddled plane crashed near Kuhua Island. It is thus possible that the guns of a PT boat were the first to draw blood in the Pacific war.[2] Shortly, the two PT gunners shot down a second torpedo bomber, the last aircraft crashing near Halawa, behind the submarine base.[3]

Below decks on *PT 23*, Ens. Edward I. Farley was sound asleep, having returned at 4:30 a.m. from the Royal Hawaiian Hotel. Awakened by the boat's chattering machine guns he sleepily hurried on deck clad only in his undershorts to stare in horror as Japanese torpedo planes swept in low with practiced precision to drop one torpedo after another aimed at the defenseless battleships. Two miles from the submarine base, the second six boats of Squadron 1 were in the process of being loaded aboard the U.S.S. *Ramapo*, an oiler slated to transport the boats to the Philippines. Four boats, *PTs 27, 29, 30* and *42*, were already on cradles secured on the ship's deck. *PTs 26* and *28* were in cradles still on the dock alongside the ship.

In preparation for the voyage, as part of shipping procedure, their gun turrets had been immobilized. After considerable effort, the frantic PT crews managed to get the guns into action, but there is no confirmation they brought any of the enemy down.[4]

By now Pearl Harbor was a nightmare of burning ships and exploding bombs. Within three minutes of the start of the attack, the battleships *Arizona* and *California*, along with 1200 American sailors were doomed. Aboard the *Oklahoma*, crewmen heard a crump and a boom as a torpedo hit; then a second torpedo hit and the ship's lights went out. The massive vessel began to list to port. Within twenty minutes, the battleship began to roll over, finally coming to rest with her bottom and screws out of the water, her superstructure resting on the mud bottom about twenty-five feet below.

Within thirty minutes, the Japanese had achieved their primary goal; the destruction of the United States Pacific Fleet's battle line. In addition, the attack had damaged the Army and Marine Corps air bases on Oahu, and destroyed thirty-three aircraft on Ford Island, plus Army aircraft. In a little over an hour and forty-five minutes, American air power in Hawaii, along with the Navy's battle line had been virtually destroyed. In all, the United States had lost 2,403 killed with 1,178 wounded. Japanese losses numbered a mere twenty-nine planes and pilots. Studying the incoming reports, Vice Admiral Chuchi Nagumo, commanding the carrier strike force, remarked to his staff, "We may conclude that the results we anticipated have been achieved.[5]

Back at Pearl Harbor, Lt. Comdr William C. Specht, the commander of PT Squadron 1, breathed a sigh of relief: all twelve of his boats had survived the devastation around them. But wild rumors abounded: there was the pervasive fear that a powerful Japanese invasion fleet was on the way. "They could have come in canoes and we couldn't have stopped them," one soldier said later.

Later that morning, the six PTs moored at the submarine base got underway and cruised the harbor to aid in rescuing men from the debris-littered, oil-covered water and carrying them to the hospital landing. The shipment of six PTs scheduled for the Philippines was cancelled. Shortly, Squadron 1 began a round-the-clock patrol of Pearl Harbor. Their skippers were cautioned to be especially alert for submarines. In preparation for this unanticipated role, crews improvised: two long wooden slats were arranged on the sterns from which depth charges manhandled into position were dropped on the numerous periscopes sighted; however, close inspection revealed the periscopes were in fact the handles of mops floating vertically, belonging to recently sunken ships.[6]

It was early morning December 8 in the Philippines, four time zones and 5,123 miles to the west, when the telephone jangled in a dark room inside the officers' quarters at the Cavite Navy Yard, eight miles southeast of Manila. Lt. John D. Bulkeley, commanding PT Squadron 3, sleepily picked up the receiver: "We're at war," a voice blurted, "The Japs have just bombed Pearl Harbor." The voice added in a more carefully controlled tone, "the Old Man wants to see you right away." The 'Old Man,' otherwise 'the boss' in common military vernacular, was Rear Admiral Francis W. Rockwell, commandant of the Cavite Navy Yard. An alarmed Bulkeley checked his watch; it was a few minutes past 3 a.m. Like many in the U.S. military scattered across the Pacific, over the past weeks Bulkeley had expected an aggressive move on the part of the Japanese. What surprised him was that the target was far away Hawaii rather than somewhere in the much closer Philippines. Bulkeley awakened one of his young PT skippers, Ens. Anthony Akers, telling him the grim news. The soft-spoken Texan thought Bulkeley was kidding: With his eyes still closed, he mumbled, "It's a hell of a time to be declaring war!"[7]

Dressing hurriedly, Bulkeley jumped in a jeep to be driven to Admiral Rockwell's headquarters, the Commandantia, an old, thick-walled Spanish structure in the Cavite Navy Yard. Dawn was breaking when Bulkeley arrived to find the grim-faced Admiral standing outside. Staring skyward expectantly, the Admiral instructed Bulkeley to move his PTs from Cavite across Manila Bay to Mariveles Harbor at the tip of the Bataan Peninsula opposite the island of Corregidor, known as "The Rock." It was clear the Admiral expected an enemy air attack on U.S. facilities in the Philippines.

Bulkeley departed to carry out the Admiral's instructions, unaware that as a low-ranking Navy lieutenant, he had gotten the momentous news of the Pearl Harbor attack before Gen. Douglas MacArthur, commander of U.S. Army forces in the Far East: shortly before 3 a.m., the Marine duty officer had relayed a message received by his operator from a brother operator at Pearl Harbor saying it was under attack by the Japanese. The duty officer had immediately passed the information to his superior, Vice Admiral Thomas C. Hart, commanding the Asiatic Fleet, MacArthur's opposite number. Hart immediately drafted a message to the Fleet: JAPAN STARTED HOSTILITIES. GOVERN YOURSELVES ACCORDINGLY[8], thus prompting Admiral Rockwell, among other actions, to instruct Bulkeley to move his PTs out of danger in the event of an expected enemy air attack. Not until around 3:40 a.m. did MacArthur's phone ring in the penthouse at the Manila Hotel. An Army private listening to a San Francisco, California, radio station had learned of the attack; the information was quickly relayed to MacArthur. By this unusual method the general learned of the attack on Pearl Harbor.[9]

The surprised general dressed quickly and headed for his headquarters in Manila. In truth, as with most admirals of the U.S. Navy, Admiral Hart's relations with MacArthur were strained. MacArthur's paranoia and posturing, his conviction that the U.S. Navy was his enemy, had led to a virtual lack of direct contact between Admiral Hart and the general.

At around 5 p.m., following a confused and tense day, in accord with his orders, Bulkeley arrived at the Cavite Navy Yard dock where three of his six PTs were moored under the command of Lt. Robert B. Kelly, his Squadron second-in-command. Bulkeley instructed Kelly to head for Mariveles Harbor and "Remain on the alert and ready to attack 'anything' I order you to attack."[10] Bulkeley and Kelly were well aware that as the first American PT squadron to go into combat, their tactics would be based on trial and error; so new were the PT boats to the U.S. Navy that no operational doctrine for combat had yet been established.

Following a tension-filled passage through the darkness to Bataan, Kelly reached his destination, a submarine tender serving as a PT base, providing food, ammunition, gasoline, torpedoes and spare parts, all items necessary for PT operations. But now, Kelly received shocking news: the tender's skipper had orders to head out to sea toward an unknown destination to the south. Kelly's PTs would be on their own. By daylight the tender was gone.

But there was more bad news: Kelly learned that the available gasoline and oil had been sabotaged, the gas with wax to clog PT engine carburetors, the oil with sand to damage the engines. It was a problem the PT crews of Squadron 3 would encounter and struggle to cope with throughout operations in defense of the Philippines.

Later that day, fourteen Japanese bombers struck Baguio, the summer capital of Luzon, while eighteen bombers from Formosa bombed the island's north central airfields. At 12:45 in the afternoon, the Japanese struck again, bombing and strafing the airfields near Manila. These attacks on the first day of the war destroyed a third of MacArthur's Far Eastern Air Force. As a result, the Japanese had little cause to fear MacArthur's defenders.

On the second day of the war, December 9 in the Philippines, due to poor flying weather, the air over the Philippines was quiet. But early on the tenth, the weather cleared. Just before noon, Lt. Kelly at Mariveles, received word of a massive formation of enemy aircraft approaching from Formosa headed toward Manila. Immediately, Kelly led his three PTs into open water to prevent being caught like 'sitting ducks' moored to the docks. Bulkeley similarly led his three PT boats away from the docks at Cavite.

Soon a large formation of Japanese aircraft appeared, approximately fifty-two "Zero" fighters, escorting over eighty bombers. The PT crews watched as the Japanese leisurely flew back and forth at 20,000 feet for over two and a half hours, beyond range of the three-inch antiaircraft guns in the Cavite Yard. The enemy's bombing was accurate; almost all bombs fell within the Yard. From his nearby office window, Admiral Hart watched in helpless rage at the destruction of his base. Soon the entire Yard and about a third of the city of Cavite were in flames.[11]

From offshore at Cavite, the crews of the PTs stared skyward, waiting expectantly for the swarm of U.S. fighters they knew would rise from nearby airfields. But the minutes dragged by and no U.S. fighters appeared.

Offshore in the bay the PTs made easy targets. Five bombers separated from the main body and dove on Bulkeley's three PTs. The boats went to full speed, zigzagging as bombs fell nearby. The pilots made strafing runs. Bulkeley's gunners countered, opening fire with .50-caliber machine guns. MoMM2/c Joseph C. Chalker, manning one turret, fired his guns, as did TM1/c John L. Houlihan, Jr. firing from the second turret. The combined .50-caliber machine gun fire of the two men hit one attacking aircraft. The plane began to smoke, then plunged into the bay two miles away. The PT gunners continued to fire on their attackers: two more enemy aircraft went into the bay. Ironically, the PT boats designed to attack ships with torpedoes, by use of machine guns had again struck a blow against the enemy by shooting down aircraft.

Nonetheless, there was no feeling of elation. At Cavite Navy Yard, disaster followed disaster. With the Yard in flames, there would be no spare parts for the PT boats, no replacement engines; equipment, repair shops, and thousands of gallons of gasoline, all necessary for operations, were gone. The PT crews watched as the Japanese departed in flawless formation in the direction of Formosa. When Bulkeley finally led his PTs back to Cavite, he learned why there was no air opposition: there had been other Japanese targets; MacArthur's airfields were in ruins: Nichols, Clark, Nielson, Vigan, La Union and San Fernando had been devastated. For all practical purposes the U.S. Army Air Corps in the Philippines had ceased to exist. The blow dealt to U.S. forces in the Philippines was, by now, if anything, more crippling than the raid on Pearl Harbor.

Shortly after 3 p.m., Bulkeley's PTs began transporting the seriously wounded to the Canãcao hospital. Returning to the Yard, Bulkeley found Adm. Rockwell personally engaged in leading the effort to extinguish the flames at the ammunition depot. The Admiral warned Bulkeley that it was dangerous for the PT officer to be there as it could explode at any time. When Bulkeley offered to take the Admiral to the relative safety of Bataan, Rockwell replied that his job was to remain at his post and to try to save the depot.[12]

Two days after the enemy bombing, one of Bulkeley's officers, Ens. George Cox, returned to Cavite. The scene that greeted him was a horror that defied description: he estimated the enemy bombs had killed over one thousand men; most were Filipino workers. On this day, the dead were being buried. With heads, legs, torsos and assorted human parts scattered among the rubble, the American officers were having trouble collecting men to do the burying. As a solution, the officers provided huge amounts of alcohol which the workers consumed. To Ens. Cox's horror, the burial procedure consisted of collecting the various body parts and pitching them into bomb craters, then using shovels to cover them up.

With the destruction of Cavite Navy Yard, Bulkeley was forced to establish another base for PT operations. This was to be in Sisiman Bay, just east of Mariveles Harbor. There he found a small cove with a rickety old fishing dock. Nearby were *nipa* huts, decrepit straw structures mounted on stilts that could be used as quarters for the men.

Over the next week, Bulkeley's PTs patrolled regularly, alert for signs of the enemy, but no Japanese vessels appeared. However, on December 17, just before midnight, a massive explosion jarred the PT men awake at Sisiman cove. Dashing from the *nipa* huts the men ran to the shore; they saw tiny lights flickering on the dark water. Three PTs rushed to the scene to find scores of bobbing heads scattered about. Crews rigged makeshift ladders and tossed lines over the side to haul desperate people aboard. They were survivors from the 'SS *Corregidor,* a converted interisland steamship. The elderly vessel had been en route from Manila to Cebu crammed with some thousand men, women and children, largely Filipino civilians, fleeing the capital ahead of the advancing Japanese army. Among the passengers were Jack Fee, manager of the Cebu office of the Standard-Vacuum Oil Company, and his wife, Dode, three months pregnant, both of them American.

Cutting through the black waters of Manila Bay toward the exit, shortly before midnight the old vessel's engines died; in the sudden blackout, she began to drift. Then came an explosion: the *Corregidor* had struck one of the American mines guarding the entrance to Manila Bay and immediately began sinking. Chaos erupted as masses of people struggled in panic to climb in the life boats or find life jackets.

The lines the PT crewmen tossed were immediately grasped by desperate hands of people who were then pulled aboard. The young PT crewmen pulled until their arms were numb but still there were people to be rescued.

When it finally appeared that all survivors were aboard, Bulkeley gave the order to head the boats for shore. By now the PTs were laden with oil-covered Filipinos. Only after the survivors were ashore did the PT men learn they had rescued 296 refugees; among them were Jack and Dode Fee. Bulkeley's boat alone delivered 197 refugees to safety. "The miracle of the loaves and fishes has been repeated," the squadron commander observed.[13]

The first Japanese landings in the drive toward Manila had occurred on December 8, well away from Manila, which explains why Bulkeley's PTs in Manila Bay saw no signs of the enemy. A second assault followed on the tenth. On December 12, additional enemy troops landed at the tail end of Luzon. MacArthur estimated the enemy's main landing would be in Lingayen Gulf, 125 miles north of Manila, then there would be a drive southward over the central plain of Luzon to the capital.

Since Japanese air forces now completely controlled the air over Manila Bay and with the enemy advancing, MacArthur realized further defense of Manila was hopeless: on December 24, to buy time while he urged that Washington send reinforcements, MacArthur decided to withdraw to Bataan where he would fight a delaying action; meanwhile, he would move his headquarters to Corregidor. That same day, Admiral Hart decided to withdraw his fleet from the Philippines, and move his headquarters south to the Dutch East Indies. As he explained to a bitter MacArthur, who again felt betrayed by the Navy, with the destruction of the general's air force, U.S. ships in the Philippines were helpless against the continued enemy air assaults. For the ships to remain would only mean their eventual destruction.

On Christmas Eve, Admiral Hart held his final conference in the Philippines with his flag officers; all would be leaving for Java, he explained, taking with them every U.S. vessel except a few small craft: three gunboats, a few tugs and the six PT boats of Squadron 3, all deemed expendable. Admiral Rockwell, with headquarters on Corregidor, would remain behind to command them. After these vessels had been expended, the crews would be disbanded to fight as infantrymen with the ground troops. It was hard to believe: just three weeks had passed since Pearl Harbor.[14]

For the men of PT Squadron 3, conditions were already going from bad to worse. Owing to the extreme food shortage afflicting MacArthur's defenders, naval personnel were limited to two meals a day. Hunger was thus an added problem.

Among MacArthur's staff, the mood was equally grim: late Christmas Eve, at dusk, with Japanese troops closing on Manila, MacArthur, his family and staff along with a hundred others, boarded the interisland *Don Esteban* at the Manila dock for the trip to the blacked-out island of Corregidor, thirty miles away. Off the vessel's port bow, Cavite still burned. A dense pall of smoke drifted over Manila, the odors of burning oil and cordite filled the air. Aboard the small vessel there was only silence, the only sound to be heard was the hiss of water against the vessel's bow and the chugging of its engine. It was hard to believe it was Christmas Eve.

For the next three months, the tadpole-shaped, two-and-a half mile long island of Corregidor, two miles south of the Bataan Peninsula in the mouth of Manila Bay, would be MacArthur's headquarters. MacArthur had barely arrived before he summoned one of his staff officers, ordering him to return to Manila to retrieve some documents, adding, "while you're in my apartment, look in the drawer of my bedside table. You'll find my Colt .45—the one I carried in the First World War." The officer carried out MacArthur's instructions riding aboard one of Bulkeley's PT boats.[15]

On the night of December 31, Bulkeley and his men finally got a chance to strike a blow at the enemy. But it was a mission far removed from the intended role of a PT. Taking one boat, with engines muffled, Bulkeley headed into Manila Bay. His orders were to sabotage what shipping was in the harbor.

With Manila illuminated by flames, the single PT slipped soundlessly into the harbor. In the darkness, to the tense crew, almost every vessel in the harbor seemed a likely place for enemy snipers. Ashore the crew could see the orange glow and the death pall of smoke hovering over the doomed city once known as the Pearl of the Orient. They were so close they felt certain they glimpsed the silhouetted helmets of the enemy moving through the Manila streets. Dimly the PT men discerned the outline of the Army and Navy Club ashore where American officers had previously spent many a pleasant social hour; now the building stood dark and silent. Suddenly, lights flashed on inside: Ens. Akers, standing beside Bulkeley in the boat's cockpit, became suddenly angry. "Goddamn them!" he exploded in a stage whisper. "I had to leave my spare uniforms in a locker there. I hope none of them fit the bastards."[16]

At a few minutes before 9 a.m., crewmen began clambering from the PT's deck into smaller craft moored in the harbor; using axes they smashed holes in the bottoms leaving them to sink. To the Americans, it seemed the sound of the blows could be heard for miles. On the larger craft, the men placed explosives timed to detonate after they were clear of the harbor. Six hours after returning to Sisiman Cove, at 3 a.m., on the first day of 1942, the sabotage mission was complete. The PT with engines still muffled departed the harbor still undetected by the enemy.

MacArthur's initial challenge was to manage the withdrawal of his troops into Bataan. On the morning of January 10, the general traveled by PT boat from Corregidor to Bataan to visit the men and boost morale.[17] But it was clear that the situation was bad. Inside the tunnels on Corregidor, Admiral Rockwell jotted a note in his diary: "Motor torpedo boats are rapidly deteriorating due to lack of spare parts and bad gasoline...Because of [constant] emergency trips and patrol duties their crews are becoming exhausted."[18]

It was a gloomy assessment; and it was about to get worse. With Bulkeley's boats virtually the only U.S. fighting vessels remaining in the islands, the PTs continued to patrol. And wax in the contaminated gas continued to clog carburetors, which had to be cleared almost hourly; what was particularly unnerving was not knowing when the engines would stop. On Christmas Day, as a result of wax in the gas, the squadron suffered its first casualty when *PT 33* grounded on a coral reef after engine failure while on patrol south of Manila Bay. When all attempts to free her failed, she was set aflame to prevent her falling into enemy hands.

On January 18 Lt. Bulkeley was called to Corregidor. There he was handed a brief message by Capt. Herbert Ray, Admiral Rockwell's chief of staff: "Army reports four enemy ships in or lying off Port Binanga. Force may include one destroyer, one large transport. Send two boats, attack between dusk and dawn."[19] Army reports were not noted for accuracy in ship identification. In any event, it seemed as though there was finally an opportunity for the PTs to carry out a mission of the type for which they had been designed.

Bulkeley returned to Sisiman Cove to prepare for the night's mission. By now, his reputation for courage bordering on being reckless had earned him a nickname: the "Wild Man of the Philippines." If anything, his appearance more than confirmed the term: under constant stress, operating under primitive conditions for over a month, Bulkeley's shirt had been torn, his uniform was soiled and wrinkled. The squadron commander had grown a black unruly beard, and his green eyes were bloodshot due to long hours of night patrols. No less intimidating was the fact that the he was heavily armed with a pistol strapped to his hip, and a Tommy gun cradled on one arm. And from his manner, it appeared he would not mind using it. Not that his crews looked less intimidating.

For this mission, Bulkeley decided to use *PT 31* commanded by Lt. Edward G. DeLong, and *PT 34,* temporarily under the command of Ens. Barron W. Chandler, replacing the boat's regular skipper, Lt. Robert Kelly, who had been hospitalized at the Corregidor hospital with a serious infection. Bulkeley would ride on *PT 34* as officer in tactical command.

Port Binanga was located at the top end of Subic Bay, about ten miles deep, bordering the northwest shore of Bataan. The port as well as both shores of the bay were held by the enemy. Bulkeley's plan called for the two boats to enter Subic Bay and then split up, the *34* boat proceeding north along the western shore, the *31* boat making its way up the eastern shore. At the top of the bay, the two PTs would meet again outside Port Binanga. If one failed to arrive, the other would enter and attack alone; at dawn, if separated, the two PTs would rendezvous outside the minefield at Corregidor before entering Manila Bay and returning to Sisiman Cove.

It was close to midnight when the two boats arrived outside the entrance to Subic Bay. Slowing to reduce their telltale wake, with engines muffled down for silent running, they crept inside the bay, then parted as planned. But quickly there was trouble: Chandler's boat had not gone far when a searchlight ashore snapped on: its beam soon caught *PT 34* in its glare. Chandler altered course, managing to evade the light. But then came the crack of a shore battery echoing across the water. Fortunately, the enemy's aim was off and the shell passed overhead to land in the water beyond the boat. In any event, the PT continued to slip silently through the darkness. Shortly, an unidentified vessel flashed a challenge. This was ignored: then more shore batteries began firing: it appeared the Japanese feared an invasion was in progress. Again the enemy's aim was faulty—and *PT 34* continued north toward its objective undamaged.

At 1 a.m., Chandler's PT reached the entrance to Port Binanga. When after a brief wait, and when the second PT failed to appear, Chandler entered the port alone, keeping his speed at a slow 8 knots with mufflers engaged.

Inside the port it was deathly quiet. Too quiet. The tense crew sighted a massive vessel less than 500 yards away: but this was no cargo ship, nor was it even a destroyer; the silhouette was that of a massive 6,000 ton Japanese cruiser.

The *34* boat continued to slip closer. Suddenly—as if on cue, the ship's searchlights snapped on, the beams illuminating the PT in a brilliant glare. With the range down to 300 yards, Chandler shoved his throttles forward as he gave the order, "Fire." Two torpedoes leaped from their torpedo tubes. As quickly as the missiles cleared their tubes and hit the water, Chandler threw the boat in a hard right turn and went to full speed. As the PT began zigzagging its way back toward the exit, the PT crew heard a massive explosion.

Looking back, the men saw a spectacular fireball erupt at the ship's waterline and arc toward the sky.

But there was no time for elation: shells from the cruiser's guns along with those of nearby shore batteries were falling close by. Moreover, one of the PT's torpedoes had failed to fully emerge from its torpedo tube. Hanging half way out of the tube, the rising scream of the torpedo's engine was not merely unnerving; there was the possibility it would disintegrate, sending lethal hot pieces of steel slicing through the air. It fell to TM John Martino to close the valve on the runaway torpedo engine and end the danger. Emerging from the port, the crew finally relaxed a bit. They had made a successful attack and escaped. Finally back at the entrance to Manila Bay at dawn, *PT 34* again waited for the arrival of DeLong's *31* boat. When again it failed to appear, *PT 34* returned to Sisiman cove alone.[20]

Not until two days later did the mystery surrounding the disappearance of *PT 31* become known with the return of its few survivors. As DeLong reported, after the PTs split up, the *31* boat immediately ran into trouble. It began with when the engines died; the problem proved to be wax-clogged gasoline strainers. Under shielded lamps, the motor macs, working frantically, managed to clear the strainers and restart the engines; then the engines' cooling system quit. As the motor macs struggled to make the repairs, there came a grinding crunch: the boat had drifted hard aground. For three hours the frantic crew struggled to free their boat, burning the reverse gear out in the process.

By now, the commotion had attracted the attention of the Japanese ashore. A battery, possibly a three-inch gun, opened fire from Ilinin Point. As the enemy gun began to find the range the shells fell closer.

DeLong was finally forced to give the order so dreaded: "Abandon Ship!"

With no life raft aboard, the crew had to improvise: mattresses were wrapped in a tarpaulin and dropped over the side and all scrambled aboard, all that is except DeLong, who remained aboard to destroy the boat to prevent it falling into enemy hands.

With the use of a hand grenade, DeLong blew a hole in the PT's bottom and set the boat afire. That done, he tried to spot the raft in the darkness. But by now, however, the raft had drifted out of sight. With *PT 31* now burning and ammunition starting to explode, DeLong clambered off the boat on the side toward the shore and made his way across the reef to the beach, fully, as he said later, expecting to find a Japanese reception. But he was alone.

Meanwhile, lacking paddles, the men in the improvised raft were drifting out into the bay. With dawn approaching, bringing with it the danger of being sighted by the enemy, the men held a conference: nine men voted for shore where they could hide. Three who could not swim remained. The three, Ens. William H. Plant, MoMM1/c Rudolph Ballough, QM3/c William R. Dean, would never be heard from again.[21]

With the coming of daylight, moving cautiously along the shore, DeLong spotted fresh tracks in the sand. On a hunch, he followed them; they led into the brush. There he found the nine crewmen who had swum ashore. All that day the men remained concealed. Between them, their armament consisted of one rifle and six pistols, not enough to take on the many Japanese soldiers that were all around. DeLong told his men that unless they were attacked by enemy scouts, in which case the men would "club their brains out" with the butts of the rifle and pistols, they would stay hidden.

Still seeking a means of escape, DeLong spotted two *bancas,* native canoes, a few hundred yards down the beach. When investigation showed they seemed seaworthy, at dusk, the ten men crawled toward the *bancas.* Having found a board and two shovels for use as paddles, when it was dark, sometime around 10 p.m., the men shoved off. Thirty minutes later, a stiff wind swept across the bay capsizing both *bancas.* After a struggle, the men righted the craft and clambered back inside.

But they had now lost one shovel; this left one board and one shovel between the two boats, making them difficult to steer in the wind and heavy seas. For two hours, the men battled the elements, taking turns with the improvised paddles. By 3 a.m. they were exhausted. The men held a conference and it was decided that, despite not knowing where they were, whether they were opposite a Japanese or American shore, they would head for land.

Once ashore, the men were confronted by a steep cliff. DeLong decided they would wait there until daylight. At dawn, the men spotted a man standing watch with a rifle: it turned out to be a Filipino soldier; they had come ashore in the American zone. By nightfall, the exhausted survivors were back at Sisiman Cove. For the squadron, the joy of seeing the men return was tempered by the loss of the PT and three crewmen; now there were only four boats. As for the missing men, Bulkeley was not prepared to accept the fact that the men were not still alive.

By now Lt. Kelly had been released from the hospital at Corregidor. During his battle due to an infected finger, he had lost thirty-four pounds, weight he could ill afford to spare from his lanky frame. Despite all, Kelly had badgered the doctors to be released until they finally gave in. Now with Kelly back in command of *PT 34,* a few nights after the loss of *PT 31,* on the night of January 22, Bulkeley decided to make a sweep of Subic Bay in hopes of finding the three missing men.

Heading into the bay under cover of darkness, the *34* boat soon found itself under fire from shore batteries. An incensed Bulkeley recognized the guns as American. "The main problem these nights," Bulkeley told Kelly, "is trying to keep from being sunk by our own side on shore. Half the time those dumb bastards don't know friend from foe."[22]

A short time later, the *34* lookouts spotted the dim form of a vessel. As Kelly headed the PT toward the vessel, Bulkeley cautioned the gunners to hold their fire as it might be Ens. Plant and the other two survivors.

With the distance narrowing between the PT and the unknown craft, Bulkeley raised his megaphone and called: "Boat ahoy." In response, from a distance of twenty-five yards, a stream of machine gun bullets snapped past his head and ripped through the PT fourteen times. One round struck Ens. Chandler; with a cry of pain,

Chandler slumped in the cockpit bleeding profusely. A bullet had gone through both of his ankles. Immediately the PT gunners opened fire with their twin .50-caliber machine guns as Bulkeley grabbed his Tommy gun and joined in.

What the *34* boat had encountered was a motorized enemy landing barge, about fifty feet in length, loaded with helmeted armed soldiers. At its top speed of 8 knots, the barge headed for Bagac Bay. *PT 34* circled the barge at high speed three times firing into the vulnerable flanks. Sixteen minutes after the attack began, the barge had gone under. In the darkness, it was not possible to find survivors, but *PT 34* remained in the area for ninety minutes searching for more barges. Finding nothing, Kelly moved closer to shore in his search, but fire from a "friendly machine gun and a three-inch battery" forced him back out to sea.[23]

Ensign Chandler was given first aid and a shot to relieve the pain, and *PT 34* continued to patrol. As dawn approached, Kelly headed for home. At 6:10 a.m., in the faint pre-dawn light, the *34's* lookouts sighted a second landing barge three miles offshore. Having learned from his previous encounter, Kelly closed at high speed; at four hundred yards the gunners opened fire on the barge. This time they faced another problem: it turned out the vessel was heavily armor-plated and the PT's .50-caliber bullets merely ricocheted off the armor.

Suddenly the enemy vessel lost power: smoke began to billow skyward; with the barge now on fire and the engines dead she began to drift; even so it continued to return fire.

"Pull up alongside her," Bulkeley told Kelly. "I'm going to board the bastard."

As Kelly sought to ease the PT alongside the vessel, the enemy driver threw his helm hard over in a effort to ram. An infuriated Bulkeley grabbed a handful of grenades and began pulling the pins and tossing them into the barge. As the explosions died down, Bulkeley, clutching his Tommy gun, leaped aboard the smaller craft, landing in several inches of water, oil and blood.

A quick glance showed most of the Japanese sprawled in grotesque positions; some twenty-seven were dead. Three were still alive, but badly wounded, however. Each of the three was hoisted aboard the PT by a line around his shoulders.

With the barge sinking, Bulkeley quickly sorted through the mess that littered the vessel, returning to the *34* boat with his arms filled with papers and knapsacks. With that, Kelly finally headed PT *34* home.

Before returning to Sisiman Cove, Kelly paused at Corregidor where the wounded Ens. Chandler was taken ashore to be hospitalized. The Japanese captives and papers from the sinking barge were turned over to Army intelligence officers. They would prove of value. Examination of the documents disclosed the enemy planned to mount a landing involving some eight hundred to a thousand marines behind American lines on Bataan. The plan called for the enemy to hide in caves until the entire force was assembled before attacking American ground troops from the rear. The two barges engaged by *PT 34* on January 22-23 were part of that operation. By then some four hundred enemy troops were already ashore and in hiding.

Because of the rough seas and disruption caused by the *34* boat, the Japanese plan was thrown out of kilter. On the night of January 24, following the *PT 34's* engagements, Ens. George Cox departed Sisiman at the helm of *PT 41* to patrol Bataan's west shore. Approaching Subic Bay, he slowed and crept inside with mufflers engaged. About a half-mile from shore, Cox sighted a 6,000-ton enemy cargo ship. The PT commander started a torpedo run at high speed. At eight hundred yards he fired his starboard torpedo; it hit the water and made a normal run. The explosion shattered the cargo ship sending debris flying through the air. At five hundred yards Cox fired his second torpedo. But the tail fins of the torpedo hit the edge of the PT's deck as it was ejected; this caused the torpedo to run erratically and end up on the nearby beach.

As Cox turned at full speed to strafe the ship with his guns, a "friendly" shore battery began firing, forcing Cox to withdraw toward the sea as shells rained nearby. The PT boat emerged unscathed and with at least one torpedo a positive hit, the attack was deemed a success.[24]

A PT boat idles into Manila harbor, one of six boats in the understrength Squadron 3 commanded by Lt. John Bulkeley based in Manila at the outbreak of the Pacific war. Arriving at Manila in September 1941, by April 1942, Squadron 3 would no longer exist, the boats lost in a futile battle in support of MacArthur's troops against advancing Japanese. *Courtesy of WWII PT Boats Museum and Archives, Germantown, Tennessee, USA.*

CHAPTER TWO

A GENERAL'S ESCAPE

The sun was nearing the end of its plunge toward the eastern mountains of Luzon as Lt. Bulkeley backed the *41* boat clear of the dock in Sisiman Cove. By now, dark shadows blanketed the lower levels of the island. With the suddenness common to the tropics, the blackness of night would soon follow. Although the squadron commander appeared calm, he was unusually concerned. Ahead lay one of the greatest single challenges to be thrust upon a PT officer during the war.

Two weeks earlier, General MacArthur had summoned him to Corregidor, telling him in strictest confidence that the president was ordering him to Australia. Bulkeley learned the PT boats would carry the general from Corregidor to Mindanao, some 600 miles to the south. From there, MacArthur would continue on to Australia in a B-17 dispatched from Australia to Mindanao for that purpose.

For MacArthur, the decision to leave the Philippines had been difficult. Initially, he had been determined to fight to the end. But when informed by Washington that an army was in Australia waiting to be led back across the Pacific, and that this provided the best solution for preventing defeat in the Philippines, MacArthur had agreed to the escape plan.[1]

Bulkeley learned that MacArthur was to remain at Mindanao a week, long enough to organize a defense for the southern Philippines before continuing on to Australia in the bomber.

Original plans called for MacArthur to depart Corregidor on March 15 aboard the submarine *Permit,* but the vessel was unable to reach Corregidor before March 13, and there was reason to believe the Japanese had learned of the planned escape and intended to prevent it.

Indeed, that MacArthur meant to escape from the island fortress was an open secret, evaluated on American radio stations and written about in the newspapers.[2] On Corregidor, U.S. naval officers discussing the plan, assessed MacArthur's chances as one in five against.[3]

To the Japanese, with their air and sea cordon around the Philippines extending over 2000 miles outward, the idea that MacArthur might slip through and reach Australia some 2500 miles distant was ludicrous. "It was all too apparent," Bulkeley wrote later, "that the Japanese Navy not only expected General MacArthur to leave Corregidor, but would do everything it could to intercept him."[4] Days before the escape date, in a radio broadcast, the sultry-voiced Tokyo Rose, slated to become so familiar to Allied personnel in the Pacific during the war for her propaganda programs, after playing the usual popular American recordings, predicted that MacArthur, rather than escaping, would be captured, locked in a cage and put on display in a large square before Emperor Hirohito's palace in Tokyo. In a following program days later, she made a more ominous threat; she promised the general would be hanged in the Imperial Plaza as a criminal.[5]

As the time approached, signs the Japanese were determined to prevent MacArthur's escape increased. Filipine scouts reported a Japanese destroyer flotilla steaming north from the southern Philippines at full speed. Other reports told of increased Japanese activity north of Corregidor, in Subic Bay. On March 9, MacArthur again summoned Bulkeley to Corregidor, saying they would depart for Mindanao after sunset, Wednesday, March 11.

Bulkeley returned to Sisiman to brief his PT skippers: Now, for the first time his four PT commanders, Lt. Robert Kelly, (*PT 34*); Lt. Anthony Akers, (*PT 35*); Lt. George Cox, (*PT 41*); and Lt. Vincent Schumacher (*PT 32*)[6] learned about the escape plan. In what would best be described a grim atmosphere, the Squadron 3 commander explained the plan. With Japanese ground forces steadily closing in, and no help on the way, defeat was only a matter of time. The squadron officers had discussed escaping to China, some thousand miles to the northwest. Once there they meant to continue the war against the enemy. But Bulkeley's words dashed that hope. The likelihood now was, that if they survived the voyage, they would become prisoners of war confined in a Japanese stockade.

For the voyage, Bulkeley laid down three main rules: above all, the boats would remain together; second, should a boat break down, the others would continue on, leaving the stranded PT to make its own way; third, the enemy was to be avoided. If fast Japanese warships began to pursue and were overtaking, Kelly would lead three of the PTs in an attack on the pursuers, while Bulkeley with the *41* boat carrying MacArthur, made an escape. The last order was not one Bulkeley was comfortable with, but his instructions were to deliver the general to Mindanao's Port of Cagayan, on the north coast of the island at 7 a.m. Friday. Enemy engagements along the way were out. It was an order that all understood.[7]

For Lt. Bulkeley, an immediate concern was the decrepit condition of his boats. Standard practice called for the replacement of the Packard engines after 600 hours' operations.[8] But the engines in Bulkeley's PTs had four times the hours, and tired engines made for slow boats. For Bulkeley's crews, the PTs designed for 42-knot top speed was a dim memory; on average, 27 knots was the best they could manage, with some even slower. With Japanese destroyers and cruisers capable of speeds in excess of 35 knots, the threat was obvious. Furthermore, as was evident, owing to poor maintenance due to a lack of facilities and the constant patrolling over a three-month period, the boats and their equipment were less than reliable.

For the trip, Bulkeley would have to rely on charts of doubtful accuracy; for navigation, the squadron commander would be virtually dependent on a compass alone, along with dead reckoning, skills seamen had practiced in the previous century with sailing ships, but rarely needed by PT skippers operating among the South Pacific islands.

In an effort to evade enemy planes and surface vessels, travel would only be at night. Roosevelt had authorized the escape of the general only. The War Department amended the order to include wife Jean and four-year-old son Arthur. But the autocratic MacArthur had his own ideas: He would decide who and how many would accompany him.[9] In the end, the four PTs would carry sixteen passengers—fourteen Army and two Navy.[10] Rank was not the basis for the selection; one passenger was a staff sergeant, a technician. All were key personnel, however; people MacArthur felt he needed when he reached Australia to help organize the return. However, it was the presence of young Arthur's Cantonese nanny, Ah Cheu, that would provoke the greatest criticism. MacArthur justified her as a passenger on the grounds that the Japanese would view her as one of the MacArthur family and torture her to death.[11]

According to Bulkeley's plan the *41* boat would carry the general, his wife and son and Ah Cheu. The rest of the escape party were divided among the other three PTs. Even more than was usually the case, the PTs would be floating bombs. Due to the long voyage ahead, each boat carried twenty fifty-gallon steel drums of 100-octane gasoline lashed on deck for refueling purposes.[12]

By the time *PT 41* reached Corregidor it was dark. The island's cliffs rising steeply over five hundred feet above were now concealed; the devastation caused by the constant Japanese bombing was for the moment invisible, but in the daylight, one saw that much of Corregidor's green foliage had vanished under the pounding blasts from artillery shells and bombs.[13] Few buildings and trees had escaped.

Bulkeley deftly maneuvered the PT alongside the island's North Dock where MacArthur and his family stood waiting, barely visible in the darkness. Earlier, the squadron commander pointed out to the general that there was no food available on the boats for the passengers. MacArthur's wife and his naval aide had quietly collected what they could, mostly tinned food.[14]

With limited space and weight a critical factor on the PT boats, Bulkeley allowed each passenger thirty-five pounds of possessions in one suitcase. The squadron commander carried the general's luggage aboard himself. Jean MacArthur's possessions were in a valise: a dress, a pantsuit and a coat; Ah Cheu carried her possessions folded in a handkerchief. Arthur had a stuffed toy and a six-inch-long toy motorcycle. There was no room for his tricycle; it had to be left behind.

MacArthur, out of uniform for this momentous occasion, wore brown wingtip shoes with bright checkered socks, and carried his toothbrush in his pocket. His one familiar apparel was his gold-braided cap.[15]

Finally, at this most bleak and mournful moment, MacArthur stood alone on the dock, the last one to board. As the PT's engines idled, its crew stood ready to cast off its mooring lines. The general, his face pale, his back toward the boat, stared upward into the darkness that concealed the high cliffs. It was as though he was reluctant to leave.

Finally, lifting his cap in a final salute, he turned briskly and stepped aboard the PT. At the same time, as if on cue, U.S. artillery on Corregidor commanded by Col. Paul Bunker, a West Point Academy classmate of MacArthur's and an All-American halfback when the general managed its football team, opened fire, the thunder of the guns intended to provide a diversion for the escape. Col. Bunker would be among the Americans captured at the fall of Corregidor; he would die in a Japanese prison camp before the war ended.

Precisely on schedule, Bulkeley headed the *41* boat into the darkness. For security reasons, the other three boats had taken their passengers aboard at obscure points. At exactly 8 p.m., the four boats joined together.

The crews and passengers were tense. Last-minute reports warned of a Japanese cruiser and destroyer approaching Corregidor, possibly to prevent MacArthur's escape.

With the *41* leading, the other boats following, the PTs trailed in the wake of a slow-moving minesweeper making its way through the defensive minefield outside the entrance in the darkness beyond Corregidor. Once clear, the PT skippers pushed their throttles forward; the sound of twelve unmuffled Packard engines was deafening. Heading south, the boats formed a diamond formation; the *41* at home plate; Ens. Akers, (*PT 35*) at first base; Kelly (*PT 34*) at second base; and Lt.(jg) Vincent Schumacher (*PT 32*) at third base.[16]

As travel was limited to hours when it was dark, the plan called for the boats to reach Tagauayan in the Cuyo Islands, roughly midway toward Mindanao, by dawn. They would remain concealed there during Thursday, and leave at 5 p.m. to arrive Friday morning at the Port of Cagayan. Should MacArthur wish to switch from the PT boat en route, the submarine *Permit* would be waiting at Tagauayan to transport the General the rest of the way underwater.

As it turned out, virtually nothing went according to plan. The trip was barely under way before things started to go wrong. All that afternoon the seas had been building in Mindoro Strait. Bulkeley meant to skirt the islands keeping the land on his port bow where the waters would be smoother as he headed south. But huge bonfires sprang up along shores of Cabra and Apo Islands—the age-old signal that a nighttime attempt to escape through a blockade was in progress. Fearing the Japanese ahead would be alerted to their approach, Bulkeley led his force westward until they were hull-down over the horizon.

For the next few hours, hammered and tossed by stormy seas, the boats struggled to maintain their formation. But then Kelly's boat began to lag, the distance increasing steadily.[17]

Bulkeley slowed the formation in hopes it would solve the problem. It helped briefly. But at 3 a.m., the 34's engines died; the remaining PTs continued south, leaving PT 34 behind.

With the disabled PT now rolling steeply in the heavy seas, the motor macs worked feverishly to restart the engines. The source of the problem turned out to be the familiar wax-contaminated gasoline; thirty-five minutes later, the engines coughed, sputtered, and rumbled back to life. By then, however, Kelly was hopelessly behind the other boats. In any event, Bulkeley had provided an emergency plan, an alternate cove in the Cuyo Islands. With daylight approaching, Kelly headed for the cove.[18]

Meanwhile, all had not gone well for the other three. Thirty minutes after Kelly's engines died, the other boats, battling huge seas and with limited visibility, lost contact with one another. After a fruitless three-hour search, Bulkeley gave up and, now behind schedule, like Kelly, he headed for the same alternate cove. For Lt. Schumacher, the experience was the same. Unable to locate the other two boats, he also headed his PT toward the cove. At dawn, Schumacher spotted a pursuing enemy destroyer. With his boat at full throttle, the enemy continued to close. In desperation, the 32 boat skipper jettisoned the drums of gasoline stored in deck. When the enemy continued to gain, as a last resort, Schumacher prepared to fire his torpedoes. Only then did he recognize the approaching vessel as PT 41; the early morning mists had distorted the silhouette. But it was too late, the damage had been done. Without the extra gasoline in the drums, Schumacher's PT could not reach Mindanao. Worse, the pounding seas had loosened the struts holding the prop shafts and the hull was leaking; and further inspection showed that two of the three engines were finished.

Daylight found the three PTs moored in the alternate cove. As one of MacArthur's officers observed, "they were a sorry looking crew."[19] The fate of the fourth PT, commanded by Ens. Akers, was still unknown. Later it would be learned that Akers' boat had been disabled by the same wax-contaminated gas that crippled Kelly's boat.[20] It would finally reach Mindanao under its own power.

There were other problems: the huge seas and the pounding by the PT boats had caused extreme misery among the boats' passengers; particularly three of Bulkeley's passengers; MacArthur, his son and Ah Cheu, had become seriously ill, with young Arthur running a fever. Hardest hit of all, however, was MacArthur. Wracked by nausea, his stomach long since emptied of any contents and subjected to the unceasing pounding of the PT, it could have been a fatal experience for the sixty-two-year-old general.

And there was the schedule. Having been forced to take cover well short of the halfway point, they would be unable to cover the remaining miles to arrive at Mindanao as scheduled unless they risked traveling during daylight. And there was the matter of the *Permit,* waiting at Tagauayan in the event MacArthur chose to switch vessels.

Bulkeley warned MacArthur that the coming night's seas would be as bad if not worse than the previous night. Not surprisingly, the general was tempted to change to the undersea vessel. But Admiral Rockwell, one of the passengers, cautioned that the submarine might not have reached Tagauayan. Rather than take a chance, he argued that it was better to head directly for Mindanao.

After a brief period, MacArthur made the decision. Despite the risk of being sighted by enemy ships or aircraft, they would leave the cove while it was daylight and head straight for Mindanao. If all went well, they would arrive as scheduled.

At 4:30 a.m. Thursday, with the passengers and crew from Schumacher's abandoned boat divided between Kelly's and Bulkeley's boats, they got under way. This time, Kelly's boat led, Bulkeley's boat following in his wake in an effort to provide a smoother ride for MacArthur.

Twenty minutes later, they got their first fright: a Japanese cruiser appeared on the horizon. Luckily it failed to sight the two tiny boats as it headed away on another course. A short time later, an enemy destroyer was sighted on the horizon in the distance, but like the cruiser, it failed to notice the two small vessels and continued on its way.

Finally it was dark. With the two PTs passing Negros Island, the Japanese ashore, mistaking the sound of the engines for aircraft, swept the skies with searchlight beams and opened up with antiaircraft fire aimed at the empty skies while the two boats continued south undetected.

That night, as Bulkeley had warned, the seas became rough again. Huge waves repeatedly carried the PTs to their peaks, only to drop them violently into deep troughs. Men and boats suffered. Most of the passengers on Bulkeley's boat were in agony, especially MacArthur. Conditions on Kelly's boat were no better: there was the danger of injuries due to the violent motion. Crews suffered as well. As in the days of sailing ships, the rule was one hand for the task, the other hand to hang on to a part of the vessel. Men not on watch stayed in their bunks or found places providing security against the boats' movements.

Finally, the storm began to pass and the sea began to grow calm and dawn approached; with this spirits began to rise. Soon the boats passed from the Sulu Sea to the Mindanao Sea. At 6:30 a.m., following a change of course, an excited lookout sighted the light at Cagayan Point. Not far beyond lay the harbor. Against all odds, despite the unexpected difficulties, including wax-contaminated gasoline, becoming separated from one another, being forced to take cover in an emergency assigned cove, being battered by fierce storms on two successive nights, they had completed a thirty-five-hour passage, passing through almost six hundred miles of Japanese-dominated seas to arrive on schedule.

At 7 a.m. Kelly peeled off to the side and allowed the *41* to take the lead with the port charts. Thirty minutes after sighting the Cagayan Point light, the two boats entered the harbor channel.[21]

Ranged in ranks on the dock stood an honor guard of U.S. troops under the command of Colonel William Morse, a unit attached to the local garrison, representing the region commander, Brigadier General William F. Sharp.[22]

Despite the battering MacArthur had experienced and the agonizing hours of seasickness, the general was equal to the occasion. Showing no evidence of ill effects, he now stood on the deck of PT *41* with his wife and son, braided cap tilted at its usual jaunty angle, critically eyeing the waiting honor guard.

With the two PTs finally moored and engines secured, the general, assisting his wife, stepped onto the dock. By now, Jean's handbag was gone, but she had managed to retain her lipstick, compact and comb, all carried in a red bandanna.

With the passengers safely disembarked, MacArthur turned solemnly to Bulkeley, and said: "Johnny, I'm giving every officer and man here the Silver Star for gallantry. You've taken me out of the jaws of death, and I won't forget it."[23]

Suddenly at a loss for words, the embarrassed squadron commander could only stammer his thanks. But as MacArthur turned to leave he found his voice; "General," he called, "what are my orders?"

MacArthur paused thoughtfully, then answered: "You will conduct offensive operations against the Empire of Japan in the waters north of Mindanao. Good luck."

This was a tall order for two worn and tired boats. The waters to which MacArthur referred covered an area greater than that of the United States. Yet, it seemed to Bulkeley and his men, the general considered it a reasonable task. Although unable to cover it completely, they would do their best as long as the boats were operable.

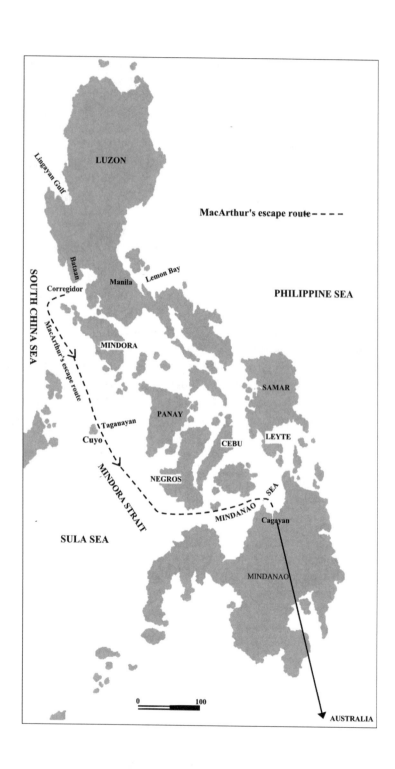

PT 32, one of Lt. John Bulkeley's Squadron 3 boats based at Manila at the outbreak of WWII. It was one of the three boats that helped rescue the survivors of the *SS Corregidor* after the steamship hit a mine while en route from Manila to Cebu loaded with passengers fleeing ahead of advancing Japanese troops. After further combat operations, she was scuttled. By then she was running on only one of her three engines. She was, indeed, expendable, as was the entire Squadron 3. *Courtesy of WWII PT Boats Museum and Archives, Germantown, Tennessee, USA.*

CHAPTER THREE

TO KIDNAP A PRESIDENT

Having successfully completed the remarkable feat of breaking through the enemy cordon and delivering General MacArthur to Mindanao, Lt. Bulkeley and his crews sought to enjoy a few hours of long overdue sleep. But this was not to be. Shortly, a messenger aroused Bulkeley with urgent instructions to report to the general at his temporary headquarters at the Del Monte plantation.[1]

Following a wild jeep ride through the night, the squadron commander arrived to find a scene of near panic. Word had reached Cagayan that the Japanese, having captured Davao on the south coast of Mindanao, and aware that MacArthur was on the island, were rushing troops toward Cagayan to capture or kill MacArthur. In the atmosphere of alarm, a jittery General Sharp had doubled the guard at the Del Monte plantation.

But this was not the cause for summoning the PT officer. Bulkeley found MacArthur on the veranda of the old clubhouse. The general's visible rage shocked the squadron commander. Throughout the period on Corregidor during the Japanese advance, MacArthur's self-control in front of junior officers and men had never wavered. But now, MacArthur's jaws were clinched, his eyes blazing, in his struggle to control his fury.[2]

The amazed Bulkeley was even more surprised by the general's words. "Johnny," said MacArthur, "I've got another crucial job for you, and I know you won't let me down." After a moment of silence, he continued: "I want you to hop over to Negros, find Quezon, and bring him and his whole tribe back here. I don't care how you do it, just get them back. We're sending Quezon to Australia to form a Philippine government-in-exile, whether he likes it or not."[3]

As a typical low-ranking military officer, Bulkeley knew little about the world of diplomacy and politics other than what appeared in the newspapers or was heard on commercial radio stations. They had portrayed the President of the Philippine Commonwealth as a staunch ally of the United States, as well as a committed foe of Japan.[4]

In realty, relations between Quezon and the U.S. were at a point of crisis: earlier, Tokyo had promised the Philippines immediate independence, their long-sought goal, if her soldiers ceased fighting alongside the Americans. Quezon had been tempted, but MacArthur argued against it, telling him, "instead of putting you in the palace, Manuel, the Japs will more likely slit your throat." The general pointed out that as an alternative, with Quezon as a figurehead, the Japanese could keep him a prisoner and issue directives in his name, making it easier for them to control the archipelago.[5]

This had settled the matter, but only temporarily. When word came that the United States planned to concentrate on the war in Europe, and no American army was being dispatched to drive the invading Japanese from the Philippines, a disillusioned Quezon declared: "...our country is being destroyed. The fight between the United States and Japan is not our fight." Quezon argued that Washington should grant the Philippines immediate independence, and all Japanese and U.S. troops should be evacuated from the islands. This was clearly an idealistic dream. Possession of the Philippines was essential to the Japanese plan to control Asia, a plan already well on its way toward completion; furthermore, the U.S. lacked the capability to either support or evacuate the thousands of Americans now trapped in the islands.

MacArthur told Bulkeley that Quezon, having retreated from Manila ahead of the oncoming Japanese, was on Negros Island, where he meant to establish a seat of government; it was only a matter of time before the Japanese tracked him down. If Quezon sided with the Japanese, the lives of American servicemen still fighting in the Philippines would be in danger. It would also be a major propaganda victory for the Japanese in furthering their "Greater East Asia Co-prosperity Sphere" concept. But as long as the brown-skinned Filipinos fought alongside the Americans, the cry would have a hollow ring.

MacArthur had already sent Quezon a message, urging him to come to Mindanao. But Quezon had refused. Now Bulkeley was to deliver a second message, telling the Philippine head of state that the United States was preparing a major offensive in Australia to be launched in defense of the Philippines before the Corregidor-Bataan situation reached its climax. Meanwhile MacArthur wanted Quezon and his family to join him in Australia.[6]

What had alarmed MacArthur was news that Japanese destroyers were thought to be en route to Negros Island, possibly after Quezon. Bulkeley's task was to get to Negros and Quezon ahead of the enemy and return him to Mindanao. As the general explained, Quezon had no choice about going to Australia. What made the mission delicate, of course, were Bulkeley's orders, that he could not take "No" for an answer: "I don't care how you do it," said MacArthur, "just do it." Bulkeley noted that MacArthur's instructions were liberally punctuated with swear words— something else he found unusual about the general this night.

At this point, a third man was ushered into the room. MacArthur introduced him as Don Andres Soriano, a Filipine national. "He will serve as your guide and interpreter in the rescue operation," said MacArthur.

Bulkeley's mind was in a whirl: "Rescue operation!" It sounded more like a kidnapping. Nothing in his training had prepared him for this. Adding to his sense of unease, he instinctively distrusted Soriano.[7]

With his instructions complete, an exhausted MacArthur warmly shook hands with Bulkeley and turned away, saying: "Don't forget, bring him back—by whatever means necessary," providing further evidence that this mission was likely to be difficult in more than one way for the PT officer. Rushing back to the dock, Bulkeley found two PTs moored. For this most momentous and delicate operation, the dependable Kelly and *PT 34* would not be available, as the boat was now laid up for repairs. Instead, Lt. Akers with his *35* boat, having arrived at Cagayan after Bulkeley and Kelly, would accompany the *41* boat skippered by George Cox.[8] With the crews' briefing complete, Bulkeley dealt with the question of the Filipino guide, Soriano: "Any monkey business, and Soriano goes down first," he instructed two crewmen. If Soriano indeed proved treacherous, Bulkeley would make certain he would not live to tell about it.

Darkness had fallen by the time the two PTs emerged from Cagayan Harbor on this most critical and unusual mission. Shortly before 1 a.m. Saturday March 4, following a tense passage, they arrived off Negros Island's port of Dumaguete. A careful check of the area revealed no sign of enemy vessels. Ashore, all was dark and seemingly deserted. As Bulkeley had no charts for the port, and the harbor waters were believed to be extremely shallow, there was the danger of running aground or striking a reef, crippling one or both boats. As Quezon was supposed to be at a house in Dumaguete, Bulkeley had no choice but to get ashore, a feat he was fortunate to manage without doing damage to the PTs.

Gripping his sub-machine gun and accompanied by Soriano and two armed crewmen, the squadron commander headed rapidly up a dark trail. Shortly they encountered a man who identified himself as a local constable.

When questioned, he told them that President Quezon had left Dumaguete that day, and his location was undisclosed. Clearly, Quezon had his own spies, and had expected company. According to the constable, any Americans who appeared were to be told that Quezon had no intention of leaving Negros with them. This was an unexpected complication. But it was not one that would stop the determined Bulkeley.

"Where did President Quezon go?" The PT commander's menacing voice, his manner and his Tommy gun frightened the constable. But Quezon's orders were clear.

"I can't tell you that," he answered.

"The hell you can't!" Bulkeley exploded, cocking the Tommy gun.

Confronted by the threatening PT commander and his three roughly dressed men, two of them heavily armed PT crewmen, the unnerved constable blurted that Quezon had gone to the village of Bais. This, Bulkeley learned, was some twenty-five miles further up the coast.

The four men hurried back to the dock. Soon the two PTs were racing north to the new destination. At Bais, Bulkeley instructed Akers to remain offshore on patrol while the *41* boat tied up at the dock. Again the squadron commander and his three-man party went ashore in search of the elusive Quezon.

Commandeering two ancient automobiles, they drove rapidly through the night to where a local informant told them Quezon was staying. It proved to be a *nipa* hut perched on the side of a hill.

Posting his two crewmen, Bulkeley had Soriano, who turned out to be a former Quezon aide, call out to the President. When first there was no response, Soriano shouted again. After another wait, a light flashed inside the hut and finally Quezon's slight figure appeared silhouetted in the doorway.

Soon the newcomers were all crowded into the hut with Quezon. It was a strange scene. Four burly, tense men confronting a defiant and sullen head of state. By now, Bulkeley's appearance had worsened; oilskins concealed his uniform. His beard and boots were caked with mud; the heavy belt strapped around his waist now held a sheathed knife, plus two pistols in holsters. And he still gripped the Tommy gun as though anxious for an excuse to use it. Not that his companions looked any different.

By now it was 2:30 a.m. Time was running out. If the "rescue" PTs were to safely cover the one hundred-odd miles back to Mindanao before daylight, avoiding the threat of attack by Japanese surface ships or aircraft, they would have to leave Bais soon. The problem was Quezon was not willing to go. He listened impassively as Bulkeley castigated the Japanese, calling the Co-prosperity Sphere and their preaching of "Asia for the Asians" a "lot of goddamned hogwash." Bulkeley disposed of Japan's promise to grant the Philippines independence in even more pungent terms.[9]

After fifteen minutes, Quezon suddenly relented. Word was out summoning his family and staff. Soon, the two vintage vehicles were packed and racing back to the dock, the guards and Soriano perched on the fenders outside. Bulkeley the President, his wife and two daughters, and Vice President Sergio Osmena, as well as the chief of staff, Maj. Gen. Basilio Valdes, along with two cabinet members crammed inside the two vehicles.[10]

Back at the dock, Bulkeley was greeted with news of a disaster. While patrolling nearby as instructed, Akers's PT had hit a submerged object and suffered so much damage it could not make the return voyage to Mindanao. It had to be abandoned and sunk.[11]

As the squadron commander was absorbing this blow, more problems arose. Seven additional members of Quezon's cabinet arrived at the dock, bringing a huge collection of assorted luggage belonging to the Quezon family and entourage. Included were bags of U.S. currency, possibly twelve to fifteen million dollars.

With space on the single PT at a premium, it was obvious there was no room for all the luggage, the *35* boat's crew, and Quezon's family and party. When this became clear, chaos broke out on the dock, with constant chattering and debates as to where individuals and their luggage would go on the boat. By now it was after 3 a.m. and time was running out.

Bulkeley, his anger mounting, finally brought it all to an end: "All right, that's it," he roared. "Everyone get aboard and forget the goddamned suitcases."[12]

With that, everyone on the dock scrambled on the boat. That is, all except one person: Quezon. The President calmly approached the squadron commander, saying, "I've changed my mind. I'm not going to go."[13]

With little sleep over the past fifty hours, Bulkeley was barely able to restrain the urge to bodily throw the President on the boat. A shouting match erupted between the two men. It finally ended with a compromise. Quezon would board the PT, but Bulkeley would take him to the tiny port of Oroquieta on Iligan Bay opposite Cagayan de Oro on Mindanao instead of Cagayan. Midway back, President Quezon approached Bulkeley again, saying he wanted to go back to Negros. The out-of-patience squadron commander replied: "Well, if you want to go back to Negros, help yourself. But you'll sure have to walk on water to get there."[14]

At 6 a.m., following a stormy passage that left all passengers seasick, with waves washing overboard what pieces of luggage they had, the boat reached the port of Oroquieta. Bulkeley had radioed ahead to the local army commander. Thus Quezon was greeted by a military honor guard in a manner appropriate to a head of state.

Stepping to the dock, Quezon, a true politician, gave a short speech expressing his joy at being a part of America's struggle against the Japanese. But Bulkeley and his men had had enough of Quezon. They departed aboard *PT 41* in the middle of the speech, headed back to Cagayan for a long period of well-deserved sleep.

On March 16, two B-17s arrived from Australia; they quickly departed carrying the general and his party on what was to be a five-hour, 1,579-mile return trip. Shortly, as MacArthur had told Bulkeley on March 13, Quezon would also leave the Philippines; he would meet MacArthur in Australia before continuing on to Washington in May, where, as the general had promised, he would form a Philippine government-in-exile, remaining there for the duration, beyond reach of the Japanese.

On a final note, Bulkeley's instincts concerning Soriano proved erroneous. "Soriano's loyalty," the squadron commander later declared, "was exceeded only by his intense desire to make the mission successful." Nor would this be the last time Soriano aided the Allies in their war against Japan on behalf of the Philippines.

On April 8, Bulkeley's remaining PTs carried out their final mission. That afternoon the general commanding on the island of Cebu, where the last two PTs were undergoing maintenance, summoned Bulkeley to his headquarters. The general had reason to believe an Allied air attack was being launched against the Japanese in the Philippines, and that the enemy would shortly be in full retreat. Also, two Japanese destroyers had been sighted headed south toward Cebu. The army officer wondered if Bulkeley would like to take a shot at the two ships. An enemy cruiser had also been sighted headed toward Cebu, but the officer confidently assured Bulkeley that aircraft would take care of it. In fact, the general had been deceived by false rumors now running rampant through the islands. No Allied "offensive" was underway and no aircraft were available to attack the Japanese ships. And certainly the enemy was not retreating.

That night, on the basis of the general's information, Bulkeley led his last two PTs from Cebu, Ens. Cox at the helm of the *41* boat, followed by *PT 34* commanded by Lt. Kelly. Bulkeley planned to lay in wait on the eastern side of Cebu for the two destroyers heading through Tanon Strait. This was the first occasion in World War II in which PT boats carried out a torpedo attack on warships in the manner envisioned by the U.S. Navy.

Bulkeley's plan was simple: there would no high-speed attack. Rather, concealed in the darkness, the PTs would lay in wait ahead of the oncoming ships, engines muffled, relying on their low silhouette and the darkness to make a successful torpedo attack. In the enemy's resultant confusion, the PTs would quietly slip away without being detected: in any event, virtually nothing went as planned.

To the astonishment of the PTs, what loomed out of the night was a massive cruiser escorted by destroyers.[15] Nonetheless, the PTs attacked. In what was to be a wild and confused action that so characterized later PT attacks on warships, Bulkeley's two boats fired a total of eight torpedoes; unfortunately, their old Mark VIII torpedoes were up to their old tricks, running erratically or failing to detonate when hitting the target. Cox led the attack, firing two torpedoes at a range of five hundred yards. Both ran erratically and missed. Cox then made a tight circle and fired his second pair of torpedoes. These ran hot and straight but proved to be duds. However, when the duds clanged against the cruiser's hull without exploding, they served to alert the enemy.[16] The cruiser's searchlights flashed on; their beams swept the surface before settling on Kelly's *34* boat. At the same time the big ship surged ahead to high speed, its guns firing on the *34,* making the cruiser a more difficult target. In an effort to divert the cruiser's fire, Cox sent *PT 41* racing close along the port side of the big ship, raking her decks with machine-gun fire. Despite the effort, as Kelly pressed home his attack the cruiser's gunners shot away the *34* boat's mast and riddled his PT.[17]

Kelly fired two torpedoes at the cruiser; both missed, passing astern of the speeding cruiser. Now dead astern of the cruiser, the most difficult of all possible torpedo shots since it offered the narrowest target, Kelly fired his last two torpedoes.

With all his torpedoes fired, Kelly turned to port at high speed to withdraw, but the cruiser turned with him; apparently the Japanese skipper hoped to block Kelly's escape. Then, two massive water spouts shot into the air amidships on the cruiser's port side. Kelly concluded that either both torpedoes had hit, or the cruiser had been struck accidentally by shellfire from one of its escorting destroyers.[18]

Whatever the cause, the cruiser immediately suffered a power failure and its searchlights dimmed. Bulkeley noted the cruiser was enveloped in a cloud of yellowish brown smoke. As an escorting destroyer raced by, its searchlight briefly illuminated the cruiser showing it to be in a sinking condition, down by the stern, its bow in the air.[19]

Pursued by three destroyers, Kelly raced for the darkness; in a desperate move he managed to elude his pursuers in the shallow waters south of Mindanao. Now separated from the *41* boat, Kelly headed toward to Cebu City to secure medical treatment for crewmen wounded during the engagement.[20] It was daylight by the time the shot-up *PT 34* reached Cebu City. There its luck would finally run out. Four Japanese float planes dove out of the sun. The first bomb exploded a mere ten feet away, blasting a large hole in the boat's hull forward. After dropping additional bombs, the aircraft made strafing runs on the PT. Slugs ripped through the throat of TM2/c David W. Harris as he returned fire. QM1/c Albert P. Ross saw his tracers hit one of the planes and it flew away trailing smoke. But moments later, a slug from another float plane tore into his leg as other slugs shattered his machine gun.[21]

With his boat riddled and holed, the engine room full of water and the PT sinking, Kelly beached the boat. With the vessel grounded and enemy planes continuing to strafe, Kelly climbed down into the engine room to aid the wounded motor mac. What he saw was horrific: CMoM Velt F. Hunter was covered with blood, one arm virtually blown off as he sought to man his post.

Kelly gave the inevitable order to "Abandon Ship." Only three of the crew were still unscathed. Two would die as a result of their wounds.[22]

At 12:30 p.m. enemy planes returned and again attacked the grounded *PT 34,* this time setting it afire. Finally the boat exploded; now Squadron 3 had only one boat.

PT 41 had only narrowly escaped destruction during the attack on the cruiser. As Kelly fled following his attack, *PT 41* also raced from the attack scene. Pursued by destroyers, Cox raced southward. Unable to outrun the enemy, upon reaching Mindanao, he managed to escape his determined pursuers by holding up in an inlet too shallow for the deeper-draft destroyers to follow.

Unfortunately, the PTs' experience on this night's action resembled those that followed later in the war: following the attack, PT officers claimed they sank a six thousand-ton cruiser of either the *Kuma* or *Tenryu*—class. Enemy records confirm a *Kuma* class cruiser was in the area, but that it was hit by a dud torpedo. This was probably one of the second pair of missiles fired by Ens. Cox. But Japanese records deny losing a cruiser that night. Although this was a typical response during wartime, the fact is that the Japanese built five Kuma-class cruisers; four were lost in 1944, the fifth was scrapped after the war in 1947. Thus, what ship did Kelly sink? Or did he actually sink a ship? The answer remains just one of the mysteries of World War Two.

Another apparent problem that night, one that would plague American PT boats throughout the war, was their flawed torpedoes: Out of eight Mark VIII torpedoes, the type arming PT boats at the start of the war, two proved to be duds, two ran erratically, two appeared to run properly but passed astern of the target, and the performance of the last two remains a mystery. Later in the war, tests of the Mark VIII torpedo disclosed the vintage missile, designed for use on World War One destroyers, was rife with flaws: duds, prematures (exploding before reaching the target), running deeper than set, taken all together, afflicted 63 percent of the torpedoes tested.[23] Even without any flaws, the heavy Mark VIII with its puny warhead and slow speed was a poor weapon for PTs engaging World War Two warships capable of speeds in excess of 35 knots. Just how ill-suited the Mark VIII torpedo was for the PTs' armament is best illustrated by the fact that a PT boat running at its designed-for speed of 42 knots was 14 knots faster than the torpedo.

There was also a question of determining the best methods to attack warships: Following the outbreak of World War Two, Britain's Royal Navy's MTBs (motor torpedo boats)—Britain's counterpart to the PT—learned that the ideal firing position for an attacking motor torpedo boat was at an angle on the enemy ship's bow, which allowed for maximum error; it also provided the enemy commander with the greatest distance to cover of he sought to evade the oncoming torpedo by a maneuver called "combing the track," meaning to turn the ship parallel to oncoming torpedo tracks, allowing the missiles to pass alongside.[24] It hardly need be said however, that firing from the "ideal" position was sometimes not possible. Firing a torpedo off the enemy's quarter, with the ship going away and offering a narrow silhouette, the quarter was the worst possible position.[25] In fact, for a PT with a Mark VIII torpedo with its slow 28-knot speed, if the target happened to be a destroyer, the torpedo might even be outdistanced by the intended target.

In any event, for a PT skipper, getting a hit with his torpedoes meant aiming at a point ahead of the target so that the torpedo speed and that of the targeted ship arrived at a given point at the same time. Making the necessary calculations was crucial to success; of course, night operations made this more difficult.

Whereas submarine and destroyer skippers were aided in making torpedo attacks by fire control systems that provided the essential data, PTs boats had only a simple "torpedo director" fitted in the cockpit in anticipation of long-range, high-speed torpedo attacks, something that rarely took place in the Pacific war. As the war dragged on, PT skippers had little need for the torpedo director since firing ranges tended to vary from as little as five hundred yards to a maximum of seven hundred fifty yards, ranges in which PT skippers relied on a "seaman's eye." In any event, after the initial months of the Pacific war, the Japanese switched to the use of motorized barges in delivering supplies and fresh troops to their island garrisons as the Japanese navy sought to reserve its destroyers and cruisers for anticipated major future fleet engagements with the American navy. PT skippers thus found there was little need for their torpedoes or the skills required to fire them successfully.

With the supply of torpedoes exhausted at Mindanao, and with the advancing Japanese occupying Cebu, *PT 41*'s use as a torpedo boat was over. Shortly thereafter, the boat was transferred to the army for use as a gunboat to deter Japanese floatplanes from using Lake Lanao in Mindanao. While being moved by truck and trailer over a mountain road, it was determined that Japanese troops were closing in, and on April 15, 1942, the army destroyed her.[26]

In the end, during its five months of operation, Bulkeley's squadron claimed four ships sunk or destroyed. Typically, the record made no reference to the number of enemy barges sunk or destroyed; thus the squadron's record was hardly imposing. However, the lessons would be invaluable for use of PTs that followed, particularly in the battles with barges and shore batteries in support of Allied ground troops.

With the end of the torpedo supply, following orders from General MacArthur, Bulkeley was flown to Australia. On April 13, also under orders from the general, Lt. Kelly, Ensigns Cox, Akers and Brantingham would be among the veterans to return to Melville as instructors.[27]

For Allied forces on Bataan, weakened by starvation and disease—malaria, scurvy, beriberi and dysentery—the end came on April 10 when 76,000 men, barely a fourth of whom were combat-effective, became Japanese prisoners of war. On May 4, the Japanese landed on the beaches of Corregidor; two days later, Maj. Gen. Jonathan M. Wainwright, who had assumed command of Luzon forces with the departure of MacArthur, surrendered the island fortress, and another 15,000 Americans disappeared into captivity.[28] A few of Bulkeley's men managed to escape to Australia by submarine. Most, however, dispersed, some joining local guerrilla forces. Thirty-eight were taken prisoner; most to be moved finally from the Manila Bay region to prison camps in Manchuria and Japan. Not until after the war would the world learn of the torture and overcrowding in which the half-starved prisoners were forced to live, or of the great efforts made by the Japanese to devise new ways of inflicting torture. For Allied captives, Japanese prison camps were far more deadly than the German; only 4 percent of American and British troops captured by German forces died in the camps. For the Japanese camps, the mortality figure for Allied prisoners, soldiers, sailors and flyers, including Australian, British, Canadians, Americans and the rest, including native troops, was 28.65 percent. And the survivors emerged as virtual skeletons. Indeed, Japanese records suggest it was Imperial policy, meaning with the authority of Emperor Hirohito, that the prisoners be exterminated to the last man. Only the end of the war and Japan's defeat foiled the effort.[29] By then, nine of Bulkeley's squadron taken captive would be dead; only twenty-nine survived to be liberated.

For Bulkeley, escaping from the Philippines to land in Australia as he did, there was cause for yet another historic controversy. One of MacArthur's first acts upon reaching Brisbane was to recommend Bulkeley to be awarded the Medal of Honor, the nation's highest award for gallantry, for his performance in the Philippines. This did not sit well with Admiral Ernest J. King, the Navy's CNO back in Washington. The Admiral declared to his aides that MacArthur would not by any means dictate a Medal of Honor to "one of my men." King would himself make any such recommendation on behalf of the Navy.[30] Thus it was that the Navy chose to make the award, the first of only two such awards to be received by a PT officer during World War Two. As a point of interest, the second award had its own unique complications inspired by the Navy's reluctance.

Bulkeley's troubles with the Navy did not end there. Reporting to U.S. naval headquarters in Australia after his evacuation from the Philippines, he was greeted by a wall of hostility. As he later recalled, officers from the senior vice admiral down to commander, berated him for not leaving MacArthur behind to die. For the second time in recent weeks, as a lowly lieutenant, Bulkeley had reason to wonder: later, he learned the U.S. Navy viewed the Pacific war as a conflict best left to the Navy. MacArthur's presence jeopardized this goal. With rare exceptions, this would be a source of dissent throughout the Pacific war.

For himself, Bulkeley found a moment for amusement. In Brisbane, he was invited to lunch with General MacArthur and Manuel Quezon, the latter on his way to the United States by way of Australia to establish a Philippine government-in-exile. On the occasion of this event, Bulkeley's appearance was that of a perfect naval officer, hair trimmed, clean shaven, wearing a regulation uniform. Quezon, in a relaxed mood, proceeded to describe in considerable detail to the guests his manner of being "rescued" from Negros Island by a gallant "American sea wolf." A puzzled Bulkeley searched his mind as to the identity of this "sea wolf."

The answer was soon apparent: Turning to Bulkeley, the president of the Philippines said, "I want to express my sincere appreciation to your father, the sea wolf, and commend him on his great courage."

A startled Bulkeley responded: "My father?" General MacArthur and the other guests roared with laughter. When it dawned on the Philippine president that he was speaking to the same Bulkeley that had "rescued" him, he joined in the laughter as well.[31]

A short time later, the general sent for Bulkeley. MacArthur told the PT officer he was to return to the States to receive the Medal of Honor from President Roosevelt personally. "When you get there," the general added, "I want you to stress to the President the vital need to retake the Philippines." Cautioning Bulkeley not to write anything on paper, MacArthur emphasized what the PT officer should say. Bulkeley was particularly elated with one part of the message:

> "I want a hundred or more torpedo boats here...two hundred boats if possible, within eight months...With enough of this type craft, hostile Japanese shipping could be kept from invading an island or a continent."[32]

For General MacArthur, this was not a sudden conviction. Earlier, in 1940, MacArthur envisioned a force of fifty motor torpedo boats swarming out to sink enemy transports steaming into Lingayen Gulf. But the Navy lacked interest in such a scheme. Since the U.S. had no such craft, the only boats available were British Thornycrofts. When Eisenhower learned the cost, he was "staggered." At $250,000 per boat, fifty boats would come to $12.5 million, the equivalent of the entire Philippine defense budget for more than eighteen months. That kind of money was not even available.[33]

Arriving back in the United States, promoted to the rank of lieutenant commander and awarded the Medal of Honor by President Roosevelt under the watchful eyes of Admiral King, Bulkeley was greeted as a living legend. For a year, he traveled the nation recruiting potential PT skippers, while the press, responding to the public's need for war heroes after a steady stream of Allied military defeats, printed fantastic stories about PT boats in the Philippines, depicting boats as being capable of incredible speeds armed with torpedoes that never missed. In these stories, Bulkeley's PTs sank battleships and cruisers with impunity. The book *They Were Expendable*, followed by the movie of the same name, added to the myth. It seemed that PT boats, if given the chance, could win the war in the Pacific alone. Indeed, in the months ahead, the PTs would come close to at least measuring up to if not exceeding the feats proclaimed in the press.

Lt. Comdr. John Bulkeley receives the Medal of Honor from President Roosevelt in the presence of Admiral Ernest King. *Courtesy of WWII PT Boats Museum and Archives, Germantown, Tennessee, USA.*

Lt. Robert Kelly, Bulkeley's Squadron 3 executive officer during the Philippines campaign at the start of World War II. In the Hollywood film, "They Were Expendable," depicting the squadron's operations, the part of Kelly was played by Hollywood star John Wayne.

Months later, during the New Georgia campaign, Kelly, now a PT squadron commander, was responsible for torpedoing and sinking the flagship of Adm. Richard Kelly Turner, commanding the invasion force.

It was a mistake in identification that so incensed Turner, known by reputation as a "fire eater," he never forgot it, later banning PT boats from his command in the central Pacific. *Courtesy of WWII PT Boats Museum and Archives, Germantown, Tennessee, USA.*

CHAPTER FOUR

LONG VOYAGES

Following the attack on Pearl Harbor, American authorities greatly feared Japanese troops would invade Hawaii. With the resultant devastation, defenses there had been virtually obliterated. In this period of uncertainty, the twelve PTs of Squadron 1 were assigned to patrol the waters of Hawaii.

But not for long: toward the end of May, U.S. intelligence detected the Japanese intended to attack Midway Island. Admiral Yamamoto, having failed to catch the U.S. Pacific Fleet's carriers in port during the December 7 raid, had devised a second plan to achieve the same result. To quote the admiral, he hoped to draw what remained of the U.S. Pacific Fleet out in defense of the outpost so he could "annihilate" it at its moment of greatest weakness, before American construction had time to replace the losses suffered at Pearl Harbor.[1]

Two square miles of coral, 1,136 miles WNW of Pearl Harbor, the outermost link of the Hawaiian chain, Midway served as an early warning outpost for Pearl Harbor. To the Americans, the expected attack portended another offensive against Hawaii and Admiral Nimitz meant to employ every possible vessel and unit at his disposal to defeat the effort.

Accordingly, toward the end of May, Squadron 1 was ordered to Midway. Accompanied by a seaplane tender for refueling, the squadron departed Pearl Harbor on what was to be the longest open-sea voyage to be made by PT boats. One boat was forced back due to mechanical problems, but the rest continued on.[2]

On the morning of June 4, shortly after the arrival of the squadron, a Midway search plane sighted the approaching Japanese fleet. This time there would be no surprise; this time the Americans were ready and waiting. In the air clashes that marked the Battle of

Midway, U.S. fighters shot down a third of the attacking aircraft. PT boats in the Midway lagoon aided in the defense, firing on low-flying Zeros. After the battle, the boats were dispatched to rescue pilots shot down in the waters nearby; they also ferried rescue parties and supplies ashore.

Shortly before midnight the PTs were ordered to search for damaged Japanese carriers thought to be broken down some distance from the location of the main battle scene: It was possible the damaged ships were within 170 miles of Midway. But although the boats searched all night, bad weather and poor visibility, not to mention the lack of radar, spoiled any hope of a contact. All they found was floating wreckage.[3]

The Midway battle had barely ended when Squadron 1 was directed to detach four boats for operations in the Aleutians. On June 7, closely coordinated with the Midway attack, 1800 Japanese troops had occupied Kiska and Attu, two islands that were the furthest east toward the end of that chain of islands.[4] In response, American forces were being dispatched to the area in defense. Among its forces, the U.S. Navy decided to send PT boats to the Aleutians on the theory that under cover of the perpetual fog common to the region, such boats could successfully make torpedo attacks on enemy ships. As it happened, PT service in this far away frozen world be among the most difficult encountered by crews.[5]

Designated Motor Torpedo Division 1, under the command of Lt. Clinton McKellar, four boats, *PTs 22, 24, 27* and *28,* were ferried to Seattle. On August 20, they departed from there under their own power on the 2500 mile voyage through the Alaska Inland Passage and Gulf bound for Dutch Harbor, arriving on September 1.[6] Continuing on, they reached Adak, completing the longest voyage ever made by PT boats.

Based at Adak, the four PTs stood ready to repel Japanese landing forces. When this failed to occur, the boats doubled as scouts and, as in the case of Midway, helped deliver supplies, this time, for the army. In what was a new wrinkle, they even served as minelayers. However, despite the navy's expectations, for PTs in the Aleutians the main enemy was the weather. Winter frost lined the PTs' hulls inside, sometimes as much as two inches in thickness. Green seas turning to spray, coated the boats with ice, weighing them down dangerously.

Guns and torpedo tubes as well as other essential equipment were covered with ice. Crewmen worked constantly keeping them cleared in the event of an enemy encounter.

On one occasion the four boats were patrolling in the midst of a snow squall when two of them collided. As the storm dragged on, all four boats sought refuge in a small cove. During the next four days as the gale raged, anchors dragged, cables parted, and three of the boats ended up in a snow bank. Help finally arrived, but to no avail. Tow lines snapped, cleats were jerked from decks, as men struggled against the fury of nature. Despite the difficulties, McKellar's boats continued operations. On January 12, U.S. troops landed on Amchitka, and PTs began operating from a base there.[7] On May 11, American troops succeeded in landing on Attu. By the end of May, after fierce ground fighting, Attu was back in American hands. Within a month of the landings on Attu, the PTs were operating out of Attu's Casco Cove in Massacre Bay.[8]

In June 1942, the U.S. staged two bombing offensives against Japanese positions on Kiska, without obvious effect, while the PTs continued to patrol without any enemy contact. From June 1 until August Allied aircraft dropped 1255 tons of bombs on the enemy despite the fog conditions. During these missions, the PTs supported the air operations, taking station as lifeguards west of Amchitka, ready to rescue any pilot and crew forced to ditch during a mission. As most air losses were operational, the presence of the PTs helped maintain morale among the air crews.

On February 28, 1943, the newly commissioned PTs of Squadron 13 commanded by Lt. Comdr. James B. Denny, having been shipped from New Orleans, were unloaded from freighters at Seattle to start the long trip to Alaska. As the first squadron equipped with the new 78-foot Higgins PT, Squadron 13 had problems with the initial boats; first, they were overweight, and second, they were below required performance in top speed. Navy officers joined plant officials in lightening the weight and making other recommended modifications to be included in the Higgins PTs to follow. After commissioning in September 1942, the squadron spent several additional months training and fine-tuning the boats before starting the trip to Alaska.

Initial Squadron 13 operations were from Finger Bay on Adak. By June, four Squadron 13 boats, *PTs 75, 77, 79* and *82* were

mounting patrols out of Attu. Soon they were joined by two more
Higgins PTs, the *219* and *224* boats attached to Squadron 16. The
balance of Squadron 16 would follow in August.[9] Soon after the
landings on Kiska, the PT base at Amchitka was abandoned after
the base was virtually destroyed by a severe storm. Finger Bay on
Adak, however, remained an operational base for PTs until May
1944, at which time the PTs were finally withdrawn from the
Aleutians.[10] To the end, the combat record for the PTs in the
Aleutians remained the same: no enemy contacts. Until the end it
was the weather that served as the PTs' foe.

In the meantime, there was action aplenty on the home front.
With the United States at war in Europe and the Pacific, there was a
sudden need for more PT boats. Having delivered twenty-nine of
their 77-foot Elco PT boats to the Navy, Elco's contract called for
delivery of twenty more of this type by mid-March 1942. In
January, on the heels of the Pearl Harbor attack, Elco laid the keel
for the first 80-footer, *PT 103*; it would be completed on May 16,
1942. On that day a gala ceremony was held at the Bayonne plant.
Public officials, assorted dignitaries and high-ranking naval officers
joined assembled plant workers and the news media for the event.
The highlight of the gathering was when Lt. Comdr. John D.
Bulkeley appeared and recounted some of his experiences in the
Philippines as commander of the expendable Squadron 3.[11]

Then, before an appreciative audience, a crane lowered the new
80-foot Elco into the water. One by one, the three Packard engines
were started and the boat roared away from the dock, capping the
event.

With new PT boats under construction and due for completion,
the Navy hurriedly began preparations to select and train new crews.
By now, the Navy had established a training facility at Melville,
Rhode Island.[12] Located on Narragansett Bay, the Navy's Motor
Torpedo Boat Training Center began operations in March 1942. The
experience of Bulkeley's Squadron 3 in the Philippines helped
shaped the course, while student instructors were largely veterans
recently returned from the first months of the war in the Pacific.
Thereafter, nearly all who served on PT boats would be both
volunteers and graduates of Melville's eight-week intensive course.

But it would all take time to select and train men, form squadrons, and ship them to the war zones. Meanwhile, as the war continued to rage, it was up to the original surviving PT crews to face the enemy as best they could with the boats available.

PT 66, a 77-foot Elco, tied up along the Morobe River, an advanced New Guinea PT base in May 1943. As an earlier boat, it lacks radar and has the older type torpedo tubes. Unlike most PTs in combat zones, *PT 66* is fitted with only two torpedo tubes, the aft tubes having been replaced with depth charges. Of special interest is the camouflaged hull, useful for operating among the islands of the South Pacific. *Courtesy of WWII PT Boats Museum and Archives, Germantown, Tennessee, USA.*

A Higgins PT, one of Comdr. Stanley Barnes's Squadron 15 boats, laying smoke in support of Allied troop landings at Salerno during the Mediterranean campaign. For months, this squadron was the only naval unit of the U.S. Navy in the Mediterranean theater. As such, it operated as a part of and under the command of the Royal Navy. The boat's number is unknown. *Courtesy of WWII PT Boats Museum and Archives, Germantown, Tennessee, USA.*

PT 103 on its trial run; judging from its wake, it is about at its top speed. Note it lacks radar and all the added guns and assorted armaments that were added before it was turned over to a squadron. Designed for a top speed of forty-plus knots under ideal conditions, this is no doubt the last time this boat reached forty knots. In combat theaters where conditions were rarely if ever ideal, and with the added weigh of men and guns, as well as tired engines, twenty-six to twenty-eight knots was more the norm. But some were slower. Since PT crews thrived on speed, to have the fastest boat in the squadron was every crew's goal. Boats returning to base from a night's patrol, once in sight of the base, would go from cruising speed to a wide-open race to see which of the boats among them was the fastest. *Courtesy of WWII PT Boats Museum and Archives, Germantown, Tennessee, USA.*

CHAPTER FIVE

GUADALCANAL

By mid-1942, PT Squadron 2, the one remaining commissioned squadron not yet committed to combat operations, was stationed in the Panama Canal area. By now, it had grown to an oversized fourteen boats.[1] In July orders came to break off eight boats. They would be designated Squadron 3, in lieu of Bulkeley's no-longer existing unit. The new Squadron 3 would be commanded by Lt. Comdr. Alan R. Montgomery, like Bulkeley, a regular Navy officer. Orders were for the new Squadron 3 to be shipped to the South Pacific in two divisions of four boats each with crews. Owing to the usual tight wartime security, the men could only guess as to their destination.[2]

The first division, *PTs 38, 46, 48* and *60* departed Panama on August 29 aboard a transport bound for "somewhere south" with Commander Montgomery along in command. The ships arrived at Noumea, New Caledonia, a major Allied rear base in the South Pacific. There the division encountered an obstacle of no small consequence. One PT skipper decribed it as a big "snafu," (situation normal, all f_____ up), a phrase used constantly among American servicemen during World War Two when referring to any form of confusion or mix-up in operations: with each 77-foot Elco PT boat weighing 50 tons fully loaded, no crane at Noumea was capable of lifting the boats from the transport's deck to the water.

Three weeks passed while port officials worked to solve the problem. The answer would come in the form of a floating crane built by the Seabees. Once the boats were in the water, the confusion continued: no one seemed to know where the boats were to go.

During the waiting period, the squadron heard stories of Japanese warships coming south to shell Marines on Guadalcanal from an island called Bougainville. Young and cocky, the crews of the new Squadron 3, fresh from training in the States, boasted that given the chance, they would "derail the Tokyo Express," as the Americans had nicknamed the almost nightly arriving enemy ships.

The squadron was to get its chance. Shortly they learned their final destination was Tulagi, a small island separated from the larger island of Guadalcanal to the south by the thirty-five-mile-wide Sealark Channel.[3] It would be the role of Squadron 3 to supply the Marines on Guadalcanal with much-needed naval support, support which thus far had been lacking.

Almost from the start, the Marines' invasion of Guadalcanal had hovered on the edge of disaster. Within hours of the landings on August 7, the first of the many setbacks for the U.S. Navy came in the naval battle known as the Battle of Savo Island. Named for a tiny island located between Guadalcanal and Tulagi, the battle lasting only thirty-two minutes; in it a Japanese scratch task force dealt the American navy its most humiliating defeat in recent history, with the enemy sinking four heavy cruisers and a destroyer, while suffering only minor damage itself. Over one thousand Allied naval officers and men perished with 709 wounded.[4] Following the battle, Vice Admiral R. L. Ghormley, COMSOPAC, with few warships available, chose to not risk any further ships in defense of Guadalcanal; it was a decision whose significance was not lost on the Marines on the island.

Abandoned in waters dominated by the enemy, the Marines faced what seemed like hopeless odds: assaults from the air and sea followed as the enemy landed additional troops on the island in an effort to drive the Americans into the sea. Even as they resisted, the Marines struggled to complete an airstrip, an airstrip upon which their survival depended.

On August 20 the airstrip, named Henderson Field after a Marine Corps pilot, Major Lofton Henderson, killed during the Battle of Midway, became operational. As an immobile aircraft carrier now supporting the defenders, Henderson Field would become the key factor in deciding the outcome of the campaign for Guadalcanal. That day, two Marine squadrons, nineteen Wildcats and twelve Dauntless dive-bombers, launched from a U.S. carrier safely positioned miles south of the "Canal" landed on the strip. By the end of the month, American aircraft operating from Henderson

Field, nicknamed the "Cactus Air Force" after Guadalcanal's code name "Cactus," were flying regular patrols in defense of the Marines. But the American dive-bombers, or SBDs, had a radius of only two hundred miles. And with the twelve-hour nights that prevailed close to the equator, the Japanese had a great advantage. Within an hour of darkness, fast enemy destroyers started their high-speed dash down from the north, bringing additional troops and supplies to Guadalcanal. By daylight, the ships would be 175 miles north and soon beyond range of the Cactus Air Force.

As a consequence, an unusual tactical situation developed: a virtual exchange of sea mastery every twelve hours. Supported by the Cactus aircraft, the Americans ruled the waters around Guadalcanal from sunup to sundown. But, with the coming of night, the bigger American ships fled south, and the smaller U.S. vessels holed up in Tulagi Harbor. For then, the Tokyo Express with reinforcements for the Japanese garrison on Guadalcanal, sometimes including cruisers or even battleships, ruled the seas. On some occasions, after delivering supplies and troops and starting their dash north, the enemy took time to lob a few shells in the direction of the hard-pressed Marines and Henderson Field.[5]

But with the coming of PT Squadron 3 based at Tulagi, for the first time, the "Express" would encounter American naval units whose task was to provide the Marines support on the islands of Guadalcanal and Tulagi. Tulagi, the first advanced PT base in the South Pacific, was a small island of some significance. About two miles long and a half-mile wide, before the war it had been the capital of the British Solomon Islands Protectorate. Government structures, including the Governor's House or regency, dotted the southeast end of the island.[6]

On the morning of October 12 after being towed part way to the island of Espiritu Santo by the newly arrived PT tender *Jamestown,* and continuing on under their own power, Montgomery's four boats arrived at Tulagi Harbor. Only hours earlier a bare fifty miles away, the U.S. Navy and Japanese warships had clashed in another of the major naval battles fought during the campaign for Guadalcanal. Termed the Battle of Cape Esperance by naval historians, it had been costly for both sides, the Americans losing one destroyer with two cruisers being badly damaged; Japanese losses consisted of a cruiser and three destroyers.[7] Ironically, the battle occurred when both sides inadvertently chose the same night to resupply their respective garrisons on Guadalcanal.

At Tulagi, the PT crews spent the rest of October 12 and the following day double checking equipment and armament in anticipation for action. On the following day, October 13, Comdr. Montgomery crossed Sealark Channel to consult with the Marine officers commanding on Guadalcanal. While there, he could not help noting the evident exhaustion of the Marine defenders; weeks of tension under attack, poor food, malaria, dysentery and a host of other tropical afflictions had had an effect. Montgomery could only marvel at the lift in spirits caused by the arrival of his four PT boats. One red-eyed youth with a captured Japanese knife in his belt doubtless spoke for all of them when he told Montgomery: "Just teach the bastards to stay home in bed at night where they belong. Just do that, and we'll remember you in our prayers."[8]

The chance for the PTs to do just that was quick to arrive. Unknown to the Americans, a major Japanese offensive to retake Henderson Field was underway. For more than a week prior to October 12, Japanese destroyers had made nightly runs between Shortland Island, a small island just south of banjo-shaped Bougainville Island and the base of operations for the Tokyo Express, and Guadalcanal, some three hundred miles south, bringing fresh troops.

Returning to Tulagi, Montgomery learned another "Express" was approaching from the north: As Montgomery recalled, "We got word the afternoon of the thirteenth that a Japanese task force was in 'the Slot.'"

Apparently it consisted of three destroyers, or a cruiser and two destroyers. Patrol planes had spotted them and word was passed along to us. "When I heard it, I went at once to General Rupertus [commanding Marines on Tulagi] to find out what he thought about it. I told him I didn't consider it wise to sacrifice our number one weapon of surprise on so small an enemy. No fooling—that's what I told him. It will give you some idea of what we thought of those boats of ours.

"The general agreed that we should wait for something really worthwhile. He smiled as he said it. Now that I look back on that little conversation, I realize why he was smiling; but at the time there was nothing very droll to me in the idea of four midget PT boats haughtily refusing to attack a trio of Japanese destroyers because they weren't big enough."[9]

Indeed, the reports could not have been more inaccurate. For the first time since the struggle for Guadalcanal began, battleships were among the ships coming south. The *Kongo* and *Haruna*, both 31,000 tons, each armed were eight fourteen-inch guns and over nine hundred bombardment shells packed in their magazines. Most were AP (armor piercing) intended for use against ships. Fired at Henderson Field, they would blow holes in the ground and render the airstrip unusable. In addition, the battleships carried 104 special Type 3 shells. Designed for antiaircraft defense, the thin casing of each shell contained 470 individual incendiary sub-munitions capable of scattering over a wide swath, equally effective in destroying fuel drums, parked aircraft and Marines.[10]

Commanding the force, part of Operation "KA," the Japanese plan to eliminate Henderson Field as a threat before an attack was made with the main forces, was Rear Admiral Takeo Kurita. His orders were to fire a barrage pattern within a 2,200-meter-square area overlapping Henderson Field at the fighter strip. Four destroyers sweeping ahead of the battleships would alert the admiral if any U.S. ships were in the area. None were there. By this time, the surviving U.S. Navy's warships that fought in the Battle of Cape Esperance were well to the south, returning to their base at Espiritu Santo. Moreover, the battered force lacked the power confront this powerful Japanese armada.

Led by the advancing destroyers, the two battleships, screened by a light cruiser, the *Isuzu* and five additional destroyers, entered Sealark Channel. At 1:30 a.m., October 14, the Japanese admiral slowed the battleships to 18 knots and eased past the south side of Savo Island before turning parallel to Guadalcanal. Moments later, *Kongo*'s guns thundered its first salvo; a minute and a half later *Haruna*'s guns roared.

Exhausted after the recent preparations for operations, Montgomery was jolted awake by the thunder of the guns. He knew immediately these were destroyers. He quickly summoned his four PT skippers, Henry S. "Stilly" Taylor commanding *PT 46*, Robert C. Wark, skipper of *PT 48*, and the two Searles brothers, John ("Jack") M. commanding *PT 60*, and Robert L, commanding the *38* boat. All were reserve junior grade lieutenants; Montgomery was the only regular naval officer present; and none had seen combat before.

It did not take long for Montgomery to outline the situation. Nor did the four skippers need any urging. All were burning with enthusiasm to engage the enemy; it was what they had longed for, what they had practiced for. Montgomery's "Let's go get 'em" sent them hurrying to their boats.

As officer in tactical command, Montgomery rode on "Jack" Searles' *PT 60*. Having contracted pneumonia during the trip from Panama, Montgomery was far from well; thin and gaunt, his body covered with painful water blisters as a result of taking too much sulfa, he refused to be put on the sick list in order to go on the squadron's first combat mission.

When Montgomery led the PTs out of Tulagi Harbor, he and his men received their first shock of the night; ahead of them lay a virtual impenetrable "black wall." Lacking radar at this early stage of the war, the four boats quickly lost contact with one another. "You had a feeling of aloneness that set in your throat like an egg," said Montgomery. Stilly Taylor recalled: "We had trained and been on many practice runs at night, but there had never been anything like this. We found out later that the Japanese would typically wait for the darkest nights to make their runs. Running by ourselves, we really had no idea 'how' we were going to find and torpedo the Japanese ships in the black of night.[11]

The orange muzzle flashes of the enemy's guns on the far side of Sealark Channel told the PT crews where the enemy ships were, but the gun flashes also hampered their night vision. Said a frustrated Taylor, "PTs should have been manned by cats. They might have been able to see what was going on that night. We couldn't. All we could see was the flash of gunfire in a tight formation which was moving down from Cape Esperance to Lungo Point at some 20 knots, swinging out and around and back again—and tracers arcing ashore."[12]

What followed was a confused melee so common to PT attacks against heavy warships: first to make enemy contact was *PT 60*, sighting a ship identified as a cruiser. Closing to four hundred yards, Jack Searles fired two torpedoes from his forward torpedo tubes: the aft tubes had been removed and replaced by depth charges on the theory that PT boats could be used to combat submarines, even though the boats lacked underwater detection gear.

With his two torpedoes launched, Searles reversed course back toward Tulagi and opened the throttles; shortly, two massive explosions shattered the night and crewmen on the PT observed two red flashes and two water spouts rising in the air from the cruiser's waterline. But for *PT 60,* the real action was yet to come. Said Montgomery, it was then that "we got the surprise of our sweet young lives. We were running wide open when Jack Searles, who was always thinking of his engines, said ever so casually, 'We can slow down now, commander. They didn't spot us'—and he eased back on the throttles. I didn't have a chance to answer him. A salvo of enemy fire burst around our ears, and we were damn near blown off the boat. Jack and I both jammed the throttles wide, practically up through the windshield, and the PT boat went soaring."[13] In turning away from the cruiser, *PT 60* had encountered the battleships' destroyer screen. About a thousand yards to the rear of *PT 60* at the time of its attack on the cruiser, and separated from one another by a few hundred feet, *PTs 46* and *48* were slowly groping their way toward the enemy ships' gun flashes when the beam of a searchlight suddenly pierced the darkness. At the far end of the beam, Stilly Taylor saw *PT 60,* but what he saw at the other end of the beam brought his heart to his mouth: looming out of the darkness, the massive curved bow of an onrushing ship was seconds from ramming his *46* boat. Instinctively, Taylor jammed his throttles forward to full speed and turned hard, narrowly avoiding disaster. Confronted moments later by the same hurtling ship, Wark also managed avoid being rammed. But not content with evading destruction, Wark decided he would attack.

Circling at high speed, Wark began to pursue the unsuspecting destroyer. It promised to be a long chase. Apparently the enemy was heading home. With throttles jammed hard against the stops, *PT 48* slowly closed the gap. Coming up on the destroyer's port side, Wark decided to first position his boat on the destroyer's starboard side before attacking. However, instead of crossing the destroyer's wake, astern of the vessel where there was plenty of room as well as less chance of being spotted by the enemy lookouts, Wark chose to cross ahead of the ship. It was a nearly fatal decision. As one of Wark's crew later commented, "We sure cut it close."

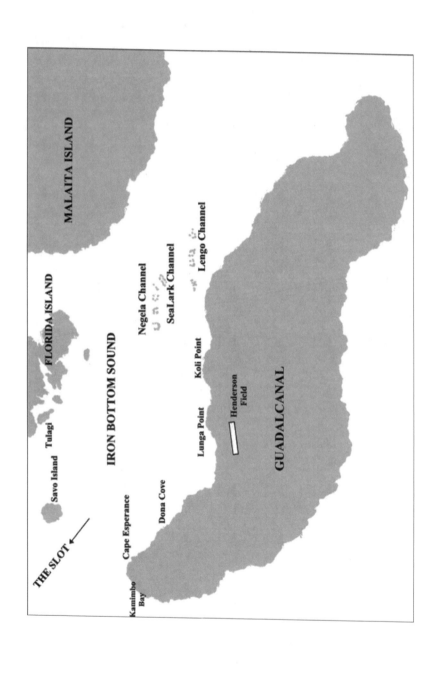

Wark's luck continued to hold: Earlier, the *48* skipper had cautioned his gunners not to fire unless the boat was fired on, since the muzzle flashes provided ideal targets for the enemy's gunners and the heavier weapons of the big warships could reduce the PT to a mass of splinters.

Now, having barely managed to cross ahead of the destroyer, Wark's attack seemed to be going as planned. Suddenly, a searchlight on the destroyer snapped on. "The beam probed and passed right over us, continuing its sweep," said one of Wark's crew. "That's when this nineteen-year-old gunner...opened up from his .50-caliber turret. That searchlight zipped right back over and pinpointed us, and I swear I could feel it burning the back of my neck. Why that kid did that I'll never know, but as far as I know, that was the last time he rode one of our squadron PT boats. When the light hit us, I figured we were really in for it. Almost immediately, three 4.7-inch shells landed 'very' close to us, one to port, one to starboard, and the last one in our wake. That's when ol' Todd opened up from the other .50-caliber turret. They say that cooks make good gunners and they were sure right about Todd. He was just as cool as could be. He poured a burst into the searchlight, and we were so close to that ship I could hear the glass shattering above the gunfire and the roar of the engines."[14]

For Wark's *PT 48,* this ended the encounter. Apparently under orders, the destroyer continued on its way. Having survived his near near-brush with disaster, Wark found he had another problem. Uncertain as to his position, he chose to secure engines to drift until daylight when he could see and make his way back to Tulagi.

Further east, having avoiding the speeding destroyer, Taylor continued to search for the enemy, but, found nothing. Like Wark, uncertain of his position, he also secured his engines to wait until daylight.

Still further east, Robert Searles had slightly better luck. Sighting a cruiser, he closed to a range of four hundred yards and fired two torpedoes. Here his luck changed for the worse: the fins of one ejected torpedo struck the boat's deck before it entered the water, assuring an erratic run and a miss. The second torpedo also malfunctioned: emerging only partially from the torpedo tube it hung, its engine screaming, adding to the sense of chaos, threatening to disintegrate and scatter shrapnel across the deck.

Even as Bob Searles's torpedo man scrambled to reach the missile and shut its engine down, Searles continued his attack on the cruiser. Closing to two hundred yards, he fired his last two torpedoes. Again there were problems: one torpedo's engine fired, but remained firmly in its steel tube; but the fourth torpedo fired cleanly. A hit at this range seemed certain.

Having done all he could, the *38* skipper shoved his throttles to wide open, sending his boat skipping across the cruiser's wake only one hundred yards astern.[15] Behind them, the elated crew heard a deep-sounding explosion and saw a red glow appear just forward of the ship's bridge. Then came a second explosion. Although Searles did not have time to see the results, he claimed a torpedo hit and a cruiser damaged. Now, faced with the same problem as the other two PTs, he also secured his engines until daylight.

For all of the drama and near-disasters occurring this far, these paled when compared to that of *PT 60*'s experience. Finding their boat suddenly under enemy fire after having torpedoed a cruiser, Comdr. Montgomery recalled how "everybody ducked," adding, "later, we got a good laugh out of it because, of course, there is nothing on a PT boat to duck behind. As we took off in the general direction of Tulagi," he continued, "there were two destroyers on our tail. Enemy shells, mostly 4.7s, screamed around us like rockets, and the gun flashes were so continuous they seemed to light up the whole place like daylight.[16]

To the amazement of the PT crew, with the boat running at full speed, they could not outrun the enemy ships. In fact, the destroyers, one of which was the *Naganami*,[17] a 2,000-ton ship with a top speed of 35 knots, was overtaking the PT boat.

With shells from the ships' guns falling continuously around the PT, Searles began to zigzag the boat, hoping to make it a more difficult target. In desperation, Montgomery ordered smoke: the smoke generator secured aft on the fantail shortly began spewing billowing white clouds blinding the destroyers and concealing the PT from its pursuers.

Despite the smoke, a shell exploded in the PT's churning wake; the concussion knocked Torpedoman Willie Uhl flat on the deck. However, the uninjured crewman regained his feet and returned to his post at the generator.

Then the pointed bow of a destroyer began to appear through the wall of smoke. "We could see the tracers streaking by us," said Montgomery, "small red balls of fire, some of which seemed to hang suspended in space for an incredibly long time as they passed us. Those Japs were good gunners, but they couldn't locate us, nor could they see where their shells were falling."[18]

Finally, with the enemy continuing to pursue, Montgomery ordered depth charges dropped, set to detonate shallow. This proved successful. Perhaps the destroyer skippers thought they had entered a mine field, or perhaps they thought they were under attack from an unseen vessel. Whatever the reason, they sheared off and disappeared into the darkness. To be certain they stayed away, Montgomery ordered the smoke generator, still spewing smoke, dropped over the side in hopes of convincing any curious destroyer skippers that the PT boat had gone down.

Having finally eluded their pursuers, the shaken Montgomery and Searles agreed it would be best not to tempt fate further. They would hide behind Florida Island until daylight, when the enemy would have headed back north. With engines muffled down, the *60* boat crept along the shore of Florida Island. Then more trouble: a Japanese destroyer was blocking Sandfly Passage. Perhaps, the Americans reasoned, it had been posted as protection for enemy's bombardment force. "There we were, and there he was," said Montgomery. "The only thing we could do was cut our engines, sit tight, and send up a fervent ten-man prayer that he would not discover our presence." Unable to retreat, unable to go forward, with no torpedoes in their torpedo tubes, Montgomery ruefully recalled his recent conversation with General Rupertus. The general's smile now held a new significance. Certainly after this night, the Tulagi PTs had ample reasons to revise their own views on Japanese destroyers.

Sometime during the night, the enemy ship departed. However, at daylight, the men on *PT 60* experienced a final disaster in what had been a long night. "We started engines," said Montgomery, "and discovered to our complete disgust that we were stuck fast. The bottom there was coral, wickedly sharp, and the ebbing tide had dropped us on the reef."

When the boat was finally hauled clear, examination revealed all three props, shafts and struts were seriously damaged. It would be some time before the boat was operational. As it so happened, following the night's operation, *PT 38* was also out of action: the hot-running torpedo that failed to fire had welded itself inside the torpedo tube.

In one night's operation Montgomery had lost the use of half his boats. But the PT crews were not totally discouraged. In their first action, they had forced the Tokyo Express to break off its bombardment of the Marines and Henderson Field, and had torpedoed and possibly sunk two cruisers.

Or so they thought. Hampered by poor visibility the crews had seen little and knew even less. First, as noted, only one cruiser had accompanied the battleships that night; it, as well as all other ships in the "Express" returned to base the following day without damage. Second, despite their belief, Montgomery's PTs had no effect on the night's bombardment. Admiral Kurita's orders called for a ninety-minute shelling. With only five minutes remaining, observing gun flashes as his destroyers engaged the PTs, the cautious Japanese admiral concluded his escort was attacking submarines and ordered a cease-fire and withdrawal.[19]

At 2:56 a.m. the Japanese task force began to depart. In any event, as Admiral Kurita guessed, by then the two battleships had accomplished their objective. Henderson Field and the Cactus Air Force had been all but wiped out. With gasoline supplies destroyed, and few aircraft left intact, there was little the American defenders could do to stop the second approaching force of eight enemy transports loaded with troops escorted by eight destroyers coming down the Slot. When Admiral Yamamoto learned of Kurita's success in destroying Henderson Field and the Cactus Air Force, he ordered the waiting invasion force waiting north to steam south to Guadalcanal and destroy the U.S. fleet he was certain would appear to defend the Marines. To Yamamoto, Guadalcanal provided another opportunity to force the Decisive Battle that so obsessed Japan's military leaders.[20]

With few aircraft on Henderson Field left to mount an attack, the American defenders on Guadalcanal now faced the threat of being overwhelmed by the fresh enemy troops approaching the island. The American warships having fought in the recent Battle of Cape Esperance, were still replenishing to the south and could not sail until the fifteenth. In any event, the available U.S. warships at

Espiritu Santo were no match for Yamamoto's Combined Fleet, as the Japanese Admiral was well aware.

It seemed Montgomery's PT boats had reached Guadalcanal just in time to be present at the defeat. A Marine Corps colonel appeared at the battered airstrip to announce for the benefit of the Army pilots, that the Marines were not sure they could hold the airstrip, that a task force of Japanese transports was headed for Guadalcanal. With gasoline sufficient for one mission only, they were to take off and bomb the Japanese ships. When that was done, they were to attach themselves to an infantry outfit on Guadalcanal.[21]

In any event, the best the few planes could do was damage one enemy destroyer, and the enemy troop transports with their escorting destroyers continued to approach.[22]

The night of October 14-15 was another bad night for the American defenders. As part of the massive plan, two Japanese cruisers, the *Chokai* and the *Kinugasa,* entered Sealark Channel and blasted Henderson Field with 752 eight-inch shells.[23] On this night, Montgomery's four PTs did not respond: *PT 60* was inoperable due to the grounding, *PT 38* had exhausted her torpedoes, and *PTs 46* and *48* were assigned to escort a shuttle boat running between Tulagi and Guadalcanal. By the time the two PTs completed their assignment the Japanese force had departed.[24]

On October 15, Admiral Nimitz at Pearl Harbor, expressed his view of the situation in three grim sentences: "It now appears that we are unable to control the sea in the Guadalcanal area. Thus our supply of the positions will only be done at great expense to us. The situation is not hopeless, but it is certainly critical."[25]

Back in Washington, officials acted as though they were preparing the public for a disaster. Navy Secretary Knox commented that he "would not make any prediction, but every man will give a good account of himself... Everybody hopes that we can hold on."[26] Others were less optimistic.

With little added resources available, Admiral Nimitz decided that Admiral Ghormley should be replaced, that what was needed was a more aggressive commander; his choice was Vice Admiral William F. Halsey. On October 16, with Admiral King's authority Nimitz acted at once. On October 18, Admiral Halsey landed at Noumea to find to his surprise, that he had been ordered to "take command of the South Pacific Area and South Pacific Forces immediately."[27]

By this time, the second division of four PTs of Squadron 3 was aboard a transport bound for the South Pacific, destination Tulagi. The appointment of a new and more aggressive South Pacific Theater commander and additional PTs based at Tulagi came at a crucial time. Indeed, unknown to the Americans, the Japanese high command had decided it was time for their army and navy to combine forces and throw the Americans out of the Solomons. This decision stemmed from a mid-September agreement reached by the Emperor's chiefs of staff that the airstrip on Guadalcanal would replace New Guinea and the Papua operation as Japan's top priority, with the latter dropping to second place. In short, the Japanese recognized that they could not risk another battle for tactically important Henderson Field until the airstrip had been captured by its ground forces.

Unknown to the Americans, the Battle of Cape Esperance followed by the clash between the PTs of Squadron 3 and the "Express" on the night of October 13 was the quiet before the storm in what would be an all-out effort by the Japanese to retake Guadalcanal. As it was, it marked the completion of the first phase of Operation "KA."

On October 15, the Japanese reinforcement phase of the plan was completed. "Y-Day," October 22, was to be the fateful day. On that day, the Japanese Rising Sun was to be planted on Henderson Field by the Japanese army commander on Guadalcanal. With the field in Japanese possession, Admiral Yamamoto's Combined Fleet circling north of the Solomons in anticipation, would head south to "apprehend and annihilate any powerful forces in the Solomons area, as well as any reinforcements."[28]

In any event, thanks to both the jungle on Guadalcanal and the determined Marine defenders on the island, another major effort by the Japanese failed. Thus the battle for the prize that was Henderson Field ended shortly after daylight on October 26 with the repulse of the enemy ground attack.

Lt. Comdr. Alan R. "Monty" Montgomery, commanding Squadron 3 based at Tulagi who led the first PT attack on the Tokyo Express in October 1942. Well liked by his men, "Monty" had to be relieved from command due to having contracted pneumonia during the voyage to the South Pacific. *Courtesy of WWII PT Boats Museum and Archives, Germantown, Tennessee, USA.*

Six Squadron 3 PT officers based at Tulagi who engaged the Tokyo Express in late 1942 during the campaign for Guadalcanal: from left to right, rear, Lt. Jack Searles, Lt. Tom Kendall and Lt. Charles Tilden. Botton row, left to right, Lt. Robert Searles, Lt. "Stilly" Taylor and Lt. Leonard Nikoloric. *Courtesy of WWII PT Boats Museum and Archives, Germantown, Tennessee, USA.*

CHAPTER SIX

PTS VERSUS
THE TOKYO EXPRESS

On October 25, the four boats of Commander Montgomery's second division reached Tulagi, completing the last stage of the trip under tow by the destroyer-minesweepers *Trevor* and *Zane*. Piled high on the decks of the erstwhile four-stackers were much needed ammunition, drums of 100-octane gasoline, and Mark VIII torpedoes.[1] As expected, the newcomers were full of questions. What they heard was not reassuring. The "veterans" of the first division by virtue of less than two weeks experience, regaled them with stories of hair-raising confrontations. Ordinarily, such tales would have been deliberately spiced for maximum effect; in this case, however, what they heard was more truth than fiction.

For the new men, the fact that Japanese destroyers were as fast as their fleet PT boats, if not faster, came as a shock. As a professional naval officer, Comdr. Montgomery described *PT 60*'s experience on the first night of operations, noting how luck was a major factor in its escape, emphasizing that Japanese destroyer crews were well trained and highly aggressive.[2] New men learned that Japanese destroyer crews tended to favor operating on the darkest nights and were skilled seamen. In short, unlike the stories they had heard back in the States, the enemy was no second-class fighter. There would be no such thing as knocking off the Japanese ships with impunity. If the PTs were to win against this foe, they would need to be no less skilled and equally aggressive.

As with the first division, the second PT division managed to reach Guadalcanal at time of crisis: on Guadalcanal, a Japanese ground attack on Henderson Field scheduled for the 22nd, had been rescheduled for the 24th due to unexpected difficulties. By the afternoon of the 25th, the ground war for Henderson Field was at its height. However, by October 27, it was clear the Japanese army's effort to retake Henderson Field had again been defeated with Japanese losses.

North of the Solomons, Admiral Yamamoto's powerful Combined Fleet had been circling, awaiting word of a victory. On the 24th, an out-of-patience Yamamoto told the army commanders that if they did not take Henderson Field quickly, his ships would be obliged to retire as fuel was running short. In the end, due to a series of confused signals between the Japanese on Guadalcanal and the Combined Fleet, Yamamoto's fleet steamed south to destroy American ships near the island. The result was the Battle of the Santa Cruz Islands, a carrier-plane battle fought on October 26. In combat tonnage lost, it proved to be yet another Japanese victory: American losses included the carrier *Hornet*. Reflecting the mood at Pearl Harbor, Admiral Nimitz observed, "The general situation at Guadalcanal is not unfavorable." Note was made that this statement was slightly more positive than the mid-October pronouncement.[3]

With the U.S. Navy's ships still at Espiritu Santo, hundreds of miles to the south of Guadalcanal, it remained for the PTs at Tulagi and the planes on Henderson Field to cope with the nightly incursions of the "Express." But the Tulagi PTs and Henderson Field held "two aces." Foremost was an excellent intelligence system: from the moment the Japanese lit their boilers at the anchorage in the Shortlands three hundred miles to the north, Allied Coastwatchers posted on nearby Bougainville sounded the alarm, radioing a timely warning to Guadalcanal. The Coastwatchers were part of a system organized by Australia to defend the lower continent from attacks by reporting sightings of the enemy, with the outbreak of the Pacific war, a few members of the Australian system remained, or were stationed among the islands; their task was to radio information on the Japanese to Allied headquarters, information on naval, air and ground forces, but to avoid combat with the enemy. Also, since Japanese destroyers intent on reaching Guadalcanal during hours of darkness had to start their three-hundred-mile dash while it was still daylight, Allied reconnaissance planes were able to report their progress.[4] Secondly, the Japanese ships coming south down the Slot had to pass through one or the other of two passages formed by Savo Island, to enter Sealark Channel, one to the south Savo, a seven-and-one-half-mile gap between Savo and Guadalcanal's Cape Esperance, the other, a fifteen-mile wide opening between Savo Island and Florida Island to the north.

By now, the PT commanders at Tulagi had devised a system: alerted as to the approaching Japanese, one PT would be posted at the entrance to each passage as a lookout, radioing the alarm when the enemy ships were sighted. The rest of the available PTs would be posted further east in Sealark Channel, ready to attack with torpedoes once the enemy ships were in the Channel. At a time when PTs lacked radar, spreading the boats out offered a better possibility the enemy would be spotted; also, owing to a lack of visibility, the use of high-speed PT torpedo attacks as taught at Melville, exposed the PTs to the possibility of colliding with one another in the darkness. Instead, the PT skippers would rely on stealth and the boats' low silhouette to maneuver into close range for their attacks.

It was not long before an opportunity came to test the theory. On the night of October 29-30, Coastwatchers reported three destroyers heading down the Slot. Newly arrived Lt. James Greene on *PT 39* drew the assignment to patrol the lower, or south passage to Sealark Channel; veteran Bob Searles on *PT 38* covered the wider passage north of Savo.

Shortly after midnight Greene sighted the silhouettes of two fast-moving ships off Cape Esperance heading toward Savo Island. Even as he radioed the sighting the ships disappeared in the darkness.

Alerted by Greene's call, Bob Searles turned toward the lower passage. In doing so, he failed to notice another destroyer bearing down on him from the opposite direction. Apparently the destroyer's intent was to ram.

At this fateful moment, a night-flying PBY dropped a flare overhead, prompting the enemy ship's gunners to fire on the aircraft. In the glare of the flare, Searles saw the charging ship. Ramming his throttles to the wide open, he fled toward Tulagi with the enemy in close pursuit. "One enemy can [Navy slang term for destroyer] coming from east through Cape Esperance and Savo," Searles radioed desperately. "Am being chased. Am being fired on, course northeast. Hurry! Hurry!" But then, to Searles's relief, the enemy ship suddenly veered away and headed for the lower passage, apparently departing Sealark Channel. But now, having heard Searles's urgent call for assistance, Lt. Greene was racing to help. Crossing the wake of a fast-moving ship heading west, Greene concluded that this was the ship Searles had reported. Determined to attack, Greene began to pursue the enemy, pushing his boat to its maximum speed.

Shortly, the dim form of a narrow silhouette appeared ahead. Slowly the distance closed. However, the narrow stern of the destroyer provided a difficult torpedo target. To provide a better chance of getting a hit, Greene angled away then turned back, firing three torpedoes off the ship's quarter. As he raced away, Greene thought he saw a hit amidships. However, Japanese records contain no record of such a hit.[5] Nevertheless, there is no doubt that the PTs' actions alarmed the enemy. That night, two destroyers, *Shigure* and *Ariake,* possibly the ships sighted by Greene, hurriedly departed Guadalcanal with part of their supplies still aboard. They left two passengers behind, however, Comdr. Ohmae, IJN, and General Miyazaki, the 17th Army's chief of staff; the two had come to the island in response to the serious threat of starvation and diseases that by now afflicted the 17th Army on Guadalcanal. Despite the efforts of the Tokyo Express, the Japanese on Guadalcanal faced a critical supply problem that threatened to weaken the Army. Describing the misery of retreating from the last failed attack to retake Henderson Field, one Japanese Army lieutenant's diary told of existing only on a tiny teaspoon of salt per day and a palmful of rice porridge; a second entry noted that "food capture(s) the mind to the degree that one is always thinking of it."[6]

Nevertheless, during the last week of October, despite the failed mid-October ground attack, Imperial Headquarters remained optimistic. First, the Imperial Army had finally agreed with the Navy that Guadalcanal was developing into the "decisive battle" between the United States and Japan. Second, there was the mistaken conviction that the U.S. Navy had lost so many ships in the Battle of Santa Cruz Islands that Japan now had a clear dominance at sea, and third was the belief that the failed ground attack in mid-October had only narrowly failed to achieve its aim. Amidst such false optimism, a three-day effort by the staff of the Combined Fleet provided the outline of a plan to finally retake Henderson Field.

Meanwhile, the Tulagi PTs maintained their nightly patrols off Guadalcanal, but lacking radar, they had little to show for it. On the night of November 4-5, Stilly Taylor encountered the destroyer *Murasame*. The enemy ship's gunners fired first, forcing Taylor to hastily retreat in the darkness before he could fire his torpedoes.

Ashore on Guadalcanal, an American ground offensive provided proved promising. As Japanese troops retreated before the advancing Americans, the 17th Army sent an urgent call for reinforcements on November 4 or at least by November 5. Unable to make a run on the night of the 4th, on the night of November 5th, the "Express" combined the effort in what was planned for the nights of November 5 and 6. As darkness fell, fifteen destroyers and the light cruiser *Tenryu* closed on Guadalcanal with throttles wide open. *Tenryu* and five destroyers peeled off to land part of the 228th Infantry Regiment at Cape Esperance. At 10:40 p.m. the remaining ten ships approached Tassafaronga to land the commander of the 38th Infantry Group, his headquarters, and the bulk of the 228th Infantry Regiment.[7]

On this night, with the PTs on the alert, Lt. Les Gamble with *PT 48* was prowling close to the shore of Guadalcanal in Sealark Channel when he encountered a destroyer off Koli Point; Gamble fired all four torpedoes at a range of four hundred yards. As he withdrew he was rewarded by the sound of two explosions. Again, Japanese records make no mention of a sinking.[8]

Two nights later, Coastwatchers reported five destroyers barreling down the Slot toward Guadalcanal. Records at Tulagi noted that was the third night out of the previous four that all PT boats at Tulagi had been ordered out. By now, both boats and crews were showing signs of stress. Long hours of night patrolling with days spent working on boats under primitive conditions, with little sleep before preparing for the coming night patrol, were wearing out men as well as boats. Fatigue was now an enemy: "You had to stay alert to stay alive out on patrol," said Lt. Gamble, "but you could actually go to sleep on your feet. I don't know whether I was dreaming or hallucinating, but I remember looking up one night and seeing a golden aircraft carrier being pulled across the sky by sixteen horses. On another occasion I was driving the boat after a long patrol, and suddenly there was a giant brick wall in front of me. Luckily, I woke up before we hit the wall."[9] On November 7, the

Japanese plan was to transport 1300 troops, the advance unit of the 38th Division, down the Slot to Guadalcanal on eleven destroyers. Commanding the "Express" was Captain Torajiro Sato. Reported by the Coastwatchers, Sato's force was attacked by forty Henderson Field aircraft, but veteran destroyer skippers were so successful in evading the attacks that only modest hull damage was reported by two ships.[10] The report of the approaching Express was then passed to Tulagi. At 9:44 p.m. Commander Hugh Robinson, having replaced the exhausted Comdr. Montgomery with the arrival of Squadron 3's second division, ordered all available PTs out. This amounted to a mere three boats, *PT 39* skippered by Lt. Greene, *PT 37* commanded by Lt. Leonard Nikoloric, and *PT 61* with Comdr. Robinson at the helm.[11]

At 9:44 p.m. PTs sighted the destroyers south of Savo Island and fanned out to attack. Greene and Nikoloric each fired two torpedoes. The alert destroyer skippers turned their vessels to parallel the torpedo tracks, offering the smallest possible targets, a maneuver referred to as "combing the tracks." Three of the four torpedoes missed. The fourth hit the destroyer *Mochizuki,* but it proved to be a dud.[12] Then it was the destroyers' turn: the inevitable enemy searchlights snapped on, their beams probing for the fleeing boats now laying billowing clouds of smoke in their wakes. With their usual accuracy, the enemy gunners opened fire. Commander Robinson vividly described what followed: "We turned away from the destroyers and were making top speed to clear the area when a shell zipped right over the cockpit—it couldn't have cleared our heads by more than a few inches—and landed on the bow, blowing a large section of it away. I kept the throttles full forward, and by making top speed we managed to keep any water from shipping in. When I pulled into Tulagi Harbor and brought the boat down off its plane, we immediately started taking water in the hole."[13]

By November 9, Allied commanders were convinced the Japanese were preparing to make yet another effort to retake Henderson Field. According to intelligence, this promised to be a major amphibious effort supported by heavy warships. For the Americans it was to be a race against time to get additional ground forces to Guadalcanal. In any event, additional U.S. troops began disembarking on the island from troop ships on November 11. In mid-afternoon of the 12th, reports were received of Japanese battleships, cruisers and destroyers 335 miles to the north of the "Canal." A second group of enemy destroyers were sighted less than two hundred miles to the NNW; in mid-afternoon, two carriers and two destroyers were sighted 265 miles to the west. And still, the Americans had no report of the approaching enemy troop convoy. In fact, impatient with previous efforts, Admiral Yamamoto's plan called for a massive operation: Eleven army transports carrying the main body of the 38th Division escorted by twelve destroyers would head down the Slot to Guadalcanal from Shortland, arriving on the 13th, Z-Day. On November 12, Z-Day minus one, the plan called for the Advance Force: two battleships escorted by a light cruiser and fourteen destroyers to shell Henderson Field in a repeat of the October 13 operation. In addition, a cruiser force would again blast Henderson Field on Z-Day. Admiral Yamamoto's Combined Fleet would also provide naval support. Rear Admiral Richmond Kelly Turner, commanding the South Pacific Amphibious Force, estimated Japanese strength of the force approaching Guadalcanal late November 12 from the north to include two battleships, two to four heavy cruisers, two light cruisers and ten to twelve destroyers, clearly too powerful a force for his convoy escort centered on five cruisers and escorting destroyers to deal with. But with ninety percent of Turner's supplies and equipment from the convoy ships now exposed on the beach, and heavy U.S. warships too far away to interfere, the overmatched U.S. escort units had no choice but to block.

What followed is the first phase of what is known as the Naval Battle of Guadalcanal, fought in the early hours of November 13 with the U.S. losing the light cruiser *Atlanta* and destroyers *Barton, Cushing, Laffey* and *Monssen.* Japanese losses were no less extensive. But what was important was that the Japanese Advance Force failed to break through and bombard Henderson Field as planned. For his failure to complete this mission, as commander of the Advance Force, Adm. Hiroaki Abe was summarily retired.[14]

But the night's battle was far from decisive. The convoy carrying enemy troops scheduled to land on Guadalcanal accompanied by its escorting destroyers continued to approach; it still would have to be dealt with. The outcome of the Japanese plan to retake the island was yet to be determined.

At 1:30 a.m. November 4, Z-Day, Japanese float planes began dropping flares over Henderson Field. Shortly, as planned, two heavy cruisers, *Suzuya* and *Maya,* screened by light cruiser *Tenryu* and four destroyers, entered Sealark Channel by the south passage before turning parallel to the Guadalcanal coast and opened fire. Each of the heavy warships carried five hundred rounds of high-capacity eight-inch shells for what was scheduled to be a thirty-seven-minute bombardment of the airstrip.[15]

On this night, only two Tulagi PTs were operable; both were skippered by veterans, *PT 38* by John Searles and *PT 39* by Stilly Taylor. They were screening the cruiser *Portland,* heavily damaged during the previous night's battle, now being towed back to Tulagi. "We were secured from this job and immediately tried to locate each other again," said Taylor. "However, before we were able to do so, the Nips began to shell Henderson Field, first putting up a very bright flare in the vicinity of the field, and naturally both of us started in on them independently.

"Apparently I was much nearer to the Japs than Jack was, because of where I had secured from patrol around the *Portland.* The best intelligence we had was that there was a Jap battleship on the way down from either Bougainville or Rabaul. It was supposed to have been accompanied by escorts, probably destroyers.[16]

"As soon as the Japs opened fire, it was obvious to us that there was at least one fairly heavy ship. We thought at the time, that it was probably the battleship referred to in the intelligence report. We could tell that it was definitely a heavy ship because of the long orange flash from its gunfire rather than the short white flash which we knew from experience was the smaller fire of the destroyers. As we started to make our run on this formation, we thought we saw a destroyer make a short scouting trip well ahead of the main formation. My quartermaster reported this, and I could never be absolutely sure that it was not his imagination. However, due to the light put up by the Nips' flares, I was able to use my [torpedo] director for the first time. I set his speed at about 20 knots and I think that he was doing slightly more than this. I kept him in the director for approximately seven salvos, and I really had a beautiful line on him."

Believing he would be spotted by the ship's escorting destroyers if he continued his run in, Taylor fired all four torpedoes at a range of about one thousand yards. Again there were problems: three of his Mark VIII torpedoes ejected smoothly, the fourth, however, remained stubbornly inside its steel torpedo tube. Having done all he could, Taylor reversed course and headed back to Tulagi, convinced, as he said later, "that at least one of them found its mark."[17]

Coming in behind Taylor, Searles sighted a destroyer crossing ahead, one of the enemy's escorts, and fired all four torpedoes at the destroyer. As he turned his PT away, his crew claimed they saw two of the torpedoes strike home. "This was an easy attack for the PTs," said Taylor later. "We were able to get within range unmolested with good visibility because of their flares and because of their gunfire. I do believe that the first they knew of our presence was when torpedoes hit them. It was the kind of attack that we all had been dreaming about. They usually came in under cover of bad weather, and we often found ourselves in the middle of them before we knew what was going on."

Alas, as on the night of October 13, the truth was that none of the PTs' torpedoes were hits; and again, as on October 13, the Japanese commander of the bombardment force never knew his ships had been attacked by PT boats. Observing fires and explosions ashore, Rear Admiral Shoji Nishimura, estimated correctly that the field was still operable. However, having dispensed 989 eight-inch shells, in accord with his orders, he departed Sealark Channel to rendezvous with the waiting Main Group for the return trip to Rabaul.[18]

Back in Washington, they were in the process of savoring news of the defeat of the enemy task force on the night of November 12-13 when officials were dismayed to learn that Henderson Field had been bombarded by heavy warships and a large force of troop transports were approaching Guadalcanal to carry out an amphibious landing. At this moment, even President Roosevelt began to have doubts.[19]

To the PT crews at Tulagi, the situation was nothing short of grim, but for other reasons. "We got word that more transports, destroyers and battleships were coming in from the northwest and that cruisers would be running through the passage south of Savo," said Comdr. Robinson. "We were ordered to go out to the west of Savo and seek targets of opportunity. They told us there was a possibility that Admiral Lee would be coming in from the south with a battleship force, but the feeling was that he would not arrive in time."[20] Admiral Willis Lee, commanding Task Force 16, two new battleships, the *Washington* and *South Dakota*, along with four destroyers, was part of a screening force for the carrier *Enterprise*, some 350 miles south of Guadalcanal. Again it would be up to the PT boats at Tulagi.

For this momentous event, only three boats were operable, *PT 57* with Lt. Nikoloric at the helm, *PT 59* skippered by Lt. Greene and *PT 61* commanded by Robinson, its shattered bow repaired. As these veterans boarded their boats this night, they held no illusions. From where they stood, three tired PTs against the entire Japanese Navy could end in only one way.

However, at the last minute, there would be a reprieve. Hours earlier, with the fate of Guadalcanal at stake, in a bold decision, Admiral Halsey had detached his two battleships, *Washington* and *South Dakota,* from his carrier task force and, led by Rear Admiral Willis ("Ching") Lee, sent them racing north with a destroyer escort to intercept the enemy armada bearing down on Guadalcanal from the north.

Nearing Sealark Channel, flagship *Washington* began to pick up radio transmissions between the Tulagi PTs. As Robinson recounted later: "About half way between Tulagi and Savo I heard a voice come over the radio and say, 'Peter Tare, Peter Tare...this is Lee...Ching Lee, Catchy?' 'Ching' Lee was the name by which Admiral Lee was known in the Navy owing to his lengthy service in China.

"I got on the radio and said, 'Ching Lee, I understand.' A voice came back, 'Peter Tare...Peter Tare...stand clear we are coming through.' I turned my boat around and headed for home."[21]

Greene followed Robinson as he headed back to Tulagi. There, crews from the two boats scrambled ashore and ran to the top of a nearby hill to watch the action. However, Nikoloric withdrew a safe distance to the northeast. "We stopped engines," recalled the young skipper. A member of crew went below and made sandwiches and coffee. Then "we all went up and sat on the foredeck, and a half hour later we were all sitting there eating tuna fish sandwiches, sipping coffee and watching from a front-row seat one of the greatest battles of the war. It was like sitting at Ebbets Field.[22]

Back at Tulagi, Robinson and his men had a no less ideal vantage point. Indeed, what followed was one of the few battleship vs. battleship duals to occur in the Pacific during World War II, this one involving the *Washington* and the *Kirishima,* sister ship of *Hiei,* lost earlier in the Naval Battle of Guadalcanal. To observers ashore, however, it was most confusing: "You couldn't tell who was who," said Robinson, "but we assumed that the two big ships to the south were Lee's battleships. It was a very clear night for a change with a bright moon shining. You could actually see the ships out in the bay. You could see the big guns fire and the shells go arcing up into sky in a bright red streak. And then they would start down and finally hit and blow the side completely out of some ship. There wasn't much in the way of cheering—we were mostly awestruck by the spectacle.[23]

By 1 a.m. November 15, the Naval Battle of Guadalcanal was over. Both sides suffered losses. Both sides claimed victory. But it was the United States that accomplished its goal, the successful landing of reinforcements and materiel on Guadalcanal. The Japanese managed to land a mere two thousand shaken survivors, 260 boxes of shells and 1500 bags of rice.[24] A captured Japanese document summed it up briefly: "It must be said that the success or failure in recapturing Guadalcanal Island, and the vital naval battle related to it, is the fork in the road which leads to victory for them or us." There it was. But the realization that the Naval Battle of Guadalcanal marked the moment when Japanese dreams of retaking the lower Solomons and Henderson Field ended, was not readily apparent, other than to the Imperial Navy, whose opinion the Imperial Army scorned. On December 1, a CINCPAC analyst noted, "It is still indicated that a major attempt to recapture 'Cactus' is in the making." And he was right.[25] It would be another ten weeks before the Japanese Army finally agreed with the Navy's position that the island was beyond recovery, and evacuation was the only logical solution.

Note: The *South Dakota* lost electric power at the outset of the battle and was forced to retire, leaving *Washington* to battle on its own.

CHAPTER SEVEN

STARVATION ISLAND

The failure of another effort by the enemy to retake Henderson Field was followed by a momentary lull in the fighting. With the period of the full moon in the latter half of November, the commanders at Rabaul temporarily suspended operations by the Tokyo Express. To the Tulagi PT crews, there was time finally for long overdue boat maintenance, no less than for boat crews to catch up on their sleep, for tightly stretched nerves to heal. Conditions were further improved toward the end of November with the arrival of PT Squadron 2 with twelve additional boats, a blend of six 77-foot and six 80-foot Elcos. By November 30, a total of fifteen PT boats, along with then tender *Jamestown,* were based at Tulagi.[1]

As was frequently the case in these early days of the Pacific war, the new squadron was the result of some last-minute adjustments. Initially Squadron 5, with a full complement of twelve new 80-foot Elco PT boats had arrived at Panama for shipment to the Solomons to reinforce the battered, hard-fighting remnants of Squadron 3. But the commander of the Panama Frontier recommended that Squadron 2, the more experienced unit already in Panama, be sent instead. Thus Squadron 5 remained behind in Panama. When Squadron 2 departed, it took with it six of Squadron 5's newly commissioned 80-footers, *PTs 109* through *114*; in their place, Squadron 5 received six of Squadron 2's older 77-footers. It was a development doubtlessly greeted with a profound lack of enthusiasm by the officers and men of Squadron 5.[2]

For the Tulagi veterans, the arrival of the first 80-foot Elco PTs in a combat theater was a source of considerable curiosity. Typically, PT crews tended to be jealous if not competitive concerning their boats' performance. When asked whether the crews of the older 77-foot Elco PTs were envious of the newcomers,

Comdr. Robinson answered, not at all. "In fact," he noted, "the men of Squadron 3 felt the 77-footers were better suited for the task at hand. With their more shallow V-bottoms, they were faster than the 80-footers and were also more maneuverable. We felt," Robinson concluded, "that the new boats were really a compromise. They were a more comfortable boat, but that didn't mean a great deal when a Japanese destroyer was on your tail."[3]

For the long-suffering First Marine Division on Guadalcanal, supported by the Tulagi PTs since October, it was also a time of change. Battle fatigue, disease, and short rations had dulled their fighting edge beyond recovery. They would shortly be replaced by Army troops.

The Naval Battle of Guadalcanal had left more than 15,000 Japanese troops stranded on the island,[4] no clear record exists as to just how many. Marine Corps Maj. Gen. Alexander Vandegrift, commanding the U.S. ground campaign, tried to follow up the recent naval victory with a push westward. But he learned that despite setbacks and a lack of reinforcements, the 17th Army was still a formidable foe.

However, with the suspension of operations by the Tokyo Express due to the full moon, the lack of food supplies for the Japanese garrison on Guadalcanal reached a crisis. By mid-November, 17th Army reports described its men as being reduced to eating wild plants and animals; on average a hundred men were dying per day, if conditions did not improve, warned the reports, the number would increase.[5]

On November 16, the Japanese command made a major decision. Since the Americans now controlled the air, which meant control of the sea, Combined Fleet ordered that the bulk of its submarine force be assigned a new mission: moving supplies to Guadalcanal.[6] The submarines would load at Bougainville, just beyond the range of the Cactus Air Force, and proceed to Guadalcanal at the rate of one per day, landing ammunition, medicines and provisions at the western end of the island. The combat-minded submarine crews hated the assignment; their officers scornfully termed it the "Marutsu" after the Japanese equivalent of Federal Express or UPS, or a "mogura" operation, so named because it operated like moles, slowly and out of sight.[7]

The Tulagi PTs managed to frustrate the first submarine landing on November 24; but on the following night, the *I-17* managed to land about eleven tons. On each night until the end of the month, submarines made runs to Guadalcanal where they surfaced under cover of darkness and sailors manhandled cargo across their narrow decks to waiting *daihatsus* sent from shore. Each load represented possibly a day's worth of food for the 17th Army.

On December 9, the "Underwater Tokyo Express" suffered its first casualty. Heretofore, American intelligence, which had generalized rather than issued precise information on enemy submarine arrivals, gave the Tulagi PTs a precise report indicating an enemy submarine would surface close to shore the next morning in Kamimbo Bay at 2 a.m. On December 9, *PT 44* with Frank Freeland at the helm and Jack Searles on *PT 59* were in position. At about the expected hour, with the two boats separated by about five hundred yards, the submarine surfaced between them. Freeland's boat was not aligned to fire, but Searles's was. He launched two torpedoes at close range, and the submarine disintegrated in a violent explosion.[8] Japanese reports confirmed the sinking of the 320-foot-long *I-3* commanded by Comdr. Ichiro Togami. She had departed Shortland Island on December 7 with a load of provisions and medicines. According to Japanese reports, all hands went down with the boat.

Back at Tulagi, Searles, having fired two torpedoes at close range, wondered aloud how it was only one was a hit. Freeland had the answer: The second torpedo, said the skipper of the *44* boat, passed under the submarine then zipped beneath *PT 44* before disappearing into the night. Only the shallow draft of the PT prevented Searles from getting a second hit, sending the *44* boat to the bottom along with the I-boat.

The loss of the I-boat caused the Japanese to suspend the use of submarines for hauling supplies to Guadalcanal.[9] The problem of supplying the 17th Army on the island in its dire straits had yet to be resolved. A strength report from the garrison dated November 20 noted that of 29,177 soldiers landed since August 7, only 12,775, by a liberal definition were capable of combat. By November 26, the 17th Army's entire stock of meat and vegetables was nearly exhausted, and even the rice and barley would be consumed by the end of the day. In forward positions, the few relatively healthy men were doing the patrolling, scouting and attacking; those too weak to walk were in dugouts in defensive positions. Before the end of November, due to lack of rations, the men of the 17th Army would be living on grass and water.[10] Compounding the problem was the lack of medical supplies to counteract the spread of diseases.

The limited success of the Underwater Tokyo Express and the conditions now prevailing in the 17th Army compelled the recourse to the use of the proven mainstay, the destroyers, termed the "Nezumi" (rat) system by the Japanese: with U.S. ships fitted with radar, ready to pounce on the destroyers as they made their runs to Guadalcanal, the "rats" had to elude them. In doing so, their best weapon was speed and elusiveness, the same methods rodents used to escape death.[11]

However, the new Express would operate with new refinements, steps that would reduce the loss of destroyers on the reinforcement mission: sailors cleaned heavy drums, normally used for oil and gasoline, and half-filled them with rice and barley, allowing the drums to float. Between 200 and 240 drums, joined in clusters by ropes, were loaded on the weather deck of each destroyer. Off Guadalcanal, the Express would merely reduce speed to 12 knots as the clusters of drums were shoved over the side close to the beach to be pulled ashore by soldiers on the shore by use of a central line. Through this method, only twenty runs per month would be sufficient to feed 20,000 men while drastically reducing the exposure period for each destroyer's time spent off the island.[12]

The responsibility for the first of five runs using the new method of supply fell to Rear Admiral Raizo Tanaka. Widely regarded as Japan's most gifted destroyer flotilla commander, following the U.S. Marine invasion of Guadalcanal in August 1942, it was Tanaka and his destroyers assigned as a Reinforcement Unit to support the Army in its effort to retake the island,[13] that the Americans would nickname the "Tokyo Express."

On November 29, Admiral Tanaka left Shortland for Guadalcanal with eight destroyers; six were loaded with 200 to 240 drums each, the two unencumbered vessels comprising a screening unit. Upon receiving word of Tanaka's departure, Admiral Halsey ordered an interception. At 10:25 p.m. on the night of November 30, Task Force 67 commanded by Rear Admiral Carleton Wright met the Reinforcement Unit off Tassafaronga. In November 1942, U.S.

naval units were still not trained properly for night combat. And like the PT boats, American destroyers were armed with inferior torpedoes. Nor did radar provide the Americans with an unlimited advantage, as in the blackness of a night battle, it caused the task force to train its guns on the nearest and biggest blip on radar screens, allowing the rest of the enemy force to slip away untouched.[14]

The Battle of Tassafaronga would be another sharp defeat inflicted on the U.S. Navy, this time by an inferior force. At the cost of one destroyer, Tanaka seriously crippled four of Wright's cruisers, and sent one, the *Northampton* to the bottom. Every American naval officer—from Admiral Halsey down—sought an explanation for the disaster, but all were hard put to find the answer. A Japanese analyst provided a useful contribution, saying in part, that having gained an initial advantage though the element of surprise, the enemy's "fire was inaccurate, shells [im]properly set for deflection were especially numerous, and it is conjectured that either his marksmanship is not remarkable or else the illumination from his star shells was not sufficiently effective."[15]

In fact, American marksmanship during the battle was abominable. In any case, the Battle of Tassafaranga was the last surface action fought off Guadalcanal in which major ships were engaged. Hereafter, the task of coping with the Tokyo Express would be left to the PTs at Tulagi and the Cactus Air Force. The major U.S. naval units would remain at Espiritu Santo, close enough to be available in the event a major enemy fleet approached Guadalcanal, but far enough away to be reasonably safe from enemy air and submarine attacks.[16]

Although the American navy's ships were defeated in this battle, the action prevented Admiral Tanaka's ships from delivering the critically needed drums of supplies. This failure enhanced the urgency for delivery of provisions to the island. On December 3, Admiral Tanaka led ten destroyers south from Shortland to Guadalcanal, seven laden with drums of supplies, three as a screening force. Again, despite attacks by aircraft of the Cactus Air Force from Henderson Field, only one destroyer was damaged by a near miss. As usual, this did not hinder the enemy's advance. Although the approach was reported by the Coastwatchers, Wright's cruiser force was too battered due to the recent clash with Tanaka to interfere; and, for some reason, word did not reach Tulagi. As a result, the Express discharged 1500 drums of supplies without interruption and retired safely to the north.[17] Back at Shortland, however, a disheartened Tanaka learned that a mere 310 barrels, only some twenty percent of the precious drums of supplies, had been recovered by the Guadalcanal garrison.

On the following day, reflecting the continuing urgency of the supply crisis, Tanaka's Reinforcement Unit was increased to thirteen destroyers. Also, the *Teruzuki,* a newly built 2500-ton destroyer capable of 39 knots, arrived. On December 7, Tanaka shifted his flag to the new ship.[18]

That afternoon, the Reinforcement Unit consisting of twelve destroyers, nine carrying drums of supplies, three providing a screening force, left Shortland for Guadalcanal under the command of Capt. Torajiro Sato. Alerted by the Coastwatchers, SBDs from Henderson Field again attacked, and again damaged one ship with a near-miss. With the crippled ship under tow back to base by a second destroyer, Sato continued to race south with the remaining ships.

Now it was up to the Tulagi PTs. On this night, one year since the attack on Pearl Harbor, the PT command at Tulagi had the luxury of having eight boats available, *PTs 36, 37, 40, 43, 44, 48, 59,* and *109,* the last skippered by squadron commander Rollin Westholm. As the *109* boat was a new 80-foot Elco, there was considerable interest on the part of the veteran PT crews to see how well it performed in combat.[19]

In accord with what was now fairly standard practice when the Express was expected, the waiting PTs were dispersed along Sealark Channel, two positioned as lookouts between Savo and Cape Esperance, while a second two-boat section cruised off the northwest shore of Guadalcanal, between Kokumbona and Cape Esperance. The balance of four boats, designated the "striking force," idled in wait in the lee of Savo.

Around 11:20 p.m., the two boats posted between Savo and Cape Esperance, *PTs 40* and *48* commanded by veterans Bob Searles and Stilly Taylor, spotted the Reinforcement Unit standing into the passage. As the two skippers maneuvered to attack, two of *PT 40's* engines suddenly died. Slowed to a crawl, the crippled PT was spotted and taken under fire by Sato's destroyers. As Searles sought to withdraw at his best speed, Taylor, throttles wide open and trailing a billowing cloud of smoke, sent *PT 48* thundering between the onrushing Sato and *PT 40,* diverting Sato, who suspecting this was the prelude to a PT torpedo attack, reversed course temporarily, thus allowing the slowed PT to reach safety.[20]

With word received from the scout boats that the Express had arrived, the four boats of the "striking force," *PTs 36, 37, 44,* and *59* moved into position to intercept. Fifteen minutes later, they sighted the silhouettes of Sato's destroyers entering the Channel. First to attack was *PT 37* firing two torpedoes at the lead destroyer. Immediately in the *37*'s wake, the battle-worn *PT 59,* commanded by John Searles, sent a second pair of torpedoes racing toward the enemy. Wheeling *PT 59* to withdraw, Searles passed within three hundred feet of destroyer *Oyashio,* suicidally close to a steel ship with 4.7-inch guns. Automatic fire punctured the PT in ten places; at what was point-blank range, Searles's gunners returned fire, inflicting as many casualties as hits received, then made it back to base.[21]

With the first two boats completing their attack, *PTs 44* and *36* closed, emptying their torpedo tubes. Unfortunately, all the PTs Mark VIII torpedoes missed.

At 12:15 a.m., in the midst of the action, drawn by monitored radio PT transmissions of the attacking boats, *PTs 109* and *43* came thundering into the area from their assigned positions. As the two boats drew closer, a violent explosion occurred. Since none of the PTs' torpedoes were hits, the likely source of the detonation was a "premature;" one of the Mark VIII torpedoes exploding during its run without hitting a target.

Whatever the source, for Capt. Sato, it was the final straw: he ordered a withdrawal without first discharging the drums of supplies, returning to base without suffering damage. Another effort by the Japanese to deliver food and medicines to the starving 17th Army had failed.

This encounter, on the first anniversary of Pearl Harbor is justly considered a PT victory. Without suffering loss, the young PT crews had achieved the considerable feat of forcing the Reinforcement Unit to retreat; only a week earlier, eleven U.S. warships had been severely mauled accomplishing no more. Moreover, it was a feat yet to be achieved by the Cactus Air Force.

But for the PTs it was still a hollow victory: after sixty days of continuous operations, the strain was starting to affect the men who had first arrived in October. As in the final days with the PTs in the Philippines, patrolling all night and working on the boats during daylight hours in an effort to keep the tired boats operating was taking its toll. Recalled Stilly Taylor:

> "Our effectiveness fell off 100 percent. We had had enough; we were no good anymore. All of us had malaria or dengue fever or dysentery. We had all lost between ten and thirty pounds and were terribly nervous. We weren't properly closing with the enemy anymore. Every time we reported in before a patrol we would be wringing with sweat. We prayed the Japs wouldn't come down. We were no good anymore. About the only thing that held us together was [squadron commander] Robbie Robinson's leadership and understanding."[22]

On the Japanese side there were also signs of strain. Following the Naval Battle of Guadalcanal, the Navy Section of Imperial General Headquarters became convinced that with the increased strength of the Cactus Air Force, there was little likelihood Guadalcanal could be retaken. But in Tokyo, the Army General Staff remained resolved to retaking of the island with the use of additional men. Convinced the battle for the island was the decisive struggle that would determine the war's final outcome, and that victory could be had with slightly more effort, the Army made a drastic realignment of its forces: thereafter 17th Army would concentrate on the Solomons, while the 18th Army assumed responsibilities for New Guinea. Both would be under the command of Lt. Gen. Hitoshi Imamura commanding both as the newly formed 8th Area Army. Since Guadalcanal was now the primary enemy target, Japanese operations in New Guinea, previously the major focus, would be limited to securing "important areas," namely air bases at key points such as Lae, Salamaua, Madang and Wewak. In support of the next effort to retake Guadalcanal's Henderson Field, the 17th Army would be reinforced by the 6th Infantry Division transported from China, the 65th Brigade, and fresh Army Air Force Units.

Newly made plans called for attacking and seizing Henderson Field on January 20, 1943. But when General Imamura arrived at Rabaul, to his surprise, he learned local Army commanders tended to favor withdrawal from Guadalcanal, a thought Imamura refused to consider since he had given his personal vow to the Emperor to retake the island.[23]

But shipment of a fresh division to Guadalcanal required ships, vessels Japan found to be scarce as well as in great demand. The continuation of the Guadalcanal campaign viewed by the Army General Staff calling for another 370,000 tons of shipping, forced the War Ministry to reassess the campaign. Meanwhile, with the 17th Army slowly starving on Guadalcanal, the Navy opted to reactivate the "Tokyo Express" using the drum method of supply.

Following the December 7 failure of the Express to complete the drum-delivery of supplies, a crucial meeting was held at Rabaul by officers of the Combined Fleet, the 8th Fleet based at Rabaul, and the 11th Air Fleet. General Imamura termed the resultant decision a "bombshell." Losses and damages sustained by destroyers at the pace experienced since mid-November, said the Navy delegation, meant the Navy would be unable to win the decisive battle to be fought against U.S. naval forces in the battle that would ultimately win the war. Effective immediately, notwithstanding conditions on Guadalcanal, all destroyer runs to that island would be halted. In the face of General Imamura's pleas, the Navy agreed to allow one more resupply run to Guadalcanal. A dismayed General Imamura appealed the Navy's decision to Tokyo, arguing this meant the sacrifice of the 17th Army.[24]

Even as the issue hung in the balance, back at Shortland Island, hurried preparations were carried out for another run. Eleven destroyers were assembled; no fewer than five would comprise the Reinforcement Unit's screen. A personal message from Admiral Yamamoto on the eve of departure emphasized the mission's importance.[25]

On the afternoon of the 11th, the force started south; this time it was led by Rear Admiral Tanaka aboard his new flagship *Teruzuki*. The passage was without incident until sunset when they were attacked by a group of bombers and fighters. One SBD was downed by ships' antiaircraft fire as the destroyers evaded the bombs, continuing on without damage or losses. Now it was up to the Tulagi PTs.[26]

When word came the Tokyo Express was approaching, five boats were all that were available: Les Gamble on *PT 37*, Stilly Taylor on *PT 40* and the Squadron 2 executive officer, Lt.(jg) William Kreiner, at the helm of Bob Searles's *48* boat would proceed to Savo Island to idle on the southeast side close to shore, hoping once again to surprise the Reinforcement Unit as it slipped through the gap between Savo and Cape Esperance. Kreiner, a veteran PT skipper in his own right, was filling in for Searles who was spending a few days on Guadalcanal as liaison officer between the PTs and Marine units on the island. Primarily, Searles's job was to inform night-flying Marine Corps pilots where the PT boats would be patrolling on a given night so as to avoid tragic accidents due to mistaken identity.[27]

The last two boats, *PT 44* skippered by Frank Freeland and Lt.(jg) Charlie Tilden on *PT 110*, were assigned to what was called the "Bitch Patrol," the choppy waters off Kamimbo Bay at the western end of Guadalcanal. All the boats were 77-footers except Tilden's *PT 110*, an 80-foot Elco.

By midnight, the five boats were in position. On this night, unlike most nights the Express chose to run, visibility was relatively good. The boats from Tulagi did not have long to wait. Shortly after midnight the Express rounded Savo slowing to 12 knots; the six drum-laden ships began discharging their cargo off Cape Esperance, casting 1200 drums afloat.

Lurking in the shadow of Savo, the three waiting PTs sighted the silhouettes of at least five destroyers. Radios crackled; at about 10 knots, the three boats began to move, trying to maneuver into firing position. Within moments, each boat fired a full spread of torpedoes. With twelve missiles racing toward the enemy, the PTs turned to slip back behind the protective lee of Savo.

As they did so, a massive explosion shattered one destroyer. Tanaka's flagship, *Teruzuki*, had been mortally hit on the port side. With the ship afire and unnavigable, leaking fuel blazed, turning the sea into a mass of flames. Fire soon reached the after magazine causing a second huge explosion and the ship began to sink.[28] Directing operations on the bridge, Tanaka was thrown violently to the deck, knocked unconscious by the initial explosion. By the time

he regained consciousness, a second destroyer, the *Naganami,* had
come alongside to take off survivors. With the help of his staff, the
bruised admiral transferred to the second ship; most of the crew
would be rescued by the *Naganami* and *Arashi,* which also came
alongside. However, both ships were forced to leave suddenly when
it was reported that more PT boats were approaching. Lifeboats
were dropped for the remaining survivors as the two destroyers
hastily got underway. Drawn to the scene by the radio transmissions
between the three attacking boats, *PT 44* roared past the burning
Teruzuki in pursuit of the enemy destroyers. Although Freeland did
not know it, at least one of the destroyers was now behind him, and
the glow of the flames made his boat an excellent target. Recalled
Lt.(jg) Charles M. Melhorn, executive officer of the *44*:

> "We were throwing up quite a wake, and with the
> burning cargo ship [mistaking the destroyer for a transport]
> lighting the whole area I thought we would soon be easy
> pickings and I told the skipper so. Before he could reply,
> Crowe, the quartermaster who was still at the wheel, pointed
> and yelled out, 'Destroyer on the starboard bow. There's your
> target, captain!' Through the glasses I could make out a
> destroyer two points on our starboard bow, distant about
> 8,000 yards, course south-southwest. We came right and
> started our run. We had no sooner steadied on our new course
> than I picked up two more destroyers through my glasses.
> They were in column thirty degrees on our port bow, target
> course 270, coming fast.
>
> "The skipper and I both saw at once that continuing our
> present course would pin us against the beach and lay us wide
> open to broadsides from at least three Jap cans. The skipper
> shifted targets to the two destroyers, still about 4,000 yards
> off, and we started in again."[29]

As *PT 44* raced toward this latest target, Melhorn spotted a
gunflash from another destroyer, previously concealed by the
darkness, and realized they were under fire:

> "By this time we were directly between the blazing ship
> and the two destroyers. As we started the run I kept looking

for the can that had fired. I picked him up behind and to the left of our new targets. He was swinging, apparently to form up in column astern of the other two. The trap was sprung, and as I pointed out this fourth destroyer the lead ship in the column opened fire."[30]

Now the target of the destroyers' guns, *PT 44* turned hard to withdraw and began to lay smoke; once in the clear, however, the *44* boat turned back for a second attack even as the lurking destroyer, aided by the illuminating flames of the burning *Teruzuki* drew a bead. "We had just come out of our turn when we were fired on," recalled Melhorn. "I saw the blast, yelled 'That's for us,' and jumped down on the portside of the cockpit."

The shell hit the PT aft in the engine room. For a few seconds, said Melhorn, nothing registered. Then he looked aft and saw a gaping hole where once there had been an engine-room canopy, the edges marked by little tongues of flame. Glancing down in the water he saw the boat had lost way.[31] With the boat dead in the water and under attack, Freeland gave the order to abandon ship. Melhorn, standing in the cockpit, glanced in the direction from which the shell had come just as the ship fired again. "I dove deep," said Melhorn, "and was still under when the salvo struck. The concussion jarred me badly, but I kept swimming underwater." Then came a tremendous explosion paralyzing Melhorn from the waist down and the water around him turned red. Said Melhorn:

> "The life jacket took control and pulled me to the surface. I came up in a sea of fire, the flaming embers of the boat cascading all about me. I tried to get free of the life jacket but I couldn't, so I started swimming feebly. I thought the game was up, but the water, which shot skyward in the explosion, rained down and put out the fire around me. From the first hit to this point took less than fifteen seconds."[32]

Melhorn managed a couple of strokes to get away from the gasoline fire that was still raging some fifteen yards behind him. As he turned to look back, he saw two heads, one still helmeted, visible in the glow of the flames. He called to them, saying he expected the enemy would be there in a short time to machinegun any survivors, and to get their life jackets ready to slip, adding that they should get clear of the reflection of the fire as quickly as possible, then proceeded to do so himself.

"I struck out for Savo, whose skyline ridge I could see dimly, and gradually made headway toward shore." Every two or three minutes Melhorn paused to look back for signs of other survivors or an approaching destroyer, but all that was visible was the burning remains of Tanaka's flagship.

As he continued to struggle on, Melhorn's efforts grow steadily weaker. His arms were like lead. The thought of sharks, known to be in these waters, haunted him. Just before dawn, a PT rumbled by, passing within twenty-five yards ahead. He was about to hail it when he saw a Japanese destroyer bearing down on the boat's starboard quarter.

Suspecting the PT was maneuvering to fire a torpedo, Melhorn remained silent, slipping out of his life jacket as he waited for the action to start. The enemy ship lay motionless as the minutes passed, then Melhorn realized it was nothing more than a shape formed by the fires and smoke.

Not until sometime between 7:30 and 8 a.m. did the PT officer reach Savo Island. About an hour later, Stilly Taylor rescued him from the beach. Two officers and seven enlisted men on *PT 44* had died. Only one man other than Melhorn survived the explosion and destruction of *PT 44*.[33]

It had been a bad night for the Tulagi PTs: another boat had run aground on a reef. There it remained until daylight when the Cactus patrol boat, *PC-476,* towed her free. On the positive side, along the way the rescuing boat discovered a deserted Japanese landing barge containing some useful charts to be turned over to intelligence.

For the enemy, it was also a bad night. Crewmen on the *Teruzuki* worked through the midwatch in an effort to save the destroyer. At 3:15 a.m. it became clear their efforts were futile, and the order to scuttle was given. Survivors made their way to Kamimbo in small boats where they found refuge. At 4:40 a.m. the flames reached the destroyer's depth charge magazine and she exploded with a roar before heading for the bottom of Sealark Channel, now nicknamed "Ironbottom Sound" owing to the number of ships from both sides resting on the bottom as a result of the struggle for Guadalcanal.

Although the Express had discharged its load of drums and returned safely, to Admiral Tanaka the mission was a personal disaster. The loss of his newest and best destroyer to "such an inferior enemy" was devastating: "I have often thought," Tanaka said later, "that it would have been easier for me to have been killed in that first explosion. Forced to remain in bed because of my injuries, I reported by radio the fact that the flag had been shifted to *Naganami*. Tanaka withheld mention of his injuries out of fear of the demoralizing effect it might have on the force.[34] To add to the irony, Tanaka's destroyer was the first heavy ship to be sunk by the Tulagi PTs during the Guadalcanal campaign.

Back at Shortland on December 12, Tanaka had further reason to be depressed. Only 220 of the 1200 drums discharged during the previous night's mission had been recovered by the 17th Army. Capping that was an order temporarily discontinuing resupply runs to Guadalcanal because of moonlit nights.[35] In fact, the destroyers would make no further runs to Guadalcanal for the next three weeks.

On the American side, *PT 44* was the first of the Tulagi boats lost in the campaign for Guadalcanal; but more would follow. During the ensuing lull lasting through the balance of December, the PTs of Tulagi continued their nightly patrols. Meanwhile, the plight of the Japanese troops on Guadalcanal worsened, prompting the men of the 17th Army to devise a mortality chart:

He can rise to his feet…30 days to live
He who can sit up…20 days to live
He who must urinate while lying down…3 days to live
He who cannot speak…2 days to live
He who cannot blink his eyes…dead at dawn.[36]

For both sides, the campaign for Guadalcanal had now reached a critical point where changes were necessary. While the Japanese high command remained locked in heated debate as to whether a final major effort to retake the island should be undertaken or the 17th Army evacuated, key changes were occurring on the American side. On November 26, Halsey became a full admiral in recognition of his success thus far and the importance of the South Pacific command. Also, following the Naval Battle of Guadalcanal, the decision was made to relieve the 1st Marines, it being noted the

Marine amphibious troops, suffering from battle fatigue, disease and short rations had lost their offensive edge beyond renewal on Guadalcanal.[37]

Plans to replace them with Army troops were made. Since the bulk of the troops on the "Canal" would soon be Army, Maj. Gen. Alexander Vandegrift, USMC, commanding the 1st Marines would be replaced by Maj. Gen. Alexander M. Patch, USA, commanding the Americal Division.

On December 7th, the date the Tulagi PTs forced the Express to retreat with its drum-supplies still aboard, General Vandegrift learned by dispatch the 5th Marines would be relieved December 9 with other Marine units following in increments. That day he issued his final division letter on Guadalcanal, a letter in which he sought to summarize the brutal months just past. In it, he expressed his pride in the men of his command, their magnificent accomplishments, self-sacrifice and high courage as displayed by soldiers, sailors and Marines who had faced the enemy; notably, among those singled out for particular tribute were the men of the PTs based at Tulagi, for "their nightly slashing attacks against the enemy."[38] Two days later, on December 9, General Patch took command, and the men of the Marines began to embark on waiting transports, destination Australia.

Shortly, other new arrivals on Guadalcanal promised to provide aid and support for the PTs. That month a "Black Cat" squadron, PBYs painted a dull black for night operations, began operating from Henderson Field. The aircraft would serve as an extension of the PTs' eyes during night operations, radioing enemy sightings to the boats, and dropping flares over suspected targets. The first PBY arrived on December 15; by the end of the month, nine Black Cats would be based at Henderson Field.[39]

Far away in Tokyo, late December saw a reluctant Imperial Army bow to the inevitable. Despite its promise to the Emperor, American strength on Guadalcanal, given existing conditions, meant retaking the island was a near impossibility. On December 23 the urgency of the situation was brought home by a radiogram from General Hyakutake, 17th Army commander on the island:

"No food available and we can no longer send out scouts. We can do nothing to withstand the enemy's offensive. 17th Army now requests permission to break into the enemy's positions and die an honorable death rather than die of hunger in our dugouts.[40]

By now, malaria affliction among the Japanese on Guadalcanal was virtually 100 percent, as it was for dysentery. Troops existed on grass, roots, and on occasion, human flesh. On Christmas Day, the Army and Navy leaders held a formal emergency meeting at the Imperial Palace. No longer was there any doubt as the need for a withdrawal from the island.[41]

A report was received about this time from nearly all front line Japanese Army and Navy commanders in the Solomons favoring a retreat from Guadalcanal; this led to an audience with the Emperor on December 28. At the meeting the heads of the Army and Navy informed His Majesty of the need to withdraw from the island. On December 31, a disappointed Emperor Hirohito approved the plan for evacuation.[42]

Meanwhile, the Tokyo Express had resumed operations. Despite the mixed success of the drum-supply method, the Japanese continued its use, but with additional improvements: kapok would be wrapped around the drums to keep them buoyant even if strafed by the enemy. In addition, destroyers would embark Army officers to be put in small landing craft to assure the ropes attached to the supply drums were handed over to the men ashore.[43]

On December 30, ten destroyers were readied for the first run to be made in 1943. Based on recent experience, the Japanese expected to encounter fierce resistance, especially from PT boats, and prepared accordingly. No fewer than half the ships would serve as escorts; these were fitted with extra 13-mm machine guns. The R Area Air Force, normally responsible for reconnaissance of the Shortland anchorage, was given four more float planes to scout ahead of the Express on the next run to Guadalcanal: they would sniff out the PTs for the destroyers.

Meanwhile, nightly PT patrols at Tulagi had continued. In the absence of the Express operation, the boats had been patrolling close to the shore of Guadalcanal, alert for enemy barges and submarines.[44] But this was about to change.

Back at Shortland, as of the end of December the Express was ready to resume running. Commanding the ten-ship Reinforcement Unit departing Shortland was Rear Admiral Tomiji Koyanagi: in December, he had relieved an exhausted Admiral Tanaka as commander of the Reinforcement Unit, with Tanaka being transferred to Rabaul. However, the PTs at Tulagi would find Admiral Koyanagi was a no less fierce and determined foe. On January 2, Admiral Koyanagi led the Express south from Shortland to Cape Esperance with food and ammunition for the starving 17th Army. Reported by the alert Coastwatchers, at 2:15 p.m. the ships were bombed from high altitude by five B-17s; one destroyer sustained damage from a near-miss and turned back with a one-ship escort. The rest of the force continued its race down the Slot as the airmen sounded the alarm.

Approaching Cape Esperance, the Reinforcement Unit was preceded by the float planes. The aircraft found the PTs' wakes easy to spot at night, even at a range of four miles. Gliding down along the tell-tail wakes of the PTs, the pilots could attack the PTs from astern without warning, strafing and dropping bombs with lethal effect.

On one occasion, eleven PT boats were waiting, but with the floatplanes reporting their presence to the destroyers, the PTs made no contacts: the Express successfully discharged its drums and returned to base. The next day the 17th Army happily reported the recovery of 540 drums and 250 rubber bags of supplies—about a five-day supply.[45]

On January 10, Admiral Koyanagi led an eight-destroyer "Express" south, again divided equally between transport and screening ships. A Coastwatcher sounded the alarm, but it was too late for the Cactus Air Force to attack. Again, it would be up to the Tulagi PTs to intercept.

On this night, the Express would encounter ten Tulagi PT boats: four boats were out on regular patrol, veteran Les Gamble on *PT 45* and Lt. Ralph Amsden, Jr. on *PT 39* patrolling the west side of the gap between Cape Esperance and Savo; Bob Searles at the helm of *PT 48* and Ens. B.J. Connolly on *PT 115* covering the east side.

With four boats on patrol, Squadron 2 commander Lt. Westholm got word that an eight-destroyer Express would arrive at Guadalcanal around midnight. He now ordered out the rest of his operable boats, six PTs. The squadron commander himself would command a three-boat "strike force," *PT 112* with Westholm as skipper, *PT 43* commanded by Charlie Tilden, and *PT 40* with Lt. Clark Faulkner at the helm. The strike force would be positioned in the sector immediately east of Cape Esperance between Doma Point and Tassafaronga, close to shore, the most likely objective of the drum-carrying destroyers. Westholm assigned the other three boats, *PTs 36, 46,* and *59,* to patrol further east off the coast of Guadalcanal.

In any event, aided by poor visibility, the enemy managed to slip by the four waiting PTs near Savo at the entrance to Sealark Channel without detection.

Indeed, first to sight the enemy was Lt. Westholm at 12:37 a.m. January 11, four destroyers, about 1,200 yards out and heading east in Sealark Channel. At the moment, Westholm's three-boat section was idling along about four hundred yards from the shore of Guadalcanal headed east as well, the three PT in column, Tilden's *43* boat leading followed by Faulkner, and trailed by Westholm as the last in line.[46]

As a beacon, the Japanese on the island had lit small fires to help guide the destroyers. With Westholm's three boats concealed by the dark mass of the island background, it was a perfect setup for a surprise torpedo attack. Westholm ordered the two skippers in his section to attack. As lead boat in the PT column, Tilden drew a bead on the lead destroyer and Faulkner took aim at the second ship in the enemy column. Westholm aligned his boat on the third destroyer. By now, the fourth destroyer had disappeared, veering off into the darkness.[47]

Closing to a range of between 400 and 500 yards, the three PTs launched their torpedoes: Tilden punched the two buttons electrically firing his two aft torpedoes; disaster followed. The PT's port tube emitted a red flash of flame as the Mark VIII torpedo emerged, in all probability caused by the black powder charge igniting the oil and grease in the tube. Whatever the cause, it provided a perfect target for the alert destroyer gunners.

Immediately, Tilden threw the PT in a hard turn and opened the throttles in an effort to escape. He might have succeeded if his torpedoes had been hits, but despite the short range and the element of surprise, both missiles either missed or were duds: The enemy's aim was accurate, however. The first 4.7-inch salvo landed close, the second shattered the *43* boat killing three crewmen.[48]

Recovering from the shock of the blast, and with the boat dead in the water, Tilden ordered the boat abandoned as destroyer machine gun bullets sprayed the water around them.

By now, Faulkner, having successfully fired all four of his torpedoes at the second destroyer, was withdrawing at top speed eastward close to the Guadalcanal shore, preferring the likelihood of hitting an unseen reef to the threat of the enemy's gunfire. Peering aft, the *PT 40* lookouts reported seeing one of Faulkner's torpedoes hit the target destroyer, throwing a massive column of water in the air followed by a secondary explosion.

By now, Westholm had fired his four torpedoes at the last destroyer in the column. One seemed to be a hit, sending the usual geyser of water skyward. With all torpedo tubes emptied, the squadron commander pushed his throttles forward to wide open and pointed his boat toward Tulagi. Unfortunately, Westholm's course took him past the rear of the enemy destroyer column. As his boat crossed the enemy column's wake, two other destroyers unseen by Westholm opened fire. Moments later, the *112* boat was aflame, hit in the engine room and on the bow by 4.7-inch shells. On watch in the engine room, MoMM1/c C. A. Craig, suffering burns on his arms, hands and face, found himself fighting a raging fire in an effort to save the boat. With the PT dead in the water and the flames beyond control, for the second time this night a PT skipper was forced to give the order "Abandon Ship."[49]

In accord with naval tradition, Westholm was the last to leave the boat, along with the painfully burned Craig. For some reason, the destroyers did not follow their usual routine of closing in and machine-gunning the PT and its survivors, thus there was time for the crew to throw the life raft over the side, climb into it and paddle away.

An hour passed, and at 1:30 a.m. with *PT 112* still afloat and no sign of the Japanese, Westholm ordered crewmen to paddle the raft back to the boat in hopes of retrieving his prized set of binoculars left behind on the bridge in his hasty departure. As the raft reached a point within about one hundred feet, however, the *112* exploded. For the record, *PT 112* was the first 80-foot Elco lost in combat in World War II.

Drawn to the battle now in progress, *PT 46* with Stilly Taylor at the helm arrived just as a destroyer's searchlight snapped on to illuminate Tilden's abandoned *PT 43*. At a range of 1800 yards Taylor fired all four torpedoes. Moments later he was rewarded by the welcome sound of a deep explosion, retribution for the destruction of the two PTs and the deaths of three crew members.

As was typical in a night naval battle, claims were inflated. During the action, other PTs reported firing twelve torpedoes without getting hits. Westholm, Faulkner and Taylor each claimed hits. But the Japanese reported only one destroyer, the 2,000-ton *Hatsukaze,* was torpedoed, the missile striking at the ship's wardroom, killing eight and wounding twenty-three crewmen. Her captain reported the ship was in "bad shape." With speed reduced to 16 knots and accompanied by three protective sisters, she finally made it back to Shortland. On the other hand, the Japanese skipper thought he had been attacked by more than eight PTs.[50]

The abandoned *43* boat ended up grounded off Guadalcanal. By dawn Japanese from the island garrison were observed crawling all over the beached vessel. A New Zealand corvette based at Tulagi finally arrived and blew the stranded PT to splinters with gunfire.

On the following morning, the PTs held target practice on 250 drums floating off Cape Esperance. On the 11th, the 17th Army reported recovering 250 drums, about thirty tons of food, medicine and ammunition. Another Express was necessary. However, it would not be the usual supply-delivery mission.

Even as the Tokyo Express made its first run in 1943 to Guadalcanal with supplies, Imperial Headquarters issued orders for the "KE" Operation, the evacuation of Guadalcanal. Set for late January–early February, it would be completed by February 10. For the operation, Admiral Yamamoto promised the full support of the Combined Fleet. The "KE" Operation called for three runs down the Slot using destroyers.

To keep the unsuspecting Americans in the dark as to the withdrawal, the Japanese successfully devised a series of feints and ploys. These included an increase in radio traffic near Java to the west and a night air raid on Australia's Port Darwin along with fake radio traffic in the Marshalls.

Nonetheless, Japanese expectations of success were largely pessimistic: General Imamura expected half the destroyers used in the "KE" Operation would be lost. And Admiral Yamamoto concealed his view that only about one-third of the 17th Army could be saved at the cost of half the destroyers engaged in the operation. As part of the first phase of the evacuation, on the afternoon of January 13, a nine-destroyer Reinforcement Unit carrying a thousand-man rear-guard force along with supplies left Shortland for Guadalcanal. Most importantly, it carried orders for the evacuation to be handed to the commander of the 17th Army with an oral reminder that it came from the Emperor. The ships were to reach Guadalcanal on the fourteenth. Commanding the force was Rear Admiral Satsuma Kumura, another destroyer commander. Kumura had replaced Admiral Koyanami, the latter now acting in a reserve capacity. In the nights ahead, the PTs at Tulagi would find Admiral Kumura the equal of the legendary Tanaka.

On the night of January 14, heavy weather shrouded the approaching Express. Again the sighting report arrived too late for the aircraft on Henderson Field to make an attack. Once more the Tulagi PTs would have to make the interception. On this night, thirteen boats were operable. However, poor visibility made more difficult by heavy rain, a night in which the skippers found even seeing the bows of their own boats difficult made locating the enemy virtually impossible. Occasional lightning flashed.

These difficulties aside, the PTs faced a threat of their own. Unknown to the PT crews, the wakes of the PTs were still visible to the R Area Air Force float planes lurking overhead. Sighting the PTs below, the float planes reported their positions to the Express commander, then attacked the boats using their phosphorescent wakes as guides. Lieutenant Gamble at the helm of *PT 45* and Lieutenant John Clagett on *PT 37* were engaging an R Area Air Force float plane with machine guns when a flash of lightning revealed five destroyers standing in between Savo and Cape Esperance. Both skippers attacked the ships with torpedoes; with their torpedo tubes empty, they withdrew pursued by the ships. Clagett made it back to Tulagi, but the aggressive destroyer skippers stayed on Gamble's tail: hampered by poor visibility, and maneuvering radically in an effort to elude his pursuers, Gamble ran aground off Florida Island. He managed to escape the destroyers but he needed a tug the following day to refloat his boat. Damage to the boat meant it would be out of operation temporarily. On this night, the rest of the PTs even failed to make contact with the enemy.[51]

By January 23, Allied aerial reconnaissance clearly showed the Japanese were planning a major operation. Over two months had passed since the Naval Battle of Guadalcanal, but there were no signs the Japanese were on the way out. The Americans had learned to respect the enemy's ability to bounce back, and there were signs that something big was in the wind. To Allied staff officers at Noumea and Pearl Harbor, the something looked like another major assault on Henderson Field. Thus Halsey, alerted to the possibility, prepared to use the full array of American naval power in the South Pacific. The result was the Battle of Rennell Island on January 29, a battle that cost the Americans the cruiser *Chicago,* the only U.S. heavy cruiser to have survived the Battle of Savo Island. However, the Americans were unaware that due to the Battle of Rennell Island the Japanese had postponed the "KE" Operation until February 1.

Finally, the evacuation began; The operation would be supported by fifty to sixty R Area Air Force float planes. Again the planes were assigned to sweep ahead of the destroyers, shielding them from the depredations of the PTs while the 17th Army was embarking off Cape Esperance.[52]

On February 1, following an air battle over Shortland, the first of the three runs needed to remove the 17th Army from Guadalcanal as part of the "KE" operation, twenty-two destroyers cleared Shortland forming up into two columns for the sprint down the Slot. Seven ships provided a screen. Commanding the destroyers engaged in the "KE" Operation was Rear Admiral Shintaro Hashimoto. Admiral Koyanami remained with the unit in reserve.

A Coastwatcher sighted the destroyers north of the island of Vella Lavella at 1:30 p.m. and radioed the alarm. To the Americans, it looked like another major effort to land more reinforcements on Guadalcanal. The Cactus Air Force scrambled two groups of aircraft, including a combination of SBDs and TBFs escorted by F4Fs. A near miss rendered Admiral Hashimoto's flagship unnavigable and two ships were detached to provide aid; the remaining nineteen ships evaded the bombs and raced on. Four American aircraft failed to return.

With the continued approach of this massive Express, the defenders at Guadalcanal feared the worst: three weapons were readied, mines, destroyers and PTs. By nightfall, three converted four-stack destroyers had laid some three hundred mines beginning at Doma Reef and extending halfway to Cape Esperance. The second instrument of opposition was a force of three modern destroyers, *Fletcher, Radford,* and *Nicholas.* Their commander planned to launch a surprise torpedo attack, but the night-flying Japanese float planes sounded the alarm, making the attack impossible. In the end, the main defense would be the PT boats of Tulagi. That night eleven boats would be waiting in what was to be the final engagement between the Tulagi PTs and the Tokyo Express.[53]

To the PT crews the situation was frightening. Being scared was a normal reaction to night patrols; a single destroyer was a lethal foe in itself. But on this night, they were told they would face twenty of these ships. As they considered the odds, there was a feeling that they would be lucky to merely survive the night. Some would not.

Every operable PT at Tulagi would be out: on this night Westholm was on *PT 109,* with Charlie Tilden with *PT 36* stationed two miles north of Doma Reef; Faulkner and Lt. Ralph Richards of the newly arriving Squadron 6 on *PT 124* and *123* respectively, both new 80-foot Elco boats were positioned some three miles south of Savo. Nearby, about a mile to the northeast were two veterans, Bob Searles and Stilly Taylor on *PTs 47* and *39.* Closer to the passage between Savo and Cape Esperance on the Savo side, were Les Gamble with *PT 48* and Lt. Clagett on *PT 111.* The final three boats, *PT 59* skippered by Jack Searles, *PT 115* commanded by Ens. Bart "BJ" Connolly and *PT 37* under the command of Ens. J.J. Kelly patrolled of Cape Esperance, considered to be the enemy's most likely destination.

Unknown to the PTs' crews, by this time thousands of Japanese soldiers had made their way over dark trails leading to designated embarking points at Cape Esperance. Despite the difficulties, by 9 p.m.—the estimated hour of arrival—the men were in place near the shore. But time crept past the hour of arrival and still the sea remained empty. Then gunfire was heard to seaward and the men on the beach saw flames offshore: apparently some vessel was on fire.

On this night, the first to make contact with the enemy destroyers were *PTs 111* and *48.* At a range of nine hundred yards, Gamble fired all four of *PT 48's* torpedoes at a destroyer—all missed.

Pursued by the destroyers, Gamble ran aground on Savo Island and escaped destruction. There he and his crew would spend the rest of the night. Clagett was not as fortunate.

Slowly patrolling in the blackness off Cape Esperance with engines muffled, he suddenly found his boat in the midst of enemy destroyers. Still undetected, Clagett began to stalk his quarry, closing slowly on the nearest ships. At a range of five hundred yards, still undetected, he fired his two aft torpedoes. As the boat lurched indicating a successful launch he fired his two forward torpedoes. Flames flickered in one of the *111's* torpedo tubes as the torpedo emerged, the flames disclosing the PT's presence. Clagett groaned. Immediately, the helmsman turned the boat hard and pushed his throttles forward to withdraw. Even as the *111* began to increase speed, shells from the lead destroyer's guns screamed overhead; the ship's searchlights snapped on probing for the target. Now under fire from the rest of the enemy ships, the *111* began to plane, approaching full speed, a massive wake astern. Enemy shells churned the sea nearby: one landed close to the bow. Clagett ordered smoke, and dense clouds began billowing behind the boat.

But the enemy had the range: At 10:54 the *111* was hit on the bow by a shell fired by the *Kawakaze,* the explosion turning the PT into a ball of fire and knocking out the engines.[54]

Blinded by the smoke from the explosion, with the boat dead in the water and on fire, Clagett found he was alone in the cockpit surrounded by flames. The heat was intense. Clagett's one instinct was to escape. He tried to walk, but his legs gave way and he was forced to crawl through a wall of flames. His mind went to the tanks beneath him with their hundreds of gallons of 100-octane gasoline that could explode at any moment. Finally, as if in a dream, he found himself at the edge of the deck. With his last strength he heaved his body over the side into the welcome blackness below.

The relief was overwhelming: immediately the cool water soothed the pain. He allowed his body to sink without resisting: "That's my last ride on a PT boat," he told himself.

Pulled back to the surface by his kapok life jacket, Clagett saw the PT drifting close by, its hull shattered, aflame from stem to stern.

Having escaped from the doomed PT boat, Clagett's problems were far from over. His body felt no pain, but his hands and feet felt numb. The heavy steel helmet weighed his head down, threatening to force his face under water. When he tried to unbuckle it his fingers refused to work; a wave of agony swept his body as his fingers touched the rough strap. He tried to lift the heavy binoculars from around his neck, but failed. He tried to unbuckle his pistol belt from around his waist, again his fingers refused to function while pain forced him to stop.

He held his hands up out of the water; now, in the glow of flames from the burning PT he saw they were swollen and dark; long white strips of skin hung from his hands and floated in the water.

"I'm burned," he told himself. "I'm burned bad as hell!"

As though in a dream, he saw a dark form approach out of the darkness. Sparkles flickered and he heard the rattle of machine gun fire and the sea was churned up nearby; an activity in which "I was mildly interested," recalled Clagett.

The he heard the familiar voice of one of his crew about a hundred yards away, yelling "They're shooting at us!"—a warning to get away from the boat.

Finally, all grew quiet. By now, the steel helmet on Clagett's head had grown heavier. He tried to float on his back, but the two-pound helmet continued to roll him over so that he was face down in the water. The PT skipper soon lost consciousness and woke up choking. He found his life jacket was not tight and he was slipping out of it. Though his eyes were swollen half shut, he could see a gleam of phosphorescence in the water beneath him. Recognizing it as a shark, he fought back the urge to panic.

In a voice he hoped sounded calm, he called out for help. Moments later, two rescuers, TM2/C Merle C. Elsass and SN1/C Walter L. Long were at his side, arriving just as Clagett's strength failed. Both men, although painfully burned, remained with Clagett, removing the troublesome helmet, tightening his life jacket, and keeping the partially conscious skipper's head above water until dawn when they were rescued by another PT boat searching for survivors.

During the night, other *111* crew members struggled to survive. Blown over the side by the explosion, RM2/c Russell J. Wackler sustained compound fractures of both legs. Although injured as well, Ens. A.E. "Whitey" White and FN2/c2/c Lamar H. Loggins stayed with the mortally wounded Wackler, fighting off sharks attracted by the blood of the wounded men. Wackler died shortly before a rescuing PT arrived. A second crewman, Lt. Philip A. Shribmen, remained missing; his body was never recovered.

The three-boat section off Cape Esperance had mixed results. Enemy float planes bombed and strafed the three boats; then, at 11:00 p.m. the three became embroiled with what appeared to be a dozen destroyers. Ensign Connolly with the *115* closed to within five hundred yards of a target and fired two torpedoes before changing aim and firing his last pair of torpedoes at a second destroyer. He evaded gunfire, probably from the *Satsuki* and *Nagatsuki,* by a combination of doing the unexpected and luck: reducing speed to avoid creating a revealing wake, and ducking into a convenient rainsquall that also concealed *PT 59.* Although virtually surrounded by destroyers, Connolly managed to beach his boat on Savo where he remained until dawn.[55] Ensign Kelly with *PT 37* closed on the destroyers and fired all four torpedoes. But as in the case of *PT 111* before he could withdraw, gunfire transformed his boat into a mass of flames. Only one crewmember, MoMM1/c Eldon C. Jenter, badly burned and blown through the side of the boat into the sea, survived the explosion. After bobbing in the water for about three hours, he was finally rescued by a passing PT boat.

At 10:49 as *PTs 124* and *123* moved in from the south of Savo, a destroyer loomed out of the darkness. Faulkner bored in with *PT 124* and fired three torpedoes before withdrawing rapidly toward Tulagi. As he retreated, the crew saw the torpedoes hit the target; Ensign Richards on the *123,* following in the wake of Faulkner's boat, closed to within five hundred yards of a destroyer, but his boat was attacked by an unseen and unheard R Area Air Force float plane that glided down behind along his wake and with remarkable skill dropped a bomb on the fantail of *PT 123.* Four crewmen died, and the rest abandoned their blazing craft.

While the PTs were hotly engaged in what was the escort destroyers, the enemy destroyer-transports moved in close to Cape Esperance. Blue signal lights flashed. The ships stopped engines 750 yards from shore but did not anchor. Landing craft emerged from the shadows loaded with men. It required little more than thirty minutes to get 5,424 men aboard the ships. On the bridge of his ship, Admiral Koyanami described the evacuees:

[they] were so undernourished that their beards, nails and hair had all stopped growing, their joints were pitifully large. Their buttocks were so emaciated that their anuses were completely exposed...[56]

Indeed, all had dengue fever. Probably they were happy, observed the Admiral, but they showed no expression. Even as the men were being taken aboard the ships, the destroyer *Makigumo* chased a PT boat almost to Tulagi, but Admiral Koyanami recalled it. But as the destroyer was returning, a huge explosion wracked her hull. The Japanese thought she hit a mine, but, as recalled, the PTs claimed Faulkner's torpedoes struck the destroyer. In any case, the ship's crew was forced to transfer to destroyer *Yugumo* after which the latter scuttled her with torpedoes.[57]

The enemy then headed back up the Slot, leaving the Americans believing the enemy had landed still more reinforcements; moreover, all ships, except the scuttled destroyer, returned safely. Back at Guadalcanal, General Patch, anticipating a renewed ground attack, continued to hold his defensive positions pending the arrival of Allied troop reinforcements. As for the PTs, it had clearly been a bad night. Fifteen crewmen had died and three boats were lost. All surviving PTs had had close calls. To the crews, the sight of so many enemy destroyers was discouraging: "We'd heard about the fall of the Japanese headquarters at Kolumbona and how the Japs on Cape Esperance were hopelessly pocketed," recalled Bob Searles. "Yet here was this armada of ships steaming down, and we didn't know why they were coming or what they hoped to accomplish, and everyone had the feeling that our part of the fighting was never going to end. Night after night for the rest of our lives we'd be doing this all over again, until the men cracked and the boats fell completely to pieces.[58]

On the night of February 4, nineteen destroyers departed Shortland headed down the Slot on the second of the three scheduled runs as part of the "KE" Operation; on this run, 4,977 men would be evacuated. This time, although Japanese aircraft combed the nearby waters, no PTs or any other ships appeared to interfere. At 9:30 a.m. February 7 eighteen destroyers left Shortland for Guadalcanal on the third and final run. Again, the Tulagi PTs were conspicuously absent; on its final trip, the Express evacuated a final 2,639 men. In keeping with the pattern of the campaign, the number of evacuees reported in the "KE" Operation varies, ranging as high as 12,805.[59]

On the morning of February 8 American ground forces approached Cape Esperance and found no signs of the Japanese other than empty boats and abandoned supplies. This was the first the Americans knew of the evacuation. General Patch's radio message to Admiral Halsey reflected his sense of relief: "Total and complete defeat of Japanese forces on Guadalcanal effected 1625 today. Am happy to report this kind of compliance with your orders 'Tokyo Express' no longer has terminus on Guadalcanal."[60]

For the PTs at Tulagi, there was an overwhelming sense of relief. Although the boats would see more action in the struggle for the Solomons as the Allies advanced north and the Japanese fought a retirement action, they would never face Japanese capital ships again in this kind of intense, violent action as experienced at Guadalcanal. In the end, one might ask just what the Tulagi PTs accomplished in their many sorties against the Express during the previous four months. Perhaps squadron commander Robinson answered the question best when he said:

> "We probably claimed more torpedo hits than we got—we found out later that many of our torpedoes were duds and that others would explode, for instance, in the destroyer's wake. But I think our major contribution to the campaign was that we posed a threat. Had we not been there, the Japanese would virtually had had their own way at sea most of the time. They would have been free to supply their troops on the island, and whether or not this would have affected the final outcome of the battle isn't nearly as important as the number of American lives that we saved because the Japanese were too hungry or too tired or too ill-equipped to fight any longer than they did."[61]

Considering those words, Robinson would have been pleased to read Tokyo's lament in a special report devoted to the actions of men such as Clagett and Kelly; "The enemy has used PT boats aggressively…on their account our naval ships have had many a bitter pill to swallow—there are many examples of their having rendered the transport of supplies exceptionally difficult." The writer urged that Japan develop a motor torpedo boat force, perceptively noting "It is necessary to assign to the boats young men who are both robust and vigorous."

Nor was the commander of the ground forces on Guadalcanal unaware of the role played by the Tulagi PTs. Shortly after the end of the Guadalcanal campaign, General Patch crossed Sealark Channel to Tulagi where he presented medals to some of those "robust and vigorous" youth. "A wonderful and touching sight," said the general, "all these fine young men, ready to go anywhere and do anything. Makes you feel humble."[62]

But it was Les Gamble who summed up the feeling of the PTs most succinctly when he said. "We were awfully glad when it was over."[63]

CHAPTER EIGHT

THE FORGOTTEN WAR

Even as the struggle for Guadalcanal dragged on, a few PT boats began to operate from bases in New Guinea, an island some six hundred miles west of the Solomons. Officially listed as detached elements from Squadron 5 and 6, as at Guadalcanal, in the absence of available heavy warships, the PTs were there to provide the needed close naval support for Allied troops engaged in a ground war against the Japanese.[1]

Diverted from Guadalcanal, doubtless their initial destination, the first boats, *PTs 113* and *114,* reached New Guinea's Milne Bay, at the southeast tip of the island, on December 17, 1942. They came by way of Cairns under tow by the PT tender *Hilo.* Two more boats, *PTs 121* and *122,* followed, reaching Carnes under tow by a Liberty ship, continuing the rest of the way under their own power escorted by the pre-war gunboat *Tulsa,* fresh from duty in China. Soon *PTs 119* and *120* arrived. The six boats, designated Division 17, began immediate operations under the command of Lt. Daniel S. Baughman.[2] By the time the New Guinea campaign ended twenty-three months later, the six boats and one tender would grow to a force of eight tenders and fourteen squadrons. By then the shore of New Guinea would be littered with the shattered wreckage of *daihatsus* and the skeletons of thousands of Japanese solders who had died due to a lack of supplies.

The largest island in the world not dignified as a country or a continent, the hot and humid New Guinea seemed an unlikely place for a confrontation between the Allies and Japan. Lying north of Australia, separated from the lower continent's Cape York by the eighty-mile-wide Torres Strait, New Guinea was a forbidding world. Shaped like a buzzard, the head facing west, the tail, or Papua, pointing southeast containing Milne Bay, the 1300-mile-long

New Guinea, was one of the least-known areas of the world. Consisting largely of steamy jungles, swamps, quicksand, mountains and gorges it scarcely seemed worth invading. Here the air reeked with vile odors; little light penetrated the matted screens of liana vines overhead where steam rose from dank marshes after the rain. Here clouds of mosquitoes and flies bedeviled man and beast.

And there were larger dangers: great winged creatures with teeth, like giant rats; pythons and crocodiles, lurking in bogs waiting for the unfortunate soldier to stumble from trails covered waist-deep in slop.

That the first six PT boats reached New Guinea was due in no small part to the efforts of Vice Admiral Arthur S. "Chips" Carpender, commanding the U.S. Seventh Fleet based in Australia, otherwise known as "MacArthur's Navy." Assuming command on September 11, 1942, the admiral quickly realized his available surface ships centered on five cruisers and eight destroyers, left much to be desired. While the interdiction of enemy operations along New Guinea's north shore called for heavy warships, with the waters under constant enemy surveillance and within easy bombing range of Japanese air bases on New Britain, the use of such ships as there were had to wait until air cover was available. In addition, the waters off New Guinea were said to be festooned with more navigational hazards than any in the world. Allied amphibious operations employing heavy ships would thus have to be delayed until an aerial survey was completed and the Allies at least had partial control of the air.[3]

Carpender thus reasoned the only combat vessels that could be risked there and along the shores of Papua, were PT boats. With their shallow draft they could not only patrol close to shore, but unlike gunboats, the PTs had the speed to reach areas as distant as one hundred miles from base and patrol under cover of darkness. Furthermore, with their torpedoes, they could attack the enemy's heavy ships when encountered. And finally, unlike destroyers and cruisers, PT boats were considered relatively expendable.

Despite their need, with few PT boats available, Admiral Carpender found getting boats difficult. Only after repeated requests, entreaties, and even threats, was he able to persuade the Navy to let him have the six boats that arrived in December 1942.

Indeed, for the first six months following their arrival, the few PT boats dispatched to New Guinea would provide the Navy's sole support for MacArthur's troops in the New Guinea campaign.

For General MacArthur, faced with the struggle to defeat the Japanese on New Guinea, the PTs would repeatedly prove crucial. Following his narrow escape from the Philippines, MacArthur arrived in Australia only to find he had been deceived by Washington. As the end drew near in the Philippines, General Eisenhower had been convinced MacArthur meant to die on Corregidor rather than surrender. But General Marshall feared he might be captured rather than killed. Along with the loss of the Philippines and its thousands of American defenders, in either event, MacArthur's loss would be a double blow to the American public's confidence as well as a Japanese victory bringing shame to the Army. In this time of imminent disaster, Marshall sought to convince the president to order MacArthur out of the Philippines. But Roosevelt was doubtful. From a political view, to the president, it seemed like a major mistake: "It would mean that the whites would absolutely lose all face in the Far East. White men go down fighting but they can't run away," said Roosevelt.[4]

But then, political concerns intruded: to strengthen relations between the U.S. and Britain at a moment when it was under stress in the Pacific, Roosevelt ordered MacArthur to Australia to aid in its defense against the onrushing Japanese. By this time Japanese aircraft were bombing Australian cities from air bases in New Guinea. But given the demands of the war in Europe, the U.S. could offer little of consequence to the Australians.

For MacArthur, the truth was indeed shattering. Not only was there no Allied army waiting in Australia as promised for him to lead back to the Philippines, there were not even sufficient Allied fighting forces on hand in Australia to defend the continent from the expected Japanese attack. It seemed he had merely exchanged one disaster for another. Lacking an air defense worthy of the name, its army in the Middle East fighting the German forces alongside British troops, Australia appeared to be doomed: "God have mercy on us," said a grim MacArthur. For one of the few times in his career he was nearly plunged into despair.

Nonetheless, concealing his feelings, in a meeting with reporters shortly after reaching Australia, the general announced: "The

President of the United States ordered me to break through the Japanese lines...for the purpose, as I understand it, of organizing the American offensive against Japan, a primary object of which is the relief of the Philippines. I came through and I shall return." It was the last three words that captured the public's attention and became the most famous spoken during the Pacific war by a commander.

Although MacArthur meant every word he said, he realized the problem was not "how to get back to the Philippines—that army was doomed;" his problem now was to defend Australia against a Japanese offensive that at this time in the war seemed unstoppable.

Convinced that if the enemy were ever to establish a beachhead on the coast of Australia, the continent would be lost, MacArthur decided on a radical strategy: "We'll defend Australia in New Guinea," he told his amazed staff, adding that the jungle of New Guinea was just "as tough and tenacious an enemy as the Japanese." Better a head-on grinding collision with the Japanese on Papua, he reasoned, than a battle of maneuver in Australia where he lacked the troops for such a battle. In the months ahead, given the jungle-fighting skills of the Japanese Imperial Army, MacArthur's troops would need every advantage they could get. It was in this context, the PT boats would play a key role in MacArthur's war in New Guinea.

Events developed rapidly: On April 18, Australian Prime Minister John Curtin appointed MacArthur supreme commander of all Allied forces in the Southwest Pacific. On May 8, a Japanese invasion force, after steaming southeastward from Rabaul with troops to be landed at New Guinea's Port Moresby was intercepted by a U.S. task force. The result was the Battle of the Coral Sea, fought off the coast of Australia in which the U.S. Navy lost the carrier *Lexington* and the Japanese lost a smaller carrier. On the basis of tonnage sunk, the battle was an American defeat. But it forced the enemy to cancel the intended invasion of Port Moresby by sea, making it rightly a strategic victory for the United States. But with Port Moresby still the enemy's objective, MacArthur knew the battle was just only starting. The next effort to take Port Moresby by the Imperial Japanese Army would be from the land side, over the Kokoda Trail.

To counter this, on September 15, 1942, slightly four months after the fall of Corregidor, MacArthur began landing his available troops at Port Moresby. By now, Japanese garrisons stretched back over a thousand miles along the north coast of New Guinea, and in typical fashion, the enemy was prepared to defend them to the last man. But troops, skilled and dedicated or not, as shown at Guadalcanal, need supplies and reinforcements. In the end, for both sides, the battle for New Guinea would be one of attrition, and as at Guadalcanal, the rampaging PT boats supporting American the ground forces would make the difference.

By the time the first PT boats reached Milne Bay, the heaviest ground fighting was some two hundred miles to the northwest along the coast of New Guinea, between Buna and Tufi. Given the short range of the boats and their thirst for gasoline, Milne Bay proved useful only as a rear PT support base. Commander Edgar T. Neale of the PT task group, found an ideal location for an advanced PT base close to the fighting, at Tufi, an Angau station in a deep, mountain-rimmed estuary. Cool and clean, it was a marked contrast to New Guinea's typically torrid temperatures with its mass of mosquitoes. Within easy range of the fighting, Tufi was also well camouflaged from the air by natural jungle growth. Here, PT crews had a unique opportunity to witness native life at its best. Moreover, a sympathetic Angau director and his staff provided hospitality and native labor to handle refueling of the boats, a tedious chore done by hand, along with other heavy work required.[5]

On December 20, the *Tulsa* made its initial run from Milne Bay to the new base with supplies. Immediately nightly PT operations began from Tufi in support of MacArthur's troops on New Guinea. For the Japanese, plagued as they were by a shortage of warships and cargo vessels, the Imperial Navy was forced to rely increasingly on barges, or *daihatsus,* as well as submarines for delivery of supplies to their New Guinea garrisons. Thus, the *daihatsus,* landing barges between thirty-five and forty-nine feet in length with a low freeboard, became the PTs' primary target. With a capacity of around 35 troops with equipment, or three to four tons and eighty men, or eight tons for the larger craft, such vessels were usually powered by diesel engines that provided a top speed of six to eight knots. Armament was light, generally one or two machine guns.[6]

At first glance, *daihatsus,* as slow moving as they were, seemed easy prey for the fast-moving PT boats armed as they were with torpedoes, machine guns and 20-mm cannon. But the shallow-draft barges were immune to torpedoes, the PTs' primary weapon, and the sturdily-built craft, generally of wood construction, could withstand considerable punishment from bullets and cannon shells before sinking. Barge passengers also tended to be armed soldiers, who added their guns in defense. Additionally, barges tended to travel in groups and close to shore.

In contrast, PT boats were vulnerable to small arms fire, their plywood hulls offering no protection to crewmembers from bullets, and a bullet in a PT gasoline tank with its 100-octane fuel could prove catastrophic. Worse, PT skippers had no established doctrine upon which to rely in this unexpected form of combat, a type of conflict unanticipated by Melville or the Navy with their emphasis on attacking ships with torpedoes. PT skippers thus had to devise a barge-fighting doctrine by trial and error in combat. Success, when it came, would be at a cost.[7]

The Tufi-based PTs were quick to make their presence known to the enemy. On the night of December 21, the Japanese submarine I-4 commanded by Lt. Comdr. Toshitake Ueno arrived off the coast of New Guinea, but due to patrolling PT boats, was unable to surface and unload its supplies intended for Buna's garrison. On its way back to Rabaul, the I-4 was sunk by the American submarine Seadragon.[8]

On Christmas Eve, the Tufi PTs had better luck. Patrolling off Buna near the mouth of the Kamusi River, PT 122 commanded by Ens. Robert F. Lynch sighted the conning tower of a surfaced submarine. The I-boat was preparing to unload supplies for the Buna garrison. Closing to a range of a half-mile, Lynch fired two torpedoes; one detonated, probably a "premature" since the submarine showed no sign of damage. A determined Lynch continued his attack, firing his second pair of torpedoes at a range of five hundred yards. This time, the shock of two sudden explosions rolled across the water; the submarine appeared to break in half before sinking amidst a cloud of smoke and flames. Japanese records confirm the loss of the 2180-ton I-18 sunk that night off the Kamusi River by a PT boat.[9]

That same night, in what would become a more typical action, using machine guns and 20-mm cannon, PTs 114 and 121 sank two daihatsus filled with reinforcements bound for Buna. In the nights that followed, the Tufi PTs continued to engage barges. On the night of January 17-18, while patrolling near Buna, *PT 120* encountered three *daihatsus* crammed with Japanese soldiers, departing from Sanananda, a village near Buna. The *120* boat attacked all three barges with guns; the enemy responded in kind, mortally wounding a *120* motor mac. But the PT's guns managed to sink two barges and set the third afire.

On the following day, Sanananda fell to advancing Australians, and Buna was declared also secured. For the first time in the war in the Pacific, the Japanese Army had suffered a major setback: Guadalcanal was not declared an Allied victory until February 9.

These events did not go unnoticed. In Tokyo, an Army hothead accused the Navy, declaring, "You landed the Army without arms and food and then cut off the supply. It's like sending someone on a roof and taking away the ladder." Ordered to withdraw all troops from Buna by sea, the local Japanese commander found this was impossible due to a lack of barge transport. To prevent a repeat of the Guadalcanal debacle, the Japanese would launch a massive barge-building program, but it would be too late to help the Buna garrison. That the Tufi PTs had influenced the outcome was confirmed by comments made following the fall of Buna:

According to Major Mitsuo Koiwai, the only field officer grade of Japan's South Seas Detachment known to have survived the campaign, when interrogated at the end of the war, he declared that supply strangulation caused the Japanese defeat. "We lost at Buna because we could not...supply our troops, and because our navy and air force could not disrupt the enemy supply line."

Speaking even more bluntly for the Allied side, Col. J. Sladen Bradley, Chief of Staff of the U.S. 32nd Infantry Division, declared, "the successful conclusion of the Buna campaign was brought about by the mere fact that the American and Australian troops were able to *'exist'* longer than the Japs. That the Allied troops took Buna as a result of superior leadership, arms, and tactics is sheer fantasy. Attrition worked both ways, but our supply, (although meager) was better than the Japs' supply as they were completely isolated. We lived the longest and therefore took our objective.[10]

But it remained for Australian Lt. Gen. Edmund Herring, commanding Allied troops in New Guinea, to make the point most emphatically. In a late December memo, the general wrote:

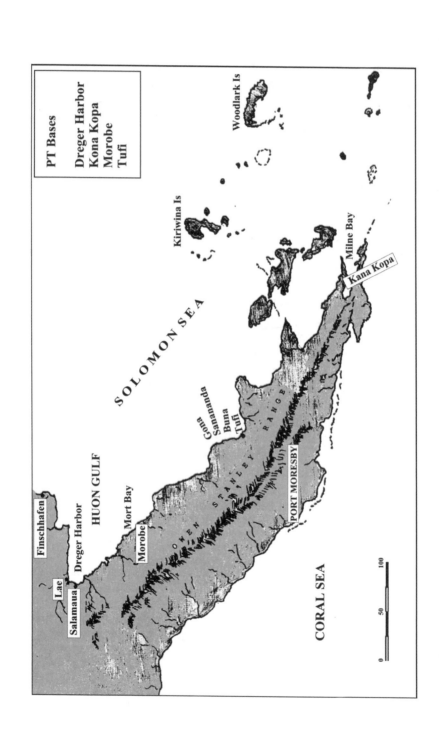

PT Bases

Dreger Harbor
Kona Kopa
Morobe
Tufi

SOLOMON SEA

Woodlark Is

Kiriwina Is

Milne Bay

Kana Kopa

HUON GULF

Finschhafen

Lae

Salamaua

Dreger Harbor

Mort Bay

Morobe

Gona
Sanananda
Buna
Tufi

OWEN STANLEY RANGE

PORT MORESBY

CORAL SEA

0   50   100

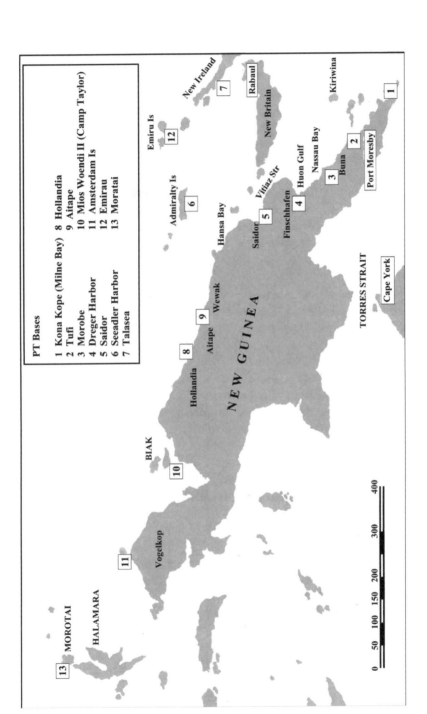

PT Bases

1 Kona Kope (Milne Bay)	8 Hollandia
2 Tufi	9 Aitape
3 Morobe	10 Mios Woendi II (Camp Taylor)
4 Dreger Harbor	11 Amsterdam Is
5 Saidor	12 Emirau
6 Seeadler Harbor	13 Moratai
7 Talasea	

MOROTAI

HALAMARA

BIAK

Vogelkop

Hollandia

NEW GUINEA

Aitape

Wewak

Hansa Bay

Saidor

Finschhafen

Vitiaz Str

Admiralty Is

Emiru Is

New Ireland

New Britain

Rabaul

Huon Gulf

Nassau Bay

Buna

Kiriwina

Port Moresby

Cape York

TORRES STRAIT

0 50 100 150 200 300 400

"Enemy is reduced in numbers, short of ammunition, food and supplies, whilst our air force and PT boats are preventing any large reinforcements or delivery of supplies. He is weak in artillery, has no tanks, and has suffered a series of defeats.

"He has been attacked by our air force and artillery and has no adequate counter measures."[11]

General Herring added, "We have unchallenged air superiority," and at sea, PT boats are "effectively protecting Allied convoys," enabling them to land supplies close to the front. Note should be made that General Herring's admiration did not extend to other American fighting forces. Earlier, during the battle for Buna, the general suggested to MacArthur there was a need for more troops. When MacArthur suggested bringing the U.S. 41st Infantry Division over from Australia, Herring along with another Australian general, told MacArthur that on the basis of what they had seen this far, they did not think much of the fighting qualities or leadership of the U.S. 32nd Division then in New Guinea, and asked instead for an Australian force. As an American army officer, this was a bitter blow for MacArthur; but he agreed to fly to the battlefield the Australian 21st Brigade, then in training in Port Moresby. He also took severe steps to remedy the problem with the U.S. troops in New Guinea.

For the Japanese in New Guinea, it was to be another Guadalcanal. Cut off from supplies, starved and weakened by diseases, Japanese troops continued their battle against the jungle and advancing Allied troops as PT boats maintained their nightly patrols offshore, providing an effective naval blockade.

With the Buna defeat, PT boats, still the U.S. Navy's sole representatives in the Solomon Sea, found fewer enemy contacts. Still the boats maintained their nightly patrols, sinking some barges and running others ashore. In the absence of action, as was common in all South Pacific theaters, PT skippers aggressively prowled close to the enemy beach to strafe Japanese bivouacs, using information provided by Coastwatchers and friendly natives. Enemy supply dumps were also targeted by PT machine guns and cannons, all of which added to the enemy's misery and sense of isolation. Submarines were occasionally sighted, but with the PTs' lack of underwater detection gear, the escape of the enemy vessels once submerged was virtually certain.

In any event, it was obvious the PTs served their purpose as a miniature "fleet in being." Knowing they were there, the enemy chose to reduce his barge and submarine resupply operations accordingly.[12]

Further evidence that the Tufi PTs' efforts were effective was confirmed by a recovered diary: according to notes written by Sergeant Kiyoshi Wada, a medical corpsman stationed in a village near Munda, disease and starvation stalked the Japanese at Buna. He described how as December passed, he and his fellow soldiers had been reduced to eating crabs raw, and even snakes. By January his diary notes that he and his comrades were eating grass. "We are just like horses," he wrote. By January 10, "all the grass and roots have been eaten in the area." Stricken by malaria and tortured by hunger, he called New Guinea "the island of distress and sorrow."[13]

On January 12, an urgent Japanese radio report from Munda to Rabaul noted the soldiers at Munda were starving. Most had dysentery, said the report. If reinforcements were not sent immediately, "We are doomed," the message concluded.

As a consequence, Rabaul ordered its 18th Army to withdraw westward to Lae and Salamaua; barges were to transport the sick and wounded. On January 19, General Yamagata, as senior officer in the area, ordered the withdrawal. When the last of his men disappeared into the darkness, General Yamagata and his supply officer, Colonel Yoshinobu Tomita, each smoked a final cigarette then shot themselves.

However, for the PT boats, the close-to-shore patrolling, so effective against the enemy, came at a stiff price. Bad weather, flotsam drifting offshore, including waterlogged-tree trunks and uncharted reefs, caused bent props and gashed hulls. The scarcity of tools, parts and even gasoline added to the PT crews' own sense of isolation resulting from being at the end of a very long supply line. Milne Bay's code name, "Fall River," added to the problem as badly needed parts and other such items often ended up at Fall River, Massachusetts.[14]

But help for the PTs was on the way. At Kana Kope, on the southwest shore of Milne Bay, known locally as Gili Gili, the PT tender *Hilo* was moored as a place of repair. At first, only basics, such as engine changes, were handled. But even this was an improvement. Previously, this meant a boat trip to Gili Gili to borrow an Army crane. To repair bent props or struts, or check a boat's bottom for damage meant a trip to Samarai, in the Louisiades. There, encouraged by raucous blasts from a conch shell, natives cranked the boat up a dilapidated marine railway. Such procedures added to the time a badly needed PT was unavailable for patrol.

In February, the PTs at Tufi got another break. Commander Morton C. Mumma, Jr., former skipper of the submarine *Sailfish,* recently appointed naval liaison officer to MacArthur's headquarters, was made commander of New Guinea based PTs. On March 15, the New Guinea PT boats were designated Task Group 70.01 (Motor Torpedo Boat Squadrons Seventh Fleet). As commander, Mumma's task was relatively simple, but reflected a major difference between PT operations in New Guinea and those in the Solomons. As commander of a unit of the Seventh Fleet, under MacArthur's command,[15] Mumma and his PTs were not subject to the orders of any and every passing naval flag officer without the general's prior approval. In contrast, PTs operating in the Solomons were in the nature of a seagoing cavalry that could be ordered to "charge" by any admiral passing through.

By now, with more PTs reaching New Guinea, including boats from Squadron 8, a mixture of 77- and 80-foot Elcos skippered by Lt. Comdr. Barry K. Atkins and Squadron 7 with twelve 80-foot Elcos under the command of Lt. Comdr. John Bulkeley of Philippine fame, back in the South Pacific for a second tour of duty, a new PT main base had been established at Kana Kope.[16]

By now, also, the PTs of New Guinea had friends overhead: PBY patrol planes painted black; built by the United States, based at Milne Bay flown by the Royal Australian Air Force, the "Black Cats" as in the Solomons, provided night support to patrolling PTs by dropping flares on suspected targets and scouting for the boats.

By March, the Tufi PTs were still experimenting with ways to attack the *daihatsus.* Some skippers, influenced by their Melville training, or by personal choice, preferred high-speed strafing runs, subjecting the enemy vessels to a barrage of machine gun and cannon fire as they swept past. Other skippers tried a different approach. On the night of March 16, two skippers, Lieutenants Frank H. Dean commanding *PT 114* and Francis H. McAdoo, Jr., on

PT 129, decided to try an idea they had used back home in the woods when hunting for game, called the "still hunt."

Suspecting that a tiny inlet along New Guinea's Huon Gulf was being used by the enemy as a barge terminal, the two skippers approached after dark with engines muffled. Once in the inlet, they secured their engines and settled down to wait. But McAdoo became impatient and left Dean behind while he looked around outside. Dean, more patient, dropped anchor to prevent the persistent tide from carrying his boat from its place of concealment near the shore. What the PT men did not know was that a group of *daihatsus* had already arrived and were inside the inlet unloading supplies. As each vessel was emptied it backed clear to idle offshore awaiting the rest of the barges. A driving tropical rainstorm and the darkness concealed the two sides from one another.

The first indication Dean and the crew had something was amiss was when their boat was nudged in the darkness by another craft. Had McAdoo returned, they wondered? Then they froze: the sound of Japanese voices coming from the unseen quickly settled the question. Two *daihatsus* had harmlessly bumped into the PT. As the Japanese occupants continued to chatter, it was evident the enemy believed they had merely nudged another barge.

Dean's crew made quick preparations. Since the barges were too close for the fixed guns to bear, hand guns were passed out to the crew. At a signal, the men opened fire on the barges as the PT's engines were started and a crewman ran forward and cut the anchor line, thus allowing the boat to move enough for the .50-caliber turret guns to fire. Meanwhile, Dean wasted no time: shoving his throttles ahead, he sent the PT surging ahead riding over one of the barges that was ahead under the bow, breaking the smaller craft in two.

Once in the clear, Dean pointed the boat toward the shore and made a strafing pass, as McAdoo, attracted by the sound of the gunfire, came roaring back into the inlet. Together, the two PTs dispatched four more *daihatsus* before departing.[17]

By February, the Japanese command at Rabaul had decided that, given MacArthur's successes thus far, it was time for a major response. The result would affect the entire New Guinea campaign and involve the PTs in one of the most controversial operations of the war. Since Lae, some 150 miles west of Buna, MacArthur's next likely objective, was garrisoned by a mere 3,500 troops, General

Imamura ordered 6,900 men of the 18th Army shipped to Lae as reinforcements. Such a large force would have to go by ships. With their experience in reinforcing Guadalcanal, the Japanese planned to use the weather for cover along with heavy fighter cover. Admiral Mikawa commanding the 8th Fleet based at Rabaul, estimated that at the very worst a well-organized convoy could deliver at least half the force. Eight transports would make the voyage from Rabaul accompanied by eight destroyers, the entire convoy under the command of Rear Admiral Masatomi Kimura. Departing Rabaul on the night of February 28 under cover of a weather front as planned, the ships followed a counterclockwise course around New Britain into what was soon to be known as the Bismarck Sea.

But MacArthur's forces were on the alert. Allied reconnaissance planes had noted the unusual concentration of ships in Rabaul's Simpson Harbor. Earlier, a number of Fifth Air Force B-25 medium bombers were modified, the bombardier position removed in the aircraft's nose and replaced by eight .50-caliber machine guns firing forward. The aircraft were also fitted to carry five-hundred-pound bombs with a five-second delay fuse. Thus equipped, the B-25s were to approach the Japanese ships at sea level, first firing the nose guns, then dropping their bombs as they neared the ships; the five-second delay in bomb detonation, called "skip-bombing," allowed planes to escape the blast.[18]

On the afternoon of March 1, unfortunately for the Japanese, the weather cleared. A Fifth Air Force reconnaissance plane sighted the convoy north of New Britain, headed west. Contact was lost at nightfall, but on the following morning, March 2, a B-24 reestablished contact; the convoy was now thirty miles north of Cape Gloucester, estimated speed 9 knots.

March 3 was a fateful day for both sides. In Japan, March 3 is Girls' or Dolls' Day. On that day, little girls dress up their dolls and display them to friends and neighbors. To remind the troops of their kid sisters at home, candy was issued to all hands on the ships. But on this day, the Huon Gulf would be no place for a joyful celebration. With daylight came MacArthur's air force. Bombed and strafed, by midday the convoy was shattered, the ships scattered about the Gulf, many stopped and sinking. Only four destroyers survived. Fishing out what survivors they could, they fled back to Rabaul. Behind them they left thousands of men still alive in the water. For the Tufi PTs, there had been two days of anxious waiting as the convoy made it way toward New Guinea. In anticipation of the action, Commander Mumma brought three PTs up from Milne Bay. On the afternoon of March 3, with the convoy finally in range, Commander Atkins, having replaced Lieutenant Baughman as commander at Tufi, led ten boats from the base toward the open sea and the shattered convoy. For the PT boats it was likely to be a hazardous mission. They would be operating in the open sea with at top speed on average of 28 knots, less than that of which Japanese destroyers were capable; and their armament, the Mark VIII torpedoes, were none too reliable. As a result, once in the open sea, they would be easy victims for the enemy destroyers if such were encountered. Equally hazardous was the likelihood of damage: shortly, two boats struck submerged objects and were forced to return to base. But the remaining eight PTs, a mixture of 77- and 80-foot Elcos, continued on, battling heavy seas and rain squalls. At 10:50 p.m., Atkins sighted a burning ship. Thirty minutes later, *PT 143* commanded by Lt.(jg) John S. Baylis and *PT 150* skippered by Lt.(jg) Russell E. Hamacheck had closed sufficiently to make out the burning hulk of the 6,493-ton abandoned transport *Oigawa Maru*. Both skippers fired a single torpedo and the ship disappeared beneath the surface in a cloud of smoke and steam.[19] A further search by the PTs that night proved fruitless. But daylight brought another problem. With the loss of twelve ships, the sea was alive with survivors, some clinging to wreckage, some in life rafts and others in rubber boats. As the men were within paddling or swimming distance of New Guinea, military necessity would not permit them to reach shore to confront Allied troops. And Japanese Bushido culture prohibited surrender. Both the returning Allied aircraft that morning and the PT crews had no option but to go about the sickening task of machine-gunning the survivors. Not that there was much thought given to any other course of action. Stories of wounded or captured Japanese using hidden grenades to kill themselves and their rescuers were common among Allied military personnel in the Pacific, as was the Japanese habit of torturing captives before beheading them.

On March 5, the two PTs that sunk the *Oigawa Maru* were dispatched on a rescue mission to the position of a reported downed Allied pilot. Shortly they came upon a surfaced *I-boat* twenty-five miles off Cape Ward taking survivors aboard from three *daihatsus*. The PTs attacked with torpedoes: the missiles missed and the submarine crash-dived, leaving over a hundred men behind to their fate.[20] Governed by the same necessity of war noted earlier, the PTs machine-gunned the stranded survivors. When the vessels were littered with bodies, the two PT boats raced by hurling depth charges, the explosions finally sinking all three barges. Termed the Battle of the Bismarck Sea, the Japanese credited PT boats and strafing aircraft with the deaths of three thousand men. Japanese destroyers and submarines managed to rescue a reported 2734 men; nevertheless, several hundred Japanese managed to swim ashore; for more than a month afterwards, for the headhunting natives on nearby islands it was open season on the survivors. One group of eighteen made it to Kiriwina Island in a small boat, one of the Trobriand Group, only to be captured by *PT 114*. Following the Battle of the Bismarck Sea and the losses, the Japanese would never again risk sending a ship larger than a coastal vessel or a barge into New Guinea waters. The garrisons in New Guinea had to further tighten their belts and do without.

With daylight and Allied air power dominating the waters off New Guinea, whatever supplies the Japanese hoped to get to New Guinea would have to come by submarines from Rabaul or barges dispatched to the island garrisons by way Cape Gloucester. Before the war ended, workers in China, Malaya and the Philippines would have built over four thousand *daihatsus* for the Japanese. And because they swarmed down from Rabaul like ants, the Japanese termed it the "Ari" (ant) system. But no matter how hard they worked, what got through to the hard-pressed garrisons was never enough. Nonetheless, for the PTs of New Guinea, the barges were flexible foes, adding guns as heavy as 37-mm cannon as well employing makeshift armor plating to protect the coxswain and the engine compartment from the guns of the lurking PT boats.

With the steady advance of MacArthur's New Guinea ground forces westward, it was necessary for the PTs to abandon Tufi for a base further west and closer to the fighting. While based at Tufi, the PTs had accounted for one submarine and eighteen *daihatsus,* plus two possibles.[21] The next base would prove to be even more productive.

Located eighty miles northwest of Buna and a mile up the Morobe River, the new base allowed the PTs to easily patrol the Huon Gulf, intercepting *daihatsus* passing through these waters. Concealed from aerial observation by the heavy jungle, for the PT crews used to conditions at Tufi, Morobe was an unpleasant shock. At first glance, the base looked like a Hollywood jungle scene; in fact, its primitive setting was more the norm for PT advanced bases in the South Pacific. However, as one of the most primitive advanced PT bases established in the war, Morobe seemed more like a throwback to the Stone Age. Extending back from the river beneath a thick jungle canopy where sunlight rarely filtered through, it appeared to be infested with all the bugs and smaller creatures common to New Guinea that crawled or flew, the most bothersome being flies, the most lethal the malaria-bearing mosquitoes. In the cloying heat, PT base personnel, radiomen, motor macs and all the rest so essential in keeping the boats operating, lived and worked. When it rained, the ground became a quagmire where men plodded in ooze up to their ankles, a dim world where men moved about dressed in foul weather gear.[22]

But there was no getting around the fact that Morobe was a hot spot for the PTs. And it was about to get hotter. On March 12, Washington issued a directive for Operation "Cartwheel" calling for Admiral Halsey to advance north through the Solomons while General MacArthur fought his way west through New Guinea. The target of this two-pronged Allied drive was Rabaul, Japan's main base of operations in the Southwest Pacific. Furthermore, the Joint Chiefs of Staff declared there would be no added reinforcements for the South Pacific while the war in North Africa against the Axis forces was in doubt. On March 29, a JCS Directive declared the two Trobriand Islands, Kiriwina and Woodlark, north of Milne Bay to be Allied objectives. To MacArthur, their only value was as air bases. An airstrip on Kiriwina, 125 miles from New Britain and 200 miles from Bougainville, could provide fighter protection for bombers carrying heavier loads of bombs. MacArthur's bombers were pounding Rabaul, but having little effect, as the long range and required fuel meant they carried insufficient bombs to do real damage.

On April 15, 1943, Admiral Halsey, whose advances from Guadalcanal north through the Solomons meant he would be operating in the Southwest Pacific under General MacArthur instead of the South Pacific Theater under Admiral Nimitz at Pearl Harbor, flew to Brisbane to talk with his new superior. The complex plan hammered out by MacArthur and Halsey called for a series of attacks aimed at Rabaul as defined by the JCS, the two commanders coordinated their advances to keep the Japanese off balance. MacArthur would start by capturing Lae and the remaining Japanese-held positions in northeast New Guinea. Halsey's first step up through the Solomons was the island of New Georgia. In fact, three islands figured in his immediate plans: New Georgia and Kolombangara in the Central Solomons, and Bougainville, at the western end of the chain. By seizing part of Bougainville, Halsey would be at the top of the Solomon chain, a mere 150 miles from Rabaul, within bombing range. The simultaneous movements by MacArthur in New Guinea and Halsey in the Solomons, would each call for the use of PTs boats.

In New Guinea, amphibious landings for Operation Cartwheel began on June 30 with two simultaneous landings, at Nassau Bay and the Trobriand Islands. Earlier, Commander Mumma aboard one of the PT boats had been poking about the little-known shoreline of Huon Gulf; he had found an excellent landing beach at Nassau Bay, virtually under the nose of the Japanese position at Salamaua. Mumma reported his find to MacArthur's headquarters, pointing out the advantages of having an all-weather supply route with a terminus near Salamaua, a mere sixty miles below the Japanese base at Lae. The idea was approved.

On the eve of the landings, four PT boats under the command of Commander Atkins departed Morobe for the embarkation point. At 5 p.m. three of the PTs came alongside a jetty, and troops from the U.S. 41st Infantry Division commenced boarding. *PT 143* and *PT 120* took seventy men aboard; *PT 142* took ten more aboard; as the escort, *PT 168* carried no passengers keeping its decks clear in case of action. The balance of the invasion force, the 162nd Infantry Regiment, was distributed among three dozen landing craft manned by the 2nd Engineer Special Brigade.

The unique invasion force, the first instance in World War Two in which PT boats carried troops as part of an amphibious invasion, put to sea in the teeth of a raging storm featuring high winds, lashing rains and low visibility. *PT 168* soon lost contact with the force and proceeded independently. The other three PTs wallowed on for the forty-mile trip averaging 7 knots, matching the speed of the landing barges.

Leading the first wave, *PT 142* overshot Nassau Bay, now nicknamed "Mort Bay" in honor of its discoverer. In reversing course, the *142* boat accomplished the near impossible feat of running into *PT 143* leading the second wave. The startled landing craft scattered like frightened minnows.

Lt.(jg) Carey, commanding *PT 142* soon rounded them up, however, and led them back to the beach where they landed their troops. With the storm intensifying the landing craft of the second and third waves broached in the twelve-foot surf. Nevertheless, all the invasion force got safely ashore.

That is, nearly all: unable to land their passenger troops due to the unexpected difficulties, the three PTs returned to the staging area, their passengers still aboard, by now a thoroughly miserable group of men.[23]

Despite setbacks, the Nassau Bay landings proved to be an immense success: nearby Japanese troops, hearing the sound of grounding landing craft, mistook them for tanks coming ashore and fled into the jungle. Two days later, Commander Atkins returned to Nassau Bay; while his PTs strafed the nearby villages, reinforcements from eleven landing craft arrived under their own power, together with several others towed by trawlers, landing additional troops. Still more troops were landed on July 4th and 6th. By this time, the beachhead was secure and Australian troops were pushing on toward Japanese held Salamaua.

On June 30, MacArthur's second landing, supported by PTs under the command of Lt. Comdr. Bulkeley and Lt. Pat Monroe, timed to take place at the same as the Nassau invasion, was also carried out successfully, with five thousand troops led by Lt. Gen. Walter Krueger's U.S. Sixth Army, dubbed the Alamo Force, landing unopposed on the islands of Woodlark and Kiriwina.[24] Once more the PTs had demonstrated their versatility.

An advanced PT base in New Guinea. Screened by trees, such bases were hewn out of the jungle and typically lacked any amenities. *Courtesy of WWII PT Boats Museum and Archives, Germantown, Tennessee, USA.*

CHAPTER NINE

GUADALCANAL NORTH

Admiral William F. Halsey was a man in a hurry. On January 23, Admiral Nimitz had cautioned him that should the enemy retreat from Guadalcanal, no permanent installations should be constructed on the island. Rather, the emphasis would be on a rapid advance upward through the Solomon chain. Nimitz shrewdly guessed that given the time, the Japanese would shift to a strategic offensive and the Americans would be faced with another grinding struggle for yet another island in the chain.

Responding to Nimitz's urging, Halsey took aim at the Russells, a small group of islands a mere thirty miles northwest of Cape Esperance, soon to be famous to many Allied servicemen for its mud, rain, and coconut trees. During the struggle for Guadalcanal, the groups of islands had served as a staging point for the enemy's barge line between Shortland and the "Canal." With the Japanese retreat from Guadalcanal, the islands were abandoned as well.[1]

Called Operation "Cleanslate," the Allied occupation of the Russells would provide the short-ranged PTs with a new advanced base close to the next expected enemy opposition; here also, American engineers would construct a radar site along with an airstrip to cover future advances north through the Solomons.

The two largest islands were Pavuva and Banaka. The first, with an area of roughly eight by seven miles, featured a 1,500-foot jungle-covered hill useful for positioning radar; the second, about eight miles long and two miles wide, separated from Pavuva by a half-mile-wide strip of water called Sunlight Channel, possessed two inlets facing the Slot, ideal as an advanced PT base.[2]

On February 23, 1943, some four thousand troops of the U.S. 43rd Division under the command of Maj. Gen. John H. Hester, began landing in the Russells. Naval support for what was an unopposed landing, included eight PTs designated TG 61.2 under the command of Lt. Allen H. Harris.[3]

With the occupation of the Russells, Tulagi was relegated to the role of support base. Immediately, nightly PT patrols were initiated, but without effect. The only enemy reaction to the occupation of the Russells came fifteen days later, when the Japanese launched a series of air raids with little result.

For the PT crews, the Russells provided one of the rare occasions during the war when the action was scarce and there was time to indulge in a bit of relaxation. At first, swimming was favored, but nearby cruising sharks dampened most of the interest in that form of activity. Exploring the nearby islands and native villages proved of interest, but U.S. Navy orders put native villages off limits to crews. Furthermore, such explorations could be risky. Crocodiles were to be found dozing on the muddy banks of streams or lurking watchfully in the murky water leading back into the jungle. When the more daring crew members approached a native village, they were met by half-naked native men armed with spears and clubs, forcing them to make a hurried retreat.

But all was not lost. There was always the favored pastime of PT crews, brewing an alcoholic beverage. Although difficult to come by, five-gallon cans of 190-proof alcohol used in torpedoes was available. To prevent such misuse, the Navy had added a pink-colored chemical nicknamed "pink lady" rendering the fluid nonpotable. The PT men countered with a simple still, a canteen fitted with copper tubing and coils. With the canteen on a hotplate, the coils were run through cold water. At the end of the tubing a tin cup collected the pure distilled alcohol. Mixed with readily available canned pineapple juice the results were ready for consumption.[4] Meanwhile, back in Washington, the JCS directive for Operation "Cartwheel" was about to end this period of relative relaxation for PTs in the Solomons.

For Admiral Halsey, the first objective as part of the operation would be New Georgia, code named Operation "Toenails." Northwest of the Russells in the Central Solomons, the forty-five-mile-long New Georgia, was thirty minutes flying time from Guadalcanal. Naval support would be provided by destroyers and PT boats.[5]

In a deliberate effort to unbalance the enemy, the invasion would be carried out on June 30, the day General MacArthur landed at Nassau Bay in New Guinea.

New Georgia had first drawn the attention of the Allied command in November 1942, when Japanese troops landed there and in December, constructed a 4,700-foot airstrip on the island's Munda Point. Thus it was the airstrip that was the major objective. As long as the enemy held the airfield and had planes based there, Halsey's advance north would be in jeopardy. If the Allies could take the airstrip, however, the enemy could be denied access to everything below Bougainville, the big island at the top of the Slot. As in the case of Guadalcanal and Henderson Field, an airfield was the focal point, but now the roles would be reversed; Japanese troops would be defending and American ground forces attacking, hampered by a jungle, if anything, more dense than that encountered on Guadalcanal. And unlike the Japanese on Guadalcanal, veterans as they were of previous campaigns, the Americans would be fresh from the United States training camps, well equipped but still green men.[6]

Halsey's key landings on June 30 would be on the small island of Rendova, south of New Georgia, separated from the larger island by five-mile wide Blanche Channel. Rendova Harbor, a calm sheltered body of water provided the ideal PT base, with easy access to the Solomon Sea via Blanche Channel. Like Tulagi, in the battle for the Central Solomons, Rendova was fated to become a part of World War Two PT history.

In mid-1943, Japanese commanders at Rabaul, alerted by increased Allied radio traffic, and by the occupation of the Russells, grew convinced the enemy was preparing an assault somewhere in the middle of the Solomon chain. In any event, the Japanese stationed submarines north of the Russells as lookouts. One such submarine was the *RO-101* commanded by Lt. Comdr. Zenji Orita. As commander of a Japanese submarine in combat, Orita's experience would typify the problems submarines faced when confronted by PT boats.

In the small hours of June 30, the date of the invasion of the island of New Georgia, Commander Orita was patrolling northwest of the Russells. With supplies running low and nearing the end of his period on station, Orita was beginning to work his way toward

Rabaul, the *RO-101* cruising on the surface when, about ninety minutes prior to sunrise, his listening gear picked up the sound of approaching PT boats. Orita submerged and a short time later, peering through his periscope, he sighted a massive armada of ships headed toward New Georgia.

As soon as the ships were safely past, Orita raised his antenna above the surface and radioed Rabaul: "Group of enemy landing craft sighted, heading west, at 5:45," adding the position and time of his transmission.[7]

As it was now daylight, Orita remained submerged, his radio antenna extended awaiting orders. Just before noon he monitored a radio transmission from the garrison on Rendova Island. "Enemy troops are landing with amphibious tanks in the lead. We are exchanging fire with them."[8]

Finally, at 4 p.m., Rabaul responded: the delay was possibly caused by Rabaul being distracted by the simultaneous Allied landings at New Guinea's Nassau Bay and in the Kiriwina Islands. Rabaul instructed Orita to attack the enemy convoy, unloading troops off Blanche Channel. Orita was to attack from the west, the *RO-107,* a sister submarine patrolling nearby, from the east, through Blanche Channel. Rabaul added that submarines *RO-100, RO-103,* and *RO-106* were departing Rabaul at once as support.

Accordingly, Orita headed the *RO-101* northward. By dawn July 1 he was thirty miles from the target area. Peering through his periscope, he sighted two PT boats about 500 to 1000 yards ahead. To Orita, it seemed as though they were providing him an escort. Convinced the two boats carried underwater detection gear, Orita ordered "silent running" and went deep.[9]

After allowing the two PTs time to move on, he returned the *RO-101* to periscope depth, only to find more PT boats. When they remained close by, a frustrated Orita again took the submarine deep.

At 2 p.m. Orita tried again. Twenty miles from the convoy he had to break off his approach: the *RO-101's* batteries providing power for his engines' underwater operations had to be recharged. Thus Orita was forced to slip away and spend the night surfaced. On the following morning, with the *RO-101's* batteries recharged, Orita again headed toward the convoy's position. However, once again fast approaching PTs forced him to submerge; this time Orita believed the PTs' radar had detected the surfaced submarine.[10] For the rest of the day, *Orita* sought to reach the convoy, but it seemed that PT boats were always near. Late in the day, Rabaul radioed, instructing the *RO-101* and *RO-107* to return to Simpson Harbor. The *RO-101* returned as ordered, but the *RO-107* was never heard from again. According to U.S. Navy records, on July 1 she was sunk by the U.S. destroyer *Radford*.

The Allied invasion force had been spared a submarine attack by the presence of PT boats. But this unknown accomplishment would go unrewarded. Indeed, the PTs supporting the New Georgia invasion would shortly find themselves so deeply in the proverbial "doghouse" that, in the eyes of some traditional U.S. naval officers, they would never recover.

It began at 3 p.m. June 30, when initial landing operations at New Georgia were complete; Rear Admiral Richmond Kelly Turner, commanding the amphibious force, ordered a retirement south. Thirty minutes later, the ships were attacked by a formation of twenty-five torpedo-armed "Bettys" escorted by twenty-four "Zekes." About ten of the torpedo planes broke through the convoy's air cover and flak to drop their fish. Only one was a hit. Ironically, the ship hit was Admiral Turner's flagship, the transport *McCawley*, known as the "Wacky Mac." The *McCawley* lost power and drifted to a stop with eight wounded and fifteen crew members dead.[11]

With the rest of the convoy continued south, Turner shifted his flag and staff to an escorting destroyer while a second destroyer took off most of the wounded vessel's crew; only a salvage party remained behind in an effort to prevent the *McCawley* sinking.

With the transport *Libra* towing the *McCawley*, and escorted by two destroyers, the group of ships slowly headed south. By nightfall, despite the efforts of the damage control party, the *McCawley* was clearly sinking and the men of the party were taken aboard the destroyer *McCalla*. A Navy tug, the *Pawnee*, arrived to take over the tow, only to have the tow line part. Rear Admiral Wilkinson, commanding the salvage effort, believing the odds were against saving the "Wacky Mac," decided to put no more salvage personnel on the ship, but rather, to tow it until it sank.

At 8:23 p.m., as the *Pawnee* was preparing to secure a second tow line, two torpedoes slammed into the crippled ship sending her to the bottom.[12] Seconds later, lookouts on the *McCalla* sighted two torpedoes approaching the destroyer, however, the *McCalla* managed to comb the tracks, successfully evading both missiles.

Concluding the source of the torpedoes was a reported enemy submarine in the area, Admiral Wilkinson instructed the *McCalla* to run down the tracks and make an attack. As the destroyer sought to respond, she encountered a number of PT boats. When informed by the destroyer's skipper that the presence of the PTs interfered with the attack on the submarine, Wilkinson canceled the attack and ordered *McCalla* to rejoin the *Libra* and *Pawnee* as they continued south.

On the following morning the mystery as to the source of the torpedoes was resolved; entering Rendova Harbor with six PTs was Lt. Comdr Robert B. Kelly on *PT 153*, the former executive officer of Bulkeley's Squadron 3 during the final days of the Philippines. Back in the Pacific for a second tour as commander of Squadron 9, Kelly reported to the commander of the naval base at Rendova, describing the previous night's action. The report sent shock waves through the base. To his dismay Kelly learned that he had torpedoed and sunk a friendly vessel; worse, of all the "friendly" ships in the Pacific, the PT squadron commander learned he had sunk Admiral Turner's flagship *McCawley*. Kelly's statement that he had first questioned Rendova prior to the attack and been assured no friendly vessels were nearby did nothing to calm the storm.

Known as "Terrible Turner" throughout the Navy with good reason, the admiral, described once by an ensign as "the meanest man I ever saw," was famous for his stormy temper and bullying behavior toward subordinates who fell short of measuring up to his exacting standards. For a lowly PT officer, a type vessel the admiral had no love for, the sinking of his ship by PTs would more than qualify as a cause of his wrath. Under the circumstances, bearing in mind that the early PT radar sets left something to be desired, Commander Kelly's report is of some significance:

"At 2014 *153*'s radar detected a very large target distance 800 yards surrounded by eight smaller targets, apparently landing craft. The first [PT] section closed range to about 600 yards. Targets appeared to be a large destroyer, a 7,000-10,000 ton transport and a small destroyer or transport. [They] were seen to have converged. The large transport was lying to, the other ships were circling behind it. At 2016, *PT 153* fired four torpedoes at the transport and radioed for all boats in the first and second sections to press home the attack. *PT 153* continued on the same course and at the same speed to allow other boats to fire undetected. When *PT 153* was 300-400 yards from the transport, four torpedoes were seen to strike it in succession; one forward, two amidships and one aft. *PT 153* then reversed course to the left and retired at slow speed. The first two torpedoes hit 4-5 seconds apart; the last two simultaneously. *PT 118* on the starboard quarter of *PT 153* fired two torpedoes at a small transport or destroyer and observed two direct hits. As the *PT 118* retired followed by *PT 153*, her target appeared to be sinking by the stern.

PT 158 fired two torpedoes no hits observed changed her course and fired her last two torpedoes these torpedoes were seen to straddle the target. *PT 160* fired one torpedo but it missed. *PT 159* fired two torpedoes both of which missed.[13]

As one observer noted, it was fortunate that the PT skippers were poor shots. Out of thirteen torpedoes, only two were really hits. Still in question was Kelly's report that six torpedoes were hits, resulting in the sinking of two ships. The likely explanation is the Mark VIII torpedoes were up to their old tricks, the detonations being "prematures;" as for the rest, much like pilots engaged in stressful combat where visibility is limited, imagination did the rest. The negative consequences of this incident, as noted, coupled with other tragedies involving PT boats, particularly in the Solomons, would be long-lasting.

As a consequence of the torpedoing of the *McCawley,* Admiral Turner placed the PTs of New Guinea under his direct command, appointing a liaison officer to keep him informed of the PTs' actions.[14] As expected, this had a dampening effect on Kelly. Just how dampening was soon apparent. Only hours later, on the night of July 1, the Tokyo Express made its first visit to New Georgia, the light cruiser *Yubari* with nine destroyers entering Blanche Channel to bombard the recently landed American troops and supplies on Rendova.

Patrolling nearby with *PTs 156, 157* and *161*, Kelly observed the gun flashes, reaction to the sinking of the *McCawley* still ringing in his ears, he was naturally inclined to be cautious about attacking too quickly. Doubtful as to the identity of the ships, he even crossed ahead of the enemy in an effort to confirm whether or not they were friendly. The Japanese commander, having no such doubts, dispatched four destroyers to dispose of this threat. By steering erratic courses and by the use of smoke, Kelly's PTs managed to evade the pursuing enemy, and in the process, even managed to fire six torpedoes. As it turned out, they got no hits, but at least they could claim they forced the Express to retreat.[15]

The original plan called for the establishment of a PT base at Viru Harbor on the southern side of New Georgia. But the plan was abandoned because the harbor was found unsuitable as a base. But it still served a purpose as it came to possess a small marine railway built by the Seabees, useful for repairing PT boats that so frequently suffered damage to hulls, props and shafts caused by running into reefs in the poorly charted waters.

Instead of Viru Harbor, an advanced PT base was established at Rendova; boats based there covered the waters to the west. To patrol the Slot, a second PT base would be established at Lever Harbor on the northeast coast of New Georgia within easy cruising distance of Kula Gulf. During the New Georgia campaign, four PT squadrons, 5, 9, 10 and 11, a total of roughly fifty-two Elco boats, operated from the two bases. Headquarters for the New Georgia PTs was Rendova under the command of Captain E. J. ("Mike") Moran, former skipper of the cruiser *Boise*. Commanding the Lever Harbor boats would be Lieutenant Commander Kelly. As a point of interest, Moran's impressive title, Commander Motor Torpedo Boat Squadrons South Pacific,[16] was less than accurate: first, New Georgia and Rendova were not in the South Pacific Theater but the Southwest Pacific Theater, as shown by Halsey being subject to MacArthur's authority; thus Moran's authority over PTs at best, was limited to the squadrons in the area of New Georgia. In any event, there is little evidence he a was more than a commander in name only; second, since New Guinea and Rendova were both in the Southwest Pacific and under the command of MacArthur's 7th Fleet, Moran hardly had authority over the New Guinea PTs. Nonetheless, although the PTs of Bulkeley's in the Philippines and the PTs at Tulagi were later determined to have provided largely mythical victories, in the Central Solomons as in New Guinea, PT boats would find their true role as the scourge of Japanese barges. By the end of the campaign, the bedeviled Japanese would be writing treaties on how to deal with this menace.[17]

After the initial clash between Kelly's PTs and the Tokyo Express on the night of July 1, for a time PT contacts around New Georgia were scarce. But the condition was only temporary. With the Allied invasion of New Georgia, Tokyo declared the island a key outpost to be "held at all costs"; four thousand troops were readied for transport down the Slot to Munda. With the end of the struggle for Guadalcanal, the U.S. Navy had made some changes. While the Tulagi PT boats and Henderson Field had been responsible for intercepting the Tokyo Express during the campaign for the "Canal," the U.S. Navy's heavy ships, now based at Tulagi, would handle such interceptions in defense of the Central Solomons. Reflecting Admiral Turner's negative attitude regarding PT boats, Rear Admirals W. L. "Pug" Ainsworth and A. S. Merrill, commanding cruiser task forces based at Tulagi, insisted that Kelly's Lever Harbor boats stay home during their frequent sweeps up the Slot to Kula Gulf "lest they foul things up."[18] The irony was that later, it would be determined that the Navy's heavy ships were not only prone to exaggerate the number of vessels sunk in battle as did the PT boats, a problem shared as well by the Japanese, but in combating *daihatsus*, U.S. warships were a virtual failure. Worse, despite the advantage of radar, and usually prior notice the Express was running, the heavy ships of the U.S. Navy rarely prevented the enemy's reinforcement efforts.

Evidence of this was not long in coming. Japanese plans to reinforce New Georgia called for destroyers to transport reinforcements from Rabaul to Vila Plantation, the staging point on the shore of the island of Kolombangara facing Kula Gulf. From there the supplies and troops would continue on to New Georgia's Munda by barge. All four thousand men would safely get as far as Vila Plantation. The first contingent for Vila headed down the Slot on the night of July 4-5 aboard three troop-carrying destroyers. As was so often the case in the Solomons campaign, the Americans picked the same night to land troops in a nearby area. When the two sides clashed in what was an inadvertent battle, the U.S. force of three light cruisers and nine destroyers, commanded by Admiral Ainsworth, lost the destroyer *Strong*. Hit by a torpedo launched by a retreating Japanese destroyer, American losses numbered forty-six men, including the *Strong's* skipper; 241 crewmen survived. For Admiral Ainsworth, the mystery was the source of the torpedo. With the Japanese destroyers on the far side of Kula Gulf, Ainsworth concluded the torpedo had been fired by a submarine. The reality was that at this late date, the U.S. Navy was still unaware of the capabilities of the Japanese Type 93 torpedo, aptly known to naval historians as the "Long Lance."

Having been thwarted on the previous night in their effort to land troops at Vila, the Japanese made a second attempt the following night: ten destroyers, seven loaded with 1600 troops with three escorting, departed Shortland at sundown. Warned by his intelligence, Admiral Halsey ordered Ainsworth to intercept the Vila-bound enemy. The result was the Battle of Kula Gulf. In it, Ainsworth lost the cruiser *Helena,* sunk by Type 93 torpedoes. Japanese losses consisted of two destroyers, one due to running aground. Despite the advantage of radar, the element of surprise, as well as possessing a superior force of ships, Ainsworth failed to prevent the reinforcements from reaching Vila. Worse, in all sincerity, he claimed a massive victory, the sinking of nine enemy ships instead of the two the Japanese actually lost.

Eight days later, on July 12, Halsey's intelligence again sent Ainsworth up the Slot. A formidable Express, nine destroyers were reported departing Rabaul. In fact, four were destroyer-transports laden with 1200 troops to be landed at Vila; five destroyers provided escort. Leading the Express was the light cruiser *Jintsu.* It was the *Jintsu* the Tulagi PTs had attacked on the night of October 13, 1942, in their first action; as noted the cruiser had returned home that night unscathed.

In the Battle of Kolombangara about to be fought in much the same waters as the recent Battle of Kula Gulf, the *Jintsu's* luck would run out, but the Japanese would again succeed on their mission. Furthermore, the Americans would lose the destroyer *Gwin,* and suffer serious damage all three of Ainsworth's cruisers as a result of torpedoes: two cruisers would be out of action for several months, the third out for the rest of the war.

Disheartened as he was by his losses, Admiral Ainsworth was nonetheless cheered by the belief that during the battle he had sunk an additional five ships. In fact, as in the Battle of Kula Gulf, he was wrong. This time Japanese losses were limited to a single ship, the *Juntsu*. And as noted, the Express had managed to land the reinforcements destined for Munda's defense.

For the New Georgia PTs, the first brush with the enemy occurred after July 21 and involved PTs operating out of Rendova; the first encounter of note occurring involving the Lever Harbor PTs did not take place until August 1. As the PTs still lacked radar, given the blackness of the nights, this is not surprising. Typical was the July 21 clash in which three PTs from Rendova prowling Blackett Strait intercepted three barges, sinking one with gunfire and chasing the other two northward. The encounter delayed a barge rendezvous with troop-carrying destroyers which were forced to depart with the troops still aboard. Three nights later, three Rendova PT entered a running gun battle with six *daihatsus*. During the exchange of gunfire, the PT crews noted their .50-caliber bullets and 20-mm shells bounced harmlessly off the barges' makeshift armor. Emerging from the battle with bullet-punctured plywood hulls, the Americans were now on notice. Clearly, the wooden-hulled PTs would need heavier guns if they were to cope with this foe. For the PT skippers, the solution would be 37-mm anti-tank guns obtained from friendly local army units to be mounted on the PT's bow.

However, it was not barges that first proved lethal to PT crews. And as with the *McCawley,* faulty communications was the problem. On the morning of July 20, *PTs 164, 166,* and *168* were returning to Rendova from a night patrol. One boat had hit a log during the night, and the boats had been forced to reduce speed as a result. Thus, instead of being far to the south near Rendova, daylight found the PTs still miles from home.

Standard procedure called for Henderson Field to send a flight of B-25 Army Air Force bombers on an early morning sweep. The three PTs were just emerging from Ferguson Passage when a flight of four B-25s returning from the morning reconnaissance flight, sighted the boats. The airmen had been told that only enemy vessels would be found in these waters during daylight hours. The PT crews easily recognized the approaching aircraft as American; they saw no cause for alarm, that is, until machine gun bullets began churning the sea near the boats. In an effort to demonstrate they were "friendly," the crews tried radio contact, fired signal flares, and frantically waved their arms, all were futile. The B-25s continued their strafing attack.[19] The skipper of *PT 168*, Lt. Edward MacCawley, III, held his gunners under firm control, refusing to allow them to return fire. Without orders, however, the gunners of the other two PTs opened fire. One of the attacking B-25s began trailing smoke before crashing in the sea five miles away. Somehow, by now, the remaining air crews had recognized the vessels as PT boats; but already *PT 166* was ablaze. The crew, some of whom were wounded, managed to abandon the doomed vessel before she exploded and sank. *PT 168* was also afire, but her crew managed to extinguish the flames.

The *168's* enraged skipper and crew raced to the downed B-25. But what they found dispelled the anger and added to the tragedy. They found the pilot of the aircraft dead, along with two crewmen; three others in the B-25 had been injured. In what was a shocking end to a dismal event, the surviving PTs headed south to Rendova, carrying the dead from the B-25, and the wounded, including eleven PT men.

Word of the disaster spread through the New Georgia PT bases and Henderson Field like wildfire. Angry PT crews declared that being attacked by enemy aircraft was bad enough, but to be attacked by friendly planes was unthinkable. Arguments raged as to the proper response, whether or not PTs should return fire in self-defense. To some, the act of shooting back at other Americans was simply wrong. In the end, the Navy made no firm decision. In effect, it would be up to each individual PT skipper, if attacked by friendly aircraft, to decide what course of action was proper under the circumstances. This was not the last time PT crews would be confronted by this frustrating problem.

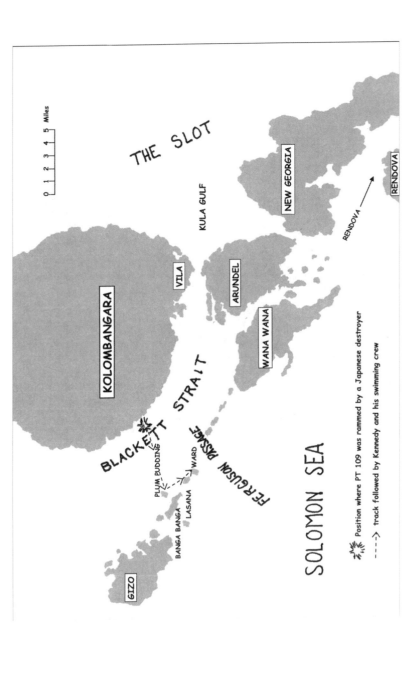

THE SLOT

KOLOMBANGARA

VILA

KULA GULF

ARUNDEL

WANA WANA

NEW GEORGIA

RENDOVA

RENDOVA

BLACKETT STRAIT

PLUM PUDDING

WARD

LASANA

FERGUSON PASSAGE

BANGA BANGA

GIZO

SOLOMON SEA

0 1 2 3 4 5 Miles

※ Position where PT 109 was rammed by a Japanese destroyer

- - - > track followed by Kennedy and his swimming crew

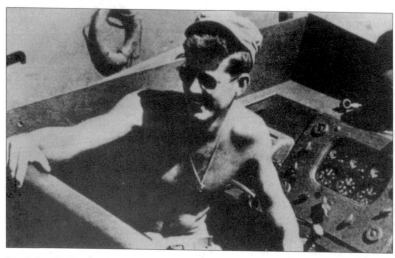

Lt. John F. Kennedy at the helm of *PT 109. Courtesy of WWII PT Boats Museum and Archives, Germantown, Tennessee, USA.*

CHAPTER TEN

PT 109

It was mid-July and the campaign for New Georgia was at its height when orders came for *PT 109,* commanded by Lt.(jg) John F. Kennedy, to proceed northward from the Russells for duty at the advanced PT base at Rendova. For the young skipper, this was the long-awaited moment.

Indeed, it had required no small amount of effort on his part, and to a lesser degree, the influence of his father, Joseph Kennedy, for him to be assigned to a combat area. In October 1941, Kennedy, recently commissioned an ensign in the U.S. Naval Reserve, had been ordered to the Pentagon assigned to naval intelligence, a task the action-minded officer found to be a complete bore. With the December attack on Pearl Harbor, like so many young naval officers, he sought a transfer to sea duty. Instead he found himself posted to headquarters, 6th Naval District in Charleston, South Carolina, responsible for protecting war plants from enemy attack, a duty he found no more to his liking.[1]

In the summer of 1942, he got a break from an unexpected source: while attending a Naval Reserve Officer's Training School at Northwestern University, he learned that two officers, Lieutenants John Bulkeley and John Harllee, both PT veterans, would be visiting the campus interviewing potential candidates as PT officers. By this time, with the publishing of the best selling book "They Were Expendable," an account depicting the heroics of Squadron 3 in the Philippines, PT boats and Bulkeley's fame were well known. For his part, Lieutenant Harllee was now a senior instructor at the Navy's recently established Motor Torpedo Training Academy at Melville, Rhode Island.

As it so happened, Kennedy proved to be the kind of officer the two veterans were looking for. A graduate of Harvard, he had been a member of the swimming team, evidence of the competitive spirit considered essential for PT officers. Moreover, Kennedy had grown up around water handling small boats, as well.

On October 1, John Kennedy reported to Melville to begin an eight-week training course that would turn him into a PT officer. That same month, he was promoted to the rank of lieutenant junior grade (jg). It seemed everything was finally going as he wished. Completing the course in November, however, Kennedy learned to his great disappointment that due to his excellent record, Harllee had recommended he be retained at Melville as an instructor assigned to Squadron 4, the base training unit.

Kennedy was given command of *PT 101,* one of the few 78-foot Huckins boats in the service, a type of PT the Navy was less than impressed with; as a result Huckins boats had been relegated to Melville and other non-combat areas.[2]

When word was received that a number of Squadron 4 PTs were to be shipped to Panama, a desperate Kennedy called upon his father to use his influence to get him assigned to combat. This time he got his wish: on March 6, he departed from San Francisco aboard a navy transport bound for Espiritu Santo as a replacement skipper; once there, along with other officers and men he boarded an LST landing craft headed for Guadalcanal.

By April 1943, much had changed; both Tulagi and Guadalcanal were rear-support bases for the forces preparing to start the drive up through the Solomons. Recently, an advanced PT base had been established in the Russells. Back at Tulagi, the tender *Jamestown* was moored available for minor repairs with PTs nestled alongside. Other PTs were moored beneath overhanging brush along the banks concealing them from roaming Japanese aircraft.

Once at Guadalcanal, Kennedy shortly learned of his assignment. He was to take command of *PT 109,* whose skipper was due to return to the states. Anxious to leave, he took Kennedy on the boat for a few rides and then said goodbye.

Also departing at the time was the rest of the boat's crew, with one exception, Ensign Leonard J. Thom.[3] A blond giant with the looks of a Viking, Thom was another former university athlete, having played tackle on the 1939-1940 Ohio State football team. Kennedy decided Thom would be the *109*'s executive officer; the two then set about to form and train a new crew for the *109* preparatory to going into combat.

The log of the *109* shows that on April 25, 1943 at 1100 hours, Lt.(jg) J. F. Kennedy assumed command.

After nine months of hard service at Tulagi, unlike the trim, well-maintained Melville boats, the *109* was a stained and scarred veteran. Her three Packard engines were well past being due for replacement, and the boat's performance was accordingly below par.

Kennedy selected his crew members from the Melville-trained men arriving at Tulagi from the States. Three of the men reported aboard the day he took command. As was typical of PT crews, all had joined the Navy following the attack on Pearl Harbor: GM1/c Charles A. Harris was a slightly-built, wiry, dark-complexioned 20-year-old from Kennedy's home state, a graduate of the Watertown, Massachusetts, High School. Ten years his senior, MoMM2/c Leon Drawdy, a native of Florida, tall and lanky, with a narrow face, possessed a drawling voice and a kindly manner. He had been working in Chicago as a machinist at the time of the attack on Pearl Harbor and immediately quit the job to enlist. The third was MoMM2/c Edmund T. Drewitch; also thirty years old, Drewitch hailed from Pittsburgh. A musician and a bandleader in high school, he had gone on from there to hold a number of jobs before joining the Navy.

On May 1, two more men arrived: twenty-one-year old GM3/c Maurice L. Kowal, from Uxbridge, Massachusetts, was the second crewman to arrive from Kennedy's home state. Of Polish descent, Kowal was working in factory near Boston building engines for Victory ships. In the eyes of some, Kowal would become the *109*'s leading wit. TM2/c Andrew Jackson Kirksey, a native of Reynolds, Georgia, attended high school in Columbus, Georgia. After completing the 10th grade, he left school; at the time he enlisted on July 1, 1942, he was working as a refrigerator engineer. Unlike the typical PT enlisted man, the twenty-five-year old Kirksey was married and had a son, born three months after he enlisted.[4]

On May 5, twenty-six year old RM2/c John E. Maguire reported aboard. A native of Dobbs Ferry, New York, Maguire grew up on the banks of the Hudson River. Following the Pearl Harbor attack, Maguire's brother, William had joined the Navy and volunteered for

PT boats. He liked it so much that he persuaded his brother to follow his example. Both would end up serving on PTs in the Solomons.

Next to arrive was Seaman 1/c Edgar E. Mauer. A survivor of a ship recently sunk by the Japanese, Mauer was another exception to the rule in that he had never attended the Melville training course. As a further exception, Mauer arrived with only the clothes he was wearing, the rest having gone down with his ship. Immediately, Kennedy personally accompanied the newcomer, obtaining shoes, and extra clothing. When he learned Mauer had done some cooking for his brothers back home in St. Louis, with no cook assigned to the boat, he appointed Mauer the boat's cook. The quick-learning Mauer would soon became proficient as a signalman and quartermaster as well.[5]

Even before he had a full crew Kennedy began work on the boat and training the men. For PTs based at Tulagi, patrols were largely carried out as a precaution to assure no Japanese were lurking about. By the end of May, the crew was becoming the team essential to survive in combat.

With the invasion of New Georgia scheduled for the end of June, destroyers and landing craft began arriving in Sealark Channel from the New Hebrides, the vessels staging at Tulagi, then continuing on to the Russells, eighty miles to the west, roughly a third of the distance to New Georgia.

Among the first vessels to leave Tulagi were the PT boats. Not all headed for the Russells, however. An order to send six boats to New Guinea arrived. During the selection, the question arose as to whether *PT 110* commanded by Lt.(jg) Pat Munroe or Kennedy and the *109* should go. Both wanted the assignment, as rumor had it that the New Guinea campaign would provide the most action. To decide the matter, Munroe flipped a coin; when Kennedy lost the call, Munroe left for New Guinea leaving Kennedy in the Solomons.

The *109* was ordered to depart Tulagi at dawn May 30; for the next month and a half, Kennedy would operate from the advanced PT base in the Russells. As at Tulagi, the PTs were moored close to shore concealed from enemy aircraft by overhanging jungle growth, while continuing their nightly patrols. As noted, this was one of the rare times in the war when operating PTs failed to score.

On June 30, the Russells PTs were ordered to support of the amphibious convoy headed for New Georgia. The *109* was assigned to patrol the area between the Russells and New Georgia but found no sign of the enemy. Nevertheless, the patrol turned out to be difficult as well as costly. The PTs encountered huge seas as a storm sweeping through the area battered the boats. By morning it was a challenge to stand on the plunging vessels. Men not on watch took to their bunks; those on duty had the age-old sailors' problem of hanging on to a permanently secured fixture while carrying out their tasks with one hand.

Having completed his patrol, Kennedy was heading back to the Russells when a massive wave slammed into the boat's port side with such force that one of the depth charges was torn from its rack; crashing through the deck, it landed on the upper bunk in the crew's quarters below.

Asleep in the lower bunk a startled Drewitch leaped to his feet just as the *109* was hit by a second wave. Hurled bodily across the compartment by the force, the dazed motor mac crashed head-first into the boat's opposite bulkhead, suffering injuries to his face and body.

Back at the base, Drewitch was taken ashore to be hospitalized as carpenters began the job of patching up the *109* boat. Although none suspected it at the time, Drewitch would never see the *109* again.[6]

By now, two new men had joined the crew. Both were motor macs; both were older than the typical PT crew member. At age 37, MoMM1/c Patrick McMahon, "Pappy" to the crew, would be the oldest of the men. From Wyanet, Illinois, since his early boyhood days he had been fascinated by engines. During the 1920s, he had been a mechanic working on race cars competing on Southern California's dirt tracks. At the time of the Pearl Harbor attack, he was a mechanic for the Detroit Street Railway Company. Despite problems with the Navy eye test, he managed to enlist. After attending the Navy Diesel school at the University of Missouri, he volunteered for PT boats because he thought his skills as a mechanic might be of use on the small boats.[7] William Johnston, the second motor mac, had the distinction of being the only South Pacific veteran in the crew. From Dorchester, near Boston, the 33-year-old Johnston was the third man in the crew coming from Kennedy's home state. At the time of the attack on Pearl Harbor, as the driver of a truck and trailer rig for the Union Oil Company, he had been attending a union meeting. That same week he joined the Navy; soon he was serving in the South Pacific. Expecting finally to be rotated home, a dismayed Johnston found himself assigned to Kennedy's *109*. He had arrived just in time. With the campaign for New Georgia bogged down, Kennedy was ordered to the advanced PT base at Rendova.

Following a ten-hour passage from the Russells, *PT 109* entered Rendova Harbor. Approaching the base, the *109* crew noticed a small jetty. Above it, a conspicuous sign drew their attention: "Todd City." The eight black letters mounted on eight white-painted oil drum heads, was suspended on a line strung between two palm trees. They learned the sign was in memorial to Leon E. Todd, Jr., an officer attached to Kelly's Squadron 9, the first man to die attached to Rendova.[8]

Unlike Tulagi, a former center of British colonial government before the outbreak of the Pacific war, Rendova was starkly primitive. Base headquarters was a square dugout in a clearing set back from the beach with four palm trees and a foundation of sand-filled fuel drums. Stacked sandbags served as walls, with the roof a pyramidal Army tent. Inside were bare essentials; tables, chairs, maps, typewriters, radios, coding equipment, and an Army field phone, evidence of the close operating relationship between the PTs and the local ground forces. Close by were tents for use as a sick bay and a mess hall, the latter containing little more than C and K rations. Scattered around were more tents for base personnel, motor macs, radiomen, torpedomen, gunners' mates, carpenters, all technicians necessary to keep the boats operating.

Lister bags hanging conveniently nearby, contained drinking water obtained from streams flowing down 3400-foot high Rendova Peak, then chlorinated. Foxholes dug in the nearby sandy ground provided a visual reminder of the ever-present likelihood of enemy air attacks. Small black lizards slithered over mangrove roots, land crabs scuttled among the rotting coconut husks and dead palm fronds that littered the ground; the heat from the blazing sun combined with incessantly buzzing flies, provided a constant reminder that the South Pacific islands were not necessarily as pleasant as depicted by Hollywood movies.

Reporting to base headquarters, Kennedy was greeted by the base commander, Lt. Comdr. Thomas G. Warfield and Lt. Arthur H. Berndtson, base executive officer. Warfield had replaced the previous base commander, Lieutenant Commander Kelly, who now commanded the Lever Harbor PT base.[9] Like Kelly, Warfield was a veteran naval officer. A 1932 graduate of the U.S. Naval Academy, before the war he had served aboard battleships, at the time of the Pearl Harbor attack he was in Manila. In the wake of the destruction of the Pacific Fleet on December 7, Warfield was given the challenging task of sailing a cargo ship from the Philippines to Australia before the Japanese could sink her. With a multi-lingual crew, during the thousands of miles distance, he had dodged Japanese warships and minefields to reach Darwin safely. Continuing on to San Francisco, he left the ship with it scheduled to be converted to a troop ship, while he went on to Melville for training as a PT officer before returning to the South Pacific.

Warfield explained the local problems and objectives of the Rendova PTs to Kennedy: Rendova's patrol area, Kennedy learned, extended some fifty miles from the base, running northwest to Vella Lavella Island, north across Vella Gulf, southeast to Kolombangara, a massive jungle covered island with an extinct volcano, and finally south past the western tip of New Georgia to Rendova. Within this area lay islands such as Gizo and its satellites, plus Blackett Strait, a deep body of water separating Kolombangara from Gizo, as well as Ferguson Passage, connecting Blackett Strait with the Solomon Sea.

Kennedy learned the Japanese held two key positions within the area; one was Munda and its airstrip, where the Japanese defense showed little signs of weakening, the other was north, on Kolombangara's east shore at Vila Plantation facing Kula Gulf. To hold Munda and the Central Solomons, the enemy had to retain possession of Vila, which he was making a desperate effort to do.

Warfield explained that Japanese reinforcements and supplies were coming down the Slot on destroyers to Vila by way of Kula Gulf. From there, troops and supplies were making their way to New Georgia and Munda by barges through Blackett Strait. The Rendova PTs' mission was to intercept the nocturnally operated barges, thereby depriving the Munda garrison of supplies and reinforcements necessary for its continued defense. In short, the role of the PTs was the same as it was at Guadalcanal and in New

Guinea. Kennedy learned that after the run through the Solomon Sea from Rendova, the route of the PTs took them into Blackett Strait by either of two passages. The nearest one to Rendova was Ferguson Passage, cutting between the Gizo Island reefs and the Wana Wana Island reefs west of New Georgia, the farther one, Gizo Strait, separated Gizo from Vella Lavella.[10]

At Rendova, Kennedy noted some fifteen to twenty PT boats moored in the harbor in "nests," three to a buoy. With the briefing ended, Warfield assigned the *109* to one of the nests.

That night, despite having just completed the trip earlier that day from the Russells, *PT 109* was assigned as the second PT of a two-boat patrol. For Kennedy and his crew, aware this was an area where enemy contacts were frequent, it. was a time of extreme tension. With all the islands north of Rendova occupied by the Japanese, to the crew of the newly arrived *109* it seemed especially important that they stick close to the lead boat as it crept slowly along close to the shore of an enemy island, the *109* gunners firing at the same time and in the same direction as the lead boat's gunners.

With the night ended without incident and the two boats speeding back toward home at their customary 25 knots, as the crew sipped cups of coffee and relaxed with cigarettes, the crew of the *109* agreed it had not been bad. In fact, soon Kennedy and Thom would become familiar with these islands as well.

Kennedy's crew soon settled into the Rendova routine. With the battle for Munda at its peak and the enemy continuing to reinforce the New Georgia garrison, in what was a repeat of conditions at Tulagi, the bulk of the PTs were out every night; sleep became a luxury; as at Tulagi, days were spent maintaining boats and equipment. At sundown as time for night-patrol neared, the tension began to increase as crews began final preparations for the departure.

Departing Rendova in pairs or in groups of three as dusk approached, the PTs faced on average a trip lasting an hour at 25 knots. Once on station, the boats slowed to their 8-knot patrolling speed and, with engines muffled down, closed in on the island. Then began the long night as they searched for signs of the enemy. During the night's patrol, half the crew stood watch while the other half dozed nearby on deck, the watch changing every two hours.

There were frequent interruptions to sleep as "General Quarters" was called whenever lookouts sighted a suspicious form that bore a resemblance to a vessel. While on station, whatever the weather conditions, PT crewmembers were not allowed below decks, allowing instant response to an enemy sighting; the exception was when off duty, crewmen were allowed to go below when not on watch to grab a cup of coffee and a cigarette. Night after night the routine was the same. The hours of tension and uncertainty all tended to put a strain on the crews' nerves. Sometimes tracers from nearby PTs' guns arced through the darkness in the direction of a suspected enemy; sometimes the target was a barge which returned fire, at other times it was merely a shadow. In this uneasy form of combat, since the results of their gunfire was generally unknown, it was a rare event when a PT crew could enjoy the certainty of victory. Perhaps the barge driver, having sighted the PT, had beached his craft and was concealed beneath the overhanging jungle growth along the shore, or maybe he had slipped into a convenient cove to wait until the PTs went on their way and he could resume the trip to his destination. With the coming of dawn, there was a slight easing of tension as the boats turned away and increased speed for the return trip home.

For the hunting PTs, there was also the fear that comes from being hunted. One night, as the *109* was slowly patrolling off Gizo, two aircraft identified as PBYs, began making runs over the *109*.

"Ask that guy what's going on up there," Kennedy said to Maguire, who as the radioman was standing nearby.

Even as Kennedy gave the order, there was a nearby explosion.

"Tell them they nearly hit us," Kennedy shouted to Maguire. A confused radio exchange followed between aircraft and PT boat, with one PBY saying he would call his partner off and leave. Then Maguire received a radio report advising a Japanese float plane was in the area. Ever since Tulagi, PT crews had learned to dread the float-equipped Zeros ahead of all other enemy threats.

An alarmed Kennedy ordered Maguire to tell the PBY pilots that he would fire on the next plane that came over. Following that, the night proved uneventful. As one *109* crewmember remarked, Kennedy's last words broke up the party.[11]

On the night of July 19, the *109* was less fortunate: patrolling off Gizo with a second PT positioned off its port quarter, the pair of boats were idling back and forth on station between Gizo and Kolombangara. The hours had thus far dragged by without incident. It seemed as if it would be a night of boredom like so many before.

Although most PT skippers preferred to take the helm only under extreme conditions, typically Kennedy was at the helm. As usual, visibility was poor, but on this night clouds hung oddly low over the water.

Suddenly an aircraft emerged from out of the clouds on the *109*'s port beam, the rising sun visible on its wings in the reflection from the clouds. To Drawdy, who first spotted the aircraft, the pilot seemed no more than a hundred feet above the water.

Two explosions shattered the night accompanied by two orange flashes just after Drawdy's warning shout; bomb fragments sliced into the *109* from stem to stern. One huge chunk ripped through the boat from the port side leaving a gaping hole above the waterline on the starboard side. Another hot piece of shrapnel severed the gas line then welded it together again. The engines died. McMahon, on watch in the engine room, frightened first by the two explosions, and then the engines cutting out, fearful of another air attack, quickly restarted the engines and Kennedy immediately jammed the throttles ahead to full speed, throwing the boat into a hard turn to port.

Hit in his left arm and hand by flying steel splinters, Drawdy lay sprawled on the deck near the engine room hatch. Kowal discovered a piece of steel sticking in his leg below the knee. Both were given first aid in the dim light of the chartroom by Mauer. The enemy had inflicted his first casualties on the crew of *PT 109*.[12]

As Kennedy felt the wounds were not serious, the boat continued on patrol until dawn when it returned to Rendova. There Drawdy and Kowal were both taken ashore for hospitalization. Like Drewitch, they would never see the *109* again.

Back at the base in the light of day, the crew was finally able to see how badly the boat had been hit, and how lucky they had been: A piece of shrapnel had gashed the steel ladder to the engine room, barely missing Drawdy who had been standing on the ladder ready to drop down into the engine room if the duty motor mac needed assistance. The concussion, blowing him bodily out through the hatch prevented him from being mangled. Others, including Kennedy, were narrowly missed by fragments that holed the *109*'s superstructure. Base carpenters had to place a patch twelve inches square over the hole in the starboard side of the hull near the waterline.

On another night, the *109* was patrolling well up in Vella Gulf. The boat was idling along with mufflers engaged for silent running, patrolling slowly to keep the wake reduced to a minimum. All was pitch black. Suddenly a bright flare popped overhead; there it hung, illuminating the men and boat as if on a stage, their faces frozen staring upward, eyes wide with shock, fearful of an attack by an unseen enemy that would destroy them. As it so happened, the flare had been dropped by a "Black Cat" checking their identity. But frayed nerves were not easily relaxed, nor was calmness of mind quickly regained. The July 20 attack by B-25s on *PTs 164, 166,* and *168,* three Rendova-based boats in which one boat was sunk, did nothing to calm the PT crews. The combination of constant night patrols, the threat of air attacks, the lack of sleep, and the ongoing threat of the unseen and unexpected were causing a strain that began to tell on both officers and men.

As the battle for New Georgia continued to rage, the Japanese increased their efforts to get troops and supplies through to Munda. Every afternoon, Warfield received orders from TF31 on Guadalcanal. At about four o'clock each afternoon, an LCVP would make the rounds in the harbor to collect the PT skippers from the moored boats. When all were assembled in the dugout headquarters ashore, Warfield would brief the officers, issuing instructions as to which boats would patrol which areas, the waters off Gizo, Vella Lavella, or Kolombangara. On July 21, the Tokyo Express, carrying reinforcements and supplies to Vila, arrived by a different route. Having regularly encountered U.S. Navy heavy warships in the Slot at the entrance to Kula Gulf as they sought to reach Vila, of late, in an effort to evade the Navy's warships, the Japanese had decided the Express should depart the Slot at Vella Gulf, steaming between Kolombangara and Vella Lavella Island before entering Blackett Strait, arriving at Vila from the opposite direction, from the southeast.

With the success of the first run following the changed route, the Japanese command at Rabaul was encouraged to repeat the operation with a larger Express. Three destroyers serving as transports, each packed with three hundred soldiers with one as escort would depart Rabaul on July 29 following the same path. The ships' schedule called for them to pass through Blackett Strait on August 1 after dark. The night was deliberately chosen because there would be no moon, making it difficult to sight the ships. In support of the run, Admiral T. Samejima, commanding the Eighth Fleet at Rabaul, scheduled a bombing raid by eighteen aircraft on the Rendova PT base for August 1.[13]

For the unsuspecting PTs at Rendova, August 1 promised to be a routine, even a quiet day. There had been a lull in the long-range bombardment of Munda by the Army 155-mm guns positioned on Rendova Island. Prior to noon, *PT 164* returned from Tulagi carrying much-needed spare parts: propellers, armatures, magneto points, and other items, all necessary to keep the PTs operable. As the day wore on, its crew and base personnel would carry out the task of unloading the cargo. Aboard the moored *PT 109* out in the harbor, the crew was preparing an experiment in weaponry. By now it was common for skippers to procure a 37-mm anti-tank cannon from nearby army units. Mounted on the foredeck of their PTs, the guns measurably increased the boats' firepower, enabling them to better cope with the *daihatsus,* now the most frequently encountered enemy vessel while on patrol. Around noon, Kennedy approached the *109* in a Higgins boat carrying a 37-mm cannon. The crew was in a good mood. Having been on patrol on several successive nights, they were finally scheduled to spend the night of August 1-2 in the harbor. Once the Higgins boat was alongside, eager hands lifted the cannon to the PT's deck, along with a couple of 2x4 planks. The planks were laid together on either side of the foredeck, and the gun lifted in place, its wheels having been removed, and placed with the axles resting on the planks to await the arrival of the base carpenters, who would nail the planks to the deck and bracket the axles to the planks.

By now, the crew of the *109* included a number of new faces. Ensign Thom, Harris, Maguire, Mauer, McMahon, Kirksey and Johnston were still aboard, but with the departure of Drewitch, Drawdy and Kowal, replacements had arrived.

At age 29, TM2/c Raymond Starkey had already experienced a harsh life. After graduating from high school, Starkey worked as a commercial fisherman out of Newport Beach and other California ports before going to work in the oil fields. Following the attack on

Pearl Harbor, he enlisted in the Navy and was shortly serving on a PT boat in the South Pacific. Sharkey had transferred to the *109* because he could not abide the skipper of his previous PT whom he termed an "Ivy League snob."

Replacing Drawdy in the engine room was MoMM1/c Gerard E. Zinser. At age 21, Zinser was the *109*'s only career Navy man. After graduating from high school, he joined the CCC [Civilian Conservation Corps] in northern Illinois. In 1937 he enlisted in the Navy taking pride in the fact that his uncle had sailed aboard the USS *Monterey* in the Great White Fleet. During the late 1930s, Zinser saw the world on the cruisers *Cincinnati* and *Trenton.* In 1941, he volunteered for PT boats and was sent to the Packard plant in Detroit to familiarize himself with the engines before transferring to a PT squadron, then at the Brooklyn Navy Yard.[14]

A third new arrival was MoMM2/c Harold W. Marney. One of three children, the nineteen-year-old Marney was another crewman from Kennedy's home state. Born in Chicopee, Massachusetts, he had grown up in Springfield where his father was employed by Westinghouse. Young Marney made it through the tenth grade of a trade school before enlisting in the Navy at age 17, a month before the attack on Pearl Harbor. As his battle station, Kennedy assigned Marney to the port turret replacing Kowal.[15]

The fourth and final new crew member was Seaman 2/c Raymond Albert from Akron, Ohio. In appearance and behavior, the twenty-year-old Albert was typical of the countless sailors seen sauntering cockily along the sidewalks of cities like San Francisco, Seattle, or in Times Square with a girl on one arm, wearing a fresh tattoo, his white cap cocked on the back of his head. Originally the Navy had sent him to radio school at Texas A&M, but he volunteered for PT boats before completing the course.

The first sign that the day was not going to be so routine came in early afternoon when a message from the commander, TF 31, Guadalcanal arrived at PT headquarters on Rendova, relayed from the base station across the harbor. Decoded, the message to Commander Warfield created a sense of urgency. "X" in the message stands for period. "Love" denotes local time, Area Baker (B) refers to Blackett Strait:

FROM: CTF
TO: (ACTION COMMTBRON [Rendova] APC: 28:21 MAR
RD
REG:

TO (INFO): COMSOPAC CTG 31.2: ATFC SOPAC
MOST SECRET INDICATIONS EXPRESS MAY RUN
TONIGHT ONE DASH TWO (1-2) AUGUST X ALSO
HEAVY BARGE TRAFFIC TO BAIROKO OR SUNDAY
INLET X WARFIELD OPERATE MAXIMUM NUMBER
PETER TARES (PT) IN AREA BAKER (B) X KELLY
OPERATE ALL AVAILABLE PETER TARES (PT) IN
KULA GULF SOUTH OF LINE BAMBARI DASH RICE X
BURKE WITH (6) DESTROYERS GOES UP SLOT
ARRIVING NORTH OF KOLOMBANGARA AT ZERO
ZERO THIRTY LOVE (0030L) AUGUST SECOND (2ND)
X IF KELLY'S BOATS FORCED TO RETIRE TO LEVER
DURING NIGHT ROUTE THEM CLOSE IN NEW
GEORGIA SHORE X JAP AIR OUT TO GET PETER
TARES (PT) X WARFIELD KELLY EACH
ACKNOWLEDGE AND ADVISE NUMBER OF BOATS
THEY WILL OPERATE TONIGHT X RICE
ACKNOWLEGE [16]

With both Rendova and Lever Harbor boats committed, in terms of numbers, this promised to be one of the largest PT actions of the war. Also, of note was the intent of the Japanese to single out the PTs for destruction. Warfield barely had time to absorb the implications of the message before he was told that an air raid on Rendova was imminent. Admiral Samejima's bombing raid was about to begin. Scarcely had the base air raid siren began to wail when the roar of aircraft engines and machine-gun fire sent men diving into foxholes.

Aboard the PTs moored in the harbor, surprise was complete. McMahon, dozing on the deck of the *109* by the engine room hatch, woke with a start to see a plane slanting down on the harbor. "A Marine Grumman," he said with relief. The aircraft altered course and McMahon saw its Rising Sun markings and his blood turned ice cold.

A Japanese plane under fire from the PTs, burst into flames and crashed off Rendova, exploding with such force that water thrown high in the air seemed to remain suspended forever.

To Radioman Maguire, the sight that caused his heart to stop was the geyser of water and smoke rising from the PT "nest" containing *PT 103,* nearly half a mile away, whose radioman was his younger brother, Bill Maguire.

As enemy aircraft dived and zoomed overhead, Kennedy, who had been waiting for the carpenters to arrive, leaped into the cockpit and ordered the engines started. Even as the Packards sputtered into life, an enemy bomber plunged straight down, crashing into one PT nest: *PT 164,* a boat that had survived the B-25s' strafing attack on July 20 blew up sending its load of spare parts into the water, killing two crewmen. The second boat, *PT 117* was left sinking, and the third was only damaged.[17]

Amid the chaos, Kennedy pushed his throttles forward and joined other PTs maneuvering through the harbor and away from the area of attack toward safety. Finally, the all-clear sounded and the boats were able to return to the harbor, now a scene of devastation and shattered PT boats.

Immediately Warfield assembled the shaken PT skippers at base operations. In the tension-filled atmosphere, he read the message from CT31 to the officers. By now they had learned that due to the damage suffered in the air raid, only fifteen boats were operable. Warfield then described how the available boats would be formed into four divisions, with each division led by a PT fitted with a recently added radar set.

For maximum effectiveness, as had become the case at Tulagi, each division would be assigned to patrol a given area: Division "A" commanded by Lieutenant Berndtson on *PT 171* would patrol opposite the village of Gatere; Division "B" commanded by Lt. Henry J. Brantingham with *PT 159* would be off the village of Vanga Vanga; Division "C" led by Lt. George E. Cookman on the *107* boat would patrol Ferguson Passage ready to intercept any ships using the channel to reach Blackett Strait; and Division "R" commanded by Lt. Russell W. Rome with the *174* boat would be east of Makuti Island. In this arrangement, Brantingham's Division

"B," the farthest out in Blackett Strait, was likely to make first contact with the enemy. Brantingham's division included *PT 157* skippered by Lt.(jg) William F. Liebenow, Jr.; Lt.(jg) John R. Lowrey with *PT 162*; and *PT 109* skippered by John Kennedy. As senior skipper, Brantingham would command all Rendova PTs during the operation.

For the night's mission, Rendova's call sign was "Oak Zero." Each boat would have a radio call sign as well. Kennedy's *PT 109* would be "Oak 14." Brantingham's career as a naval officer began before the war, starting in 1939 when he was graduated from Annapolis. At the time of the attack on Pearl Harbor, Brantingham was attached to Bulkeley's Squadron 3 assigned to Kelly as executive officer on *PT 34*. Based on his actions this night, one would be inclined to suspect his lack of qualifications beyond those of executive officer.

Leaving the briefing, Kennedy encountered Ens. George Henry Robertson Ross, a twenty-five-year-old officer and acquaintance from his Melville days. Big and amiable, Ross had been executive officer on *PT 166*, the boat sunk on July 20 by the B-25 bombers. Now shore-bound and restless, he asked Kennedy if he could ride along on the *109* for the night's mission. Kennedy responded by asking Ross if he knew how to fire a 37-mm cannon. Ross's "Hell no, but I can learn," prompted Kennedy to give his OK.[18]

Back on the *109* moored in the harbor, Kennedy's words "We're going out tonight at 1630" brought disappointed groans from the crew. Observing Ross's arrival and Kennedy's instructions to the newcomer on how to fire the 37-mm cannon to be secured near the bow, caused crewmembers who were suspicious-minded to declare the new man on the boat to be an evil omen.

By now, crews on the other PTs moored at the buoys across the harbor were in the process of completing the final tasks necessary before departure. On the *109*, with the 37-mm cannon not yet secured, Kennedy ordered the gun tied down on the foredeck and assigned Ross to the bow as lookout. Meanwhile, below decks in the boat's small galley, Mauer, having completed securing the loose items and making coffee for the crew, climbed the short ladder leading to the chartroom with a cup of coffee; there he found Kirksey.

Mauer noted the torpedoman's hands shook so badly he had to put his coffee cup on the chartroom table to sip the liquid from it. Notably calm and steady, over the past few days, Kirksey had changed, becoming increasingly nervous, telling Harris that he, Kirksey, would not be going home, asking the gunner's mate to take care of his things. Harris's efforts to reassure him had failed. A sympathetic Mauer urged Kirksey to skip the night's patrol, but the unhappy crewman believed that to do so would be letting the crew down. At a loss as to what else to do, Mauer approached Kennedy, requesting he speak to the troubled crewman. But the results were the same. The unhappy Kirksey was still aboard when the *109* departed for the night's mission

By 9:30 p.m. the boats were on station. In a departure from Warfield's theory of using the radar-equipped PTs as a basis for improving the chances of a successful interception, Brantingham divided his four-boat division, one two-boat-section consisting of his radar-equipped boat and *PT 157,* the second pair of boats lacking radar, *PT 162* and *109,* patrolled separately.

By sundown, the four Japanese destroyers having departed Rabaul at noon, had passed through Bougainville Strait between Bougainville and Choiseul Island. The threat of Allied aircraft kept the crews alert. Now, with dusk approaching, and the ships entering the Slot, tension aboard the four ships increased.

Aboard the *Amagiri,* escorting the three troop-carrying destroyers, the skipper, thirty-four-year-old Lt. Comdr. Kohei Hanami, remained on the bridge. A 1928 graduate of Etajima, Japan's equivalent to Annapolis, Hanami, a stocky, muscular officer with close-cropped hair, was a veteran. At the time the war began, he was commanding a destroyer, the *Asanagi* in the Marshall Islands. He had taken part in the invasion of the Gilbert Islands, Wake Island and New Britain. In September 1942 he was made skipper of the destroyer *Akebono.* In June 1943 at Rabaul, he was given command of *Amagiri,* a gray-colored two-stacker displacing 2090-tons, 388 feet in length, capable of 34 knots. With a normal complement of 197, the *Amagiri,* a *Fubuki*—class ship, was reputed to outclass all other destroyers in the world.[19]

With Commander Hanami on *Amagiri's* bridge was his superior officer, forty-four-year-old Captain Katsumori Yamashiro, commander of the 11th Destroyer Flotilla. An officer of vast experience in his own right, Captain Yamashiro had been born in a naval family at the Yokosuka naval base. Graduating from Etajima in 1919, for some years he had commanded a gunboat at Canton, China. Following the outbreak of the Pacific war, he participated in the conquest of Hong Kong, and transported troops to Guadalcanal in the campaign for that island. Only a month earlier, he had assumed command of the 11th Flotilla. However, the only destroyer in the four-ship-force attached to the 11th Flotilla was the *Amagiri*. Nonetheless, despite the fact that he was senior to Hanami in rank, aboard the *Amagiri* the responsibilities for the ship, her crew and the mission rested with Hanami.

For the PTs lying to or idling slowly along on station, with radio silence in effect, time dragged. With Division "C" patrolling outside Ferguson Passage, all others were patrolling Blackett Strait. A large body of water some twenty-four miles long, at its narrowest point between the Gizo Islands and Kolombangara to the northwest, it is a minimum of five miles wide; it was here that Warfield had concentrated the Rendova PTs.[20]

On the PTs the men on watch noted the hour of midnight had passed. It was now Monday, August 1. As usual, Kennedy was at the helm of the *109*.

"Radar contact!" The call from the *159*'s radio room brought Brantingham scrambling down from the cockpit. Peering at the screen, the PT skipper saw four luminous spots in column, close to the shore of Kolombangara. As small as they were he guessed they were the barges referred to in the report read by Warfield at the briefing. He estimated the range to be two to three miles.

With the dots continuing to approach, convinced they were barges, Brantingham decided on a strafing attack. In fact, the four dots were the *Amagiri*, leading the column formed by the three destroyer-transports *Hagikaze, Arashi*, and *Shigure*. The ships were on schedule and minutes away from their arrival at Vila.

In the action that followed, Brantingham's failures coupled with flawed Mark VIII torpedoes and torpedo tubes, would arguably make this the least successful and most botched PT operation of the war. Without first reporting the enemy sighting to either the other PTs under his command or Rendova, a grievous omission, Brantingham closed on what he still concluded were enemy barges, intent on a strafing attack. When the destroyers opened fire, the flash of their guns served to alert Brantingham, and he instantly switched to a torpedo attack, firing his two aft torpedoes at a range of 1800 yards before firing his two forward torpedoes. Unfortunately, as had occurred on occasion at Guadalcanal, the grease in one of the forward torpedo tubes ignited as the torpedo was ejected, the flames providing the enemy ships' gunners with an easy target.

By this time, Lieutenant Liebenow, accompanying Brantingham's PT, had managed to launch two torpedoes. Now under heavy enemy fire, both PTs turned and safely fled across Blackett Strait behind a smoke screen.

However, none of the six torpedoes proved to be hits. And the enemy ships continued their race toward Vila, unscathed.[21]

Shortly, radar images flickered on the screen of *PT 171*, leading Division "A." Unaware of the earlier sighting and attack by Brantingham, Lieutenant Berndtson nonetheless sensed these were ships and decided to make a torpedo attack. As he closed at a slow 10 knots, the destroyers fired star shells illuminating Berndtson's boats and the surrounding sea in an iridescent glow. Berndtson fired all four torpedoes at the second ship in the column. To his dismay all four torpedo tubes erupted in flames as grease ignited, providing the enemy another ideal target. With shells now churning the sea on all sides and screaming overhead, the *171* roared across Blackett Strait toward Gizo Strait where it was finally out of range. Remarkably, like Brantingham, in the excitement of the attack, Berndtson failed to alert his own division or Rendova concerning his radar contact or his own attack; one result is that he left his own three boats of his division behind as well as unaware of his actions.

The experience of Division "C" led by the radar-equipped *PT 107* was much the same. Unaware the Express was approaching until it appeared on the *107*'s radar, Lt. Cookman outran his division to launch all four torpedoes, all of which missed. With that the Express faced one final obstacle. The three PTs of the last division, having noted the tracers arcing through the night sky as the destroyers fired on the attacking PTs, headed toward the scene. A strafing float plane and salvos fired by the destroyers' main batteries failed to prevent all three boats from firing all their torpedoes; twelve missiles raced toward the enemy ships. But again there were no hits. By now the PTs had fired more than thirty torpedoes without success.

Arriving at Vila at around 12:30 a.m., the three troop-carrying destroyers were rapidly unloaded while the *Amagiri* remained on guard offshore ready to counter any attack by the enemy.

Less than an hour later, the unloading was completed and the order to start back was given.

The roughly forty-five minutes had seemed like an eternity to Commander Hanami. With great relief he ordered the *Amagiri* to take the lead and head back through Blackett Strait.[22]

Throughout these events, Kennedy and Lowrey had continued to patrol Blackett Strait. Brantingham's instructions to Lowrey were to monitor his radio for instructions and for Kennedy to stick with Lowrey. As noted, neither were aware Brantingham had attacked the enemy and then gone back to Rendova, or that the Express had already passed through and reached Vila. They knew something was happening, however, because they could see gun flashes and star shells in the distance, but guessed they were shore batteries firing on the PT boats. Under the circumstances, Lowrey headed further up Blackett Strait toward Vella Gulf.

Still bothered as to the source of the gun flashes and star shells, Kennedy, who had been following the other boat, pulled the *109* alongside within hailing distance of the *162*, calling to Lowrey if he had any information in what was going on. Lowrey replied that they were probably shore batteries, possibly firing on patrolling PTs; but the *109*'s radio had picked up snatches of transmission between PT boats indicating something else was going on.

As the two boats continued to slowly make their way up Blackett Strait a third PT emerged from out of the darkness. It was *PT 169* commanded by Lt. Philip A. Porter, Jr. attached to Berndtson's Division "A;" he had become separated from Berndtson as well as the other two boats of the division.

The three boats huddled; clearly the tactical plans laid out by Warfield had gone wrong. The question on all their minds was the whereabouts of the other Rendova PTs. The three skippers decided it was time to break radio silence and call Rendova, thirty miles away, for instructions. The answer they received was a terse "Resume patrol."

With *PT 109* now in the lead as per Lowrey's decision, the three boats slowly started back through the Strait toward Vanga Vanga. To Kennedy, it seemed the best way to relocate the missing PTs.

Standing on the starboard side of the *Amagiri's* bridge, Commander Hanami peered through his binoculars, straining to penetrate the blackness ahead, anxiously looking forward to reaching the broader waters of Vella Gulf; an equally concerned Captain Yamashiro paced the bridge on the port side. By now the ship had been at general quarters for hours. In view of their earlier attacks by PTs, Lt.(jg) Shigeo Kanazawa, a gunnery officer, was poised on the cover of the bridge. In the forward gun turret, like other crewmen aboard, Petty Officer 2/c Mitsuaki Sawada wondered if they would make it back to Rabaul without difficulties. Standing between Commander Hanami and Captain Yamashiro on the bridge was Lt.(jg) Hiroshi Hosaka. As the torpedo officer, he was prepared to pass any orders to his men; at the helm stood Coxswain Kazuto Doi, equally alert for orders.

Aboard the *109* boat as well as the other two PTs slowly trailing astern, part of the crew was on duty. Ensign Ross was standing watch near the bow by the 37-mm cannon, Marney was in the starboard turret beside the cockpit, Starkey was in the port turret aft, McMahon as duty motor mac, was in the engine room. As usual, Kennedy was at the helm with Maguire standing to his right. Mauer, aware Kennedy was looking for the missing PT boats, stood behind the cockpit staring intently into the darkness ahead. Those men off duty were trying to rest. Thom was dozing on the port side of the cockpit, close to Kennedy if he was needed; the rest were dozing close to their combat stations or trying to relax between watches. Harris, off duty, was asleep on the deck between the day room and the aft port torpedo tube. As was typical, he had removed his kapok life jacket to use as a pillow. Johnston was asleep on the starboard side near the engine room hatch. Zinzer was standing close by; Kirksey was asleep lying aft on the starboard side.

Ship ahead!" the shout aboard the *Amagiri* by a lookout riveted Commander Hanami's attention. When the sighting was confirmed, Hanami ordered the forward turret to open fire. But by then the fast-steaming destroyer was so close to the smaller vessel that the gunner Petty Officer could not depress the barrel sufficiently to bear.

With the report indicating the vessel to be an American PT boat, Hanami decided his best protection from attack was to ram the small craft.

"Hard a-starboard," he ordered.

Based on discussions heard as to the best tactic to be used under these conditions, Coxwain Doi expected the order: turning in helm to starboard he aimed the *Amagiri* at the *PT 109.*

"Ship at two o'clock!" The shout to Kennedy came from Marney in the PT's starboard gun turret. Glancing off the starboard bow Kennedy saw a shape darker than the darkness looming out of the night followed by a huge phosphorescent bow wave. For a moment he thought it was a PT boat, as did Mauer, and as did some of the men on the two PTs following in the *109*'s wake. But no PT had so massive a curved bow.

To Ross, it seemed initially the destroyer was on a parallel course; then he saw the vessel heel as it turned toward the *109*, confirming his worse fear.

Back in the cockpit, Kennedy called to Maguire, telling him to sound General Quarters as he spun his helm in a futile attempt to evade destruction. But with the PT moving at slow speed, its response was sluggish.

The onrushing steel pointed bow of the *Amagiri* slammed into *PT 109* on the starboard side at the cockpit at a sharp angle, slicing through the boat. Marney, having recently replaced Kowal in the starboard gun turret, was doubtless crushed at the initial impact. Only the angle of the collision prevented Kennedy from being crushed as well: the impact tore the wheel from Kennedy's grasp, hurling him bodily with his once-sprained back against a steel reinforced brace. With the *109* skipper prone on the deck, the destroyer sliced from the starboard gun turret, behind the cockpit several feet from Kennedy, severing the aft portion of the PT from the forepart.

On watch in the engine room, McMahon, with no warning of impending disaster, was suddenly hurled sideways against the starboard bulkhead to land sprawled on the deck, and, from there, as in a dream, he watched as a river of fire cascaded into the engine room from the day room ahead. Logic said this was impossible; but with the bulkhead ripped asunder and the gasoline tanks under the day room ignited by friction sparks, liquid fire poured into the engine room, rising in a flood around McMahon. Instinctively, he held his breath to keep from inhaling the flames. But he could do nothing to protect his body: flames seared his face and hands, and his legs which were exposed by his rolled up jeans.[23]

Then suddenly, he was in a black, watery world: sheared off from the forward part of the PT, the engine room, weighed down by the three Packards, was headed for the bottom of the Strait.

McMahon instinctively fought his way free of the engine room. In the black depths of the Solomon Sea, only the wavering glow of the PT's burning gasoline on the surface offered a guide to life. His kapok life jacket helped drag him upwards; suddenly, he found himself bobbing on the surface in a sea of fire.

Johnston's experience was no less horrific. Dozing on the starboard side near the engine room hatch, as noted earlier, the impact tossed him bodily into the sea still asleep. Wearing heavy shoes and dungarees, he awoke as if in a nightmare to see the *Amagiri's* steel hull sweeping by just before the destroyer's churning screws dragged him beneath the surface. Tumbled head over heels he was forced down toward the bottom by water pressure. It flashed through his mind that he was living his last moments. But, then the pressure of the water began to weaken and he felt a surge of hope. Guided by the glow from the burning gasoline above, he began a desperate fight upward. He managed to reach the surface just as he was unable to hold his breath longer, and was thus unable to avoid swallowing gasoline and inhaling the deadly fumes on the surface.

On the *Amagiri,* the impact with the PT caused concern: scarcely ten seconds had elapsed since the sighting followed by the crash. Captain Yamashiro smelled what seemed like smoldering cotton; on the bridge, Lieutenant Hosaka felt the heat of the flames from the PT; Petty Officer Yoshitaka Yamazaki heard someone shout that a PT lay ahead, then felt a thud, saw a burst of flames and was gripped by the thought that the Americans had fired a torpedo and hit the *Amagiri.* In the destroyer's starboard engine room, Petty Officer Shigeo Yoshikawa felt a shock run through the ship, and Lt. Shigeru Nishinosome noticed the ship's engines started to vibrate.

The problem was worse in the port engine room. Petty Officer Yoshiji Hiramatsu heard a scraping propeller shaft, and thought the ship had hit a reef. In fact, part of the blade of the *Amagiri's* starboard propeller was sheared off by the collision. A dent in the bow was the only other damage the destroyer sustained in the collision. By reducing speed to 28 knots from the customary 33-35 knots, Commander Hanami found he could steam with less vibration. The four destroyers continued on through Vella Gulf and up the Slot, finally returning to Rabaul without further difficulties.

On this night, the Rendova PTs had fired thirty torpedoes without getting a hit.[24] As noted earlier, PT skippers did not acquire such skills easily. Following the war, Comdr. Robert J. Buckley, Jr., not to be confused with John Bulkeley of Philippines fame, observed: "This was perhaps the most confused and least effectively executed action the PTs had been in. The chief fault of the PTs was that they didn't pass the word. Each attacked independently, leaving the others to discover the enemy themselves."[25]

Commander Buckley might have added that it was also one of the few occasions following the Guadalcanal campaign in which a large number of PT boats were assigned to attack warships. Clearly, attacking barges with guns with only two or three PTs involved, provided little in the way of practice or skills to make the infrequent demand for coordinated torpedo attacks on fast-moving, heavily armed warships. The same difficulties, as noted, plagued the PTs at Tulagi when attacking the Tokyo Express. Being armed with a reliable torpedo might have helped. In any case, following closely on the heels of Kelly's unintentional sinking of Rear Admiral Turner's flagship *McCawley*, coupled with the communications problem existing between the PTs and Allied aircraft and destroyers in the Solomons, a pall was cast over the PT boats. For U.S. admirals, it was enough to reaffirm the belief that PT boats were of little value. It would be an image with a long-lasting effect.

CHAPTER ELEVEN

ORDEAL

Like all PT men, Kennedy's first fear was that with the fire the *109* would explode. But there was no explosion. A fire was immediately ignited but the gasoline burning on the water's surface was at least twenty yards away from the floating forepart of the PT, the fire burning brightly for fifteen to twenty minutes before dying out. It was believed that the wake of the destroyer carried away much of the gasoline.[1]

Once the fear of the explosion passed, Kennedy, Mauer and Maguire swam back to the bow and climbed on its deck. At Kennedy's instructions, Mauer got out the blinker, a two-foot-long tube containing a light, and began walking around flashing the light as a guide to any surviving crewman in the water.

With the exception of Mauer and Maguire, Kennedy had no idea whether any of his men had survived. Impatient for the arrival of the other two PTs, he removed his shirt, shoes and sidearm and dived into the water wearing his rubber lifebelt to search for his men.

Still on the hulk, Maguire and Mauer were the first to learn that there were other survivors when Zinser called, saying Thom was drowning. Maguire, dreading swimming back into the gasoline fumes; nonetheless got a line from the rope locker in the bow. With one end tied around his waist, the other to a broken torpedo tube, with a prayer, he stepped into the black water and began to swim in the direction of Zinser's voice. Mauer was now alone on the remains of *PT 109*, shipwrecked for the second time in three months. Zinser never saw the approaching *Amagiri*. He had heard the shout "General Quarters" just before he found himself flying through the air; before fainting, he saw flames.

Like Zinser, Starkey never saw the *Amagiri*. Heading toward his battle station at the aft starboard torpedo tube, he was sent reeling; he thought the *109* had been hit by a shell. Falling into a smashed compartment of the boat now in flames he passed out. Maguire, swimming toward Zinser, had no difficulty in locating the motor mac and Thom, who by now had regained his senses and been joined by Ross. For Harris, relief came in the form of voices, evidence that he and McMahon were not alone. Leaping into the water just in time to prevent being crushed by the onrushing destroyer, Harris found at first he was alone in the water. He noticed there was pain in his left leg, the result of a blow received while diving from the *109*. Bobbing in his kapok, he spotted something drifting out of the flames. It was McMahon, in shock and in pain.

Harris's desperate calls for help brought Kennedy to the side of the two men. With McMahon too badly injured to swim, the motor mac suggested Kennedy go back without him, saying "I've had it." But the *109* skipper grabbed McMahon's kapok life jacket and began to swim, towing the motor mac in the direction of the bow.

At first, despite his injured leg, Harris remained close by. But then he began to fall behind. Kennedy would call to him to keep up, and momentarily Harris would do so, then giving up, he would allow himself to drift. Shortly, he heard a splashing of water and Kennedy's voice: having safely deposited McMahon on the bow, Kennedy had swum back for Harris.

Again, the *109* skipper urged Harris to swim. When the gunner's mate wearily responded he could go no further, Kennedy snapped, "For a guy from Boston, you're putting up a great exhibition out here."[2] Finally, the two men reached the bow.

Meanwhile, Thom, who had swum out to rescue Johnston, was having problems. Only partially conscious, his brain clouded due to swallowing gasoline and inhaling its fumes, the motor mac was nearly helpless. Like Harris, Johnston wished merely to go to sleep. And like Kennedy with Harris, Thom kept urging the wounded man on. A poor swimmer himself, he did what he could to help the motor mac. In time, the two reached the still floating bow.

Among the last to appear was Starkey. Sighting the bow about a couple of hundred yards away, he swam to it and joined the other men, now either lying on the bow's deck, or drifting in the water while hanging on to it. Two men, Marney and Kirksey, were missing, however. For Kirksey, the premonition had proved true.

During the long hours of darkness that remained, most of the survivors managed to climb up on the hulk and brace themselves on the sloping deck. To the survivors, the question of why the two following PTs had not appeared to effect their rescue was a prime point of concern. However, the two PT skippers, convinced no one had survived the explosion from the impact and fire, were already miles away to the south on their way home to report the *109* disaster.

Three miles from the bow on Kolombangara, on a hillside about 1400 feet high overlooking the Strait, two Coastwatchers, Sub. Lt. Reginald Evans of the Australian Navy, and his assistant, U.S. Army Corporal Benjamin Franklin Nash, were on watch that night. Earlier the two had been alerted by the commander of the Solomon Islands Coastwatchers network, Lt. Comdr. Hugh McKenzie, from his headquarters on Guadalcanal, to watch for Japanese ship movements through Blackett Strait.[3]

For the two Coastwatchers, intermittent gun flashes rather than the series of flashes indicating a naval gun battle had made it an unusual night. A sudden burst of flame spreading across the water had drawn their attention. Peering through his binoculars, Evans saw a burning vessel and reasoned it was perhaps a Japanese barge.

With the coming of daylight, he focused his 15-power telescope on an object floating in Blackett Strait, but still could not identify it. In his morning radio report to New Georgia and Guadalcanal, call letters KEN, Evans noted:

ALL FOUR [destroyers] WENT WEST OWE TWO TWO OWE X PLANE DROPPED BOMBS NEAR SAMBIA AND LATER NEAR GATERE X SMALL VESSEL POSSIBLY BARGE AFIRE OFF GATERE AND STILL VISIBLE[4]

The bombs dropped by aircraft were doubtless the floatplanes attacking the final division of three PTs that unsuccessfully launched twelve torpedoes at the four destroyers near Vila. At 9:30 a.m., Evans received a radio message from the Coastwatcher at

Munda, call letters PWD; note is made it indicated the presence of
Ross on the *109* was not yet known:

PT BOAT ONE OWE NINE LOST IN ACTION IN
BLACKETT STRAIT TWO MILES SW NERESU COVE X
CREW OF TWELVE X REQUEST ANY INFORMATION[5]

From the start of the campaign in the Solomons, as recalled, the
PTs and the Cactus Air Force had had the advantage of being alerted
by Coastwatchers as to the approaching Express, its makeup and
estimated time of arrival.

Although the initial purpose of the Coastwatchers was to watch
and report the movements of the enemy, they soon provided another
service: when the battle for the Central Solomons grew more heated,
and U.S. planes ranged further north, slashing and bombing
Japanese shipping, staging points and airstrips, inevitably American
pilots were shot down. The rescue of these downed airmen and
sailors from sunken ships became another Coastwatcher
contribution.[6] The crew of *PT 109* would be the first to attest to that.

Developed by the Royal Australian Navy, as noted earlier, the
network had gradually expanded to include the rest of the strategic
islands that girdled Australia's northeast coast, including New
Guinea and the Solomons. Equipped with "portable" radios, the
entire setup requiring natives to carry, the true role of the
Coastwatchers was simply to watch and report. To drive the point
home, the network was called "Ferdinand," after the famous
fictitious bull who preferred flowers to fighting.[7]

With the outbreak of the Pacific war, the Japanese drive south
through the Solomons proved to be a "spear aimed at Australia's
heart."[8] Control of the Solomons ultimately meant control of the
approaches to the Australian ports of Brisbane and Sydney, severing
supply lines to the United States, isolating Australia before the
onrushing Japanese.

Initially, only eight stations were scattered along the Solomon
chain behind Japanese lines bordering the Slot, providing the PTs at
Tulagi and the Cactus Air Force with reports on the approach of the
Express. But with increased Japanese activity at Vila in support of
Munda's defense, Australian authorities decided to add a

Coastwatcher station on Kolombangara. Shortly, Evans arrived and recruited a team of local natives as scouts. With his portable radio, call sign GSE—his wife's initials, he was soon on the air radioing messages to Guadalcanal, headquarters for the Solomon Islands Coastwatcher network.[9] By August 1943 Reginald Evans, a thin pleasant man in his late thirties, had been stationed on the island more than four months. A former purser on an interisland steamer, Evans knew the islands well. Corporal Frank Nash, USA, Evan's assistant, had the distinction of being the only American member of the Coastwatchers; a radio operator with a desire for adventure, he had only recently persuaded the Australians to use him as part of the service against all U.S. Army regulations. Arriving on Kolombangara May 17 with the Coastwatcher Network's view that with all the added activity enemy activity, Evans could use the help, Nash had quickly proved his value.

With the launching of Operation "Toenails" at the end of June, and with Vila the staging point for troops and supplies being ferried to New Georgia, GSE was soon radioing a flow of reports concerning barges observed, along with occasional destroyers. On August 1, Evans's attention was drawn to the four destroyers that would deliver 900 troops and 120 tons of supplies to Vila.

Despite Evans's reference to a small craft fire in Blackett Strait that night, neither KEN or PWD considered the likelihood that the object floating in Blackett Strait was the shattered remains of a PT boat. What followed was a maddening sequence of messages and events in which the fate of Kennedy and the surviving crewmembers hung in the balance.

Upon receipt of the message from PWD concerning the missing PT boat, Evans immediately went into action. Natives were sent out to search the coast for survivors. They found nothing except an unusual number of beached American torpedoes.[10] Since once armed, torpedoes are designed to detonate upon contact with any object of substance, here was mute confirmation that many of the PTs' torpedoes were duds.

As for the mysterious floating object in Blackett Strait, it was too far out for the natives to investigate by canoe in daylight. At 11:15, Evans radioed he had found nothing so far, noting that the "object" was still in sight, adding that three torpedoes had been discovered at Vanga Vanga.[11]

At 1:12 p.m., Evans received a report from Guadalcanal's KEN:

DEFINITE REPORT PT DESTROYED LAST NIGHT BLACKETT STS APPROX BETWEEN VANGA VANGA AND GROUP OF ISLANDS SE OF GIZO X WAS SEEN BURNING AT ONE AM THE CREW NUMBERS TWELVE POSSIBILITY OF SOME SURVIVORS LANDING EITHER VANGA VANGA OR ISLANDS[12]

Someone had at least assumed that there might be survivors, and they might have made it to a nearby island.

For the *109* survivors, perched on the listing bow, daylight brought a new fear. Although there was an increased likelihood of being sighted by rescuers, it served to remind them that they were surrounded by Japanese-held islands. In fact, they were in sight of the enemy garrisons on Kolombangara, where buildings were visible, and Gizo, where, according to pre-patrol briefings, enemy troops were stationed. If the enemy should decide to investigate, the men faced a hard decision. Logic required they have a plan on how to react, whether to fight or surrender. By now it was commonly accepted that capture, or surrender to the Japanese meant death by execution, probably preceded by torture. As a matter of fact, during one of her recent radio programs, Tokyo Rose had ominously promised that PT crewmen, if taken alive, would get "special treatment."

Kennedy told his crew that should enemy soldiers approach, since some of them were married and had children, and as he was single and had nothing to lose, they should decide on how to respond. But even if they decided to fight, there was little to fight with. A submachine gun was found in the chartroom; Kennedy had a .38-caliber revolver, issued to him on his way to the South Pacific, and six of the men had .45-cal. automatics. But all the weapons had been immersed in water and there was a question as to whether they would fire.

Regardless, none of the men favored surrender, at least at the outset. Mauer argued they should fight, unless the enemy was too strong, in which case they should surrender, but he agreed to go along with whatever Kennedy decided. Despite the agony from his burns, McMahon flatly opposed surrendering. The others debated but could reach no agreement. In the end, Zinser had the last word, suggesting they make no final decision until they saw the size of the approaching enemy force.

In hopes of attracting less attention, Kennedy had the men slide off the bow into the water on the side away from nearby Kolombangara; only the seriously burned McMahon and Johnston remained atop the bow. At 10 a.m. the bow capsized but remained afloat. The men helped McMahon and Johnston reach a position back on the overturned bow.

As the hours dragged by, the bow appeared to be settling; the survivors now faced a new threat. If it went under during the night, the men would become separated in the dark, and some were sure to drown. If they stayed with the drifting bow, they might be carried into the arms of the enemy. Considering the options, Kennedy decided they should abandon the bow and swim to one of the nearby islands while it was still light. Although Kolombangara, two miles distant was closest, Kennedy rejected it as a choice as it was the location of the enemy base at Vila; more importantly, Kolombangara lay on the side of Blackett Strait opposite from Ferguson Passage, far away from the normal route followed by the Rendova PTs as they prowled the area, too far for them to have a chance of being rescued by the passing PTs.

The problem was to find an island large enough to hide eleven men but too small for the Japanese to have lookouts posted.[13] To the west lay Kennedy's objective, about three and a half miles away, off the southeastern tip of Gizo. A small group of islands in the shape of an anchor, they had the advantage of being out of sight of enemy garrisons, while the main reef bordered Ferguson Passage, waters regularly traveled by Rendova PTs. Typically, these islands were known by varied names. In any event, any island chosen was a gamble.

Around 1 p.m., Kennedy briefed the men. His words aroused little enthusiasm, but all understood the dangers of remaining where they were. Keeping the men together along the way was essential. To Kennedy, the solution was to use one of the planks originally intended as a base for the 37-mm cannon. Now floating nearby secured by a line to the bow, the plank, with four men on each side buoyed by their kapok life jackets, would be pushed and pulled, the men hanging on with one arm and paddling with the other. Thom would be in charge. Kennedy would take McMahon with him. Before starting out, the men who still had shoes removed them and tied them to the plank. The *109's* battle lantern, a ten-pound, gray flashlight, was wrapped in a kapok life jacket to keep it afloat and tied to the plank.

To Harris and Maguire, plagued as they were by the ever-present fear they were being watched by the Japanese, being in the open water with merely a plank meant that if the Japanese came there would be no chance of putting up a fight. For them, this was a moment of despair.

To the now helpless McMahon, death now seemed a certainty, even as a silent Kennedy helped him slip into the water and grasped the three-foot-long strap extended from the top to a buckle near the bottom of McMahon's life jacket. Cutting the strap with his knife, Kennedy clamped the loose end in his teeth and using the breaststroke, began towing McMahon; the two men back-to-back, the motor mac on top, the PT skipper below. It would be a long swim. Kennedy's objective was Plum Pudding Island, a green oval-shaped piece of land about a hundred yards long and seventy yards wide. Encircled by a sandy beach, with its green canopy of *naqi naqi* trees, its chief inhabitants were birds.[14]

It required nearly four hours for the men to reach the island. By then, Kennedy's jaws ached and he was weak with exhaustion. He managed to crawl up on the beach before vomiting and collapsing. Despite his pain and swollen hands, McMahon was finally able to drag the inert body of the PT skipper as far as the underbrush for concealment. Minutes later, the rest of the crew arrived, dragging the plank up on the sand before making their way into the underbrush. They were lucky. Moments afterwards, they heard the sound of a diesel engine approaching and a Japanese barge appeared, between two hundred and three hundred yards offshore, occupied by three or four men, the barge moving slowly.

The survivors of the *109* held their breath: was this an enemy search party after them, or was this just a chance event? There was also the possibility that it was a routine patrol. In any event, only a few minutes had made the difference between death and safety. The incident served to heighten their almost paranoid fear of capture. Would the barge be back? Were there other Japanese out searching for them? By now the survivors were virtually defenseless. The submachine gun had gone to the bottom of the sea during the swim to Plum Pudding Island. After the long hours in the water, there was even less chance their remaining guns would fire.

By now they had been without food 24 hours, and there was need for medical attention for the injured. McMahon and Johnston were especially in agony. Hungry, exhausted, stranded miles behind Japanese lines, the dispirited men slumped to the ground and stared across the water at Kolombangara, five miles away across Blackett Strait. That they had been given up as dead, fortunately, never occurred to them. Back at Rendova, PT officer Paul Ray, a student at Melville when Kennedy was there as an instructor, wrote a letter to his sister, saying that "Ensign George Ross had lost his life for a cause that he believed in stronger than any of us, because he was an idealist in the purest sense. Jack Kennedy, the Ambassador's son, was on the same boat and also lost his life. The man that said that the cream of the nation is lost in war can never be accused of making an overstatement of a cruel fact."[15]

At 4:45 p.m., Evans radioed KEN from Kolombangara:

THIS COAST BEING SEARCHED X IF ANY LANDED OTHER SIDE WILL BE PICKED BY GIZO SCOUTS X OBJECT NOW DRIFTING TOWARDS NUSATUPI IS[16]

Evans evidently presumed his Gizo scouts would pick up any survivors that landed on the other side of the strait. At the time, it was a reasonable expectation.

Later, Evans sent his final message of the day: Having observed Allied aircraft passing overhead, and assuming they were also looking for the survivors, he radioed KEN:

WILL YOU PLEASE ADVISE RESULT OF SEARCH BY P FORTYS OVER GIZO[17]

With the day drawing to an end, Kennedy, Thom and Ross drew aside. The question was, how were they to get back home? The single answer seemed to be by intercepting a PT on patrol. But the difficulties involved made the thought ludicrous. It meant walking the two- or three-mile-long reef, virtually all of it underwater in the darkness, to a point where it bordered Ferguson Passage, then swimming out into the Passage. Once there, if timed right, the swimmer would have to attract the attention of the passing PT boat. As Kennedy calmly explained the idea to Thom and Ross, he decribed how he hoped to use his revolver and the battle lantern to attract the PTs' attention.[18]

Ross thought the plan absurd. Kennedy was determined, however. Returning to the men he explained how he would swim out that night into Ferguson Passage and signal the PTs. McMahon thought the idea was suicidal. Other crewmembers tried to discourage Kennedy from his plan, but without success. Kennedy told them to keep watch.

"If I find a boat," he said, "I'll flash the lantern twice. The password will be 'Roger;' the answer will be 'Willco.'"

With the approach of darkness, Kennedy stripped off his uniform. Wearing only his skivvies and his shoes as protection from the coral, he strapped the rubber lifebelt around his waist, hung the .38 by its lanyard around his neck with the revolver swinging at his waist. Then, with the battle lantern wrapped in a kapok life jacket, he stepped into the water to confront a challenge as daunting as any faced by a PT officer during the war, in part because he faced it alone. Few places are as remote as Blackett Strait after dark, an area possessing more unknown and unseen perils for a swimmer.

As night descended, Kennedy found the reef difficult to follow. The depth of the water over the reef varied widely. One moment he would be walking in water waist deep, then suddenly the reef would drop away and he would find himself swimming until his feet again made contact. In the blackness of the night, there were no landmarks for guidance; Kennedy had to rely on his sense of direction. Sometimes he slipped, on one occasion cutting his leg on the coral. Large fish and smaller creatures would suddenly dart from under his feet; one of them approached. Stories of mutilated swimmers flashed through his mind. Kennedy kicked hard, churning the water, and the fish disappeared into the darkness.

Floundering along, with the moaning wind and the lapping waves the only sound, he reached the point he believed to border Ferguson Passage. Removing his shoes and tying them to his belt, he stepped off the reef and began swimming toward the blackness of the Passage, towing the battle lantern. When he guessed he was about at the center, he began to tread water, listening for the approach of PTs. But there would be no PTs passing through Ferguson Passage this night as Warfield had routed the boats to the southern tip of Vella Lavella.[19]

Convinced finally that no PTs were coming through, a weary Kennedy faced the ordeal of getting back to the island. Suddenly overcome by exhaustion, his strength fading, he was forced to lighten his load, dropping his shoes, although he knew the torture he would have to endure when it came time to retrace his steps on the reef.

But Kennedy would never make it back to the reef. In fact, the current carried him out of Ferguson Passage into Blackett Strait. At dawn, after long hours in the water, with his last strength, he crawled up on a tiny piece of sand, Leorava Island, possessing a single tree and a patch of bushes. There he collapsed into a deep slumber.

Even as Evans and his natives searched for signs of the PT survivors, the Japanese were on the move. That night, as Kennedy waited in Ferguson Passage in a vain hope for the PT boats to come through, some three hundred Japanese soldiers landed on the north coast of Gizo Island. As a result, early the following morning, two of Evans's scouts began a trip, paddling their dugout down Blackett Strait to Kolombangara where they would report the news to Evans. For Evans, it would indeed be a busy day. He radioed KEN:

SEARCH NEGATIVE EXCEPT ONE MORE TORPEDO
AT PILPILI[20]

The word back from Guadalcanal was no better. That morning Evans finally received an answer to his query concerning the aircraft he had observed the previous day. He learned the aircraft were involved in an unrelated mission.

Indeed, aircraft had conducted a search the previous day, but it had been later in the day, about the time the *109* survivors were reaching Plum Pudding Island. The negative air search had an effect, however. If aircraft could find no trace of survivors, what logic was there in risking PT boats in a further surface search where the skies were dominated by enemy aircraft? When the skipper of *PT 171* requested permission to proceed to Blackett Strait to search for survivors, Warfield denied the request.[21]

The two natives, headed toward Kolombangara to report to Evans about the newly arrived Japanese soldiers on Gizo Island, paddled some distance without observing anything unusual. But off Bambanga Island, they retrieved a box from the water containing shaving cream, a shaving brush, a razor, and a letter. Unable to read the letter, they took it to Benjamin Kevu on Wana Wana, Evans's principal scout in the area. The district officer's clerk at Gizo before the coming of the Japanese, the older Kevu spoke and read English well. He now served as a perfect bridge between Evans on Kolombangara and about a dozen scouts operating in Wana Wana Lagoon. Reading the letter, Kevu noted it was signed by Raymond Albert, but he naturally had no idea who Albert was, or what the letter meant. The two native scouts then continued on by canoe to Kolombangara to report to Evans.

Meanwhile Kennedy awoke in broad daylight on Leorava. He felt ragged and worn out. He still had nearly a two-mile swim ahead before he reached Plum Pudding Island. He tried the battle lantern. When it failed to work he discarded it.

Wading into the water he began swimming. Later that morning, to the joy and relief of his men, Kennedy staggered up on the beach at Plum Pudding Island. The night's effort had left its mark; Kennedy's eyes were bloodshot, his hair matted; he had a beard and his sun tanned skin had taken on a yellowish hue. Exhausted, he fell into a deep sleep. Once he awoke long enough to tell Ross that he would have to try again that night.

Convinced the plan was futile, Ross nonetheless made preparations. Profiting from Kennedy's the previous night, Ross wore his uniform trousers to conceal his white skin, which he feared could attract sharks or barracuda. Concerned about getting lost after dark due to the lack of landmarks, taking Kennedy's revolver with him, he started to walk the reef around four o'clock while he could still see.

Alternately slipping and stumbling, swimming and walking, Ross was alarmed by the sight of sharks, some three or four feet in length. But he pushed on. Thanks to an early start, it was only dusk at the time he reached the point where he should start swimming out into the Passage, too soon for the PTs from Rendova to arrive. While waiting, he stood chest-deep in water, balanced precariously on a piece of reef. Soon it was the pitch black of a tropic night. Waves washed him off his perch, but each time he managed to grope his way back to the spot.[22]

To Ross, swimming out into the blackness of Ferguson Passage was made possible only because of the example set earlier by Kennedy. "If he can do it I can do it," was the driving force for Ross, providing the basis on more than one occasion for men to do what under normal circumstances they would have shunned.

Having struck out blindly for about twenty minutes, Ross concluded he had reached the right position and began to tread water. The estimated time the boat should arrive came and went. After waiting a long time, Ross raised the .38 and fired one shot, then two more shots at intervals. But there was no one to hear. This night, the PTs had again gone to Vella Lavella.

Finally, Ross started to swim back to the reef, and like Kennedy he was carried by the current out to Leorava Island. There the exhausted Ross promptly fell asleep.[23]

By the time Ross awakened, the two natives scouts paddling to Kolombangara with news of the Japanese landings had reached the island. When Evans asked them if they had seen or heard of the PT survivors around Gizo, the two scouts answered no. At 10:25 a.m., the Coastwatcher radioed PWD:

NO SURVIVORS FOUND AT GIZO[24]

A message from Guadalcanal received slightly over an hour later, at 11:30 a.m., thus baffled Evans:

WHERE WAS HULK OF BURNING PT LAST SEEN X IF STILL FLOATING REQUEST COMPLETE DESTRUCTION X ALSO REQUEST INFORMATION IF ANY JAPS WERE ON OR NEAR FLOATING HULK[25]

For Evans, Guadalcanal's unexplained leap to the conclusion that the "object" last reported floating in the passage was a PT was, at best, questionable. At 5:05 p.m. he responded:

CANNOT CONFIRM OBJECT SEEN WAS FLOATING HULK OF PT X OBJECT LAST SEEN APPROX TWO MILES NE NAMBANGA DRIFTING SOUTH X NOT SEEN SINCE PM SECOND P FORTYS FLEW LOW OVER IT AND GIZO SCOUTS HAVE NO KNOWLEDGE OBJECT OR ANY JAPS THAT VICINITY.[26]

By this time, Ross had recovered from the night's exertions and had made his way back to Plum Pudding Island. He found Kennedy much improved, but disappointed by the second failure to make contact with the PTs. The condition of the men was continuing to deteriorate. They had had no water since Sunday night and it was now the middle of Wednesday. The second failure was a blow to everyone's spirits. Still unsuspecting that authorities at Rendova considered them dead, most were discouraged, others were openly bitter toward the Navy. While maintaining an optimistic attitude in front of his men, Kennedy revealed his anger to Thom and Ross.

In search of an answer to their plight, Kennedy decided to change islands, to move to one closer to Ferguson Passage where there was a better chance of intercepting a PT boat, Kennedy's next chosen island was Olasana, a mile and three-quarters southwesterly from Plum Pudding.

Again the men dragged the plank into the water, and once again, with the strap of McMahon's life jacket clenched in his teeth, Kennedy began towing McMahon. Although the distance was less than that successfully negotiated to Plum Pudding Island, the current seemed stronger and the men weaker. Again it required hours to reach their goal.

As it turned out, Olasana was at least twice the size of Plum Pudding Island.

Speaking in hushed tones, the men wondered if Japanese sentries were stationed there. Deciding it was too dangerous to explore the island, they quietly gathered nearby coconuts for food, but after eating them, some of the men grew ill. Ross tried eating a live snail, but it tasted terrible. Zinser attempted to dig for fresh water, but the effort was a failure.

By darkness, all were exhausted. Hungry, discouraged and miserable, this night they huddled together on the southeastern tip of Olasana, fearful of the presence of the unknown enemy that might be on the island. This night, no one went out into Ferguson Passage, and on this night the PTs came through and were on station in Blackett Strait by 9:30 pm.

Although *PT 109* was by now a mere dim memory for the eleven survivors, it was now the focus of the messages between Evans and Guadalcanal. In response to the message received at 5:05 p.m. the previous day, at 9:40 a.m. August 5, Evans radioed KEN:

SIMILAR OBJECT NOW IN FERGUSON PASSAGE DRIFTING SOUTH X POSITION HALF MILE SE GROSS IS X CANNOT BE INVESTIGATED FROM HERE FOR AT LEAST TWENTY-FOUR HOURS[27]

Two hours later Evans added:

NOW CERTAIN OBJECT IS FOREPART OF SMALL VESSEL X NOW ON REEF SOUTH GROSS IS[28]

A mere half-hour later, Evans added further details in a second message:

HULK STILL ON REEF BUT EXPECT WILL MOVE WITH TONIGHTS TIDE X DESTRUCTION FROM THIS END NOW MOST UNLIKELY X IN PRESENT POSITION NO CANOES COULD APPROACH THROUGH SURF[29]

On Olasana, for the survivors, dawn of August 5, the fourth day of their ordeal, promised to be another grim experience. It seemed that everything was conspiring against them. Maguire was increasingly convinced the Japanese were preparing to swoop down and take them captive. Given the sense of disaster, someone suggested they ought to pray together. Thom disagreed, saying since they did not ordinarily do so, it would be hypocritical under the circumstances.

A troubled Kennedy beckoned to Ross and Thom and walked away from the men. "What do we do now?" he asked the two officers. They had switched islands, swum out into Ferguson Passage, posted lookouts; was there anything else they could try, if only for the purpose of keeping the men's morale up? As they sought a solution, Kennedy's eyes fell on tiny Naru Island, separated from Olasana by a half-mile wide strip of water. A narrow piece of land a mere four hundred yards long covered by brush and trees, Naru bordered directly on Ferguson Passage. On impulse, Kennedy told Ross to swim over to the island with him, leaving Thom in charge. Although no Allied ships passed through during daylight hours, it would do no harm to take a closer look.

Shortly before noon, the two PT officers waded ashore on Naru and cautiously made their way through the trees to the opposite side of the island. From there they could clearly see Kolombangara, and visible thirty-eight miles to the southeast, Rendova Peak.

After first assuring there were no Japanese on Naru, Kennedy and Ross began to walk along the beach facing Ferguson Passage. Offshore, they noted the wreckage of a Japanese cargo ship on a reef. A short distance later, they came upon a crate washed ashore. When they opened it, they found hard candy. To the two men it was like Christmas. A few yards further on, as they were sucking candy, they discovered a dugout canoe with a large tin of water concealed in the underbrush. Unknowingly, they had stumbled across one of a number of native scouts' caches scattered among the islands. They sat down and sipped water. It seemed their luck was improving.

Then disaster: as the two officers stepped back on the beach from the brush, they spotted two men standing on the wreckage staring in their direction. Thoroughly panicked, Kennedy and Ross leaped back into the brush. Who were the men? Had the men seen them? Would they alert the nearby enemy garrison? The joy of a moment ago was now forgotten.

In fact, the two men Kennedy and Ross saw were no less frightened. Having arrived at Kolombangara with news of the Japanese troops landing at Gizo, Evans's two scouts were returning home when they noted the wrecked cargo ship. The two scouts, Biuku Casa and Eroni Kumana, curious to see if the vessel contained anything of interest, anchored their canoe and climbed aboard. Finding Japanese rifles, each took one. As they stepped back on deck, they saw two men on the shore, Kennedy and Ross.

Terrified, believing that if caught by the Japanese they would be shot as looters, they bolted for their canoe; in his haste, Eroni dropped his rifle. Scrambling into their canoe, the two paddled furiously toward Blackett Strait and home.

Had they continued on, the story about the *109* in all probability could have ended with the purported loss of the crew along with the boat. With the men already believed dead, history without John F. Kennedy as President would obviously have been different. But Biuku decided he was thirsty from his exertions, and persuaded Eroni, who was the aft paddler, to head the canoe toward the closest point of Olasana for a drink from a coconut.

While awaiting Kennedy's return from Naru, Thom and the men were resting on the island concealed by the brush. The sight of the approaching canoe shocked them, however. Were these Japanese scouts from Gizo? Had their luck finally run out? Capture and death, a constant concern, seemed suddenly close at hand.

Although the paddlers were natives, there was no assurance they were friendly. The nine Americans debated in hushed tones: there was still time to slip back further into the brush to avoid being seen. In that event, the natives would have satisfied their thirst and departed.[30] With the canoe still thirty feet from shore, Thom made a decision. Rising to his feet, he stepped out of the brush in sight of the two scouts.

The sudden appearance of a blond giant seeming to materialize out of the thin air stunned the scouts. In sheer panic, Biuku and Eroni back-paddled furiously. Running to the water's edge, Thom beckoned to them. But still fearful of encountering the Japanese, the two natives were concentrating on getting away, thereby creating a potential crisis for the Americans. Whatever happened now, this might be the last opportunity to be rescued.

"Navy, Navy," a desperate Thom pleaded. "Americans, Americans." By now, the two scouts were a safe distance away and were able to pause and listen. The problem was they did not understand English. "Me no Jap," Thom called to the scouts, seeking to reassure them. Still doubtful, the two natives kept their distance. Thinking fast, Thom tried a new approach. "White star," he said, pointing upward. "White star."

These words, signifying U.S. aircraft, were something the Coastwatchers drilled into their scouts as a matter of routine— meaning friend—someone to give help.

With that, the scouts paddled back to shore where the men helped them drag their canoe behind the bushes for concealment. Now, although the language problem hindered communication, Biuku and Eroni made it clear to the shocked Americans that Japanese were on Naru Island—referring of course to Ross and Kennedy. To Thom and the men, this meant Kennedy and Ross had been captured and would not be coming back.

In fact, events were slowly beginning to swing in favor of the survivors. Evans had recently become convinced that his lookout spot on Kolombangara did not afford him an adequate view of Blackett Strait and the activities of the Japanese. That afternoon, Evans had radioed KEN:

ANTICIPATE MOVING TOMORROW X FINAL ADVICE AM[31]

Evans also sent word out to all the natives that on the following day, he planned to move to a new station on Gomu, one of several smaller islands north of Wana Wana in lower Blackett Strait, a mere seven miles east of Naru, known to Evans as Gross Island. That same day, August 5, he received an advisory message from PWD, one that finally closed the chapter on what remained of *PT 109*:

AIRINTEL ADVISE THAT HULK WAS EXAMINED BY PLANE TODAY AND WAS THAT BADLY DAMAGED

THAT IT WAS NOT WORTH WASTING AMMUNITION[32]

Back on Naru Island, following a tense period of waiting, Ross and Kennedy emerged cautiously from concealment. When they saw no sign of the canoe or the two men, they resumed their exploration of the island. Finding nothing further, Kennedy decided to use the canoe discovered in the brush. He would paddle out into Ferguson Passage to intercept the PTs coming from Rendova that night. But while it was still light, he decided to take the candy and water back to the men on Olasana; tearing a slate off the crate to use as a paddle, he told Ross to wait on Naru.

Kennedy's return to Olasana was a momentous event. Finding two natives with his men, it did not occur to him these were the same two men he and Ross had observed earlier on the ship. Thus he was at a loss to explain what they meant when they indicated there were Japanese on Naru Island.

In any event, after distributing the candy and water to his ravenous crew, Kennedy returned to Naru. That night, with the newly possessed canoe, Kennedy planned that he and Ross would paddle out into Ferguson Passage in yet another effort to waylay a PT boat. But this night stormy seas and high winds swept the passage. Under theses conditions, with only slats for paddles, Ross opposed the idea; however, Kennedy insisted. The effort failed when the canoe was capsized, throwing both men into a raging sea, finally hurling the craft and men back across the reef to land in the shallows off Naru.

Making their way up on the beach, as the two shaken men slept the sleep of the exhausted, the Rendova PTs rolled through the heavy seas of Ferguson Passage to be on station in Blackett Strait at 9:15 p.m.

On Friday, August 6, back on Olasana Island, Kennedy was still wracking his brain in search of an idea for escape. Without a definite plan, by use of sign language, he indicated to Biuku that he accompany him in paddling over to Naru. Still unaware of the existence of Evans and his Coastwatcher operations, he stared toward Rendova Peak and decided that the only practical way to get help was to send the two natives to Rendova with a message.

Pointing toward Rendova, Kennedy indicated he wanted Biuku to go there, and then he led him to a clearing; there he picked up a coconut and had the native quarter it. Using his knife, on the coconut's polished surface Kennedy inscribed:

NAURO IS
NATIVE KNOWS POSIT
HE CAN PILOT 11 ALIVE NEED SMALL BOAT
KENNEDY[33]

Back on Olasana, Thom had hit on a similar plan. Using a stub of a pencil Maguire found in his pocket and a blank invoice of the pre-war Gizo branch of Burns Philp (South Sea) Company, Limited, on the back of the invoice, Thom wrote:

To: Commanding Officer—Oak 0 From: Crew P.T. 109 (Oak 14) Subject: Rescue of 11 (eleven) men lost since Sunday, Aug 1st in enemy action. Native knows our position & will bring P.T. boat to small island off Ferguson Passage off NARU IS.

A small boat (outboard or oars) is needed to take men as some are seriously burned. Signal at night—three dashes (- - -) Password—Roger—Answer—Wilco

If attempted at daytime—advise air coverage or PBY could set down. Please work out suitable plan & act immediately. Help is urgent and in sore need. Rely on native boys to any extent. L. J. Thom Ensign, U.S.N.R. Exec 109[34]

When Kennedy returned with Biuku, both messages were entrusted to the two natives who embarked on the trip to Rendova by canoe. Along the way, they stopped at Raramana, on Wana Wana, where they told Benjamin Kevu about the survivors. Aware that Evans was in the process of moving to Gomu Osland, Kevu dispatched a scout to Gomu to wait there and give him the news. Meanwhile, Biuku and Eroni continued on foot to another village on the island, where they persuaded a third native, John Kari, a frequent visitor to Rendova, to accompany them on the overnight paddle to the PT base. That night, arriving at Gomu, Evans received the verbal report concerning the survivors. On the following morning, he dispatched a large canoe to Naru with seven natives; the leader was Benjamin Kevu. The canoe also contained food. In addition, Benjamin Kevu carried a penciled note:

> 'On his Majesty's Service' To Senior Officer, Naru Is. Friday 11 p.m. Have just learnt of your presence on Naru Is. & also that two natives have taken news to Rendova. I strongly advise you return immediately to here in this canoe & by the time you arrive here I will be in radio communication with authorities at Rendova & and we can finalize plans to collect balance of your party
> A. R. Evans Lt R A N V R
> Will warn aviation of your crossing Ferguson Passage[35]

With the information provided by Biuku and Eroni, Evans's scouts knew the survivors were on Olasana Island. After paddling more than two hours, they grounded the canoe on the beach. With no sign of the Americans, the natives soon discovered the survivors in a clearing.

To Kennedy and his men, their appearance seemed unbelievable. Having little reason to smile during the past week, after reading Evans's note handed to him by a half-naked black man as if he, Kennedy, was at his father's embassy in London, rather than a half-starved, unwashed castaway on a miserable patch of ground surrounded by Japanese and sharks, Kennedy's smile was all the more radiant. Adding to the sense of unreality was Benjamin Kevu's command of the English language as he addressed Kennedy.

The contents of the canoe virtually overwhelmed the starved Americans, yams, potatoes, rice, boiled fish, C rations, K rations with roast beef. Moreover, some of the natives scampered up palm trees like monkeys to fetch coconuts; others lighted kerosene burners for cooking, and still others collected palm fronds and built a hut for McMahon.

When the survivors finished eating, Benjamin Kevu suggested it was time to leave for Gomu. Since Evans had requested only the "senior" should return, that meant Kennedy.

Climbing into the dugout, he lay down with his feet toward the bow. Benjamin Kevu covered him with fronds and knelt at his head, paddling and on occasion conversing with him.

Midway back, Japanese aircraft approached and flew low, circling the canoe. After some hesitation, Benjamin Kevu stood and waved at the planes. Finally satisfied, the aircraft flew away.

That morning, Biuku, Eroni and John Kari arrived at Rendova. By then the PT base was in a state of rare excitement. After dispatching the canoe to Olasana, at 9:20 a.m. Evans radioed KEN:

ELEVEN SURVIVORS PT BOAT ON GROSS IS X HAVE SENT FOOD AND LETTER ADVISING SENIOR OFFICER COME HERE WITHOUT DELAY X WARN AVIATION OF CANOES CROSSING FERGUSON[36]

At 11:30 a.m., after a meaningful delay, PWD radioed Evans:

GREAT NEWS X COMMANDER PT BASE RECEIVED MESSAGE JUST AFTER YOURS FROM SURVIVORS BY NATIVE X THEY GAVE THEIR POSITION AND NEWS THAT SOME ARE BADLY WOUNDED AND REQUEST RESCUE X WE PASSED THE NEWS THAT YOU HAD SENT CANOES AND WITHOUT WISHING TO INTERFERE WITH YOUR ARRANGEMEMNTS WANT TO KNOW CAN THEY ASSIST X THEY WOULD SEND SURFACE CRAFT TO MEET YOUR RETURNING CANOES OR ANYTHING YOU ADVISE X THEY WISH TO EXPRESS GREAT APPRECIATION X WE WILL AWAIT YOUR ADVICE AND PASS ON[37]

At 11:45, Evans replied:

COULD ONLY MAN ONE CANOE SUITABLE FOR CROSSING X NO SIGN ITS RETURN YET X GO AHEAD AND SEND SURFACE CRAFT WITH SUITABLE RAFT OR DINGHIES X IF THEY ARRIVE HERE LATER WILL SEND ANOTHER ROUTE X PLEASE KEEP ME INFORMED[38]

Back at Gomu, Evans waited anxiously. Shortly before 6 p.m. as he peered through his binoculars, he sighted the approaching canoe. When the canoe finally touched the beach, Kennedy raised his head through the palm fronds, smiled at Evans, and said, "Hello. I'm Kennedy." Evans introduced himself and the men shook hands, and Evans invited Kennedy to join him in a cup of tea.

The two men walked to an old wooden house, Evans wearing shorts, the PT skipper barefoot clad only in his underwear.

As the two discussed rescue plans, Evans showed Kennedy the last message received from Rendova relayed by PWD:

THREE PT BOATS PROCEED TONIGHT AND WILL BE AT GROSS ISLAND ABOUT TEN PM X THEY WILL TAKE RAFTS ETC X WILL INFORM YOU WHEN WE RECEIVE ADVICE OF RESCUE[39]

Evans suggested that the natives paddle Kennedy back to Rendova while the PTs carried out the rescue. But the PT skipper rejected both plans.

It would be virtually impossible, he argued, for anyone who did not know exactly where the men were, to find them in the dark. Furthermore, Kennedy pointed out that he was responsible for his men, and it was his duty to remain with them until they were safe. Instead, he would meet the PTs on their way to pick up the men and go with them. Accordingly, he and Evans worked out a superseding plan. At 6:50 p.m. Evans radioed a message to PWD for relay to the Rendova PT base:

LIEUT KENNEDY CONSIDERS IT ADVISABLE THAT HE PILOT PT BOATS TONIGHT X HE WILL AWAIT BOATS NEAR PATPARAN ISLAND X PT BOAT TO APPROACH ISLAND FROM NW TEN PM AS CLOSE AS POSSIBLE X BOAT TO FIRE FOUR SHOTS AS RECOGNITION X HE WILL ACKNOWLEDGE WITH SAME AND GO ALONGSIDE IN CANOE X SURVIVORS NOW ON ISLAND NW OF GROSS X HE ADVISES OUTBOARD MOTOR X PATPARAN IS ONE AND A

HALF MILES AND BEARS TWO ONE FOUR DEGREES
FROM MAKUTI[40]

By shortly after 8 p.m., it was time for Kennedy to get in a canoe
to be paddled to the rendezvous point with the PTs. As the night
was cool, Kennedy borrowed a pair of coveralls from the
Coastwatcher until he boarded the PT. Then, just before leaving,
Kennedy recalled he had only three rounds left in his .38 revolver.
Since the plan called for four shots in response to the PTs, Kennedy
borrowed a Japanese rifle from Evans, promising to leave both the
coveralls and the rifle in the canoe.

Not until shortly after ten o'clock did Kennedy hear four shots.
Standing up in the canoe, Kennedy fired three rounds from his
revolver, then fired the rifle, the recoil of which nearly knocked him
backwards into the water.

Soon the canoe was gliding alongside Lt. Liebenow's *PT 157*
looming out of the darkness. "Hey Jack!" a voice called.

"Where the hell have you been?" a not yet ready to forgive
Kennedy responded.

"We've got some food for you," another voice said.

"Thanks," Kennedy answered dryly, "I've just had a coconut."[41]

But shortly he was aboard the PT and surrounded by happy
friends and he briefly forgot the hours of treading water in Ferguson
Passage and days of misery and frustration. Aboard were Biuku and
Eroni, and with their help, Kennedy piloted the boat through the reef
to Olasana. Soon the tattered survivors of *PT 109* were safe aboard.

The trip back to Rendova was as bizarre as any return PT trip
during the war. As expected, Kennedy and his men were in for a lot
of ribbing for failing to be able to evade a destroyer.

The first hint of dawn was starting to tint the sky when *PT 157*
curved into Rendova Harbor. Back at the PT base, Lt. Liebenow
was one of those who queried Kennedy asking how a big ship was
able to ram a more nimble PT boat. A thoughtful Kennedy answered
evenly: "Lieb, to tell you the truth, I don't know." Considering all
the trials and tribulations experienced by Kennedy and his men
during their week of suffering, this was merely one of a number of
questions Kennedy would ponder.

CHAPTER TWELVE

TARGET: VELLA LAVELLA

While the *109* survivors struggled to make their way home, the campaign for Munda continued. On August 5, reports indicated the Express would be making another run to Vila. Rear Admiral Theodore S. Wilkinson, having relieved Admiral Turner on July 15 as CTF31, prepared a welcome. With Ainsworth's cruiser force not yet rebuilt following the recent battle and Merrill's force too far away to reach the area, the Admiral chose a six-destroyer division trained in radar-controlled night torpedo attacks, to make the interception. Reflecting his poor opinion of the PTs, he assigned Kelly's Lever Harbor boats to patrol southern Kula Gulf, a different body of water, as back up, in case the Japanese got through Blackett Strait.[1]

After the successful run to Vila on the night of August 1-2, the Japanese dispatched another four-destroyer Express from Rabaul to Vila by the same route.

By noon the 6th, four ships were north of Bougainville heading southeast at high speed. The cargo included fifty tons of supplies and 1150 soldiers. The Express commander was Captain Kaju Sugiura, flying his flag on the 2,000-ton destroyer *Hagikaze*.

Noting he was being shadowed by an American search plane as he entered the Slot, Sugiura nonetheless pressed on. A typical Japanese destroyer commander, Sugiura had courage and determination; furthermore, the Express had run the gauntlet four nights earlier. Sugiura was confident he could duplicate the success.

But all would not go as Sugiura hoped. Anticipating the opposition would be the same PTs posted in Blackett Strait, the Express fell victim to the torpedo attack launched by Wilkinson's destroyers after entering Vella Gulf, well short of the Strait. The result was the August 6-7 Battle of Vella Gulf in which the Japanese suffered a disastrous defeat, the Express losing three of its four destroyers; only the *Shigure* survived to escape back to base. Awed PT sailors in Kula Gulf, twenty-eight miles to the south, sighting the glow of flames thought the volcano on Kolombangara had blown.[2]

After the battle, the skipper of the U.S. destroyer *Lang,* sweeping the water with his night glasses, observed the surface was dotted with bobbing heads, and also heard weird human voices. Believing his crew was jeering the enemy, he ordered them back to their stations. But as *Lang* edged deeper among the mass of heads and floating wreckage, the skipper noted the sound was like a chant in unison coming from the water; to the *Lang* skipper, it sounded like "Kow-we," repeated, blended with shrieks of pain and terror. A Japanese officer later ventured the word heard by the *Lang* skipper was "kowai,"—"terrible"—meaning terrible to let yourself be captured.[3]

The *Lang's* orders were to haul a few Japanese from the sea for intelligence purposes; for thirty minutes the destroyer maneuvered slowly among the enemy survivors, ready to toss any willing Japanese a line, but as was true with the PTs in their encounters with *daihatsus,* not one was willing. Whenever they heard English, someone blew a whistle, the chanting halted and they swam away. At 2 a.m., after a fruitless effort, the *Lang* followed the other U.S. destroyers down the Slot to base. Some 1500-odd Japanese sailors and soldiers would be lost along with the three destroyers. Following the victory, U.S. destroyer crews, long impatient for the chance to go it alone, without being tied to the cruisers, were jubilant. They believed they had sunk three destroyers and one cruiser, without suffering damage. And they were at least partly right.

On the Japanese side, destroyer officers returning to Buin near Bougainville, voiced a number of complaints, including the lack of radar on their ships, the lack of available accurate charts making it unsafe to navigate close to shore. Their one consolation was the illusion that it had taken a combination of cruisers, seven destroyers, PT boats and planes to beat them.[4]

For the American destroyer crews the glow of victory would soon be dimmed. Three nights later, Admiral Wilkinson, receiving another report of an Express due to reach Vila by way of Vella Gulf, again ordered his destroyers to intercept. This time, however, the American ships scoured the waters for hours, finding nothing larger than barges.

Finally, three destroyers, *Lang, Sterett,* and *Wilson,* closed on a group of three *daihatsus.* At a range of a half-mile they opened fire with 5-inch guns. Far from being intimidated, the barges replied with .25-caliber machine guns, denting the superstructure of the *Lang,* and circling tightly to confuse the American gunners. The destroyers kept firing, and in the end sank one or two barges.[5]

Later that night, when it was obvious the Express would not appear, the U.S. destroyers had two more brushes with *daihatsus.* All told, it was a frustrating experience, much like shooting at cockroaches with a pistol.

In contrast, the New Georgia PT boats in the role of "barge busters" were experiencing measurable success. From July 21 to the end of August, Rendova PTs claimed eight barges and one auxiliary ship sunk as well as three barges and one auxiliary ship probably sunk, and six barges and one auxiliary ship damaged.[6]

Kelly's Lever Harbor PTs, starting later to score, on August 3 claimed three barges destroyed, one forced to be beached and eight to sixteen barges damaged. When American troops advanced into territory previously held by the enemy, they found more destroyed barges than actually claimed.[7] That the PTs were having the desired strangling effect on the enemy was confirmed earlier, on July 23 when they attacked a group of *daihatsus,* sinking one and chasing two others back toward Vila. A recovered Japanese message told of how twelve PTs had made the attack. In fact, only three boats were involved, *PTs 117, 154,* and *155.* But the enemy was far from defeated. On the night of July 26-27, the enemy countered; three boats, *PTs 106, 117,* and *154,* attacked six barges that were so well protected by armor that the PTs' .50-caliber machine gun bullets and 20-mm cannon shells had no apparent effect. It was obvious that in this see-saw battle the PTs had to have heavier guns.[8]

On August 5, as the *109* survivors were in the process of being rescued, the New Georgia campaign began to wind down as the last

Japanese defender was blasted from the bunkers next to the Munda airstrip. That day General Griswold, commanding Allied troops on New Georgia, radioed Halsey, "Our ground forces today wrested Munda from the Japs and present it to you...as the sole owner." A week later the field was ready for Allied planes.[9] With Munda taken, Halsey and his staff eyed the northern Solomons. However, with only 1671 dead Japanese out of an estimated 5,000 under Maj. Gen. Sasaki, responsible for the Munda defense having vanished into the jungle, until the Americans controlled the enemy's supply lines from Vila to New Georgia, Sasaki was still a threat. Not until August 18 did U.S. Army units, combined with Marine raiders, force the Japanese to destroy their equipment at Bairoko and evacuate their soldiers by barge; nineteen bargeloads of troops and critical supplies made it through to Vila. As at Guadalcanal, the enemy slipped away only hours before the Americans reached Sasaki's empty encampment on August 24. After further clashes, the Japanese finally retreated north and peace came to New Georgia.

The campaign for the Central Solomons ranks with Guadalcanal and Buna as a time of human tribulation; a time in which Allied strategy and tactics in the Pacific were among the least successful.[10] The attempt to take Munda, viewed as a quick operation by a single division, finally required the elements of four; some 5,000-odd Japanese, standing off nearly 40,000 Americans, had set the Allied timetable back by a month. As Halsey wrote later, "...we controlled the air and the sea; we outnumbered the enemy 4 or 5 to 1; we bombed his positions every day and supported our troops with ships' fire on request.... When I look back...the smoke of charred reputations still makes me cough."[11]

Worse, six months after the fall of Guadalcanal the Allies were still only two hundred miles closer to Rabaul. And a few miles north of New Georgia Island lay Kolombangara, another jungle-covered island with another Japanese airstrip defended by at least another ten thousand Japanese troops, many shifted from New Georgia for that purpose.

"The undue length of the Munda operation and our heavy casualties made me wary of another slugging match," Halsey wrote, "but I didn't know how to avoid it. I could see no victory without Rabaul, and no Rabaul without Kolombangara."[12]

Plans called for a step-by-step advance upward through the Solomon Islands, 365 miles from Guadalcanal to the big island of Bougainville at the top of the chain. Indeed, the Japanese anticipated that this long, drawn-out process would weary the American public, permitting the Japanese government to obtain a negotiated peace that would allow Japan to keep the areas now won in the Far East.

But now Halsey's staff came up with the idea he found irresistible: in their advance south, the Japanese, seeing no value in Vella Lavella with its lack of a good harbor, had used it merely as a stopping point for barges on their way south to Kolombangara and New Georgia.[13] Why not bypass Kolombangara and land on Vella Lavella? From there, Allied ships and planes could harass the Japanese supply route from Rabaul to Kolombangara, blockading and starving out the Japanese on Kolombangara.[14] At the least, with the garrison isolated the Emperor would have ten thousand fewer troops for defense as the Americans advanced toward Japan.

Having come into their own as "barge busters" during the New Georgia campaign, the Allied tactic of leap-frogging, by-passing one island to land on another, meant the PTs would be used in additional multiple roles. With Vella Lavella the next Allied objective in the Solomons, Admiral Wilkinson was badly in need of intelligence. On July 21, he dispatched a Rendova PT to Vella Lavella carrying a mixed Army, Navy and Marine Corps reconnaissance party. That night the PT boat crept in close to the island with engines muffled, and the scouts slipped ashore in rubber rafts to explore the island. Six days later, on the 28th, a PT arrived at Vella Lavella, bringing the scouts safely back to base.[15]

As a result of the information, Admiral Wilkinson designated Barakoma, a shallow bay on the eastern foot of Vella Lavella, as the invasion point; the invasion to be carried out on August 15.

On the night of August 12-13, four PTs raced from New Georgia to Barakoma with a scouting party of forty-five men to mark the beaches and select bivouacs. A Japanese float plane bombed and strafed them along the way, planting a near-miss astern of *PT 168* commanded by Ens. William F. Griffin, riddling it with shrapnel and wounding four men, forcing the boat to return to base. The other three PTs continued on, however, landing their scouts as planned.

Ashore, the advance party found several score Japanese sailors roaming the island, survivors of the recent Battle of Vella Lavella. As a result, four more PTs raced north to Barakoma with reinforcements, preceding the invasion convoy by only hours. Not surprisingly, the Japanese failed to associate the appearance of PT boats with an invasion force. On August 15, 4600 Allied troops were landed at Barakoma; Allied losses were limited to twelve killed and fifty wounded, all due to enemy air attacks. Through such use of PT boats, Admiral Wilkinson had stolen a two-hundred-mile march on the enemy. The usual airstrip and PT base were soon to be established on Vella Lavella, the latter at Lambu Lambu, facing the Slot.

Although the Japanese were expected to make the typical counter attack as they had on Guadalcanal, there would be no such attack. On August 13, Imperial Headquarters, in a change of policy, forbade any further drain of the Emperor's troops down the Slot. Troops already in the Solomons were ordered to fight holding actions as long as possible and then withdraw by barge or destroyers. Commanders were to continue to strengthen the defensive positions around Rabaul, especially on Bougainville, in preparation for the expected Allied attacks. Thus when word was received at Rabaul of the landings at Barakoma, Admiral Kusaku and General Imamura saw Vella Lavella as an island not to be defended, but a mere nuisance on the evacuation route from Kolombangara north. As for the Imperial Army, its commanders ruled out the use of a one-brigade counter-landing as akin to "pouring water on a hot stone." Any force larger than a brigade was too much for naval transportation to handle. Rather the commanders at Rabaul decided to establish and defend a barge-staging point at Horanui, on the northeast shoulder of Vella Lavella, as a means of evacuating troops from Kolombangara.[16]

On the morning of August 17, the Japanese command dispatched two companies of soldiers and a naval platoon of thirteen barges to Horanui. Four destroyers provided distant coverage. Alerted by a reconnaissance plane, Admiral Wilkinson ordered his destroyers to intercept. Shortly after midnight, August 18, the destroyers of the two sides met. Both sides uncorked salvoes of torpedoes, but neither side scored. The Japanese admiral, declining to give battle, withdrew to Rabaul, explaining to his superiors that barges and men were more easily replaced than destroyers; forty of these ships had been lost in the past fourteen months, and Japan's shipyards were unable to replace them.

During the brief encounter, the barges dispersed. With the departure of the enemy ships, the U.S. destroyers discovered a lone *daihatsu,* which they sank. As on previous occasions, however, the American destroyers proved ineffective when dealing with barges. After a fruitless search, they returned to Tulagi.[17]

Typically, the *daihatsus* remained concealed, hiding on the north coast of Vella Lavella until darkness, then continued to Horanui on the night of August 19 to land 390 men. Within a week a barge depot was established for the evacuation of troops on Vella Lavella and Kolombangara.

Meanwhile, the New Georgia PTs continued their nightly patrols, with exceptions. On August 22, in a disastrous departure from usual practice, PT boats were ordered to carry out a daylight operation in the Solomons: They were to land Army demolition teams in a cove on the coast of Kolombangara near Vila.

Three PT boats were to carry out the mission. Commanding was Lt. David M. Payne riding on *PT 108* skippered by Lt. Sidney D. Hix. At 7:30 a.m. *PT 108* followed by *PT 125* skippered by Lt. Murray, cautiously entered the cove; the third boat, *PT 124* commanded by Lt. Leighton C. Wood remained outside to cover the entrance.

Inside, the cove was deathly still. Tense crewmen noted the thick, brush-covered shoreline, but saw no signs of the enemy. Suddenly the cove seemed to explode as machine guns, concealed all around the shoreline, opened fire. Caught in a murderous point-blank crossfire, the thin-skinned PT boats were at the mercy of the enemy.

As lead boat, *PT 108* was the major target: struck almost immediately, Lieutenant Payne fell dead into the chartroom. Seconds later Lieutenant Hix standing at the boat's helm, hit by another round, managed to throw the wheel hard over before crumbling to the deck. He died moments later. QM2/c James G. Cannon, wounded in the face, shoulder and arm and only half conscious, crawled to the vacated wheel, pulled himself to his feet, and standing astride the body of his skipper, steered the boat back toward the entrance to the cove.

Meanwhile, the *108* gunners were blazing away at the unseen guns ashore. In the exchange of fire, one gunner, SC2/c Jack O. Bell, was killed; all other gunners were wounded except one. Sgt. J.E. Rogers of the Army's demolition team, saw the *108*'s forward gunner on the 37-mm cannon downed by an enemy slug. Crouching over, he edged toward the wounded man to give assistance. But a bullet tore into Rogers's body and he fell dead on the deck. Only one officer and two crewmen on *PT 108* escaped being hit.

With the dazed QM Cannon at the helm, *PT 108* finally emerged from the cove. But several fires were blazing below. Crewmen who could still move went below and extinguished the flames that threatened to cause the bullet-riddled boat to explode.

With *PT 125* trailing the *108,* Lieutenant Murray initially sought to come to the aid of the lead PT when the enemy opened fire, but when the *108* turned sharply, Murray was forced to do the same; thus his boat, shielded as it was by the lead boat, was spared the worst effects of the enemy's fire, being merely punctured with bullet holes with one crewman wounded in a leg.[18] On September 14, American troops on Vella Lavella captured Horanui, forcing the Japanese there to retreat northwestward.

With the loss of Horanui, the *daihatsus* began plying between Kolombangara and Japanese held Choiseul Island. On September 20 the enemy dispatched over a hundred *daihatsus* from Bougainville; they would reach Kolombangara on the moonless night of the 28th. Eleven destroyers supported and screened the barges; meanwhile the Vila garrison made its way by foot and canoes to Tuki Point on the north shore of Kolombangara for evacuation.

Admiral Wilkinson guessed correctly that the Japanese would attempt to withdraw during the dark of the moon. Beginning September 22 he sent a force of two cruisers and four destroyers to prowl the Slot north of Vella Lavella, strengthened by a second group of ships as the moon waned. Nothing happened until the night of September 25-26 when a torpedo fired by a Japanese submarine narrowly missed the cruiser *Columbia.* With the ever-present night-flying enemy float planes broadcasting the Americans' position to submarines in the Slot, Wilkinson decided the risk to the cruisers was too great. On the night of September 27-28, he sent five destroyers to patrol the Japanese barge routes north from Kolombangara to Choiseul and Bougainville.

On this night, *daihatsus* cluttered the Slot, but the U.S. Navy's destroyers again fell short in this form of naval warfare: first, the usual enemy float planes belled the stalking destroyers, illuminating them with flares and float lights with such success that they managed to sink a mere four barges. On the following night, September 28-29, during a major evacuation, eleven barges carrying 1691 men crossed the Slot from Kolombangara to Choiseul's Sumi Point, and four Japanese destroyers picked up 2115 sick and wounded at Tuki Point and rushed them to Rabaul escorted by no fewer than nine destroyers. That night, no American vessels were there to interfere.

On the third night, September 29-30, four U.S. destroyers returned to cruise the waters north of Kolombangara. On this occasion they sank a few *daihatsus* and traded long-range salvoes with enemy destroyers. On the night of October 1-2, the U.S. ships were back, still with limited success. Eight destroyers cruised the Slot astride the barge routes. Despite soupy weather, Japanese float planes succeeded in dropping bombs close to the destroyer *Saufley,* killing two men and wounding eighteen.

By October 3-4, with the enemy evacuation of Kolombangara nearly complete, the U.S. destroyers had yet to truly score: in five days, *daihatsus* had retrieved 5400 men and the supporting destroyers another 4000, including Major General N. Sasaki, the commander of the Munda garrison.

Admiral Halsey and his commanders in the Solomons were well satisfied. But they did not know the truth.[19] Despite its best efforts, the U.S. Navy had managed to destroy only a third of the enemy barge fleet and less than a tenth of the evacuated force. With the U.S. ships fitted with radar and the barges forced to follow a definite evacuation route, the ships should have done better, as they thought they had. Clearly, Japanese evacuation operations still posed a challenge for the U.S. Navy. On the basis of experience in New Guinea, confirmed in the Solomons and later in the Philippines, a squadron of PTs fitted with radar positioned hard by Tuki Point, would have been more effective. Unfortunately, the traditional view held by big-ship American admirals, confirmed by the disastrous episodes in the Solomons involving PTs, precluded their being used. The last incident again involved poor communications. Shortly after dawn, September 30, during the Japanese evacuation of Kolombangara, four PTs under the tactical command of Lt. Craig C. Smith were returning to Lever Harbor after an uneventful night when three Marine Corsairs appeared. Two of the pilots recognized the PTs for what they were, but the third dropped down for a strafing run.

Slugs from the F4U ripped through *PT 126,* killing one officer and two crewmen. The PTs' return fire was equally lethal; the Corsair continued a short distance, before exploding in midair.[20]

Nevertheless, the fact was that Kolombangara—"King of the Waters"—no longer belonged to the enemy; but the evacuees had slipped away, and in their advance to Tokyo, Allied troops could expect to face them again on some other Pacific island.

With the loss of Kolombangara, the Japanese were left with only two islands in the Central Solomons, Choiseul and Vella Lavella. They saw no reason for concern regarding Choiseul, but on Vella Lavella, advancing Allied troops made immediate action necessary. The six hundred men forced to retreat from Horaniu had to be evacuated. For this the Japanese navy marshaled nine destroyers and a dozen small craft. Alerted to the impending operation, Admiral Wilkinson ordered his destroyers to intercept. The result was the Battle of Vella Lavella on the night of October 6-7, another in the series of major naval clashes between the two sides in the Solomons campaign; in it both sides lost a destroyer. During the battle, the subchasers and *daihatsus* of the evacuation force successfully embarked 589 waiting men and sailed for Buin.

After the battle, destroyers of the two sides headed for home. Left behind were the survivors of the sunken Japanese destroyer *Yugumo,* one of the lucky ships that had survived the disaster in the Battle of the Bismarck Sea. The thirty-fourth destroyer to be sunk in the campaign for the Solomons, one of her sailors would soon strike one more blow for the Emperor. After daybreak, a group of PT boats were dispatched to search for enemy survivors for interrogation.[21] One boat, *PT 163* commanded by Ens. Edward H.

Kruse, Jr., picked up a number of survivors who submitted only when crewmembers pointed guns at their heads.

The prisoners were ordered to strip and lie on the PT's foredeck and a crewman was stationed on each side of the cockpit with a machine gun as guard. At dusk, as the boat neared its base, a prisoner, one who had been the toughest to persuade to surrender, appealed to one of the guards for a drink. The good-natured guard fetched a cup of water and handed it to the prisoner.

Instead of taking the cup, the man grabbed the submachine gun slung around the guard's neck. The guard struggled desperately, but the prisoner had the advantage of the element of surprise. Forcing the barrel against the guard's chest he pulled the trigger as several other prisoners leaped to their feet. It was their last act. The second guard shot every man standing, including the killer of the guard, twenty-year-old, fun-loving Albert, one of the *109* survivors, now reassigned to *PT 163*.[22]

With the exception of Choiseul Island, the Central Solomons were now in Allied hands, and the Allies were two hundred fifty miles closer to Rabaul. However, the reality was that Tokyo was still three thousand miles away; three months was too long to spend on a two-hundred-fifty-mile advance, which scarcely dented the Imperial Army or the Combined Fleet.

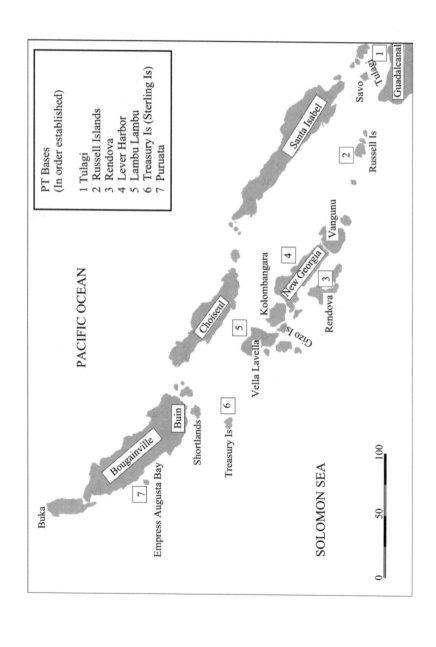

PT Bases
(In order established)

1 Tulagi
2 Russell Islands
3 Rendova
4 Lever Harbor
5 Lambu Lambu
6 Treasury Is (Sterling Is)
7 Puruata

PACIFIC OCEAN

Buka
Bougainville
Empress Augusta Bay
Buin
Shortlands
Treasury Is 6
Vella Lavella
Choiseul
5
Gizo Is
Kolombangara
New Georgia 4
Rendova 3
Vangunu
Santa Isabel
2
Russell Is
Savo
Tulagi 1
Guadalcanal

SOLOMON SEA

0   50   100

CHAPTER THIRTEEN

THE RETURN OF JOHN F. KENNEDY

Following the rescue of the *109* survivors, after a brief stop at Rendova, the men were brought to the sick bay at Tulagi. In the thatched-roof sick bay, Kennedy brooded over the fate of the *109*. Though promoted to full lieutenant and awarded the Purple Heart and Navy and Marine Corps Medal for gallantry toward his shipwrecked crew, he did not feel his career in the South Pacific amounted to much. As August dragged on and the war continued, Lieutenant Cluster, commanding Squadron 2, reminded Kennedy that Navy custom permitted an officer who had been shipwrecked to go home or at least to get another assignment to his liking until transportation was available. However, Kennedy declined the offer; he had come all the way to the Pacific, he explained, and he had not accomplished anything. What he wanted was another PT boat, if possible.[1]

Lieutenant Cluster had a thought; he asked Kennedy if he would be interested in forming a crew and taking over an experimental PT due to be converted into a gunboat as a more formidable vessel against enemy barges. As might be expected, Kennedy eagerly accepted the assignment, and Cluster appointed him skipper of *PT 59*, an old 77-foot Elco that was part of the contract awarded to Elco before beginning to build the new 80-footer.

In essence, converting the PT boat meant removing its four torpedo tubes and replacing them with additional machine guns and armor shields. In the absence of torpedoes, its main weaponry would be two 40-mm Bofers cannon, one mounted on the stern, the other on the foredeck. The PT would also have radar, by now equipping all PTs in the Pacific.

Kennedy's immediate problem was to assemble a crew. By now, with the loss of the *109,* most of that crew were now scattered and reassigned. Thom, who has also been awarded the Navy and Marine Corps Medal for his actions involving the loss of the *109,* had received a promotion and been given command of a PT. Ross was unavailable, having been assigned as executive officer on another boat.

On September 1, Kennedy and his new executive officer, Lt.(jg) Robert Lee Rhodes, Jr., reported aboard their new command.[2] Unlike other officers serving on PT boats during the war, the twenty-one-year-old Rhodes had never received training at the Melville PT Academy. Nonetheless, Kennedy had chosen the lean, alert officer as Thom's replacement. At the time the Japanese attacked Pearl Harbor, Rhodes was on the point of completing a course at the California Maritime Academy. Appointed an ensign in the Navy in June 1942 as navigator on a Liberty ship, he was aboard when the ship was sunk by a Japanese submarine between San Cristobal and Guadalcanal on June 23, 1943. He was rescued from a lifeboat by the destroyer *Skylark* and taken to Espiritu Santo. From there he went to Noumea, where, probably having had his fill of being on a large, slow target, he had volunteered for PT boats and been shipped to Tulagi.

With his new executive officer, again Kennedy faced the task of assembling and training a crew for combat able to survive in battle.

McMahon and Johnston, physically unfit for further action, were thus not available. Albert, as recalled, was now dead. Of Kennedy's old *109* crew, only five were available: Maguire, Mauer, Koval, Drewitch and Drawdy.[3] All were quick to volunteer to serve on a boat commanded by Kennedy, however. In the end, the roster of *PT 59* would list new names to round out the crew.

It took more than a month for workmen to convert the PT boat. In the meantime, the war in the South Pacific dragged on. New PT bases were established in both New Guinea and the Solomons as Allied ground forces leap-frogged past enemy strong points, leaving thousands of Japanese troops isolated in the Southwest Pacific, cut off from supplies, unable to retreat or escape. Starvation would be their final option, and again in this the PT boats were would be their nemesis.

At the end of September, following the landing of Allied troops on the island of Vella Lavella, Squadron 11 commanded by Lt. Comdr. Le Roy Taylor, moved forward to Lambu Lambu Cove on the northeast coast of the island. With remaining Japanese troops in the Central Solomons finally isolated on nearby Choiseul and occupying Bougainville, in mid-December, two Higgins-equipped squadrons, 19 and 20, would arrive at Lambu Lambu to begin operations.[4] Ultimately Squadron 11, with its twelve 80-foot Elcos, would move from Vella Lavella to Puruata Island off Cape Torokina to blockade Bougainville. From there the squadron would move on to operate from bases closer to Japan. Throughout this period, its role would be as a blockade squadron; its primary foe enemy barges and shore batteries.

Meanwhile, back at Tulagi, while waiting for the completion of work on *PT 59* making it a gunboat, Kennedy and Rhodes lived on a repair ship. Most of the crew amused themselves with the sights at Tulagi and listening to the broadcasts of Tokyo Rose. October 7, the refitting complete, they departed Tulagi for the Russells, first stop on the way north to the combat area, continuing on to Rendova Harbor on October 10.

Kennedy found the base greatly expanded, with many more ships in the harbor. After a week at Rendova, during which time Kennedy continued work to get his crew in shape for combat, on October 18, they left Rendova, cutting through familiar Ferguson Passage and Blackett Strait and crossing Vella Gulf to finally reach Lambu Lambu Cove.

Even considering conditions at Morobe, Lambu Lambu was arguably the most primitive advanced PT base in the South Pacific. In actuality on the verge of being a swamp, Lambu Lambu Cove leads back into a small river the natives called the Katapaqu; a dark and fetid stream flowing sluggishly from among blackened mangrove roots to emerge from a cavern-like jungle; it could as easily have been the Styx, that mythical river of Hades. Until the outbreak of the Pacific war, Lambu Lambu was a small Chinese trading post with a single thatched hut on stilts. Now, except for a dock of uncertain vintage, no installation worthy of the name remained.

Foot-long green lizards crawled over damp mangrove roots. The screech of strange wild birds echoed through the jungle. At night, the howl of wild dogs could be heard; some said the dogs could detect approaching aircraft sooner than manmade devices.[5]

LSTs arrived from the south to toss fuel drums on the shore; from there sweating sailors had to manhandle them over tangled mangrove vines to the dock. Food was scarce and monotonous, consisting largely of K rations; clothing and blankets were never quite dry: rain showers and humidity caused everything to mould and have a musty odor. Men slept on the PTs or lived in tents ashore, connected to the moored boats by catwalks thrown across the rat-infested mangrove roots, and scorpions were known to drop from the overhanging jungle growth above the decks of the moored PTs. Men awakening in the morning learned to check their shoes before putting them on as it was not unusual to find a land crab had taken up residence there during the night. But the base was valuable as it faced the Slot as well as Choiseul Island, still occupied by the Japanese.

The base commander was Lt. Arthur Berndtson, moved up from Renova. And on his exploratory rounds ashore, Kennedy was surprised to meet an old friend in this most isolated of places, Lt.(jg) Byron R. "Whizzer" White. Formerly of the University of Colorado, a halfback and an All American football player on the school's team, the two had met in London before the war when White was a Rhodes scholar and Kennedy was there with his father. Now as Berndtson's intelligence officer, White was assigned to Lambu Lambu.[6]

As was true when based at Rendova, the maximum number of available PTs were out every night. On the night of October 18, the day of Kennedy's arrival, *PT 59* accompanied two 80-foot Elcos, *PTs 169* and *183*, attached to Squadron 11, patrolled off the northwestern tip of Choiseul at the entrance to Choiseul Bay, called the Emerald Entrance on the maps, known barge depot. Typically, the PTs' mission was to prevent reinforcements or supplies reaching the enemy island garrison.

However, by this time, with the Allies having advanced well into the Central Solomons, closer to the Japanese stronghold of Bougainville to the north with its numerous airstrips, it was not barges that were the PTs' problem. That night, when the boats were five miles south of Redman Island, a single-engine "Pete" appeared out of the darkness dropping two bombs, exploding to starboard of the *59* boat. Instantly, Kennedy shouted the order "Commence Firing," but the PT's gunners failed to down the intruder before it disappeared into the darkness.

Continuing to patrol, the PTs turned south, slowly skirting the Choiseul coast, approaching the Warrior River, a stream winding down the western slope of the island to empty into Salovai Harbor bordering the Slot. A half-mile off the river's mouth, the PTs' radar detected two aircraft a couple of miles to seaward; the crews were called to General Quarters, but after some tense moments the aircraft faded off their radar screens.

But as they headed back to Lambu Lambu, the PTs were attacked again by a lone aircraft. The enemy pilot dropped a single bomb that landed in their midst, then circled in the darkness and made a second run. This time two bombs exploded, churning the sea and raising columns of water; but again they were misses. Clearly the hunters had become the hunted. Despite the PTs' return fire, the plane disappeared in the darkness to the north without apparent signs of damage. For the crew of *PT 59*, this first night had provided more than its share of excitement.

"Were you scared?" Kennedy asked Rhodes.

"Hell, yes," was the fervent response.

"So was I," Kennedy admitted.[7]

Two nights later, on October 20-21, the *59* boat again departed Lambu Lambu at 7 p.m.; the crews were prepared for more attacks by enemy aircraft; a sudden red flare appeared about twenty miles away, but no aircraft appeared as the PTs made their run to Choiseul Bay to patrol the islands offshore. That night *PT 59* and accompanying boats went as far north as West Cape and Poroporo. On the following night Kennedy's PT and other Lambu Lambu boats again made the run to Choiseul Bay and patrolled the entrance. However, with the weather squally, again the night proved uneventful. On October 26, the Lambu Lambu boats were back off the entrance to Choiseul Bay; on this night the PTs were again bombed by enemy planes, and again all escaped damage.

Even as the PTs continued to blockade Choiseul Island, plans were in the making that would involve Kennedy and the crew of *PT 59* in a key operation, one with far-reaching effects. Following the landings on Vella Lavella, to Admiral Halsey and his staff it became time to choose their next island objective. First to be considered was Choiseul Island and the Shortlands, home of the notorious Tokyo Express. As in the Munda campaign, like the American defense of Henderson Field on Guadalcanal, the Japanese had shown a marked tenacity in defending their air bases. Any direct assault on any presently built Japanese air base on Bougainville was bound to be costly in both time and men.

However, the leap-frog operation from New Georgia to Vella Lavella, bypassing Kolombangara, although not perfect by later standards, had proved fruitful. With MacArthur's approval, Halsey decided to bypass the Shortlands and Choiseul, and in a further application of the leap-frog theory, land an invasion force on an isolated portion of Bougainville, thus bypassing the enemy's well-defended airfields in the south end of that island. Also, in a departure from previous practice, Halsey planned to carve an airfield out of the jungle, and from it launch air raids to pound Rabaul into submission.

The largest of the Solomon Islands, one hundred twenty-five miles long and about thirty miles wide, with narrow beaches and swamps, a tangled jungle and a ten-thousand-foot-high mountain range with two active volcanoes, Bougainville was indeed a major challenge. Even the scattered native population, unlike other islands in the Solomons, was largely hostile to the Allies, supporting the occupying Japanese.

By November 1, 1943, having retreated from Guadalcanal, then New Georgia, and finally Kolombangara, Bougainville, was defended by some forty thousand men of the 17th Army, along with twenty thousand naval personnel, as well as the combat-hardened and notorious 6th Division that had sacked and raped Nanking, China, in 1937. These were now in well-prepared positions to defend the airstrips on Bougainville, in both the north and south ends of the island. In the twenty-one months since they had seized the island, the Japanese had made good use of the time.[8] Airfields had been constructed in the north and south portions of the island, with still more being added or planned. The Japanese 8th Fleet based at Rabaul was prepared to provide naval support when and if the Allies attacked.

Once it was decided to land on a small section of Bougainville where the enemy had no airstrip and was not present in force, after consideration, the final choice became Cape Torokina, Empress Augusta Bay, about halfway up Bougainville's west coast. On October 12, Admiral Halsey designated November 1 as D-Day.

Halsey preceded his landing at Empress Augusta Bay with several moves designed to confuse the Japanese as to his real target. Again, PT boats were pressed into use as support. On the night of October 21-22, a few nights after Kennedy arrived at Lambu Lambu and made his first operational patrol, a PT boat landed a reconnaissance party on Mono Island, the larger of the two Treasury Islands south of the Shortlands; it returned the men with accurate information on enemy positions and numbers there. A second PT boat brought an advance party which cut the wires between the enemy's observation post at the entrance to Blanche Harbor[*] and the enemy's main body on Mono Island.[9]

The Japanese in the Treasuries, with their seaplane and naval base a mere twenty-five miles south of the Shortlands, were caught completely by surprise when Allied troops landed on October 27. A PT base was immediately established on Sterling Island, and Blanche Harbor became a staging point for Bougainville.

In order to encourage the enemy's belief that Bougainville was not the target, that same day the 2nd Parachute Battalion, 725 men of the First Marine Amphibious Corps, commanded by Lt. Col. Victor H. ("Brute") Krulack headed for Choiseul Island. Disembarking from four destroyer-transports into rubber boats manned by Navy crews, the Marines landed at Voza on the Slot side of the island just before midnight October 27.

Initially, all went according to plan, with the Marines' main body causing concern on the Japanese side. Problems arose when two

---

[*] Blanche Harbor is the channel between Mono and the smaller Sterling, the two islands that comprise the Treasuries.

Marine platoons as a further distraction, separated from the main body and staged northwest along the coast aboard two LCPRs to the Warrior River. When the LCPRs entered the mouth of the river, although charts showed the water was deep enough for small schooners, the shallow-draft landing craft ran aground. As the Navy coxswains gunned the engines to free the vessels, threatening to alert any nearby Japanese, twenty-six-year-old Maj. Warren T. Bigger, commanding, decided the Marines should disembark on the riverbank there, allowing the LCPRs to retire a few miles up the coast to await the Marines' return.[10]

By mid-afternoon, however, instead of following a preplanned course that would bring them back to their starting point to be picked up by the waiting landing craft before dark, the Marines, guided by a native, who it turned out was unfamiliar with this part of the island, were bogged down in a swamp. By then Japanese troops, possibly alerted by the engines of the LCPRs, had moved in between the Marines and the point at which they were to recontact the LCPRs. Alerted to the potential disaster, Colonel Krulack radioed an urgent call for fighter cover and PT boats.

A few days earlier, a Marine-officer messenger had arrived at Lambu Lambu with a sealed envelope for Lieutenant Berndtson. The message informed the base commander that the 2nd Marine Parachute Battalion stationed on Vella Lavella was about to invade Choiseul as a diversionary attack. It listed the Lambu Lambu PTs as supporting units to be on call in the event an emergency arose.[11]

Now, in mid-afternoon, November 2, a radio message was relayed to Lambu Lambu for Berndtson marked "Urgent." The Lambu Lambu PTs were being summoned to assist in the rescue operation.

With only a few hours of daylight remaining, Berndtson dashed down the trail leading from the primitive operations shack to the dock. His entire "fleet" consisted of five boats: one was laid up for repairs. Two were out on patrol in accord with standing instructions from CTF31. That left two boats. Berndtson could only hope they were refueled, a time consuming process carried out manually by crews.

Reaching the dock, he found *PT 59* in the process of being refueled. Standing on the dock, Kennedy, dressed in shorts, a khaki shirt and Army fatigue cap, was observing his crew wrestling fuel drums over the mangrove roots toward the boat.[12]

"Jack, look at this," Berndtson called to Kennedy between breaths. "How much gas have you got aboard?" Berndtson asked, as Kennedy scanned the message.

"How much have we got on now, Drawdy?" Kennedy called.

"Seven hundred gallons," came the answer.

With a capacity of 2200 gallons this was a mere fraction of what was needed on a normal patrol.

"That would get you over," Berndtson said helpfully.

"Yes, we could get over," Kennedy replied. The problem was getting back. Seven hundred gallons was not nearly enough for a high-speed run across the Slot and a return trip. Furthermore, one boat alone could not provide space for eighty-seven Marines. On inquiry, Berndtson found the other boat was fully fueled. Would it be feasible, he inquired, for the two PTs to go to the rescue with the understanding that when Kennedy's boat ran out of fuel, as was certain to happen, couldn't the other boat take it in tow?

After talking it over, the officers agreed that in such an emergency it had to be tried.

"Get going, then," Berndtson urged.

"Wind her up," said Kennedy to the motor macs as he hopped aboard.

Kennedy told his crew what he knew, which was simply that they were headed across the Slot to Choiseul Island to pick up some Marines in trouble. He knew nothing more except the mission was urgent. Indeed, the information relayed from Guadalcanal did not specify the location on Choiseul where the Marines were trapped. Instead, it provided a compass bearing to steer to the Choiseul shore where a guide boat would be waiting to lead the PTs to the encircled Marines. Berndtson had marked the point on a chart, which Kennedy handed to Rhodes, who the crew believed was the best navigator.

Nevertheless, as the boats sped across the Slot, the PT crews were apprehensive. Rhodes worried, concerned about being able to locate the guide boat in the darkness after a sixty-five mile run with only a compass bearing. For PTs, operating in waters close to island shores, as was common in the Solomons, they had very little use for a finely adjusted compass. Rhodes worried about the compass on *PT 59* and wished they had taken better care of it. Drawdy in the engine room, calculating the gasoline consumption at the speed they were traveling, tried to guess how soon the tanks would be dry. Standing at the helm as usual, Kennedy feared for the safety of the Marines, praying they would arrive in time.[13]

Approaching Choiseul at dusk, a disturbed Kennedy observed there was no guide boat in sight. Rhodes assured him they had hit the island at the spot indicated on the chart: It did not help. The knowledge that the Marines were in trouble dwelled on Kennedy's mind.

Perhaps they were too far down the coast: Turning north, Kennedy led the other PT in that direction, pushing up the speed, making Drawdy wince. Their gas supply was already down to half, and they had yet to make contact.

Approaching an island Kennedy and Rhodes recognized as Moli, slightly less than halfway to Warrior River, they decided they were too far north; Kennedy now wheeled the boat about and the two PTs started back south. Approaching the indicated contact point again, they sighted a U.S. landing craft about three hundred yards off Choiseul. It was the guide boat they had been searching for.

Nearing the vessel, Kennedy was surprised to recognize a fellow PT officer, Lt.(jg) Richard E. Keresey, standing on the boat's gunwale looking as if he were ready to leap the fifty feet separating the two vessels. It so happened that the landing craft had been damaged and thus delayed in arriving due to a need for repairs.

"Dick, what are you doing over there?" Kennedy asked as he maneuvered the PT alongside the barge and the other officer leaped aboard.

"Never mind that," said Keresey. "We've got to get up the line in a hurry. Some Marines are in real trouble."[14]

The two PT officers had met at Tulagi Harbor that spring when Kennedy had given Keresey's *PT 105* a tow after his boat was damaged by striking a reef. That summer the two had been based at Rendova; indeed, Keresey's *105* boat was one of the Rendova boats assigned to intercept the four destroyers in Blackett Strait on the night the *109* was rammed and sunk.

As the two PTs raced toward Warrior River, Keresey told Kennedy how he had been sent to reconnoiter the coast for a base in case it was decided to operate PT boats from Choiseul. He gave Kennedy what information he had on the Marines' plight; their only chance to survive was to be evacuated by LCPRs. The role of the PTs would be to serve as a covering force during the evacuation.

By now the Marines at Warrior River were in desperate trouble. In an exchange of gunfire, two Marines had been killed, and a third, Cpl. Edward Schnell, had been critically wounded in the chest.

At what was the critical moment, the two LCPRs that landed the Marines, initially appeared out of the darkness. Shortly the Marines wading out from shore filled the first LCPR and it immediately departed for Voza. Other Marines, several carrying the wounded corporal, were taken aboard the second LCPR and it soon headed out to sea. To the shaken passengers in the second barge, it seemed they were finally safe. But this was not so.

The sea had been rising as darkness approached, and soon the second LCPR sprang a leak. At first, the problem seemed insignificant. But as the barge headed toward the open sea and away from the island, water began flooding the engine compartment. Soon, with the combined hammering of the waves and the increased flooding, the LCPR began to sink. When the engine died, fear gripped the occupants. With the other LCPRs well away toward Voza, and the waves carrying the disabled landing barge back toward Choiseul Island and the waiting Japanese, their hopes for survival seemed doomed.

At that fateful moment, the familiar silhouette of a PT loomed out of the darkness, its 40-mm guns pointed toward Choiseul Island, helmeted crewmen at battle stations. With engines of *PT 59* idling, Kennedy maneuvered the boat, placing it between the Japanese ashore and the foundering LCPR, ready to open fire if any opposition was offered from the enemy shore. As the PT crewmen aided the soaked Marines climbing aboard from the landing barge, Kennedy tried not to think of what an ideal target they made for the enemy a mere few hundred feet from the island.

With the PT's deck crowded with some forty to fifty Marines, Kennedy had the wounded corporal carried below to his own quarters and placed on his bunk. Mauer gave the grateful Marines what food and hot coffee he could from the PT's tiny galley; down in the engine room, Drawdy worried about the amount of gasoline remaining in the tanks.

Finally, when assured by Maj. Bigger that all the men from the LCPR were safely aboard, Kennedy finally headed the boat away from Choiseul and toward Voza as ordered. The heavily overloaded PT responded sluggishly. For Kennedy, there was concern that as an old boat with hours of operations behind it and the added load of Marines it could come apart under the pounding of the heavy seas.

Frequently the PT skipper dropped down from the bridge to his quarters, anxious to see how the wounded Corporal Schnell was faring. He found the Marine attended by a pharmacist's mate and a medical officer attached to the Marine unit. He asked if he could assist in any way, but found he could do little.

At Voza, the Marines were transferred from the PTs to waiting landing craft, all except Corporal Schnell. His condition was so critical that it was decided he should not be moved; he would remain on the PT to be returned to Vella Lavella.

It was past midnight when *PT 59*, its mission accomplished, finally started back across the Slot. At 1 a.m. November 3, with the medical officer holding his hand, Corporal Schnell died quietly in Kennedy's bunk.[15] Climbing the short ladder to the PT's cockpit, the medical officer gave Kennedy the sad news. The PT skipper merely shook his head, but remained silent. At 3 a.m. *PT 59's* tanks finally ran dry. As planned, the second PT passed a line over and towed Kennedy's PT the rest of the way to Lambu Lambu.

On the following night, with the mission of the 2nd Marine Battalion completed, five PT boats, including *PT 59*, returned to Choiseul Island to escort three landing craft evacuating additional Marines from the island. On the night of November 8-9 Kennedy joined three other boats prowling off Choiseul Bay in an uneventful search for barges. On this night of November 11-12, while on his way north from Moli Island to Choiseul Bay, Kennedy's lookouts sighted two barges emerging from the Emerald Entrance, but the two turned back and disappeared in the safety of the harbor.

Two nights later Kennedy was sent to the Choiseul Bay area to strafe Sipasa and Guppy Islands. The action apparently attracted some attention. On the way back to Lambu Lambu, at 4:35 a.m. a plane approached from astern, but the alert PT's gunners drove it away, the aircraft disappearing in the darkness.

By now, the trauma and strain of events were beginning to cause Kennedy problems. In fact, the disc between his fifth vertebra and his sacrum had been ruptured. The massive stress caused by the impact of the destroyer ramming the *109* and the extensive swimming that followed would cause lasting damage to his adrenal glands. In addition, he had contracted malaria. Finally, he consulted a Navy doctor on Vella Lavella, continuing to command the PT while the doctor considered his case.

Finally, Kennedy received the answer: he was no longer fit for action. His final patrol in World War II came on the night of November 16-17 when he crossed the Slot to patrol off Redmond Island. Following an uneventful night, *PT 59* returned to base. The log of *PT 59* for November 18 contains the following entry:

> Moored at base. 0800 Mustered—no absentees. 0900—took aboard 700 galls. fuel at Lambu Lambu. (Ensign J. Mitchell took over as Capt. of PT 59)[16]

Biloa was in southern part of Vella Lavella where the Allies had established an airstrip. When *PT 59* docked there that morning, a pale and thin Kennedy prepared to bid farewell to the crew. Walking along the deck he quietly shook hands with each man. It was a particularly difficult moment for Kennedy and the men from the *109,* Mauer, Kowal, Drawdy, Drewitch and Maguire.

"If there is ever anything I can do for you, ask me," he told them. "You will always know where you can get in touch with me." With that, he turned and stepped from the PT and headed down the path leading to the airstrip. Once back in the States, Kennedy stopped briefly in the outskirts of Los Angeles where he visited friends. From there he telephoned Mrs. McMahon, who was living in the city. He wanted to see her, but did not feel up to going into Los Angeles. Instead, she came to where Kennedy was staying, the two spending the afternoon visiting. He told her the full story of how the *109* was rammed by an enemy destroyer in Blackett Strait and gave her a detailed account of McMahon's ordeal on Plum Pudding and Olasana Islands. But he assured her that when he last saw McMahon at Tulagi, her husband was healing nicely. Indeed, in time, McMahon would recover completely from his burns.

Back in Miami, where he was briefly assigned as an instructor in a PT training program, Kennedy did what few returning naval officers would consider doing; he pecked out a letter on a typewriter to Maguire, an enlisted man and former member of his crew:

> "Went up before the Survey Board the other day—and I'm on the way out. It's going to seem peculiar paying full prices at the movie theaters again. It won't seem quite right until everyone is out, I don't think. I'm going to spend Christmas with the folks..."[17]

Kennedy called the Kirksey family in Georgia to express his condolences, and he had Johnston, now back in the States on his way to Melville, make a trip to visit Marney's in Springfield on his behalf.

In the spring of 1944, Kennedy, his weight down to 125 pounds, was admitted to the New England Baptist Hospital for the first of two disc operations, an event that did not fail to evoke a boisterous reaction from Johnston who, on entering his hospital room, asked, "Hey, have they converted you?" The Marneys also visited Kennedy in the hospital.

In the meantime, the war continued without respite. One final note concerning Kennedy's service in the South Pacific; none of the Marines rescued from the sinking LCPR off Choiseul that November night, including Major Bigger, was aware of the identity of the skipper commanding the PT boat that arrived at the critical moment, that is until a historian doing background research on Kennedy, then President of the United States, happened to disclose the information.

CHAPTER FOURTEEN

PTS VERSUS *DAIHATSUS*

Despite setbacks in New Guinea, Imperial Headquarters had clung desperately to the hope that its forces could push MacArthur back if Lae and Salamaua were reinforced. Plans for such an offensive had already been drafted when MacArthur's troops landed at Nassau Bay on June 30. The startled Japanese reacted to this small landing as though the entire campaign was at risk. The commander at Lae and Salamaua appealed to General Hatazo Adachi at Rabaul, commanding the 18th Army, for more men, and asked that a barge line be set up to operate between New Britain and the threatened New Guinea bases to provide reinforcements.[1] In fact, MacArthur planned to take all three Japanese bases along the Huon Peninsula, Lae, Salamaua and Finschhaven. A two-pronged advance by Australian ground troops targeted Lae. Finschhaven, fifty miles east of Lae, could be taken at leisure once Lae had fallen.

While Allied commanders in New Guinea prepared for the Lae-Salamaua operation, MacArthur's Fifth Air Force controlled the sea by day and the Morobe-based PTs took over the task at night. The Morobe patrols extended northward along the Huon Peninsula into Vitiaz Strait. During July and August, the shoreline of Huon Gulf and the Strait were ablaze with gunfire: on the night of July 27, PTs *151* and *152* sank four barges on the Lae-Finschhaven line.[2] On the following night, the Morobe PTs did even better: with the weather dark and rainy, PTs *149* and *142* were patrolling the Vitiaz Strait, the narrow body of water between New Britain and New Guinea, when they found themselves in the middle of thirty barges heading from New Britain to Finschhaven. Alerted by light signals, the two PTs opened fire with every gun. In the following chaotic minutes, with the barges returning fire, both PTs were damaged. One barge tried to ram, and the PT evaded the attempt by mere inches. Another barge was sunk by concentrated gunfire a mere ten feet from *PT 149*.

Realizing that in a fight with so many *daihatsus* the PTs were bound to suffer, the two skippers pulled away; behind them they left six sinking barges. The cost to the PTs was one wounded crewman and a bullet-riddled engine on *PT 149*. By the use of surgical tape, pots, pans and raincoats, the motor macs were able to effect repairs. Such was the night action off New Guinea.[3]

By July, encounters with barges caused the PT skippers to increase their boats' firepower. As in the Solomons, the solution was a 37-mm cannon anti-tank gun donated by local army units, the guns mounted on a PT's foredeck. With a range of almost nine thousand yards, firing an incendiary tracer or high explosive shell weighing five ounces, the weapon was ideal for barge busting.

On the night of August 28-29, *PT 142* commanded by Lt.(jg) John L. Carey, and *PT 152* skippered by Ens. Herbert P. Knight, departed Morobe. Aboard the *142* as officer in tactical command was Lt. Comdr. Bulkeley. The two PTs patrolled Vitiaz Strait all night but encountered no Japanese barges. On their way back, however, while passing Finschhaven, lookouts spotted three *daihatsus*. The two PTs charged, sending one to the bottom with gunfire. But the PTs' bullets and shells seemed to ricochet off the other two barges. Ensign Knight made a wide circle and raced in to drop depth charges next to both barges. The two explosions and the cascading water seemed to have no effect on the tough vessels. Lt. Carey's boat raced in, dropping two more depth charges; this sent the second barge to the bottom. But the third, although dead in the water, remained afloat.

In an action unique to Bulkeley, the Squadron 7 commander ordered Lt. Carey to go alongside the third barge. Bulkeley, Lt. Joseph L. Broderick and Lt. Oliver B. Crager, with .45 automatics drawn, dropped to the deck of the smaller craft. Spotting a helmeted figure near the wheelhouse, Bulkeley fired and the figure dropped.

An inspection of the *daihatsu* disclosed twelve armed Japanese soldiers aboard—all sprawled grotesquely in death. The three officers clambered back on the *142* and the two PT boats pulled clear and, while the PTs lay to, the 37-mm gunner on the *142* fired eight rounds into the hull of the barge; finally, the craft disappeared beneath the surface. On the night of the 29th, three PTs, in another display of determination, braved enemy shore batteries to get three more barges. Morobe PTs got so good at ferreting out the elusive *daihatsu* "trains" that one Japanese noted thankfully in his diary after reaching Finschhaven on August 29 that he had made the only trip "when barges were not attacked by torpedo boats." But the PTs got his barges on the return trip.[4]

But, as noted, the Japanese were flexible adversaries. More and more barges were armor-plated and armed with heavier guns. In addition, the Japanese were installing coastal gun batteries and machine guns along the barge routes and at the depots as a defense against the marauding PT boats.[5]

With PTs and planes blockading Huon Gulf and the Straits, Australian troops pushed west toward Salamaua. The advance caused the Japanese to transfer troops to Salamaua; as a result the latter had eight thousand defenders, four times as many as Lae.

On August 20, for the first time, heavy warships of the U.S. Navy operated in support of MacArthur's ground troops. On that day a dispatch from Admiral Carpender at Brisbane to Captain Jesse H. Carter at Milne Bay read:

> "Inasmuch as there is good reason to believe that the enemy is moving both supplies and troops from Finschhaven to Salamaua, you will select four destroyers and make a sweep of the Huon Gulf—during darkness 22-23 August—and follow this with a bombardment of Finschhaven. Targets of opportunity are to be destroyed."[6]

In the Solomons, such a mission would have been routine, but during the previous eighteen months no such naval bombardment had occurred. Reference has been made to the reasons for this delay—a shortage of ships, fear of air attack, a need for hydrographic data. But with the destroyers fitted with SG radar and good sound gear useful for avoiding unseen reefs, why hadn't the Navy's heavy ships provided more support after the Solomon Sea was surveyed? One reason is the survey ships had not yet covered the waters beyond Morobe. Another reason was the reluctance of MacArthur's Fifth Air Force to assure fighter cover. Nonetheless, it seemed past time for the U.S. Navy's warships to do something other than escort merchant ships and guard the approaches. As one member of Admiral Carpender's staff remarked: "It will be worth while to prove the Navy is willing to pitch in, even if we get nothing but coconuts."[7]

At 1:21 a.m. August 24, the Japanese on New Guinea underwent their first naval bombardment; 540 five-inch shells were fired in ten minutes and produced, as expected, nothing but shattered coconuts. Seventeen hours later, the ships were back at anchor in Milne Bay. If nothing else, they proved that as in the Solomons, warships could support MacArthur's troops if and when the Navy felt so inclined.

Fortunately for MacArthur, two new PT squadrons, Squadron 12 commanded by Lt. Comdr. John Harllee, and Squadron 21 led by Comdr. Selman S. "Biff" Bowling, both fitted with new 80-foot Elcos, were now headed for New Guinea. They would arrive between August and November, replacing the older boats of Squadrons 7 and 8 which would now be gradually withdrawn. As it turned out, as combat-minded leaders in the mold of John Bulkeley, Commander Harllee and Commander Bowling would set new standards for PT squadrons in aggressive patrol tactics. Graduating from the Naval Academy at age twenty, the son of a Marine Corps brigadier general, Commander Harllee was no stranger to the Pacific war. Attached to PT Squadron 1, he had been at Pearl Harbor on December 7 when the PTs fired their first rounds at the start of the war in the Pacific. Assigned to Melville as an instructor, in early 1943 he was made commander of the newly forming Squadron 12. At his request, the squadron executive officer would be another veteran and member of Squadron 1, Lt. Edward I. Farley, as recalled, who had been awakened by the attack on Pearl Harbor.[8] Commander Bowling, the skipper of Squadron 21, was a newcomer to PT boats, however. A graduate of the Naval Academy, Bowling was a communications officer on the staff of the South Pacific Amphibious Force. In late 1942, at the time the Tulagi PTs were locked in combat with the Tokyo Express, he wrangled rides on the PT boats during their patrols. Bitten by the PT bug, he badgered his superiors to be transferred. When the request was granted, he reported to Melville for training before being appointed commander of the newly commissioned Squadron 21.

The first boats to reach Morobe were attached to Squadron 12, arriving in late August. The new 80-foot Elcos were equipped with the latest technological PT boat advances; included were radar, fitted on all twelve boats, allowing their skippers to "see in the dark." Not only would this give them a better chance to ferret out the elusive *daihatsus*, but it would make it easier for the PTs to maintain station with reference to one another and the shore when the weather reduced visibility. Less obvious was an improved gyro-stabilized compass providing the helmsman with a true course, even when the boat was pitching and rolling in heavy seas.[9]

The astonished Morobe veterans had further cause to be envious: rather than the usual 20-mm cannon mounted aft, four Squadron 12 boats were fitted with a 40-mm Bofers cannon. They had been mounted on the boats before leaving the United States as an experiment. With a shell weighing two pounds and a range of ten thousand yards, the Bofers was ideal for coping with the enemy's barges. It would not be long before PT skippers of the older boats obtained their own 40-mm cannon from local army units. With its success, in due time the Bofers would join the 37-mm cannon as standard factory armament for PT boats assigned to the Pacific.[10]

As if radar and 40-mm cannon were not enough to awe the Morobe veterans, Commander Harllee's PTs were fitted with another eye-popping technological development: since the early months of the war, the Navy, aware of the problems associated with the PTs' torpedo tubes, had been seeking an improved torpedo launch system. Legend has it that the solution was the result of a barroom discussion by two Squadron 12 officers, Lieutenant George Sprugel, Jr., and Lieutenant James Costigan. Noting reports of flawed launches from PT torpedo tubes, the two officers reasoned that the Navy's newly developed Mark XIII torpedo, designed to be dropped from aircraft, owing to its specialized gyro, could also be launched from a light-weight, roll-off rack on a PT, similar in principle to that used by the PTs for depth charges. A model test rack was made by the New York Navy Yard based on the sketches provided by the two officers. The new system, manually operated, used a series of cables and pulleys, allowing the torpedo to simply roll off the rack into the sea, fired by a cable hooked to the firing lever. When the test was successful, the Navy immediately ordered all Squadron 12 boats torpedo tubes removed and replaced with racks with Mark XIII torpedoes. All subsequent PTs would be similarly armed, as well as PTs already in combat theaters.

With the old Mark VIII torpedo weighing 3050 pounds each and the heavy steel torpedo tubes having been replaced by the lighter weight Mark XIII torpedo weighing a third less, it was hoped that the PT boats would be capable of increased speed and better maneuverability. But, unfortunately, with the added guns, such as the 40-mm, plus additional crewmen to man the guns, the boats' performance remained the same.

But it was Commander Harllee in combination with the new boats that made the impact. On September 21, the Squadron 12 commander summoned twenty-two-year-old Ens. Rumsey ("Rum") Ewing, skipper of *PT 191*, to the Morobe operations shack, telling him he was to make his first combat patrol that night. The *191* would be accompanied by *PT 133*, a veteran Squadron 7 boat commanded by Lt. Robert R. ("Red") Read.

For the tall, husky ensign, it was the moment of truth. After the long hours of training missions at Melville and the Panamanian waters, plus briefings after arriving at Morobe, he was about to finally face the real thing.[11]

However, Ewing was reassured when Harllee told him he would be aboard the *191* as officer in tactical command.

Darkness was approaching when the two boats emerged from the mouth of the narrow Morobe River and increased speed toward the Vitiaz Strait. As the *133* lacked radar, Ewing's radar-equipped *191* would lead.

The first few hours of patrol were uneventful. But just after midnight the circling wand on the *191*'s radar screen detected a target, ten miles off Vincke Point. With the crews at battle stations, they closed on the target; it was a 125-foot diesel-powered enemy cargo ship. The two PTs roared in, the *191* leading, making a strafing pass with guns and setting the vessel afire. Moments later,

Harllee received a disturbing radio warning: Japanese float planes were in the area, and could be drawn to the scene by the fire, if they had not already been summoned. It would be wise if the two PT boats quickly cleared the area. But Commander Harllee, determined as he was to sink the vessel before leaving, ordered a depth charge attack.

With Ewing at the wheel, and Ens. Fred Calhoun, the *191*'s executive officer at the stern beside the depth charge rack, the *191* thundered toward the burning vessel. A torrent of water shot into the air as the depth charge exploded twenty feet from the ship's hull. Read, with the *133* following close behind, did the same. When the water finally settled from the explosions, however, the burning ship, dead in the water, was still afloat. "Closer," Harllee ordered, "Get closer."

Ewing and his crew eyed one another. How much closer could they get? When Ensign Calhoun assured Ewing he could do it, the *191* skipper turned the wheel over to him and took Calhoun's place at the stern by the second depth charge. Once the run began, Ewing had second thoughts, but it was too late. Fortunately for the *191* crew, Calhoun proved equal to the task. The second depth charge leaping through the air and exploding close to the ship's hull this time was sufficient. As the two PTs raced away, the crews saw fresh flames leap skyward just before the ship disappeared beneath the sea. With the *191* skimming across the dark waves, Ewing turned to Calhoun saying, "Cal, you're going to get into big trouble with Tojo. You scraped a lot of paint off that ship when you went past it."[12]

On the night of September 30, Ensign Ewing with the *191* was again on patrol. This was his first night as lead boat of a two-boat section. The second boat, *PT 68,* was a 77-foot Elco commanded by Lt. Bob Lynch attached to Squadron 8. Even though, as before, the second PT crew was the more experienced, the *191* was lead boat due to its more advanced equipment, particularly its radar.

For the first few hours, all was routine, the crews rotating, half on watch, while the other half dozed near their battle stations. As usual, with engines muffled, the boats slipping silently along at 5-6 knots, time seemed to drag. With the watch changing every two hours, there had already been a couple of watch changes with no sightings. Ewing and his lookouts, peering through binoculars, continued examining each suspicious silhouette for signs of the enemy.

At 1:15 a.m. as the two boats were passing a small cove, Ewing suddenly stiffened: he had sighted the silhouettes of two *daihatsus* to seaward, moving slowly. With his crew at General Quarters, helmeted and wearing life jackets, *PT 191* led the charge, the two boats pouring gunfire into the leading barge, which quickly sank.

Ewing then circled wide and, followed by Lynch, sped toward the second barge, now making a run at its best speed for the blackness of the cove. With the *daihatsu* less than a hundred yards from the beach, the *191* swept by, then turned sharply, its gunners raking the fleeing barge with bullets and cannon shells. Lynch followed, but then came disaster: when the second PT tried to turn, there came a loud crunching sound as it hit an unseen reef hard, a mere forty yards from the enemy shore.

Unaware of the *68* boat's plight, the *191* boat, having continued on and now laying further out to sea, received an urgent radio call from Lynch: "We've run aground on a reef just off shore. Stuck fast. Can't get her to budge. Japs all over the beach."

For the first time, the *191* crew noticed fires on the shore, about one hundred yards apart on both sides of Lynch's boat. Apparently, when the two PTs were firing on the second barge, some of their rounds had passed over the target and hit the shore beyond; perhaps it was a Japanese storage depot and the PTs' rounds had started a fire.

Cautiously, Ewing edged *PT 191* toward the grounded boat to give aid. The anchor line was passed to *PT 68*; the idea was to secure the line to the bow of the grounded boat so the *191* could pull her free. In the meantime, the fires on the nearby beach were growing larger by the minute.

Suddenly, large numbers of Japanese appeared on the shore, the figures eerily illuminated by the flames. Dashing about, to the PT men, they seemed excited or, perhaps, confused. Possibly this was a depot garrison, the original destination of the two barges.

For the two PT crews, it was a tense situation. Several times, the *191*'s engines churned the sea to a froth in an effort to pull *PT 68* free, but the grounded boat refused to budge. By now, many of the

Japanese were lining the shore, their jabbering voices heard on the boats.

When additional efforts to free the grounded PT proved futile, Ewing, Lynch and the executive officers of the two PTs held a quick conference. In the midst of their conference, however, three shore batteries opened fire.

That ended all discussion. The crew of the *68* quickly scrambled aboard the *191* boat and a crew member pulled in the anchor line. Already some of Japanese holding rifles had started to wade out toward them shouting what sounded like, "Srender! Srender!" Apparently someone had figured out what was happening and was attempting to capture the boats and their crews.

With the *68* boat abandoned, Ewing backed *PT 191* clear. It seemed they had been there forever rather than a few minutes. Ewing turned so that the starboard side of the PT was toward the shore and the grounded *PT 68,* allowing the 80-foot Elco to fire its full battery of guns. The abandoned PT boat was now directly between Ewing and the Japanese. At Ewing's command, with the thunderous roar, every gun on the *191* opened fire; the result was an awesome demonstration of the PT's firepower: multiple rapid-firing guns, .50-caliber machine guns, 20-, 37-, and 40-mm cannon: the riddled and abandoned PT boat burst into flames. More flames broke out on the shore caused by the *191's* incendiary rounds. In the glow of the flames, frantic Japanese could be seen scrambling to evade the hail of death-dealing slugs churning the water and ripping through the jungle beyond. With the *68* destroyed, Ewing gave the order, "Cease fire." With its guns silent, *PT 191* headed away toward the open sea. Looking back, crewmen noted with grim satisfaction the series of fires ashore had become a major conflagration.[13]

In early November Squadron 21 began arriving at Morobe. It was the first squadron to be shipped from the states with all boats fitted with a 40-mm Bofers cannon, radar and new Mark XIII torpedoes. Yet, what astonished the Morobe veterans was size of the squadron's officers. In fact, for the thirty-six-year-old Commander Bowling, commanding Squadron 21 had provided the opportunity to put into practice a theory: specifically, that highly competitive, tough athletic men made ideal PT officers. As a result he had recruited a number of football stars, men like Ens. Ernest S. Pannell, All-American tackle from Texas A&M and professional player for the Green Bay Packers; Ens. Alex Schibanoff, of Franklin & Marshall College and the Detroit Lions; and Ens. Bernard A. Crimmins, an All-American from Notre Dame. In addition Bowling persuaded Ens. Steven J. Levanitis of Boston College and the Philadelphia Eagles, as well as Ens. Louis E. Smith, University of California halfback; Lt.(jg) Paul B. Little, captain of the Notre Dame team; Ens. Kermit W. Montz from Franklin & Marshall; Ens. John M. Eastman, Jr., from Texas A&M; Ens. Stewart A. Lewis, University of California; Ens. William P. Hall, from Wabash; and Ens. Cedric J. Janien, from Harvard, all to volunteer. Not content with football players, Bowling had persuaded stars from other sports, men like Kenneth D. Molloy, All-American lacrosse player from Syracuse University; Ens. Joseph W. Burk, holder of the world's record as a single-sculls champion; Lt. John B. Williams, Olympic swimmer from Oregon State; and Ens. James Foran, swimmer from Princeton.[14]

As MacArthur's offensive intensified, and his Fifth Air Force dominated the sea by day and the PTs by night, it became increasingly difficult for the Japanese to resupply their garrisons. The attempt to reinforce Guadalcanal and the New Guinea garrisons had been tried in four different ways. First, with large-scale efforts with transports escorted by warships, with the Japanese losing too many of such ships in the battle for the Solomons and the early part of the New Guinea campaign to continue this method. Second, the Imperial Army sought to assemble groups of ten to twenty small cargo vessels and *daihatsus* carrying ten to twenty tons of food and ammunition, at Shortland Island. At an average speed of 6 knots, the boat operators hiding in coves and inlets during the day, it had taken more than a week for these vessels to cover the three hundred miles to Guadalcanal, and even longer to complete the four-hundred-odd-mile passage from Rabaul to New Guinea, a method, as noted, referred to by the Japanese as the "ant" system. The PTs sank many of them; and those that made it through delivered insufficient supplies and reinforcements. Thus Admiral Yamamoto made the difficult decision to employ destroyers on supply runs, a method the Americans nicknamed the "Tokyo Express." But destroyer losses in the Solomons finally forced the Japanese to virtually discontinue this method.

As a third solution, the Japanese pressed their submarines into service in the Solomons for a brief period, but experience at Guadalcanal caused the Navy to cease to use such vessels. But given the desperate situation in New Guinea, the submarines would again be employed, but with a new wrinkle: rubber bags partially filled with various supplies, then inflated while lying on the submarine deck. Lashed in place, they could be released and the submarine submerged, diving out from under them, allowing the bags to float on the surface to be recovered. This plan, coupled with partially filled steel drums, would be used in New Guinea. As in the case of the Tokyo Express, full-moon periods were avoided whenever possible, with arrivals timed after dark.[15] Some forty to fifty tons of supplies could be carried inside the submarine. In an emergency the steel drums of supplies on deck could be rolled overboard, and rubber bags allowed to simply float clear as the submarine submerged, some twenty to thirty tons of supplies being delivered in this manner.

It was a difficult method. It required two days to load an I-boat for a supply run, the run taking seven days for the round trip. I-boats traveled submerged the first day; the boats were scheduled to arrive the third day out, returning to Rabaul as soon as they were unloaded.

Thus in addition to barges, in New Guinea, the Japanese continued to rely on submarines to resupply the island. Such operations were highly successful. Between December 1942 and September 1943, Japanese submarines landed 3500 tons of supplies at the cost of one submarine, the *I-18,* sunk by *PT 122* on December 25th, 1942 off the Kumusi River.

During the last week of August as Commander Harllee's Squadron 12 arrived for operations from Morobe, MacArthur's ground troops prepared for the final drive aimed at the Huon Peninsula. Bypassing Salamaua, on September 4, Allied troops landed at Lae, a small village and peacetime mineral and agricultural outlet with a good anchorage and airstrip. Left to starve were the defenders of Salamaua. By September 16, Lae was in

Allied hands, the Japanese defenders retreating west. Acting quickly MacArthur set D-Day for Finschhaven as September 17.

Meanwhile, at Rabaul, submarine resupply operations for the New Guinea garrisons continued. On September 21, the *I-177* commanded by Lieutenant Commander Orita was departing Simpson Harbor bound for Finschhaven with supplies when he met the *I-176* returning from New Guinea. Its commander hailed Orita, signaling a warning: "PT boats are constantly patrolling near Finschhaven Bay; it would be best if you tried to make your run right into the bay while still submerged rather than entering on the surface.... Good luck."[16]

With their shallow draft, PT boats were virtually immune to the Japanese submarines' fearsome Type 95 torpedo, a modified Long Lance that had so battered the U.S. Navy's heavy ships in the Solomons. Japanese submarine skippers bringing supplies to New Guinea complained that the PTs with their low silhouette and small size were hard to see against a dark shoreline background. They noted PTs could hide under the smallest cover or cloud or in a cove, darting out to attack with machine guns, torpedoes and depth charges before racing away at high speed. When a Japanese submarine detected a PT boat, they argued, the only thing the submarine could do was dive and run away.[17]

The *I-177* reached Finschhaven September 23 and, as cautioned by the skipper of the *I-176,* remained submerged until inside the bay. In thirty minutes, all supplies were unloaded onto waiting barges and the *I-177* was on its way back to Rabaul having sighted no PT boats, arriving home on September 26. On October 2, Finschhaven fell as MacArthur's advancing troops occupied the village. The first phase of the retaking of the northern shore of New Guinea was nearly complete with the expulsion of the enemy from the Huon Gulf area. As one Japanese spokesman said, the Allies had "inflicted an annihilating blow on us without engaging in direct combat."[18] Thus far the Japanese had failed to land a telling blow against the oncoming invaders. But this was about to change.

With MacArthur's air force bombing the Japanese, and Allied ground troops advancing, Captain Jesse Carter directed a destroyer sweep off Finschhaven for the night of October 2-3; the target was Japanese submarines lurking in the Gulf. Destroyers *Reid, Smith* and

Henley, then at Buna, drew the assignment. In mid-afternoon they steamed into Huon Gulf at 20 knots, their sonar searching for the underwater vessels. At sunset, the ships were darkened: radar screens remained clear and monotonous ping of the sonar aroused no echo. Since the I-boats were supposed to be much further north, and since at 20 knots ships were usually safe from submarines, Comdr. Harry H. McIlhenney on *Reid,* as officer in tactical command, ordered a straight course without a zigzag.

At 6:18 p.m., twenty-five miles north of Cape Ward Hunt, the gun control officer on *Smith,* the second destroyer in the column, sighted three torpedo wakes abaft the port beam. Immediate action by the helmsman swung *Smith* to the right, parallel to the torpedoes, permitting the ship to "comb their wakes." But *Henley* was not as fortunate. A torpedo hit her amidships; in fifteen minutes the ship, a shattered hulk, was on the bottom. A total of 241 men out of 258 men in the crew were rescued.[19]

Following that disaster, the heaviest burden of providing naval support for MacArthur again fell to the Morobe PTs; they shot down a couple of "Bettys" and in a further expanded use of PTs, while continuing to hunt for barges and submarines, took soundings in channels off beachheads, and even battled destroyers.[20]

On the night of October 8-9, *PT 194,* a Squadron 12 boat, and *PT 128,* attached to Squadron 7, lay-to in Dampier Strait off the New Britain coast, looking for some target upon which their passenger, Mr. Richard Patton of the Raytheon Corporation, could test their new SO radars. At 1:15 a.m., lookouts sighted a puff of black smoke rising in the clear night sky over the Strait. Deciding to investigate they headed toward the smoke with engines muffled. Off New Britain's Grass Point, the radar showed two pips moving seaward, then separating and heading toward the PT boats. At 2:20 at a distance of three miles the two ships demonstrated they were hostile by dropping a 5-inch shell so near the *194* that the concussion threw everyone on the deck flat. Then searchlights snapped on illuminating the boats and 5-inch shells straddled the PTs. The two boats turned south at top speed and began to lay smoke; however, this failed to spoil the aim of the enemy destroyers—which is what they were.

Naturally anxious to fire their torpedoes, the skippers sought to maneuver, but each time they turned to increase the target angle, the enemy turned with them. The *194*'s 40-mm gun crew shot out the enemy searchlight, as a near-miss lifted the PT's stern out of the water, spraying the boat with shrapnel, killing the gunner and wounding two other men. As *PT 194* continued to maneuver at high speed, the civilian engineer coolly rendered first aid to the wounded. The two PTs finally escaped by doubling back through their own smoke to emerge from the northern end of the Strait.[21] Judging from the accuracy of the Japanese destroyers' gunners, it is speculated they were assisted by radar detectors, using the PTs' radar signals as targets. Notably, between the Nassau landings and the Finschhaven landings the New Guinea PTs fired not one torpedo.

On October 16, Japanese troops, moving by land, and barges from the sea, launched an attack on Australian positions at Finschhaven. On October 17, the Japanese 20th Division from Madang reached the area: Japanese infiltrations forced the Australians to withdraw toward the beach. But Allied reinforcements soon caused the Japanese to withdraw; by October 26th, the exhausted Japanese, weakened by battle and malaria, and short of supplies, had suspended the offensive. The Aussies buried their dead and prepared their own offensive.

During October, while the land battle raged, the Morobe PTs continuing their nightly patrols, claimed nine *daihatsus* destroyed. In the following month, the total rose to forty-five, with the boats ranging as far as one hundred miles westward in search of the enemy. Several factors were responsible for this spectacular increase: first there was the increase in barge traffic, but the fact that more PT boats, in particular, Squadrons 12 and 21, were now based at Morobe, were having an impact; furthermore, by now, most PTs were armed with the 40-mm Bofers. And notably, by November, most PTs also had the SO radar designed for PT boats, a luxury the Japanese lacked.[22] Even so, after eighteen months, the battle for New Guinea was yet to be won. While Australian troops held Lae, Salamaua and Finschhaven, and the enemy had been cleared from the Huon Gulf, the Japanese were dug in on the peninsula itself; and Japanese efforts to supply these forces continued. Thus the grimmest period of the campaign still lay ahead.

Lt. Commander Barry Atkins, PT Squadron 8 Commander. *Courtesy of WWII PT Boats Museum and Archives, Germantown, Tennessee, USA.*

PT 196, commanded by Lt. Alfred G. Vanderbilt, son of the Vanderbilts of New York City. *PT 196* was one of two PT boats that engaged six barges loaded with Japanese soldiers and through use of machine gun and cannon fire destroyed them all. Tokyo Rose, as a result, called them butchers, and promised retribution for any PT crew that might be taken captive. *Courtesy of WWII PT Boats Museum and Archives, Germantown, Tennessee, USA.*

For General MacArthur, the problem remained: how to break through the Bismarcks Barrier in order to push westward. The answer: to make bold leaps along the New Guinea-Mindanao axis, bypassing enemy strong points. By now, Allied troops held Finschhaven and had control of the Huon Peninsula. But Dampier and Vitiaz Straits and Rooke Island remained a threat. Dampier Strait was dangerous for heavy ships but ideal for enemy barge traffic. In any event, the general wanted to control both straits before his next advance involving a leap to the island of New Britain. And this required landing forces on the island of New Britain.

Jungle-covered, mountainous, 250-miles long, New Britain lacked roads other than in the area where the Japanese base was located; 80,000 to 90,000 Japanese troops were on the island, largely in the vicinity of Rabaul.

At New Britain's Cape Gloucester, at the northwestern end of the island facing Dampier Strait, the Japanese had about 7500 troops stationed to defend an airstrip under construction. MacArthur believed, and the commander of the Seventh Fleet agreed, that Cape Gloucester had to be taken. The date for Allied troops to land was set for December 25.[23]

One afternoon during the first week in December, Lieutenant Commander Atkins stepped aboard Lt. Edward Farley's *PT 190,* telling the Squadron 12 executive officer to be prepared for an urgent mission. The *190* boat would depart at 4 p.m. to transport an American and Australian scout, along with nine natives who had undergone training, to a beach near Cape Gloucester. They would be put ashore under cover of darkness to reconnoiter enemy positions and determine his strength around Cape Gloucester. That was all Atkins knew—or was prepared to tell Farley.

The mission promised to be especially hazardous since all waters near Cape Gloucester were under enemy control.[24] If captured, Farley and his men could not reveal to the enemy what they did not know. To add to the hazard, in an effort to reach Cape Gloucester, the trip led through the Siassi Straits. Success in getting through this treacherous strip of water was dependent upon Lt. Eric N. Howitt, Royal Australian Navy, who would act as pilot for the PT. Prior to the war the fifty-five-year-old Australian had been a copra plantation operator and had sailed the coastal waters of New Guinea and New Britain for more than fifteen years.

As scheduled, *PT 190* departed base at dusk. As expected, the trip through the Siassi Straits was slow and nerve-wracking: at the boat's helm, Farley carefully heeded the continuous flow of instructions from the calm, and seemingly imperturbable Howitt. It required more than an hour to negotiate the six-mile-long Straits.

Just before 11 p.m. the *190*'s radar detected targets approaching from the opposite direction off the port bow. Shortly, lookouts spotted the dark silhouettes of four barges. Although the enemy passed the PT at a distance of less than fifty yards, Atkins allowed them to continue on without firing. Tonight's mission was too important to be jeopardized by engaging barges.

Approaching Cape Gloucester with mufflers still engaged, the *190* lay to, one hundred yards of the enemy shore. The night was ideal for the mission. The American and Australian scouts, their faces blackened, gear taped to prevent any telltale sounds, assisted the natives sliding rubber rafts from the PT's deck into the water.

Soon the rafts disappeared in the darkness, the men paddling toward the shore. Once there they would hide the crafts in the underbrush, then vanish into the jungle.

Farley had arranged for a brief radio signal from the party on their walkie-talkie once the men were safely ashore. A long twenty minutes passed in silence. Then came the words: "Okay, Yanks, we're all set," blaring so loudly on the walkie-talkie on the *190* that all aboard winced: it seemed that every Japanese on New Britain must have heard the words. "Good Luck!" Lt. Walbridge, the *190*'s executive officer whispered in his walkie-talkie in response. "Now," said Commander Atkins, "let's go get those goddam barges we passed."

For Ed Farley, reflecting on the men being left behind, being on a PT boat was a better deal than being stranded hundreds of miles behind enemy lines on an island with over 100,000 Japanese; he was certain the Australian and the American with their eager scouts were lost forever.

On the way home, *PT 190* searched for the four barges until dawn, but without success. Back at Morobe, Atkins, still determined to sink the four barges, possibly on their return trip home, ordered two Squadron 12 boats, *PT 195* commanded by Lt. Ray Turnbull and *PT 196* skippered by Lt. Alfred G. Vanderbilt, the latter none other than the famous scion of the wealthy and socially prominent Vanderbilts of New York City, to undertake a search for the vessels. Using the detailed instructions provided by Farley, the two PTs departed base. What followed was a bloody encounter so typical of PT clashes with *daihatsus*. With no moon, the two boats prowling the waters with engines muffled, placed their faith in radar. Shortly after midnight, the crews heard the faint voices of singing men borne to them on a light wind. Soon, two *daihatsus* emerged from the darkness: clearly the Japanese had no thought there was danger this close to New Britain. It was a fatal miscalculation. The broadsides fired by the PTs' guns at close range, smashed into the singing soldier-passengers, crews and barges, without a shot being fired in defense.

Spotting two more barges, Turnbull's gunners opened fire, sinking both, leaving scores of Japanese soldiers floundering in the sea. Meanwhile, Vanderbilt's *PT 196* was engaging a fifth barge, shells and bullets from its guns setting the craft afire. Even as its passengers and crew fought the flames the barge was sinking. A 40-mm shell from the *196* exploding at the waterline hurried the *daihatsu's* trip to the bottom.

With three barges disposed of, Turnbull and Vanderbilt turned their attention back to the first two barges. Though still afloat and in difficulty, the two crews were far from defeated. Having lashed their craft together, possibly to transfer men and supplies from the more seriously damaged vessel, at the approach of the two PTs, the two *daihatsus* separated; one charged with the evident intent of ramming *PT 195.* The boats' concentrated firepower managed to sink the onrushing *daihatsu,* but only after it was within a boat-length of the PT. The final score: five barges sunk and an indeterminate number of Japanese soldiers killed by gunfire or by drowning, with no PT damage and no American crewman wounded or dead.

This action reverberated all the way to Tokyo; Tokyo Rose took time out while broadcasting records to issue new threats at the PTs. Having labeled them the "Butchers of the Bismarck Sea" a result of that operation, she denounced this last action, terming it an "atrocity," promising that in the future, PT crews, if captured, would not be treated as honorable prisoners of war, but as war criminals.[25]

Two weeks after the trip to Cape Gloucester, *PT 190* made the return passage. Few of the crew expected to find anyone waiting. But to their great surprise and joy, although exhausted from their ordeal, they found each and every member of the party awaiting the PT's arrival. Forty-eight hours later, the American and Australian scouts were at MacArthur's headquarters in Brisbane with critical intelligence information for use by the general's staff, information on enemy troop positions, strength and fortifications around Cape Gloucester.

Before the scheduled landing set for December 25 was carried out, three more boats, PTs *327, 325,* and *110* would each make a similar trip to Cape Gloucester, each carrying a reconnaissance team for the purpose of obtaining data useful in the forthcoming invasion of Cape Gloucester. All returned without incident; except on December 21, during the final trip, *PT 110* had a brush with *daihatsus.*[26]

With the waters north and west under Japanese control, in view of the enemy's capabilities, General MacArthur deemed it essential to secure the Vitiaz and Dampier Straits before commencing further advances westward. About November 23, MacArthur directed that Arawe be taken—target date December 15—ten days before the Cape Gloucester landings. Arawe, an island plantation on the south coast of New Britain, is some sixty miles cross-country from Cape Gloucester. Arawe's shallow-water harbor was suitable only for shoal draft vessels. Its defense consisted of a few hundred troops, coast-defense guns and beach defenses; the Japanese were using the harbor only as a *daihatsu* depot.

MacArthur's official object in taking Arawe was declared to be "the establishment of light naval forces"—PT boats—"to protect the southeastern flank of our forces in the impending seizure of the Gloucester Peninsula." But Morton C. Mumma, commanding the general's PT boats, would have nothing to do with Arawe. Mumma declared he had all the bases he could use, and the bulk of the *daihatsus* traffic was mostly off the north coast of New Britain. It is said that Mumma spent days "camping on the Seventh Fleet's doorstep" to protest against setting up a PT base at Arawe, departing only when assured by the admirals that he would not have a PT base at Arawe if he did not want it.[27]

Early in December, Morobe was abandoned and a new advanced PT base was established at Dreger Harbor near Finschhaven. In time, Dreger Harbor would take over from Kana Kopa as the main PT supply and repair base in New Guinea. For the moment, however, it reduced by sixty-five miles the distance that the PTs had to travel before reaching their patrol areas. But this did not last long.

On December 15, the first Allied contingent of forces under General MacArthur's command waded ashore on Arawe, a total of 1904 troops being successfully landed, with additional troops and supplies following on the 16th. Immediately, Dreger Harbor PTs began nightly patrols off Arawe. In the meantime, the PTs continued to patrol westward along the coast of New Guinea. At about this time, the number of PTs operating in New Guinea increased: several boats of Squadron 7 and 8 joined Squadron 12 and 21 at Dreger Harbor, and three new squadrons, 18 skippered by Lt. Henry M.S. Swift, 24 led by Lt. Comdr. N. Burt Davis, Jr., and 25 under the command of Lt. James R. Thompson, began to arrive.[28]

That the PTs were hampering enemy operations was shortly confirmed. One of the least-known secrets of the Pacific war was the existence of an intelligence unit in Australia, the Allied Intelligence Bureau (AIB). An umbrella unit supervising activities from information collection to guerrilla warfare, one of the operations was code named "Belconnen," the newly constituted Australian-American code-breaking unit at Melbourne.[29] During the first week in December 1943 duty a Navy operator began copying a secret message being sent from Tokyo to field commanders in the Southwest Pacific. Decoded it read:

AT ALL COSTS, AMERICAN PT BOATS MUST BE SMASHED BEFORE WE CAN REINFORCE GARRISONS NOW DEFENDING NEW BRITAIN AND NEW GUINEA[30]

Indeed, MacArthur's leap-frogging strategy, bypassing enemy garrisons to wither on the vine, was leaving thousands of enemy troops facing the possibility of starvation. A number of Japanese writings following the war suggest that with supplies cut off, a number of Japanese troops committed acts of cannibalism in New Guinea during the war. An example is a 1987 Japanese documentary file entitled "Yuki Yuki te Shingun" (Onward Holy Army) in which veteran Japanese survivors confessed to engaging in cannibalism during the New Guinea campaign. Also, a number of autobiographies by Japanese veterans explicitly detail cases of cannibalism on New Guinea between December 1943 and March 1944 when Japanese forces were retreating in the north central part of island.[31]

On December 24, *PT 191* with Ens. Rum Ewing in command, now a veteran PT skipper, and Ens. Herbert Knight commanding *PT 152,* were returning to Dreger Harbor after dawn following an uneventful night. With the sun blazing and the heat of the tropics, it was difficult for the men to believe that this was Christmas Eve. Approaching a small opening to a harbor near New Guinea's Gneisenau Point, the two PT skippers decided to take a look inside, "just for the hell of it." Previous Allied air reconnaissance had discovered nothing but the PT men were curious.

As the PT boats edged cautiously through the narrow entrance, the crews were astonished at what they saw: a Japanese submarine, between 100 and 125 feet long, apparently unmanned, lay moored alongside the beach. A heavily loaded *daihatsu* was moored close to the sandy shore. On the opposite side of the submarine was a picket boat, seemingly awaiting repairs. Without hesitation, the two PTs attacked, making a high-speed approach. At the sound of the PTs' engines, Japanese figures appeared on the shore as if by magic, shouting and gesturing toward the onrushing PTs before fleeing into the nearby jungle.

The PTs' machine guns and cannons delivered a torrent of destruction that punctured the submarine's hull, causing it to settle by the bow to the bottom as well as riddling the other two vessels. Before departing PT gunners raked the living and supply straw shacks on the shore. As the boats withdrew, their crews were elated to see a blazing inferno ashore with smoke rising in a column in the clear sky.[32]

Later that morning back at Dreger Harbor, Lieutenant Commander Harllee sent for Ewing and Knight. After first reading the two skippers the riot act for their "impulsive behavior" that could have "endangered boats and crews," Harllee let them know he was really pleased, adding, "off the record, that was goddamned good work."[33]

Ewing's crew had good reason to celebrate. Before leaving the States the previous May, Ewing's father, a St. Louis insurance executive, had promised them one thousand dollars should their PT sink a submarine or destroyer, or a ship of comparable size, the money to be split equally. Forbidden to write specifics on any action, Rum Ewing wrote his father: "Christmas Eve was payday for us from you."

The answer was immediate, a check for one thousand dollars, no small sum in 1943, along with a letter from Ewing's father saying, "I have never been so pleased to be a thousand dollars lighter." Three weeks later, when Allied troops overran Gneisenau Point, Lieutenant Vanderbilt, the Squadron 12 intelligence officer, confirmed that a Japanese submarine was sunk in the harbor, heeled over on its side in eight feet of water.

It was soon after the Arawe landings that the PT boats had one of the outstanding fights with enemy aircraft during the war; to most everyone's surprise, the results showed that PT boats were more than able to hold their own against hostile aircraft. With Allied troops landing in Arawe on December 15 and the PTs doing nightly patrols off Arawe, it became the practice for the Dreger Harbor PTs to refuel at Arawe before starting the night's patrol. On the morning of December 26, PTs *110* and *138* returning from an uneventful patrol, stopped at Arawe to pick up wounded soldiers to be taken back to Dreger Harbor. Suddenly the two boats were attacked by fifteen enemy dive-bombers from Rabaul, the bombs falling before the gunners could open fire. The near-misses damaged both boats and wounded several crewmen. But before the dive-bombers departed, one was downed by the 20-mm gunner on the *110,* Stephen P. Le Febure. However, this was merely a prelude to what was about to happen to two other Dreger Harbor PTs a mere twenty-four hours later. It was shortly after sunrise and *PT 190* skippered by Lieutenant Farley and *191* with Ensign Ewing in command were returning to Dreger Harbor after a fruitless night of prowling off the southern coast of New Britain at Cape Peiho. Aboard Farley's boat as officer in tactical command was Lt. Henry "Swifty" Swift, the recently arrived commander of Squadron 18. Also aboard Farley's boat was Lt. Eric Howitt, the Australian naval officer who had guided Farley to Cape Gloucester on the first reconnaissance mission.[34]

Reluctant to return from the patrol empty-handed, the two boats paused long enough to take a look inside Marije Bay; but finding nothing, and realizing they had already tarried too long, with an hour's sailing time ahead, at 7:25 a.m. they finally headed for Dreger Harbor.

With the patrol over and the boats skimming over the water homeward bound, Farley turned the wheel of the *190* over to his executive officer, Lt. William N. Bannard, son-in-law of the PT builder, Preston Sutphen of the Electric Boat Company, New Jersey. Aboard the *191,* Ewing remained at the wheel while his executive officer Fred Calhoun went below and stretched out on the bunk in his quarters.

It was nearly 8 a.m., about twenty-five miles northwest of Arawe when the first enemy plane dove from a cloud bank on the two boats and a bomb separated from the aircraft. The explosion seemed to lift Farley's boat out of the water. On Ewing's boat, the sound of the exploding bomb brought Ensign Calhoun scrambling up to the bridge. Peering northward and to the west, the PT crews sighted what they figured were thirty to thirty-five aircraft, a mixture of Zeros and Vals, no one had time to determine exactly how many there were, but all agreed there were too many for the PTs to handle.

With the Japanese attacking in groups of two and three as the others circled awaiting their turn, Ewing broke formation, forcing the enemy to divide his force. As the aircraft attacked, the two boats began zigzagging wildly at full speed, often waiting until the pilot had dropped his bomb before turning hard: In each case the bombs missed, exploding either to the left or right of the intended targeted boat as the PTs' gunners put up a constant hail of lead, blowing four of the attackers out of the sky, one of them possibly the enemy's leader.[35]

In the meantime, as the PTs' radiomen were frantically calling for air support, and trying to cope with the problem of poor communications, the enemy was beginning to score. With Ewing's PT bearing the brunt of the attack, twenty-two-year-old GM

Edmund "Buzz" Barton in the port turret blasted away at an attacking Zero, with its cannon blazing. On of the enemy's shells tore into Barton's twin-fifties knocking one gun off its base; the concussion bowled Barton over. Miraculously he was unhurt. But a jagged sliver of shrapnel ripped into Ewing's abdomen and emerged from his back. Paralyzed, the PT skipper slumped to the deck in shock where he lay, unable to move a muscle, yet fully aware of the howling aircraft overhead.

Standing near Ewing, Calhoun was also hit, a chunk of shrapnel tearing into his hip. With blood flowing down his leg, Calhoun struggled to reach the helm of the now out-of-control PT. Then, standing over the prostrate Ewing he grasped the wheel and continued to zigzag the boat.

Manning the 20-mm aft were Chief Machinist Mate Thomas D. Dean and MoMM August Sciutto. An enemy shell from a strafing plane struck the barrel of their cannon and ricocheted into the magazine, exploding six or eight shells: instantly the men's faces were transformed into masks of blood. Slivers of steel slashed into Sciutto's face below each eye, and another lodged in his brain. Dean was struck in the forehead, stomach, foot and the fingers of his left hand were mangled. Despite his wounds, he insisted that he be allowed to continue to fight. But he was taken below by MoMM1/c Victor A. Bloom for fear that, in his pain and shock, he would fall overboard as the PT continued to twist and turn in its effort to evade the attacking aircraft.[36]

By now, *PT 191* was riddled by bullets and shrapnel, an eighteen-inch hole had been blown in the port side. Another threat no less potentially lethal arose; bomb fragments had hit the water jackets on two of the engines and jets of hot water were spurting across the engine room: the boat was in imminent danger of going dead in the water. In addition, the starboard manifold had been hit; with the supercharger forcing flaming gasoline into the engine room there was a likelihood the boat would explode.

Although painfully burned by the streams of scalding hot water, Victor Bloom, the duty engineer on watch in the engine room, working against time, taped and stuffed the leaks; then with great presence of mind, suspecting the gas tanks had been hit and the leaking gasoline could burst into flames, he closed off the tank compartment and smothered the space with carbon dioxide. All the while Bloom was carrying out these tasks he could hear bullets and pieces of shrapnel striking the PT's thin hull.

By now, the PTs' radiomen had managed to contact the base: "The fighters have heard us," the *191* radioman yelled up at Calhoun from the PT's chartroom. "They say to hang on for ten more minutes and they'll be here!"

And so they were: within five minutes the PT crews recognized the familiar silhouettes of approaching Army P-47s. The new arrivals immediately sailed into the enemy group of aircraft, thus ending the threat to the PTs. The battered *PT 191* managed to limp on, arriving hours later at Dreger Harbor. *PT 190,* although buffeted by scores of bombs that missed, emerged relatively unscathed to also safely reach Dreger Harbor.[37]

That night, from the Japanese capital, Tokyo Rose related a stirring account to the Japanese public, one that the crews of PTs *190* and *191* would have found most amusing if they had heard it: "Off the southern coast of New Britain, our courageous airmen sank an entire flotilla of American PT boats without the loss of a single plane."[38]

Indeed, Ensign Ewing confounded Calhoun's prediction that the skipper was "a goner." A few days later, Ewing and motor mac Dean were lying side by side in cots in the makeshift sick bay at Dreger Harbor awaiting movement to a rear base hospital. The unconscious August Sciutto was headed for a hospital in Brisbane. He would not awaken until three weeks later; and he would continue to carry the steel sliver embedded in his brain, as doctors were unable to operate and remove it. For his skill and presence of mind in what was a highly dangerous situation, MoMM Victor Bloom received the Navy Cross.[39]

CHAPTER FIFTEEN

A BATTLE
BETWEEN GENERALS

For General MacArthur, the start of 1944 marked yet another leapfrog landing operation. With Allied troops occupying Arawe and Cape Gloucester, the general ordered the 126th Regimental Combat Team of the 32nd Infantry Division to land at Saidor at the western entrance to Vitiaz Strait near the eastern entrance to New Guinea's Astrolabe Bay. The Japanese had an airstrip there that would be of use to MacArthur's V Air Force. More importantly, there were few Japanese defenders at Saidor; on the other hand, at Sio, about seventy-five miles to the east, the point being leap-frogged, twelve thousand enemy troops garrisoned. This was in accord with MacArthur's decision following the Buna conflict to avoid further direct confrontations with the enemy.[1] The landing would take place on the second day of the new year.

On the morning of January 2, Allied landing craft disembarked 2400 troops at Saidor without suffering any casualties. By January 3, the Saidor area and the landing strip were in Allied hands.[2] Immediately, the PTs began nightly patrols off Saidor. But with the increased distance, it was the practice for Dreger Harbor boats, as in the case of Arawe, to fuel up at Saidor before starting the night's patrol.

For the Japanese, MacArthur's landing at Saidor, bypassing their prepared defenses, was a disaster. With supplies from the sea for Sio cut off, starvation and disease became the added enemy. Rabaul was forced to send supplies to Sio by submarines, the vessels returning with men too sick or weak to be treated by doctors or facilities in New Guinea.

And things got worse. On the night of January 2 at Rabaul, Lt. Commander Orita, commanding *I-177,* was summoned to submarine headquarters. There Rear Admiral Ryonosuke Kusaka told him, "Our forces at Sio are surrounded.... The enemy landed troops at Saidor today. Road communication between Sio and Madang is cut off."[3]

The Japanese command had noted with concern that Allied troops steadily pushing west from Buna, then Lae, then Salamaua and Finschhaven, were now threatening Sio. Their next strong point was Madang, about 110 miles further west. MacArthur's landing between those two places had trapped the headquarters of the 18 Army and the 18 Naval Base at Saidor, where the Army commander, Lieutenant General Hatazo Adachi and Rear Admiral Kuynizo Mori were based.[4]

Admiral Kusaka told Commander Orita that General Adachi had ordered a general withdrawal toward Madang, "but estimates that it will take as much two months to circle around through the jungle past the enemy. During that time he would be out of touch and could not direct land operations. So," Admiral Kusaka told Orita, "we have decided to use a submarine to move the general quickly from Sio to Madang."[5]

On the following day, CommanderOrita departed Rabaul for Sio. As noted, this was not the first *I-177* supply run from Rabaul to New Guinea. When MacArthur's troops overran Lae, and again when the Japanese lost Finschhaven, Orita made runs from Rabaul to land emergency supplies.

Arriving off Sio at sunset January 8, Orita's crew quickly transferred the cargo to the *daihatsus* that appeared from shore. Finally a boat started from shore carrying General Adachi and Admiral Mori. It was less than halfway to the submarine, however, a lookout shouted "PT boats." Orita's signalman blinked a quick message to the shore that he would return the following night. Crewmen secured what cargo was still aboard and the *I-177* submerged and the submarine headed seaward.

On the following night, as promised, the *I-177* returned, but found PT boats lurking at the rendezvous point. This time Orita kept the boat submerged but ran his radio antenna up and sent a message, "We will return tomorrow night, but before sunset. We will then try to take passengers aboard. Please stand by to repel enemy torpedo boats of they try to interfere." The *I-177* then headed out to sea again.[6]

In fact, by now the Dreger Harbor PTs patrolling off Sio were starting to score. On January 7, two boats, *PT 324* commanded by Ens. Ernie Pannell, the brawny Green Bay Packer tackle, and *PT 363* skippered by Ens. Frederick C. Feeser, caught four *daihatsus* loaded with perhaps 150 troops, heading from Sio toward Madang. The two PTs, charging with guns firing, were met by a withering hail of gunfire from the barges. Almost at once, GM1/c Frank C. Walker, firing the 37-mm cannon mounted on the foredeck of Feeser's boat, was hit in the stomach. Bleeding profusely, the gunner's mate staggered back to the gun where he continued to fire until the PTs ended their strafing pass, before collapsing. Crewmen carried the unconscious Walker below: placed in a bunk, he briefly regained consciousness and managed to ask the question, "Did we get them?" He was assured, correctly, that all four barges and their occupants had gone to the bottom. Walker smiled weakly and died.

That same night, other Dreger Harbor PTs were also busy. *PT 146* picked up a number of floating rubber bags containing supplies deposited earlier by a submarine intended for the Sio garrison. But it was two Squadron 21 skippers—both former athletes, Ens. Joseph W. Burk, the world's record holder for single sculls commanding *PT 320*, one of the highest scoring barge "aces" in the New Guinea campaign; and Ens. James Foran, the Princeton swimming champion at the helm of *PT 323*—who gave the enemy the roughest time. Before this night ended, few would argue that in selecting champion athletes as PT skippers, Commander Bowling had hit on a worthy idea.

It began as a typical barge-busting action, but soon grew into something more. Recalled Burk:

> At 2225, four barges were sighted one mile north of Mindire, about one quarter [mile] offshore and headed south. All barges were about 70 to 80 feet in length and one was definitely seen to be carrying troops. As the PTs closed for a port run, the troop-carrying barge opened fire with a light machine gun and a huge amount of rifle fire. On the first run

three of the barges were sunk, one exploding when hit by the *323*'s 40-mm gun. The fourth barge made a run for the beach but was destroyed by the *PT 320* on the second run. There was an explosion of what appeared to be ammunition on this barge. All barges had been loaded. The barges took no evasive tactics other than to head for the beach and to fire upon *PT 320,* which was the lead boat.

At 00.30 three barges were sighted about three quarters of a mile off the beach at Maragum, four miles north of Enke Point. By the time the *320* and *323* closed to attacking distance, the barges were a quarter mile from the beach, proceeding very rapidly. They were close aboard when both PTs opened fire, and there was no doubt about all three barges having taken plenty of hits. One was definitely hit by a 40-mm [shell]. When the PTs returned immediately after the first run, none of the three were observed floating. However, three other barges were lined up on the beach, ramps down and the sterns seaward. These barges were empty while the others were loaded. While destroying the three barges on the beach, a shore gun that seemed to be about a 3-inch in size opened fire from a position two and a half miles north of Enke Point. Both boats proceeded to close in on the shore gun at high speed, firing .50-caliber, 20- and 40-mm shells. This caused the shore battery to cease firing at both PTs, and they proceeded to finish the task of destroying the beached barges. All barges involved in this action were 70 to 80 foot length.[7]

By the time PTs *320* and *323* withdrew, they had accounted for a total of ten barges and silenced a shore battery. With the four barges sunk by Ensigns Pannell and Feeser, four Dreger Harbor PTs had sunk or destroyed fourteen barges. No less astonishing was the attack on the shore battery: standard response when vessels were fired on by a shore battery was to withdraw at high speed, as happened to PT boats on more than one occasion. By attacking the shore battery, the two PTs confounded the Japanese; moreover, such an act further enhanced the image of Squadron 21 as one of the most daring and aggressive during World War II, a squadron by which the others would be judged.

Not withstanding the PTs' successes in New Guinea, at General MacArthur's headquarters in Brisbane more than five hundred miles to the southeast, the start of 1944 was a time for grim reappraisal. It had taken MacArthur a year to claw his way 240 miles to a point northwest of Buna. With 2,240 miles still separating the general from his primary objective—Manila in the Philippines—at the current pace it would take ten years to reach the Philippines, and another five to reach Tokyo. Worse, even MacArthur's dream of returning to the Philippines was being threatened. Although the Joint Chiefs of Staff had agreed to the plan, it was clear that the U.S. Navy's carrier advance across the Central Pacific had priority. Should the Navy offensive succeed, the war could conceivably end with MacArthur relegated to the role of conqueror of New Guinea and defender of Australia rather than the Liberator of Manila. With Admiral Nimitz making bold advances westward in the Central Pacific coupled with Admiral King's hostility toward the U.S. Army, MacArthur would have to advance rapidly, taking bolder and longer leaps to keep pace and prevent the SWPA from becoming a backwater in the Pacific.[8]

MacArthur's solution involved his greatest gamble in the New Guinea campaign: He would leap to the Admiralties, three hundred miles northwest of Dreger Harbor. The largest island in the Admiralties, Manus, forty-nine miles long and sixteen miles wide, volcanic and heavily covered with a tropical rain forest, had ample space for military installations; Seeadler Harbor, MacArthur's next advance PT base, fifteen miles long by four miles wide, could also handle a large task force as well. Los Negros Island, bordering the harbor to the east, contained plenty of level land for an airfield. Whichever power held the Admiralties could deny the enemy access to the Bismarck Archipelago, and would dominate the one-thousand-mile square whose corners are Bougainville, Truk, the Palaus and New Guinea's Biak.

The proposal flabbergasted his staff. They pointed out the nearest support base was Finschhaven, too far away to reinforce the beachhead. On the basis of intelligence reports, they warned, some four-thousand-plus Japanese troops occupied the Admiralties. On February 24, following an air reconnaissance report that Manus and Los Negros seemed deserted, MacArthur decided to gamble; he ordered a reconnaissance in force to invade the Admiralties; the 1st Cavalry would be put ashore on the 29th. Anticipating little resistance, the general intended this to be an occupation force.[9]

Late in February, as General MacArthur's staff worked on the final details for the invasion of the Admiralties, newly promoted Lt.(jg) Fred Calhoun, recovered from his wound suffered during the air attack with Ensign Ewing, now returned to active duty with Squadron 12. He arrived just in time to be given a special assignment: native Coastwatchers reported the Japanese were using a mansion at Higgins Point on Rooke Island as a headquarters.

Even in this time of unusual tasks being assigned to PTs, Calhoun's mission was exceptional: using his guns, Calhoun's orders were to blast the buildings off the map.[10]

Again an Australian, this time a veteran navigator, would guide a PT boat through the treacherous reefs to a point offshore from the target, which sat on a hill overlooking the sea.

Once in position, Calhoun's PT lay to, and his gunners began firing into what proved to be a sturdy structure—.50-caliber and 20-mm, along with 37-mm and 40-mm shells—seemed to have little effect. "Raise your gunfire a little, because the lower floor is concrete," the Aussie suggested. The gunners followed the guide's advice and minutes later the structure collapsed in a pile of masonry and wood splinters.[11]

The helpful Australian next pointed to a clump of trees near the shattered structure. "You might want to send a few bursts in there," he said. "There's a building hidden in among the trees, and the Nips are probably using that, too." A torrent of bullets and cannon shells from the PT's guns now defrocked the trees making a building visible. It was soon blasted out of existence as well.

As the PT started the trip home, a curious Calhoun asked the Aussie a question: "How the hell did you know the layout so well back there?" With no sign of emotion, the Australian replied, "Because I built the place with my own hands and lived there with my family 'till the bloody Japs showed up."[12]

Late on the afternoon of February 27, MacArthur strode briskly up the gangplank of the cruiser *Phoenix* in Milne Bay. It was the first navy vessel the general had been on since he stepped off Bulkeley's *PT 41* in the Philippines. That night the cruiser departed as part of a task force: the landing of American troops in the Admiralties was now only hours away. If the general had scheduled the operation a mere twenty-four hours later, he might have reconsidered the invasion plan. On the date the *Phoenix* sailed, following a reconnaissance mission, 2nd Lt. J.R.C. McGowen of the 158th Infantry with five enlisted men found the islands "lousy with Japs;" unfortunately, the report reached MacArthur's headquarters in Brisbane too late to allow for a change in plans.[13]

The cruisers *Phoenix* and *Nashville* escorted by four destroyers would cover the Allied landing on the eastern shore of Los Negros in the small Hyane Harbor, a point chosen because it was not the most likely place for landing troops. Three APDs, plus the destroyers carried a total of 1026 troopers of the 1st Cavalry Division. Close support for the landing was provided by eight destroyers under the command of Captain Jesse Carter.

At 7:40 a.m., under covering fire from the ships, 1st Cavalry troops under Maj. Gen. Innis P. "Bull" Swift headed for shore. It took the enemy less than ten minutes to react. Indeed, far from being surprised, as a result of intercepted radio messages between talkative U.S. submarines, Col. Yishio Ezak, commanding the local garrison, had been expecting it. Machine-gun fire churned the sea near the approaching landing craft while shore batteries opened fire on the ships. Nevertheless, by 9:50 a.m. the troopers had captured Momote airstrip. So smoothly did the invasion proceed that at 4 p.m. General MacArthur went ashore to inspect the airfield and the perimeter established by the Americans.[14]

At 5:29 p.m. the supporting task force departed, leaving only two destroyers to furnish call-for fire for the men ashore. Also on hand were two PT squadrons, Squadrons 18 and 21 commanded by Lieutenant Commander Swift and Lieutenant Paul T. Rennell, respectively, operating from the PT tender *Oyster Bay* moored in Seeadler Harbor. Veteran barge-hunters, skilled at ferreting out the elusive *daihatsus,* the two New Guinea squadrons found themselves filling a new role, such as "messenger boys," salvage tugs, hydrographers, command craft for generals, as well as the familiar seagoing ambulances and pilot boats. In addition, the two squadrons provided close support to the 1st Cavalry with their guns and 81-mm mortars; like the 37-mm cannon, the mortar was a field installation with its distinct uses: where the jungle grew dense close to the water, there was virtually no weapon that could penetrate more than a few feet into the bush. A mortar on the PT boat was the answer. Also, a mortar could illuminate a target from overhead with a flare, as was sometimes done when engaging barges.

Ashore, the battle dragged on: Lorenhau Village, on Manus Island, was held by about nine hundred enemy troops. Before the Navy could use Seeadler Harbor as an advanced base, the enemy would have to be driven out. After a two-day attack on Lorenhau by B-25s, on March 15 the cavalry troopers supported by three PTs, four destroyers and three rocket-equipped landing barges, embarked from Los Negros in landing craft to be landed on Manus Island. In the action that followed, marksmen on *PT 363* knocked a sniper out of his nest; and on March 16, *PT 323* spotted a Japanese observation post along with a radio and a ladder in a tree on Rara Island and eliminated it with gunfire.[15]

Not until April 3 were the Admiralties considered to be under Allied control. Even so, several hundred Japanese remained in the interior of Manus and continued to hold two islands. Army casualties numbered 294 killed, missing or dead from wounds. But U.S. scouting planes reported almost all four thousand of the Japanese occupants had been accounted for. Only now was it possible, with the exception of the PT squadrons, to withdraw naval support. On this occasion, General Swift made a handsome acknowledgement of the role the Navy had played in the operation:

> "The bald statement, 'The naval forces supported the action,' appearing in the chronology, is indeed a masterpiece of understatement…. The Navy didn't support us, they saved our necks! All commanders firmly believe that, especially during initial phases, the balance of war was tipped in our favor by the superb support rendered by the naval forces."[16]

Hard on the heels of the success in the Admiralties, new advanced PT bases were established at Seeadler Harbor and at Talasea on the northern coast of New Britain. From Talasea, PT boats patrolled east to Cape Lambert, the dividing line between MacArthur's New Guinea area of operations and Admiral Halsey's forces in the Solomons, a mere forty miles short of the Japanese bastion of Rabaul. By April 1944, MacArthur's New Guinea PT boats were operating in four distinct areas: the northern New Guinea coast, patrolled by boats based at Saidor; the Admiralties, based at Seeadler Harbor; and northern and southern New Britain.

By now the newly arrived Lt. Comdr. N. Burt Davis, Jr. with PT Squadron 24's twelve 80-foot Elcos was based at Saidor. Meanwhile the number of *daihatsus* sunk by the PTs remained high.[17]

At about this time, the Navy acknowledged the efforts of the PTs and the hazards of barge-fighting and its influence on the course of the war, awarding the coveted Presidential Unit Citation to Squadrons 12 and 21:

> For outstanding performance during the Huon Peninsula Campaign against enemy Japanese forces from October 1943 to March 1944. Highly vulnerable to damage from treacherous reefs and grounding during close inshore patrols, Motor Torpedo Boat Squadrons Twelve and Twenty-One spearheaded a determined waterborne attack on the enemy, boldly penetrating hostile waters and disrupting barge traffic vital to the maintenance of Japanese strongholds in the New Guinea area. Dauntlessly exchanging gunfire with heavily armored gunboats and barges, airplanes and shore installations, the boats of Squadrons Twelve and Twenty-One have successfully diverted hostile artillery fire to themselves in protection of Allied Land Forces; they have steadily destroyed the enemy's ships carrying troops, food and combat supplies; they have captured Japanese personnel, landed in hostile territory, and effected air and sea rescue missions. Tenacious and indomitable in the face of superior fire-power and despite frequent damage to boats and casualties among personnel, the officers and men of Squadron Twelve and Twenty-One have fought gallantly and served with distinction in crushing the enemy resistance in this strategically important area.[18]

Here was evidence that high-performance athletes as PT skippers, coupled with the style of leadership as characterized by Commanders Bowling and Harllee provided for a potent combination. Remarkably, only one other Presidential Unit Citation would be awarded to PT squadron, one to Squadron 3 for its actions during the Guadalcanal campaign against the Tokyo Express. Before the war ended, the PTs would earn still more awards, but not without cost.

On the night of March 6-7, at 2:05 a.m., two Squadron 24 boats based at Saidor slipped into New Guinea's Hansay Bay, a Japanese stronghold 135 miles northwest of their base. Aboard the *338* in tactical command was Commander Davis, commanding Squadron 24. Commanding *PT 338* was Lt. Carl T. Gleason; commanding the second boat, *PT 337,* was Ens. Henry Cutter.

It should have been a routine mission: MacArthur's troops had recently bypassed the bay in their advance westward. The two PTs explored the bay, in keeping with their role of preventing supplies or reinforcements from reaching the enemy as well as blocking efforts of the bypassed troops to escape and possibly reform into units that would have to be dealt with again by Allied ground troops.

At first, the bay seemed empty. With mufflers engaged for silent running, the boats crept deeper in. Finally, the sweeping wands of their radars detected a target close to shore. Continuing to close slowly, they determined finally the target was two camouflaged luggers. Then the night seemed to explode: machine guns opened fire on the PTs from the shore. The enemy had used the moored luggers to lure the PTs into a trap.[19]

Commander Davis immediately ordered a strafing run on the machine guns, but the gun positions were well-concealed and difficult targets. Then a new and distinctive boom echoed across the bay: a shore battery positioned on Awar Point dominating the entrance to the bay had opened fire. Heavy shells landed near *PT 337*; shrapnel whistled through the air. The second shell from the big gun found target. The explosion, beneath the port turret of *PT 337,* killed all three engines. The explosion also blew the gunner, MoMM3/c Francis C. Watson, out of the turret to the deck. Lurching to his feet, the dazed Watson started forward to escape the fire now raging aft. But he turned back to assist MoMM1/c William Daley, Jr., the motor mac on duty in the engine room. Hurled to the engine room deck by the explosion, and struck on the neck and jaw by shrapnel, Daley had only managed to crawl from the burning engine room.

Watson pulled Daley clear of the flames, and with the aid of TM2/c Morgan Canterbury, carried him forward, even as Ensign Cutter gave the order to "Abandon Ship!"[20]

Crewmen quickly tossed the oval-shaped balsa life raft over the side, on the side away from the big gun and jumped overboard behind it. Bleeding and in shock, Daley made it into the water but was too weak from his wounds to pull himself into the raft. When he slipped back into the water, Ensign Cutter and Ensign Robert W. Hyde swam after him, towed him back to the raft and lifted him inside. As the raft was merely seven-by-three feet in size, some of the twelve crewmembers had to remain in the water, clinging to the side.

With *PT 337* in flames, it was urgent that they get as far away from the boat before it exploded. But although the men paddled and did their best, after two hours of effort with the current against them, the raft and PT were separated by a mere seven hundred yards.

At around 4:45 a.m. *PT 337* exploded. An hour later, having never uttered a word of complaint, Daley passed away. Fellow crewmen gently committed his body to the sea.[21]

When Cutter's boat failed to follow *PT 338* out of the bay, and then failed answer to radio calls from Commander Davis, the Squadron 24 commander instructed *PT 338* to return to the bay. But as Lieutenant Gleason's boat neared the bay's entrance, enemy searchlights illuminated the PT and the battery on Awar Point began firing; the shells landing close by provided proof that the hit on *PT 337* was no fluke. *PT 338* was forced back to sea. Several times Gleason attempted to slip back, but it was no use. Each time the alert Japanese battery greeted him with falling shells. Finally, with dawn drawing near, Davis was forced to depart: he ordered Gleason back to Saidor, still uncertain as to the fate of *PT 337* and its crew.

For Ensign Cutter and his surviving crewmembers inside the bay, the outlook was not encouraging. The approach of dawn found the raft and men a mile inside Hansa Bay. Once it was daylight, the Japanese on Awar Point would spot the raft and a boat would be dispatched with armed soldiers to take them captive. As PT men, the crew of the *337* was well aware of the fate awaiting them if they were to fall in the hands of the enemy.

But when all seemed lost, the tide changed, sweeping the raft and men through the entrance to the open sea. Dawn March 7 found them a mile outside the bay. Six miles away lay small Manam Island, presumably unoccupied by the enemy. Believing the smaller island would be a safe place to find food, water for drinking, and maybe a canoe or other small craft to get them back to Saidor, Ensign Cutter ordered the men to paddle toward the island.[22]

All day, beneath a broiling sun, the men struggled, pushed and paddled the raft toward Manam Island. But each time they drew near, a mischievous current pushed them back out to sea. Finally, exhausted, thirsty and hungry, the men's spirits began to plummet. That night, two logs floated by. In hopes they could reach the island with this method, Ensign Cutter and Ensign Bruce C. Bales climbed on the logs. But after three hours of strenuous effort, the frustrated officers found themselves back at the raft: the currents had carried them in a full circle around the island.

Back on the raft the two returning officers found some crewmen were missing: about an hour after the two officers had departed on the logs, Ensign Hyde and QM2/c Allen B. Gregory set out to swim to the island. Neither was ever heard from again. The night dragged on. Suddenly, Canterbury became delirious and leaped into the water and swam away. RM2/c Harry E. Barnett jumped into the sea after him, but was unable to locate him in the darkness.

That night, the *337* survivors saw gun flashes at Hansa Bay. These were made by the guns of PTs from Saidor, returning and attacking in retaliation for the loss of the *337* and her crew. But none of the PTs approached Manam Island and the survivors had no way of signaling their presence.

By dawn, the second day on the raft, the current had carried the men to the north side of Manam Island. With the distance to the shore no more than a mile, Ensign Bales, MoMM3/c Evo A. Fucilli and TM Schmidt decided to swim to the island. None was ever heard from again. A possible answer as to their fate was provided by

SC3/c James P. Mitchell, who also started to swim for shore. When he was only fifty yards from the beach, he saw Ensign Bales walking on the shore, but he also saw several Japanese soldiers, so he swam back to the raft. This ended any idea the survivors had of getting on Manam Island. After the war, captured enemy documents showed that Japanese on Manam Island had captured one officer and two enlisted men who swam ashore. However, the three were never mentioned again in Japanese records.[23]

That night, their third on the raft, the remaining survivors had another fright: a small boat put out from the island and circled the raft at a distance of about two hundred yards. Two Japanese in the craft trained their guns on the helpless Americans; it seemed they were about to be either captured or shot. Then a sudden squall swept down on them; six-foot waves tossed the raft wildly about. But the squall drove the small boat back to the island. On the following morning, the survivors' luck finally took a turn for the better: a capsized Japanese small boat drifted by. With its length of about fifteen feet, it was a huge improvement over the life raft. When the men righted the boat and bailed it out, they got another break: a live crab was clinging to its side. The men lost no time in devouring it. A couple of hours later, the thirsty men plucked a drifting coconut from the sea, but it turned out to be dry.

By now the five remaining survivors were showing the effects of the ordeal: bearded faced, skin burned by the sun, bodies covered with salt-water sores, tortured by thirst and hunger, it seemed that despite all their efforts, final survival was not to be.

But then around noon of March 10, three Army B-25 bombers appeared in the distance. A desperate Ensign Cutter stood up and furiously waved his arms; when he was certain the pilots had spotted him, he signaled them with his arms, using semaphore, a doubtful method of communication with Army pilots; but it was the best Cutter could do. In any event, it assured the airmen that the men in the small boat were Navy survivors in need of help.

The three bombers circled the boat, then one B-25 made a low pass, dropping a box, which promptly sank. The pilot then made a second pass; this time, two boxes were dropped along with a small package secured to a life preserver, all of which landed close by. Inside the containers, the men found food, water, medicines and cigarettes. Also included was a chart showing the survivors' position, and most welcome of all, a message saying: "Catalina will pick you up."

On the following morning, after a final night adrift in the small boat, a twin-engined PBY appeared, escorted by two P-47 Army fighters. Two hours later the men were back at Dreger Harbor. There they learned that for the previous five days, Allied aircraft had been searching by day and PTs by night for possible survivors. The five men of *PT 337* who returned considered themselves to be extremely fortunate. Despite the best efforts on the part of searchers, a tiny raft remains a difficult object to spot in the vast, trackless ocean, and such searches were not always a success.

In spite of the loss of *PT 337* in Hansa Bay due to an enemy shore battery, PT crews generally considered Japanese coastal guns to be a minor threat, as in fact they were. Indeed, less than ten percent of PT boats lost in action during the war were the result of encounters with shore batteries.

Not that this made the experience less nerve-wracking. Even as the survivors of the *337* boat were enjoying their first hours back home, two PTs patrolling off the coast of New Britain were facing the same threat.

According to the diary of Lt.(jg) James Cunningham, a Squadron 8 officer commanding *PT 149*, it happened on the night of March 12; Cunningham's PT, accompanied by *PT 194* attached to Squadron 12, was patrolling the north coast of New Britain. At 11:00 p.m., a target appeared on the radar screen. The PTs closed cautiously; however, it turned out to be a small destroyed vessel that had run aground. In typical fashion, the PT gunners "destroyed it once more" before moving on.

Their objective was the other side of Garove Island. There they sighted a small vessel making its way across the mouth of the harbor. Although the two skippers were aware that part of the harbor had high cliffs, ideal for the positioning of shore batteries, the two PTs charged the target with the intent of making a high-speed strafing pass.

Suddenly, recalled Cunningham, enemy 6-inch guns opened fire from the cliffs. As noted in Cunningham's diary, the concussion of the shells "was terrific. It seemed for a while that they would blow us out of the water." Not surprisingly the two PTs disregarded the initial target and raced full speed toward the open sea behind a billowing protective smoke screen. As in the case of Hansa Bay, it appeared to have been a deliberate attempt by the enemy to lure the troublesome boats into a trap. What saved *PT 149* and accompanying *194* was the battery crew's failure to wait until the boats were deeper in the harbor; also, this time the enemy's aim proved less accurate.[24]

According to Cunningham's diary, the night's action was not yet over. On their way home the PTs' radar detected three large pips ten miles off the coast of New Britain; they were identified as destroyers. As these waters were hostile and all vessels encountered were enemy, the PTs' orders were to destroy all craft encountered.

The two PTs tracked the targets on radar until at a range of one mile the vessels were visually sighted. Preparations were made to carry out a torpedo attack on what was now observed to be two large landing craft and one destroyer.[25]

Considering this to be a major target, the PTs radioed for assistance. But as they started their torpedo runs, the destroyer fired a recognition flare identifying the three vessels as "friendly." As it turned out, they had unknowingly wandered into the PTs' grid sector. Fortunately for all concerned, the destroyer had been monitoring the PTs' radio frequency and reacted in time, thus preventing what would have been a major wartime tragedy.

For the PT boats of Squadrons 18 and 21 based at Seeadler Harbor in the Admiralties, there was also action of a sort never envisioned by the designers of PT boats. To an increased extent, as noted, this involved preventing the escape of bypassed enemy troops from their now isolated jungle garrisons; if allowed to escape, such men could reform into effective fighting units and oppose advancing Allied forces. On the night of March 11-12, two Squadron 18 boats led by Squadron commander Lieutenant Commander Swift, intercepted a native canoe near Pak Island occupied by nine Japanese soldiers. When the PTs approached, one man stood, pulled the pin from a grenade, and blew himself up along with three other soldiers. A fifth man who survived the blast refused to surrender and was shot by a PT gunner. The remaining men now surrendered and were taken captive.[26]

With an Allied airstrip now in the Admiralties, and the nearest enemy airfield 150 miles away, the PTs based at Seeadler Harbor began to operate during daylight hours. With the decrease in *daihatsu* activity, the aggressive PT crews sought action in other places. On the morning of March 20, Lt.(jg) Cedric Janien, the former Harvard football star and Ensign, commanding *PT 321,* and Lt. John F. Ganong, skipper of the *369* boat, approached Los Negros Island. Their objective was Loniu Village, a known Japanese supply depot on Los Negros Island. Die-hard Japanese still hiding in the jungle on Los Negros had a practice of sending bullets whistling past the PTs moored in Seeadler Harbor.

Approaching the village, the two PTs first cruised slowly offshore while their gunners raked the village. When the structures failed to burn, the two skippers decided to take more direct action. Boarding rubber dinghies, with several armed crewmen, they headed for the beach carrying two buckets of gasoline. Once ashore, they chose as their targets twenty-five camouflaged buildings containing thirty-one large canoes, each capable of carrying thirty men.[27]

With the village apparently deserted, the men hastily poured the buckets of gasoline on the canoes and as many buildings as possible, one of which was filled with ammunition. Setting the building afire, the men rushed back to the dinghies. Back on his PT, Janien found evidence the enemy was present: one of his officers had been shot by a sniper.

Even as the ammunition ashore was exploding in the burning structure, Hanien and Ganong obtained more gasoline and again the men paddled back to shore, but this time with considerable caution. The flames and exploding ammunition was bound to have alerted Japanese for miles around. Again they doused structures, this time those containing food and supplies and set them afire.

By the time they returned to the PTs and the boats were departing, they could see with considerable satisfaction the results of their efforts, a huge fire that threatened to consume the entire village. Here, indeed, was a use of PT boats and crews, so far removed from the role the Navy had envisaged when it decided to build these boats as to be beyond imagination.

PT 337, a Squadron 24 boat based in New Guinea commanded by Ens. Henry Cutter. On March 7, 1944, the boat was lost after being hit by an enemy shore battery. A few of the crew survived to tell the tale, five men out of twelve.

Notice the boat is an 80-foot Elco armed with Mark 13 torpedoes in racks and fitted with radar. *Courtesy of WWII PT Boats Museum and Archives, Germantown, Tennessee, USA.*

CHAPTER SIXTEEN

CHRISTMAS AT
BOUGAINVILLE

For Admiral Halsey, D-Day, November 1, the date for the invasion of Bougainville would mark the culmination of the long advance up through the Solomon chain. Having landed a small party in the Treasuries immediately south of the island, following that up by landing 725 troopers of the 2nd Marine Parachute Battalion on Choiseul Island, he now added to the enemy's uncertainty: hours before his amphibious troops landed at Empress Augusta Bay he sent a force of light cruisers and destroyers to the northern end of Bougainville to shell the enemy's airfields at Buka and Bonis. By sunrise, the ships had raced down the length of Bougainville and bombarded the Shortlands, home of the notorious Tokyo Express, as well as Ballale, a small island where the enemy had built a fifth airfield. Air raids carried out by planes from the carriers *Saratoga* and *Princeton,* steaming up from the lower Solomons, added to the havoc created by the shelling.[1]

Commanding the enemy's Bougainville defense was the same General Hyakutake who had suffered the earlier defeat on Guadalcanal; he was determined not to repeat that "mortification," as he called it.[2]

By November 1, some forty thousand Japanese army troops and twenty thousand sailors were on Bougainville and the outlying islands. They included the 6th Division. Most of Hyakutake's forces were in the southern part of the island close to the airfields and naval facilities. General Hyakutake was certain these were Halsey's objective. That the American commander would choose to land in the wilderness and build an airstrip in the interest of saving lives never occurred to the Japanese army commander.

During the pre-dawn hours of November 1, the Allied armada arrived off Empress Augusta's Cape Torokina and began landing operations. For the assault, Halsey used the fresh 3rd Marine Division and the 37th Army Division, which had fought on New Georgia. Although some three thousand Japanese troops were deployed along the shores of the Bay, only 270 men with a single 37-mm cannon defended Cape Torokina. By nightfall the initial beachhead had been secured.[3] In its wake, eight PT boats arrived and began immediate operations from Puruata Island, off the northern tip of the Bay.[4] Expectations were that with Rabaul a mere two-hundred-odd miles away, the enemy's counter would be swift. The Americans were not to be disappointed.

On November 2, Rabaul dispatched a force of three heavy cruisers and a light cruiser with six destroyers to deal with the invaders. The Japanese ships were intercepted by a U.S. task force composed of four light cruisers and eight destroyers. Following a three-hour exchange of torpedoes and gunfire called the Battle of Empress Augusta Bay, the Japanese commander, erroneously believing he had sunk two U.S. cruisers, retired at 3:37 a.m. In fact, all Allied ships had survived intact.

When word of the American landings at Empress Augusta Bay reached Truk, the Japanese dispatched their Second Fleet, seven heavy cruisers, one light cruiser and four destroyers, south to Rabaul as added support. Their arrival at Simpson Harbor promised more trouble for Allied forces at Empress Augusta Bay. Lacking the heavy ships needed to oppose another attack, Admiral Halsey ordered the carriers *Saratoga* and *Princeton* to launch a surprise air attack on the ships now gathered in Simpson Harbor. The raid, carried out on the morning of November 5, caught the Japanese by surprise. Although the air attack failed to sink any ships, the damage was sufficient to knock the Second Fleet out of the war for the time being, ending the threat posed by enemy heavy ships to the landings at Bougainville.

In response, eighteen "Kates" fanned out in search of the escaping carriers. At 7:15 in late twilight they found their prey, twenty-eight miles south of Cape Torokina—or so they thought—and attacked.

In fact, their target was a tiny flotilla consisting of *PT 167,* the zebra-striped boat and *LCI-70,* an "Elsie Item gunboat" escorting the *LCT-68.* The trio had departed the Torokina beachhead at midafternoon bound for the Treasuries. At 7:15, Ens. Theodore Berlin and his executive officer, Ens. Paul B. "Red" Fay, Jr., sighted the group of Kates against the fading twilight moments before they attacked. Once again it would be a case of PT against aircraft.

The leading torpedo bomber's pass was so low its wing struck the PT's radio antenna; the aircraft continued on a short distance before it crashed in the sea. The Kate's torpedo smashed through the PT's bow without exploding, leaving pieces of the tail assembly in the boat, the event marking the only occasion in the war in which a PT was hit by an enemy torpedo. Since both holes in the PT were above the waterline, there was no danger of sinking. A few minutes later, *PT 167*'s 20-mm cannon fire hit one aircraft in the second wave of attacking bombers. It fell in flames, smashing into the sea so close to the PT's port quarter that men on the stern were drenched by the enormous splash.

In the meantime, *LCI-70* was busy. In fourteen minutes she was subjected to four low-altitude torpedo attacks and one strafing run. Owing to her shallow draft, all the torpedoes passed harmlessly under her keel, except one that porpoised onto the engine room, killing one man and lodging there unexploded.[5]

Finally, with the departure of the aircraft, *LCT-68* passed a line to the crippled LCI and began towing her back to Torokina. *PT 167* returned ahead with the wounded. On the following day Radio Tokyo reported "One large carrier blown up and sunk, one medium carrier set ablaze and later sunk, and two heavy cruisers sunk." Imperial Headquarters commended the Rabaul air forces, terming the action "The First Air Battle of Bougainville," thus making this one of the bigger cases of falsehoods told in the entire Pacific war. For his part in the action, Ensign Berlin received a congratulatory message from Admiral Wilkinson closing with the words, "Fireplug sprinkles dog."[6]

For the PTs at Puruata Island, with the Allied landings at Empress Augusta Bay, the action was not long in coming. On the night of November 7, four enemy destroyers from Rabaul managed to land 475 troops on Torokina and departed without being intercepted by Allied naval forces. The cost was seventeen Marines dead or missing, plus thirty wounded in eliminating the invaders. This event set the stage for another crisis.

On the following night, two American destroyers, *Hudson* and *Anthony,* were patrolling the bay. They were doubly alert to prevent a repeat of the previous night. The destroyers had been told that all PTs were home. In fact, three boats were out; *PT 163* was cruising the waters and PTs *169* and *170* laying-to off the Magine Islands in the bay. Unfortunately the PT skippers had also been told there would be no other friendly vessels in the area.

When the two destroyers opened fire on what they assumed to be the enemy, the PTs maneuvered radically and, with the destroyers in hot pursuit, endeavored to make their own attacks with torpedoes: the skipper of *PT 170* radioed *PT 163* that he was "leading three Nip cans" his way, suggesting he might want to take a whack at them. The *163* skipper obliged with a long-range torpedo shot, which missed and failed to divert the pursuers.

Following a furious series of turns by both sides, the *169* and *170* boats reversed course to start a torpedo run on the "enemy;" it was then that a radio message was received from the *Anthony,* "Humblest apologies, we are friendly vessels." By good fortune the destroyer's radio operator had been monitoring the PTs' radio frequency and guessed the truth. Thus ended what became known as the Second Battle of Empress Augusta Bay.[7]

For the PTs based at the Treasuries south of Bougainville, night patrols were no less fraught with the unexpected. On the night of November 13-14, two Squadron 9 boats, *PT 154* commanded by Lt. Hamlin D. Smith and *PT 155* commanded Lt. Michael R. Pessolano were patrolling about a mile off Shortland Island, an area known to be traveled by barges.

Suddenly, the lookout saw brilliant flashes on Shortland Island; these were quickly followed by a series of "booms!" Three shells screamed through the air. One slammed down on *PT 154,* the explosion tearing a massive gap in the deck, knocking out the steering system and killing the engines. Shrapnel ripped into skin and bone; sprawled on the deck were the bodies of Lt. Joseph E.

McLaughlin and QM2/c Arthur J. Schwerdt. Seven PT crewmen were wounded, including the skipper, Lieutenant Smith. Half-conscious and in shock, Smith managed to turn command of the boat over to the remaining uninjured senior crewman, MoMM1/c John M. Nicholson. Somehow Nicholson managed to restart the engines and head the crippled PT toward the open sea and away from the shore battery.

The moment Lieutenant Pessolano had spotted the flashes and the shells began falling, he turned *PT 155* and raced toward the open sea. When he saw the *154* get hit, however, he immediately reversed course to go to the aid of the stricken PT. Since the *154*'s steering system was inoperative, approaching the wounded PT proved difficult: when Lieutenant Pessolano tried to edge his boat alongside, the two collided, the impact ripping off the *154*'s aft torpedo and tube.

Finally, with the two boats beyond range of the shore battery, Pessolano managed to successfully come alongside. The wounded were then transferred to Pessolano's boat and it immediately headed for the base in the Treasuries; Pessolano remained aboard *PT 154* and, by use of the emergency steering system, returned the battered PT to base, arriving more than two and a half hours later.[8]

By the fourteenth of November, 33,861 men and their supplies had been landed at Empress Augusta Bay. The beachhead, referred to as the Perimeter, had a circumference of a mere 16,000 yards, including the 7,000 yards of beach frontage together with Puruata Island; but for now, that was enough.

Around the beginning of the last week in November, South Pacific Intelligence began to suspect the Japanese planned to send a Tokyo Express to Buka. Although by now the Imperial Navy rightly guessed the invaders' objective was in fact Empress Augusta Bay, the Imperial Army continued to believe this was not the Americans' major landing, that it was yet to take place. As usual, where there was disagreement, the Army had its way. The Army command ordered the Navy to move 920 troops north to Buka in destroyers, and to evacuate 700 noncombat personnel.[9]

Halsey's staff immediately arranged for the Express to be intercepted on its way north from Simpson Harbor by a squadron of American destroyers at a point about thirty-five miles west of Buka.

Nine PTs led by Commander Henry Farrow would be positioned near Buka Passage to intercept the Express if it slipped by the destroyers.[10]

At approximately midnight, three PTs made radar contact on what they assumed were friendly destroyers. Mindful of recent "incidents," they headed toward shore to get out of the way. However, two ships altered course to close; at 12:30 a.m., November 25, one attempted to ram *PT 318* and both destroyers fired several 5-inch salvoes; however, the shells passed safely over the PTs.

Still convinced the ships were "friendly," the PTs scattered and sought safety in a convenient rain squall. However, *PT 64* fired a torpedo because her torpedoman misunderstood the orders, but it was not a hit. In fact, the two ships were the Japanese destroyers *Onami* and *Makinami,* the screening force for the three destroyers serving as troop transports for the Express.

When the commander of the American destroyers received the radio report of the PT contact, he accurately predicted the enemy's anticipated course. In the resultant engagement, called the Battle of Cape St. George, the American destroyer force sank the *Onami* and *Makinami* along with the *Yugiri,* one of the three destroyer-transports. Only two of the five ships departing Rabaul for Buka reached their destination.

At Rabaul, the debate among the Japanese commanders continued: did the Americans mean to stay at Torokina, or did they plan on making a true major landing elsewhere? The Army, convinced of the latter, rather than sending troops to Empress Augusta Bay, sent reinforcements north to its positions ions on the Buka Passage.

Not until sometime around December 15, was the Imperial Navy able to convince the Army that something should be done about Torokina landings. This Army's response was half-hearted; General Hyakutake sent a number of troops from the south end of Bougainville, but the Americans were waiting. PT boats, Black Cats and LCIs fitted out as gunboats, a force collectively termed the "Bougainville Navy," sank many of the troop-laden *daihatsus*; other barges simply got lost along the way. To quote one Japanese naval commander, the movement was "a dismal failure."[11]

For the Allies on Bougainville, the coming of Christmas was a great event. That day, the main objective of the landings at Empress Augusta Bay, a bomber airstrip, was completed. With it, Rabaul's doom was sealed.

But long before this, an impatient Halsey was planning his next advance. With air raids on Rabaul in progress, the U.S. Pacific Fleet engaged in operations in Micronesia, Halsey could expect no naval support for any operations before April 1. This three-month period of stagnation did not accord with Halsey's temperament. With General MacArthur's forces advancing through New Guinea, Halsey decided to take steps to "keep the offensive rolling" by securing another airfield in range of Rabaul as well as a new advanced PT base.[12]

His choice was the Green Islands, a group of atolls thirty-seven miles northwest of Buka and fifty-five miles east of East Cape, New Ireland. The largest of the atolls, Nissan, was used by the enemy only as a barge relay station. A mere 115 miles from Rabaul and 720 miles from Truk, Japan's major naval base in the Pacific and headquarters for the Combined Fleet, Nissan was also near enough to Torokina to provide fighter cover during Halsey's planned occupation.

But first, Halsey needed to know if the LSTs and other beaching craft could get through the shallow passages into the lagoon. To get the answer, he sent four PT boats from Torokina under the command of Lt. Comdr. L. Taylor on the night of January 10-11, 1944. Lead casts from the PTs showed there was seventeen feet of water through the south passage, enough for the LSTs to safely slip through.

As a result, a reconnaissance party was formed to determine how many Japanese were on the atolls and whether there was enough land there to build an airstrip. The operation was carried on the night of January 30-31. *PT 176* and *PT 178,* two of the Squadron 11 boats that made the preliminary soundings, led the landing craft as they entered the lagoon. As it turned out, only 102 Japanese were discovered, along with 1200 Melanesians, natives that were so friendly to Americans and hostile to the Japanese that the usual preliminary naval and aerial bombardment was omitted.

Upon receiving a report on the mission, Admiral Halsey set D-Day for securing the atolls as February 15. Support for the landing was provided by cruisers, destroyers, and eighteen PT boats from Torokina under the command of Lieutenant Commander Taylor, including boats from Squadron 10 led by Lt. Comdr. Jack E. Gibson.[13]

The Green Islands landings proved to be an easy operation, providing a useful link in the Allied ring around Rabaul. On February 17, an advanced PT base was established on Nissan, and Squadron 10 led by Lieutenant Commander Gibson began patrolling the nearby waters. In a larger sense, the Green Islands' base permitted the PT boats to extend their patrols to New Ireland and along the outer coast of Bougainville to Choiseul. One boat, *PT 319* commanded by Ens. Richard H. Lewin, even slipped into Rabaul's Simpson Harbor in the early hours of March 1, making it the first Allied vessel to "show the flag" in the harbor. But under the circumstances the PT didn't stay long.

Not one to rest on his laurels, Admiral Halsey proceeded to add yet another link in the ring around Rabaul. This time the choice was Emirau Island of the St. Matthias Group, situated halfway between Kavieng, New Ireland and the Admiralties. On March 14 Admiral Wilkinson received the order "to seize and occupy Emirau" at the earliest practicable date, not later than March 20. A verdant and beautiful island the Japanese had taken, Emirau was peacefully occupied by the 4th Marine Regiment on March 20. Within a month, a PT base had been established and shortly after May 1, the first airstrip was completed there.

Meanwhile, the battle on Bougainville continued. Not until the end of December had General Hyakutake become convinced the Americans really intended to stay at Torokina. The general, naming his all-effort to capture "the Perimeter" in March the "TA" operation, now ordered twelve thousand combat troops to Empress Augusta Bay, including the 6th Infantry Division, referred to previously. The commander of the Division, Lt. Gen Masatane Kanda, rallied his veterans with the words:

"We must fight to the end to avenge the shame of our country's humiliation at Guadalcanal.... There can be no rest until our bastard foes are battered and bowed in shame—til their bright red blood adds yet more luster to the badge of the 6th Division."

So confident were the Japanese Army in final victory that on March 17 the enemy planned a celebration of a glorious victory. Even the spot where General Griswold, commanding the Allied Perimeter defense, would unconditionally accept surrender, was marked on a map.

But there were obstacles: As Hyakutake's troops made their way toward Empress Augusta Bay, the U.S. Navy made every effort to prevent the use of the sea as a means of reaching the Perimeter. As usual, most night intercepts were carried out by PT boats aided by Black Cats. By now, General Griswold's defense inside the Perimeter numbered twenty-seven thousand combat troops, including the U.S. 37th Inf. Division, the Americal Division (see Glossary) and the 3rd Marine Defense Battalion. Offshore, the "Bougainville Navy" now consisted of six U.S. destroyers and PT Squadron 20, equipped with Higgins PTs, led by Lt. Comdr. Thomas G. Warfield; plus, several LCI gunboats patrolled.[14]

Rear Admiral Isamu Takeda, charged with the defense of Choiseul, the Shortlands and the northeast coast of Bougainville, boasted that, in spite of them, he managed to boat 1400 men up to Empress Augusta Bay. Maybe. But it was also true that the PTs, LCIs and Black Cats, maintaining nightly patrols off Bougainville during the month of February, alone or in combination, had twelve fights with *daihatsus*, plus, they bombarded enemy shore positions thirteen times.[15]

On March 9 the enemy's first major ground attack occurred and Japanese troops gained a toehold. Not until March 12 was the U.S. 37th Division, after bitterly fought battles, able to dislodge the enemy. Meanwhile, as naval support, the Bougainville Navy including the Puruata-based PTs patrolled each night hunting for *daihatsus* bringing enemy reinforcements, since it was known that General Kanda planned a counterlanding on the Torokina beaches. As a consequence, General Griswold credited the Navy's destroyers and PTs with preventing an attack from that quarter.

On the 17th, having failed to penetrate the Perimeter, the enemy withdrew with heavy losses. On the 27th the struggle finally ended. By actual count, enemy losses numbered 5469 dead, as against 263 Americans soldiers killed, missing or dead from wounds.

Despite the setback, General Hyakutake planned a new offensive in May. Admiral Takeda dispatched his barges along the coast of Bougainville. But again the PTs and Black Cats effectively countered the movement. By May 1, with the Allied advances, the Japanese on Bougainville were isolated as an effective force in the war. With PTs patrolling the coast at night and Allied aircraft dominating the sea at daylight, the rice ration of Japanese soldiers on the island, which had been 700 grams daily before the Americans landed on Torokina, was cut to 250 grams in April and to nothing in September. As a result Hyakutake had to employ a large part of his force raising foodstuffs. Morale fell deplorably; in his narrative, Admiral Takeda, noted robberies, insubordination and even mutiny followed. In a repeat of other bypassed islands, hundreds of soldiers deserted and wandered through the jungle, living on anything they could find, even snakes, rats and crocodiles. The admiral made no mention of cannibalism, but in New Guinea, and later in the Philippines, places at which similar conditions prevailed, the Japanese army is known to have experienced occasions of cannibalism.

In the end, with the battle for the Perimeter over, General Griswold paid tribute to his troops and the support provided by U.S. Navy destroyers, PT boats and LCIs that enabled the Americans to defeat the Japanese in this key struggle in the Allied advance across the Pacific.[16]

CHAPTER SEVENTEEN

TARGET:
DUTCH NEW GUINEA

As the campaign for the Solomons wound to an end, more PT squadrons were transferred to New Guinea. In April 1944, Squadron 24, based at Saidor, was reinforced by Squadron 10 led by Lieutenant Commander Gibson; this was the first of the PT squadrons to be transferred to New Guinea from another combat theater. By now, Saidor-based PTs ranged as far west as Hansa Bay, completing a total of 185 patrols by the end of June. Shortly, however, MacArthur's troops managed to advance so far west that for the PTs, Saidor was in turn, too far removed from the fighting.[1]

In the meantime, adding to the PTs' difficulties was the old problem of poor communications. On the morning of March 27, an Australian P-40 fighter squadron based on Kiriwina Island prepared for a flight for the usual morning sweep.

Normally the night-patrolling PTs would have been home by this time. Sadly a report indicating PT boats were still in the area this morning was misfiled by a squadron clerk: *PT 353* commanded by Ens. George H. Guckert from Squadron 25, with *PT 121* under the command of Ens. Richard B. Secrest from the veteran Squadron 8 were still out. They had entered Bangula Bay on their way home. As officer in tactical command, Lt. Crowell C. Hall aboard Ens. Guckert's *353* had orders to investigate a reported enemy schooner inside the bay.

At 7:45 a.m. four Australian P-40s flew over the two PT boats. Lieutenant Hall radioed the pilots, requesting they investigate the schooner that lay beyond the PTs on a dangerous reef. The Australians complied then informed Lieutenant Hall that the vessel had already been strafed and was not worth further attention. The P-40s then continued on their way.[2]

As the two PTs started for home, a second flight of four P-40s approached accompanied by two Beaufighters. The four P-40s and one Beaufighter attacked the two PTs, making a strafing pass. The pilot of the second Beaufighter, recognizing the two vessels as PT boats, attempted to radio his companions, but his words went unheard in the excitement of the attack.

In accord with the policy of the PT command if attacked by "friendly" aircraft not to the return fire, the commanders of the PTs held their gunners under tight control refusing to allow them to fire in defense while the aircraft riddled the boats; both boats finally exploded and sank.[3]

The first four P-40s that had earlier assisted the PTs by inspecting the schooner, upon hearing the radio transmissions of the second group of P-40s suspected the worse and turned back. Over the bay they dropped a life raft to the survivors and radioed headquarters about the disaster. Two PTs were immediately dispatched to the scene. The final toll was the worst thus far experienced by PTs due to an air attack: in addition to the two lost PTs, four officers and four enlisted men had been killed, four officers and eight enlisted men wounded, all because a clerk had mistakenly handled a report.[4]

As tragic as this was, worse was soon to follow: on the night of April 28, nearly a month to the day after the disaster in Bangula Bay, *PT 347* commanded by Lt.(jg) Robert J. Williams and *PT 350* under the command of Lt.(jg) Stanley L. Manning were patrolling off the south coast of New Britain when the *347* ran hard aground on a reef at Cape Pomas, only five miles from the line separating General MacArthur's New Guinea area of operations from Admiral Halsey's Solomons area of command.

The grounding was not in itself critical. As noted, it was not uncommon for PT boats prowling close to island shores to run aground on uncharted reefs. Most were refloated having suffered minor damage. In this case, crewmen on the second PT passed a line to the stranded *347* and began the familiar task of trying to free the grounded boat. By daylight they had yet to succeed.

At 7 a.m., two Marine Corps Corsairs appeared: the aircraft were based at the Green Islands recently seized by Admiral Halsey's forces. The pilots were making a routine early-morning sweep in search of signs of the enemy; as usual, they had been told they would encounter no friendly vessels.

Owing to an error in navigation, the Corsairs unknowingly crossed the line dividing Halsey's and MacArthur's area. The pilots attacked; this time the PT gunners opened fire, bringing down one Corsair on the first pass. But three men on *PT 350* were killed by the Corsairs' bullets and both boats were badly shot up.[5]

The PTs radioed their tender *Hilo* at Talasea, asking for air cover. The tender radioed Cape Gloucester requesting air support and dispatched a third boat, *PT 346* skippered by Lt.(jg) James R. Burk to the scene for assistance.

Back at the Green Islands, there was also a rush of activity. Word from the one Corsair pilot that the second plane had been shot down during an attack on two vessels he identified as 125-foot gunboats prompted a virtual air armada to respond: Four Corsairs, six TBF "Avengers," four F6Fs, and eight SBDs headed toward Lassul Bay, the location identified by the Corsair as the location of the attack. When the armada from the Green Islands arrived at Lassul Bay and found it empty, they also wandered across the line into MacArthur's area at Cape Pomas, just seconds in flying time away.

By then *PT 346* had arrived. When the PT crews sighted the approaching aircraft, they recognized them as American planes and, assuming they were the air cover sent from Cape Gloucester, continued their salvage efforts. Their first hint that they were wrong came when bombs began to fall. The PT crews tried every trick they knew to identify themselves as "friendly," but without success. When the attacks continued, the PT gunners opened fire, bringing down a second plane. Shortly *PT 346* and *347* went to the bottom.[6]

The aircraft group's flight commander radioed for a PBY to be dispatched from the Green Islands to pick up the downed pilot. The Catalina never found the pilot; however, it did find thirteen PT boat survivors. Their arrival back at the Green Islands was the first indication to the shocked pilots and base command officers of the tragedy. The final cost: three PT officers and eleven enlisted men dead, two pilots lost, four PT officers and nine men wounded, two PTs sunk and two aircraft lost.[7]

But given MacArthur's relentless effort to advance, there was little time to mourn. Having secured the Admiralties, the general had to decide where next to land troops while continuing to avoid strong enemy positions. To his staff, bypassing Madang and Hansa Bay and landing at Wewak, 150 miles west of Madang was the answer.

To General Adachi commanding the 18th Army with headquarters at Madang, such a plan also seemed logical. Having been forced to withdraw from Sio when MacArthur seized Saidor, Adachi concluded he should withdraw from Madang. With the Admiralties in Allied hands, PTs based at Saidor and Allied aircraft made it difficult for Japanese supplies to reach Madang. He ordered his 20th and 51st Divisions to fall back seventy miles to Hansa Bay, and his 41st Division to move back 150 miles to Wewak. When MacArthur's troops landed at Hansa Bay, as Adachi expected, the Japanese would be waiting.

It was a view Imperial Headquarters shared, to a point. In light of MacArthur's recent successes, the high command had become more concerned about the menace in New Guinea than Admiral Halsey's recent landings at Torokina. As a consequence, fresh troops had been poured into New Guinea and a partial Army reorganization was made. The Second Army, commanded by Lt. Gen. Fusataro Teshima, with headquarters on New Guinea's Vogelkop Peninsula at Manokwari was given a new division from China in December. By March, when two more divisions were ordered from China, his zone of responsibility extended to Wewak. On March 25 he ordered Adachi to withdraw his three battered divisions to Hollandia. But the commander of the 18th Army, convinced the next Allied landings would be at Hansa Bay, stalled.

In fact, General Teshima was correct; Hollandia would be MacArthur's next objective. When MacArthur learned from his intelligence of Adachi's conviction, he naturally did all he could to confirm his belief. PT boats patrolled aggressively at night near Hansa Bay and Wewak, Fifth Air Force aircraft bombed the areas heavily in a pattern suggesting imminent amphibious landings and on two occasions, destroyers covered by fighters bombarded Hansa Bay.[8]

But the entire Japanese high command was not fooled by MacArthur's ruse. General K. Anami in Davao, superior to both Adachi and Teshima, concerned by the former's failure to strengthen Hollandia's defense, on April 12 sent his chief of staff to Wewak to expedite the movement west. As a result, by the time MacArthur's leap to central New Guinea was underway, two regiments of the 18th Army were already on their way there over the jungle trails.[9]

MacArthur's plan to land troops at Hollandia, code named Operation "Reckless," probably a reflection of Brisbane's view of landing troops so deep inside enemy territory, was indeed bold. From Hollandia, the general would be in position to seize the remaining key points necessary to make his leap back to the Philippines.

With D-Day April 22, final plans called for three simultaneous amphibious landings in Dutch New Guinea. From an Allied naval point of view, with sixty thousand troops, this was the largest amphibious operation thus far to be attempted in the Southwest Pacific. Naval support would be provided by Task Force 77 under the command of Rear Admiral D.E. Barbey. Eight escort carriers and seventeen destroyers, temporarily on loan from the U.S. Fifth Fleet in the Central Pacific, augmented MacArthur's Fifth Air Force providing air support.

On April 22, troops of the U.S. 24th and 41st Divisions began landing at Tanahmerah and Humboldt Bays, separated by thirty miles. In fact, Hollandia was the American name for Humboldt Bay; Hollandia was a small village located in a bight on the west shore. At both landing sites, Allied troops soon found themselves heavily engaged.

Simultaneously, the third landing was carried out at the village of Aitape, 120 miles east of Hollandia; the purpose here was to isolate the fifty thousand men of the 18th Army. Little opposition was encountered by the initial waves. By nightfall, at the cost of two killed and thirteen wounded, Aitape had been taken by Allied troops.[10]

Soon after the landings at Aitape, anticipating heavy enemy barge movements against Aitape, Squadron 7 under the command of Lt. Comdr. Robert Leeson arrived followed by Squadron 8 led by Lt. Edward Farley, its newly appointed commander. Squadron 18 commanded by Lieutenant Commander Swift moved up from Saidor to Humboldt, followed shortly by Squadron 12 commanded by Lt. Comdr. Robert J. Buckley, Jr.[11]

Night patrols began immediately. Soon the Aitape PTs, patrolling east from Aitape began to make contact. On the night of April 28-29, two PTs, one commanded by Ens. Francis L. Cappaert, the other by Ens. Louis A. Fanget, intercepted three barges in Nightingale Bay, east of Wewak. One barge was carrying two artillery pieces and forty-five men. This time, the PTs had additional orders: owing to a need for intelligence that the Japanese preferred death to capture, the crews would need to be resourceful if they were to succeed in their effort. With the enemy swimming, survivors of destroyed barges, one method adopted called for the PT boat to be maneuvered alongside the swimmer allowing a crewman to hit the reluctant enemy in the head with a boat hook, knocking him out or dazing him so that he could be hoisted on deck. A second method had a crewman lowering a cargo net over the PT's bow: two crew members would then crawl down the net and club the defiant swimmer in the head. A line would then be slipped under the enemy's arms allowing him to be hauled aboard. As is obvious, both methods were difficult to perform in the blackness of night with a swimmer seeking to evade capture.[12]

On this night, having sunk the three barges, the two PTs endeavored to take captives. Despite their best efforts, they managed to hook only two swimmers. However, one of the men, an Army officer, proved to be an exception to the rule, telling his captors that more barges were on the way to the bay. The PTs waited with engines muffled. Less than thirty minutes later, the sound of diesels was heard; soon three barges emerged out of the darkness. Again the roar of PT guns shattered the quiet of the night; tracers arced from the PTs toward the enemy craft as a torrent of bullets and cannon shells sent the second group of barges to the bottom. Again the PTs searched for swimmers. This time the results were even less encouraging: only one swimmer was hooked and hauled aboard. The semiconscious captive, still clutching a box, proved to be another Army officer. Although he resisted, the box was taken from him and its contents examined. Intelligence officers later determined it contained secret orders for the garrison commander at Wewak.

Back at Aitape, the PT crews turned the prisoners over to intelligence officers. There, the helpful officer taken captive following the sinking of the first three barges, continued to be helpful, giving questioners a lengthy list of pending barge movements, including numbers, times, destinations and cargoes. As a consequence, PTs were assigned to positions off Wewak and Hansa Bay: during the following five consecutive nights, the PT boats sank fifteen barges and a picket boat and shot up eight additional barges.

On the night of May 2, the barge-hunting PTs from Aitape scored again, but this time there were problems: two Squadron 8 boats patrolling near Wewak intercepted and sank two *daihatsus* and shot up four more. Thus far, it had been a successful patrol. But as they started for home, *PT 114* ran aground barely four hundred yards off Kairiru Island near Wewak. With dawn approaching, the situation was critical. Preparations were made to abandon ship. But when the boat's depth charges and torpedoes were jettisoned, the second boat, *PT 144,* was able to pull it free. By now it was 6:30 a.m.[13]

With the crew of the grounded PT preparing to abandon the boat, the secret codes and confidential documents were placed in a rubber raft and the raft tied to the stern of *PT 144.*

As the two PTs belatedly headed for Aitape, an officer suddenly exclaimed" "The codes on the raft! Where the hell is the raft?" A rush to the fantail confirmed the awful truth: There was no raft there. During the excitement and confusion in refloating the *144,* the raft had apparently become untied and floated away. Were it to fall into the hands of the Japanese, the information could be highly damaging.

Back at Aitape, the two mortified PT skippers reported the loss to Lieutenant Commander Leeson. The Squadron 7 commander immediately jumped aboard *PT 129* commanded by his brother, Ens. A. Dix Leeson, and headed back to search for the missing raft.

Accompanying *PT 129* was *PT 134* skippered by Ens. Edmund F. Wakelin.

Late that afternoon, they spotted the raft, but it was on the beach in clear view of a native village on Kairiru Island. Nearby were Japanese shore batteries; and a mere six hundred yards separated the raft from an enemy structure of some type.

The PT officers held a quick conference: then, without further discussion, Commander Leeson stripped off his uniform, plunged into the sea in his underwear and began swimming the four hundred yards to the shore. With the two PTs laying-to this close to shore in broad daylight, Leeson and the crews expected to hear the chatter of machine guns or the boom of a shore battery at any minute.

Swimming rapidly the squadron commander reached the shore. A quick check showed the contents were still there and apparently untouched. With the raft in tow, Leeson charged back into the water and began to swim back to the boats. Moments after he climbed to the deck of *PT 129,* the boom of a shore battery, barely a half-mile away, echoed across the water. The Japanese had finally spotted the boats, but too late. Thanks to good luck, the raft was already recovered and the PTs were able to successfully escape to the open sea.

However, with the day almost ended, Leeson was not yet ready to go home. With darkness, he led the two PTs back toward the Kairiru shore; soon they encountered three heavily laden barges; following a fierce exchange of gunfire, two barges were sunk and the third damaged. Then a shore battery opened fire and a shell ripped into Ensign Leeson's boat blowing a fourteen-inch hole in an exhaust stack and starting a fire beneath one of the Packard engines. MoMM2/c Clarence L. Nelson on duty in the engine room, grabbed a fire extinguisher and, assisted by MoMM3/c A. F. Hall, managed to put the fire out, but both men were overcome by carbon dioxide and exhaust fumes in the process. Ensign Richard Holt dashed into the engine room to the rescue: the men were revived after receiving artificial respiration.

Despite operating on only two engines, Leeson's PT led the way back toward the shore; there the two boats unleashed a salvo of twenty-four rockets in the direction of the flashes made by the shore batteries; with the enemy guns silent, the boats finally headed for home.

The rockets used by Commander Leeson's boats that proved so effective against the shore batteries had been a recent addition. In early 1944, the Navy had begun experiments with five-inch spin stabilized rockets with a flatter trajectory and a longer range than earlier products; this gave the PTs a tremendous punch that, in theory, could disable a destroyer. Although the new weapon added more weight to the already heavily loaded boats, it was decided to equip them with two Mk 50 launchers providing a total salvo capacity of sixteen rockets with one reload. So destructive was the resultant firepower that one official field report concluded:

"Commander Motor Torpedo Boat Squadrons Seventh Fleet has requested that every rocket development be thoroughly investigated with a view to possible employment by PTs and that the development of a 'motor rocket boat' be considered. If the present ratio of launcher to projection weight is maintained, and all PT armament except the turret twin fifties is removed, it would be possible to carry 5 tons of rocket equipment and deliver 4 tons of projectiles at the target at ranges in excess of 5,000 yards. This would give PTs tremendous firepower—greatly in excess of what they now have.

"The speed of rockets as compared with that of torpedoes should make them easier to hit targets with. With the development of radar on enemy ships, it may be more difficult to close them to a few hundred yards for a torpedo hit. Also the reliability of rockets would seem to be much greater than that of torpedoes and they will not require the same painstaking care. It is believed that all these advantages, plus the greater weight of explosive which can be delivered to the target, more than compensates for the torpedoes' single advantage of underwater destructive power."[14]

In what was remarkable prescience, the writer had foreseen the development of the post-war missile boat, a small vessel similar in concept to the PT boat, one that would be first introduced by the

Soviet Navy using the 80-foot Elco and 78-foot Higgins PTs received from the United States during and after the war. Replacing torpedoes, their main armament would be four cruise missiles capable of speed greater than sound, with a range in excess of twenty-five nautical miles. Fitted with warheads and launched in pairs as was the practice with torpedoes, such missiles would have the capability of destroying a full-sized warship. But such technology was yet to be developed; the Mk 50 rockets with their advantages, as will be demonstrated, left much to be desired when employed by PT boats.

Back at Aitape there was increased tension. Word had come that General Adachi's 18th Army was moving west from Wewak, ninety miles east of Aitape. On May 2, Adachi's superiors had ordered him to move by jungle trail inland, bypassing Aitape and Hollandia to reach western New Guinea.

But Adachi had a mind of his own: he proposed another plan, to retake Aitape, and Rabaul approved. With the attack planned for June 10, the Japanese general gathered twenty thousand men, all he could muster, and started west, his men traveling by foot over jungle trails, some by barge. However, weather conditions, a shortage of supplies and the presence of PT boats lurking along the shore strafing the troops slowed his progress, causing the men to fall behind schedule.[15]

In fact, for PT boats, strafing Japanese troops, either camping or traveling along a shore, was one of their most enjoyable tasks, one that came closest to being a sport. The June 23 diary entry of Lt.(jg) James Cunningham on *PT 144*, a Squadron 8 boat, provides a vivid description of one such instance. That night, accompanied by *PT 189*, Cunningham's PT departed Aitape to patrol west:

"We closed the beach at Sowam after noticing lots of moving lights. They appeared to be trucks, moving very slow. We muffled down, hidden by a black, moonless night, we sneaked to within 50 yards off the beach and waited for a truck to come around the bend and on to a short stretch of road than ran along the beach. Here came one, lights blazing. Both boats blasted away. The last we saw of the truck (shore batteries fired on us immediately, so we got out) it was still

standing there with headlights burning and flames leaping up
in the New Guinea night. It has become quite a sport, by the
way, shooting enemy trucks moving along the beach with
lights on. The Japs never seem to learn. We fire at them night
after night. They turn off the lights briefly, then turn them
back on again when they think we have gone. But we haven't
gone. So we shoot them up some more, and they turn off the
lights again. And so on all night long.[16]

In fact, the enemy was not as incapable of responding as
Cunningham indicated. His entry three nights later tells a different
story:

June 26, 1944: PTs *144* and *149* left Aitape base, New
Guinea to patrol toward Sowam Village, where the road
comes down to the beach. We were after trucks. We closed
cautiously to three-quarters of a mile off the beach, then it
seemed that everything opened up on us, 50 and 30 calibers,
40 mms and 3-inchers. At the time they fired on us we were
dead in the water, with all engines in neutral. To get the
engines into gear, the drill is to signal the engine room where
the motor mac of the watch puts the engines in gear by hand.
There is no way to do it from the cockpit. Then, when the
gears are engaged, the skipper can control the speed by the
three throttles.

I was at the helm in the cockpit when the batteries
opened fire, and I shoved all three throttles wide open,
forgetting that the gears weren't engaged. Of course, the boat
almost shook apart from the wildly racing engines, but we
didn't move. The motor mac in the engine room below
wrestled against me to push the throttles back. He was
stronger than I was and finally got the engines slowed down
enough to put them into gear. Then we got moving fast. We
made it out to sea OK without being hit, but I sure pulled a
boo boo that time.[17]

Although slowed by such obstacles, Adachi's troops continued
toward Aitape. In any event, Allied intelligence kept MacArthur

informed as to the enemy's progress. On June 21, captured Japanese documents disclosed Adachi's plan of attack. As a result, Allied reinforcements in the form of the U.S. 43rd Division, then in New Zealand, along with the 112th Cavalry and 124th Infantry Regiments in eastern New Guinea were hurriedly shipped to Aitape.

At 11:45 p.m. July 10 General Adachi's troops launched a screaming attack on the Aitape defenders that was repulsed, with heavy losses on both sides. Thus began the bitterest and biggest jungle battle to occur in New Guinea since the Buna-Gona campaign. For a full month, the two sides fought in the thick jungle around Aitape. Despite heavy losses, Adachi continued the assault, throwing two divisions into the struggle.

Offshore, in what was a virtual replay of the Admiralties, the U.S. Navy provided key support: the PTs at Aitape, operating along the coast between Wewak and Aitape, strafed the shore, breaking up known concentrations of enemy forces along the coastal road and trails, and intercepted barges supplying Adachi's forces.[18]

As the battle raged, on July 10, Vice Admiral T.C. Kinkaid, who had replaced Admiral Carpender as commander of the Seventh Fleet, issued an order that was never heard in the Solomons: he ordered Commodore John Collins, RAN, then in Seeadler Harbor, to support the PTs at Aitape being harassed by enemy shore batteries. On July 13, Collins arrived with four Australian cruisers and two U.S. destroyers. From July 14 to the 24th, when Collins was withdrawn to cover MacArthur's landings at Sansapor, farther west, the cruisers bombarded targets inland, and the destroyers working with PT boats at night searched for barges and truck travel on coastal roads as far east as Karawop, fourteen miles northwest of Wewak. Throughout this period, no difficulties occurred due to the PTs working in close proximity to heavy Allied warships.[19]

By now, with Allied air superiority established, the Aitape PTs were beginning to run daylight as well as night patrols. The PT skippers worked out a system whereby the daylight patrols would be accompanied by P-39 fighters or the rugged and equally lethal Beaufighters based at Aitape flown by pilots of the Royal Australian Air Force.[20]

The combination proved lethal. On June 26, one of the more successful combined missions occurred when a Beaufighter pilot radioed the PTs suggesting they investigate possible enemy activity on the coast of nearby Muschu Island. Two Squadron 7 boats, *PT 130* commanded by Lt. Ian Malcolm and *PT 132,* with Ens. Paul Jones at the helm, approached the island. The enemy was certainly there; however, the PTs were almost as close as two hundred feet from shore before the crews discerned two heavily camouflaged *daihatsus* covered by nets of greenery. In fact, they had stumbled on an entire fleet. The PT boats immediately opened fire, making four passes. On the final run, they counted fourteen barges riddled, six on fire. The flames soon spread ashore; as the PTs departed to return to base for more ammunition, a tremendous explosion erupted, probably an ammunition dump set off by the fire. As the PTs headed away, flames and smoke billowed skyward.

In the early hours of the following morning, PT boats returned to finish the destruction. This time they were accompanied by four P-39 RAAF fighters, each carrying bombs. As the aircraft circled overhead, the PTs made four more strafing runs, then fired a salvo of rockets. The boats then withdrew and the P-39s finished the job, strafing and bombing the site.

On August 9, the battle for Aitape finally ended. With ammunition and supplies exhausted due to the interdiction of his supply lines, Adachi was forced to withdraw. By then he had sacrificed about half of his twenty thousand men in what had been a futile attempt to retake Aitape. But it had cost the U.S. Army a reported four hundred killed, and about 2600 wounded, to beat back the attackers.[21]

For the PTs at Aitape, after five months of operations, the record stood at 115 barges sunk, plus untold numbers of coastal installations destroyed by strafing. Considering the fierceness of the conflict, PT casualties were remarkably light, three crewmen killed and seven wounded, eleven PTs hit by enemy fire, and one boat, *PT 133,* lost in action.[22]

Even as the battle for Aitape raged, MacArthur, undeterred by the struggle, having taken Hollandia, was preparing plans to launch a series of assaults in his advance west; his ultimate objective, Mindanao in the Philippines by November 15. In barely more than three months, four operations—Wakde, Biak, Noemfoor, Sansapor, would carry MacArthur to the northwest tip of New Guinea, Vogelkop, 550 miles west of Hollandia.

As usual, MacArthur's PTs were quick to secure forward bases in what was now a breathless race back to the Philippines.[23] On the morning of May 18, troops of the 41st Division landed at Wakde Island, 125 miles west of Hollandia and two miles off the enemy-held New Guinea coast. Although Wakde Island was only about one-and-a-half miles long and a mile wide, it possessed several enemy airstrips.

Three days later, Wadke was in Allied hands. Thirty PTs then moved up from Hollandia in preparation to support ground operations further west.[24]

MacArthur's next target was Biak, 185 miles west of Wadke and 1500 miles from Brisbane. The largest of the Schouten Islands, perched in the mouth of Geelvink Bay, Biak is covered with low, flat-topped hills supporting a thick jungle growth. Most of the coast is ringed by a coral reef. The island has no natural harbors, thus adding to the difficulties facing an invading force.

Allied intelligence estimates regarding expectant enemy opposition were vague; at most, no more than two thousand Japanese troops were believed to be on Biak. In fact, on May 27, D-Day, the day of the Biak invasion, there were ten thousand enemy soldiers on the island, a number almost equal to that of the attackers. The core of the enemy's defense was the 222nd Regiment, crack troops, veterans of the campaign in China, supported by a naval special base force of 1500 men under Rear Admiral Sadatoshi Senda.

As soon as word of Allied landings at Hollandia reached the Japanese, they were certain Biak was on the Allied list of objectives. The local commander prepared a typical defense. With positions dug in caves along the cliffs and in underground bunkers, the conflict would be the sort of head-on confrontation MacArthur had managed to avoid since the Buna conflict in the early part of the New Guinea campaign.

On D-Day, following a pre-bombardment by Allied warships, MacArthur's forces began landing on Biak. Initially, the troops advanced with slight opposition. It was the quiet before the storm. Soon the battle became a slugfest. Every step was purchased with blood by GIs wielding rifles, bayonets, machine guns, flames throwers, and even knives.

Six days after the initial assault, the major PT base in New Guinea was moved forward hundreds of miles from Dreger Harbor to Mios Woendi, a small atoll ten miles south of Biak.[25] In contrast to virtually all other advanced PT bases in the South Pacific, Mios Woendi comprised a deep-water lagoon and flat, white sandy beaches, festooned with palm trees.

Not surprisingly, the arrival of the PTs at the new base did not pass unnoticed. Within forty-eight hours, Tokyo Rose let the PT crews know they were far from forgotten. After playing a number of popular American records as was her practice, she greeted them with a sultry, "Hello, you sexy fellows in PT Squadron 12; we know where you are," then added ominously, "We'll be over to see you in the morning. Nighty night."[26]

Expecting the worst, the crews spent a restless night, and at dawn manned their guns. Shortly, a Zero roared in just above the waves and dropped a bomb that exploded close to the fantail of *PT 190* before disappearing in the distance. Still uneasy, and expecting more would follow, for the next two weeks the crews manned their guns at dawn, but no further attacks were made.

Immediately the boats began to blockade Biak, preventing the arrival of barges carrying enemy supplies and reinforcements. Although the PT boats found less action than the boats at Aitape, it was still intense. On the morning of June 12, *PT 326* commanded by Lt. Ken Molloy, the All-American lacrosse player from Syracuse University, was patrolling off Biak. Suddenly, four Zeros attacked out of the sun: four bombs exploded within a boat-length of the *326.* The alert PT gunners opened fire and one Zero, hit by the PT's cannon fire, crashed in flames.[27]

Continuing on, the Zeros spotted a bigger target, the U.S. destroyer *Kalk,* one of four destroyers escorting a group of LSTs arriving at Biak. The *Kalk* was working up to flank speed when a single Zero dropped a bomb heavily damaging her superstructure and causing extensive damage in the forward engine and boiler rooms. Raging fires broke out below decks: four officers and twenty-six men were killed or missing, four officers and thirty-six men were wounded.[28]

On Mios Woendi, the PT crews had observed the action. Immediately the boats raced from the lagoon and headed for the crippled ship. One after the other, the boats edged alongside the destroyer, still under way to evade additional air attacks. With wounded transferred aboard from the *Kalk,* the PTs raced to *LST 468,* a vessel nearby carrying a surgical team.

That night, as the battle on Biak continued, two PTs patrolled off the north side of Biak where the Japanese were trying to slip reinforcements ashore. *PT 190* commanded by Lt. Bill Bannard was accompanied by *PT 146* under the command of Lt. Jack C. Higgins. Shortly, lookouts spotted the dim outlines of three barges. The firepower of the PTs' guns, .50-caliber bullets, 20-, 37- and 40-mm cannon shells quickly sent all three to the bottom with two hundred members of the 202 Pioneer (Engineer) Unit along with their commander, Lieutenant Commander Nagata.[29]

However, again, the PTs did not always emerge unscathed. Early in June, when Biak proved more difficult than expected, General MacArthur's staff searched for airfield sites further west looking for a foothold on the Vogelkop Peninsula. About midway between Biak and Manokwari lies the almost circular island of Noemfoor, about eleven miles in diameter. Like Biak, Noemfoor is jungle-covered. A coral reef surrounds the island, penetrated by only a few channels. By this time in 1944, the Japanese had completed three airstrips on Noemfoor, thus making the island an Allied prize.

On June 5, MacArthur warned General Krueger, commanding ground troops, that it might be necessary to capture Noemfoor. On the 14th, MacArthur directed his staff to prepare plans to seize the island only two weeks later; D-Day would finally be set for July 2.

Distrusting maps based on aerial photographic reconnaissance, General Krueger requested a reconnaissance by scouts. On the night of June 22-23, two Mios Woendi boats, *PT 331* under the command of now Lt.(jg) promoted from ensign, Kermit Montz, the former football star from Franklin and Marshall University, accompanied by *PT 193* commanded by Lt. Cyrus R. Taylor, once a star back on the Yale football team were dispatched to Noemfoor. Aboard was a group of Army scouts assigned to examine the beaches off Kamiri. The PTs landed the scouts successfully, but the scouts were forced to quickly withdraw when they were detected by the Japanese, accomplishing little other than alerting the enemy.

Not yet ready to head for home, the two PTs continued to patrol Noemfoor. Shortly, lookouts spotted a light ashore, then more lights. The enemy's confidence so far behind the lines had led to carelessness. The two PTs, engines muffled, slipped silently in close to shore and unleashed the full power of their guns, the tracers from the PTs' guns arching shoreward: immediately the lights disappeared, evidence of the probable carnage created ashore. For the brawny six-foot, two-inch Taylor, such aggressive action against the enemy was typical. Known to his admiring crew and the men of Squadron 12 as "The Cypress," Taylor was something of a legend owing to his bold and dashing style in attacking the enemy, no small feat in a squadron with its own reputation for boldness in action.[30]

Shortly, the two PTs detected two *daihatsus* near the shore. Typically, Taylor immediately charged with the *193*'s guns blazing. One barge sank promptly; however, the second, burning brightly, remained afloat. Followed by *PT 331*, Taylor circled wide and started a second run to finish off the burning vessel. Suddenly there was a grinding crunching sound; the two crews were staggered: both PTs had run aground on a reef a short distance from the burning barge.

With only one screw still undamaged, Montz was able to back free. But Taylor's PT remained stuck fast. Ammunition on the burning barge began to explode, continuing for the next three hours as "The Cypress" and his sweating crew, illuminated by the glow of the flames from the burning barge, struggled to refloat the *193* boat.

Suddenly, just before 4:30 a.m., the situation became more critical. Japanese trucks arrived on the shore, barely a half-mile away. To the harried Taylor and his men it was evident the enemy was preparing to set up a gun to fire on the stranded PT at point blank range.

Having no choice, Taylor ordered the *193* abandoned, and for the crew to make their way to the *331* lying close by. Most of the men scrambled into a rubber raft and paddled toward Montz's boat; Taylor remained behind with three men to destroy secret materials. That done, the *193* skipper went below and dumped gasoline in the bilges to assure the boat would be completely destroyed.[31]

Suddenly a massive explosion shattered the night. The highly volatile 100-octane gasoline had ignited prematurely. Flames shot skyward from the *193.* The horror-stricken crewmen on the rubber raft looked back to see a few heads bobbing in the water near the burning boat. Then, aboard the PT a dark figure appeared, staggering through the flames before leaping overboard. It was "The Cypress!"

Lieutenant Montz called for volunteers to go to the rescue of the four men in the water. With the boat in flames and the enemy gun ashore likely to fire at any moment, this was likely to be a suicide mission. Moments later, volunteers of the *331* were rapidly paddling a raft toward the men in the water. Quickly the dazed survivors were hauled into the raft. The last man to be reached was the badly burned Lieutenant Taylor.

Aboard the *331* the tension grew: how long would it be before what appeared to be a 3-inch gun on the beach began firing? Back alongside the *331,* the men had difficulty lifting Taylor's inert 225-pound body to the PT's deck from the bobbing raft. But desperation gave them the necessary strength.

Once aboard the PT, the *193* skipper was carried below and given morphine as the boat headed back to base at its best speed. Along the way, the *331* was met by a boat carrying the Squadron 12 commander, Lt. Comdr. Robert Buckley, who had been informed of the disaster by radio. Accompanying Buckley were a doctor and two medical aides. They treated Taylor as the boat continued on the Biak. There the burned skipper was transferred to a hospital ship for further treatment.

That night, the indestructible Taylor died. Word of his passing cast a thick pall over Mios Woendi. But the war had to go on. However, the men did what they could. They renamed Mios Woendi Camp Taylor in honor of the gallant Taylor, an officer whose passing was deeply mourned by his crew as well as the men in the squadron.[32]

Although the PTs at Mios Woendi did not encounter as many barges as the boats at Aitape, June and July were nonetheless profitable. By the time the ground troops on Biak had routed the enemy, the PTs were having to range as far as the northern shores of Geelvink Bay in their search for targets. With Japanese air power virtually nonexistent in the area, the PT boats were now commonly carrying out daylight as well as night patrols.

In the role of coping with isolated, bypassed Japanese troops, the PTs of New Guinea served a special role in MacArthur's rapid advance. Lacking supplies, the enemy expected Japanese garrisons to fight to the death, winning precious time for the home islands to prepare a defense. As a result, a number of PT squadrons remained behind "the front lines" at bases like Seeadler Harbor, Aitape, and Bougainville as MacArthur's forces continued to advance to the Philippines.

As was almost always the case, the PTs found an active ally in the form of local natives. In Dutch New Guinea, natives paddled their canoes out from shore to the idling PTs offshore to tell the crews through interpreters where Japanese camps were concealed along the coast. Armed with this intelligence, PTs strafed the locations, returning later to obtain reports from the natives as to the results of their gunfire.[33]

In fact, starving, weak from diseases, bypassed Japanese became easy prey for the natives. Desperate for food, Japanese soldiers were lured away in small groups from their camps with promises of something to eat. Once they were a safe distance away, the natives overcame them and locked them in stockades. When the PT boats returned, the still starving Japanese were turned over to the crews to be transported back to base.

With the taking of prisoners for intelligence purposes now a regular part of a mission, and the enemy's demonstrated reluctance to being taken alive, PT crews had to be prepared to deal with the unpredictable. On occasion, as noted, captured prisoners would appear docile and informative. Most, however, chose death by suicide rather than capture. Sometimes an enemy would allow himself to be captured in order to kill one of his captors before being killed himself.

On the night of July 7-8, *PT 329* commanded by now promoted to Lt.(jg) William Hall, the former football star at Wabash University, and *PT 161* skippered by Lt. Rogers V. Waugh, were prowling the New Guinea coast off Cape Oransbari when their radar detected a target close to shore. It turned out to be a 150-foot lugger, a wooden-hulled cargo craft powered by diesels, creeping along in the shadow of the shoreline cliffs. With Lt. (jg) Stuart Lewis, a former University of California football player at the helm and Hall directing the boat's gun crews, *PT 329* led as the two PTs closed with engines muffled. At the point blank range of seventy-five yards, the two PTs' guns roared.

Almost immediately the lugger went under, leaving the sea dotted with the heads of swimming Japanese. A few swimmers received the boat-hook treatment and their bodies were pulled aboard the PTs. One, an especially nimble swimmer, was finally hooked and pulled on board still kicking and cursing. It turned out to be a lieutenant colonel, probably the highest-ranking officer to be captured during the campaign.

As soon as he was on deck and on his feet, the enemy officer drew his pistol and aimed it at one of the *329's* crewmen. Immediately, Lieutenant Hall smashed his huge fist into the captive's mouth, knocking him flat on the deck before he could pull the trigger.[34]

The PT skipper saved the crewman's life, but at some cost: a few days later, Hall's hand became badly infected, requiring he be hospitalized. In a liberal interpretation of the rules, to his embarrassment and the amusement of his crew and members of his squadron, Hall was awarded the Purple Heart for being wounded "in the face of the enemy."

Lt. Cunningham's diary also provides an entry concerning the perils of taking prisoners:

> "Aug 28, 1944: *PTs 188* and *144* west toward Hollandia, with a squad of Army radiomen aboard to contact a land patrol. This is enemy-held territory and the patrol was in hopes of taking prisoners.
>
> "Just after sunrise we received a message to pick up Jap prisoners at Ulau Mission. We proceeded to the mission and I asked some P-39s that were strafing the beach to cover us while we made the landing.
>
> "Lt.(jg) Harry Suttenfield, skipper of the *188,* and I launched a life raft and headed in to pick up the prisoners from the Army patrol.

"We made it OK until we got into the surf, then the breakers swamped us. There were many dead Japs lying around, and the soldiers were burning the village. The natives took the prisoners out to the boats and then swam us through the surf, pushing the raft.

We turned the prisoners over to the Army at Aitape.[35]

For the Mios Woendi PTs, the month of August was the most successful, with twenty-six barges destroyed. But the figure dropped to eight in September. By now, having lost hundreds of barges, the Japanese were withdrawing overland from territories they had earlier conquered so easily, though this meant trekking along hazardous New Guinea trails through swamps and rivers.

Ashore, advancing American soldiers were discovering disturbing signs. Ground patrols reported the possibility of cannibalism on the part of the Japanese. On August 11, the 158th Infantry Regimental headquarters received a report of fifty enemy dead after a skirmish, adding that two of their dead who had lain behind enemy lines during the night had been cannibalized. At first there was doubt the report was accurate, but this was not the case. Late in August a captured Japanese medical officer admitted surgically removing parts of dead bodies for food. Earlier, Australian troops had reported finding the grisly remains of five Japanese cadavers that had been cut up, cooked and seemingly devoured. One captured Japanese, a virtual walking skeleton, told interrogators how the Japanese, desperate for food, sent foraging parties into the jungle, and how the search parties frequently failed to return, having possibly fallen in the hands of native headhunters.[36]

On July 2, Allied troops began landing on Noemfooor as scheduled. By August 31, the island and its airstrips were in Allied hands. But already MacArthur was planning a new movement to acquire a new base at the western end of the Vogelkop Peninsula. Once that was accomplished he would pivot and take the first step toward the Philippines, his long-awaited objective

In August 1944, even as the battle for Aitape raged hundreds of miles to the east with Allied troops supported by PT Squadrons 7 and 8 against General Adachi's *18*th Army, MacArthur prepared to make his last amphibious landing in New Guinea, to Cape Sansapor, about fifteen miles west of the Cape of Good Hope, the northernmost point in New Guinea. A few miles off Sansapor, 250 miles west of Mios Woendi, lie three tiny islands, one is Amsterdam. Here MacArthur would establish a PT base to support the ground forces landed on Sansapor, the last PT base in New Guinea.

On July 30, U.S. troops landed on Sansapor. On August 2 a small armada arrived at Amsterdam Island, a tropical paradise. Included was *LST 564,* a floating repair barge, plus a floating fuel barge, a floating drydock, and Squadron 24 led by Lieutenant Commander Davis and Squadron 25 commanded by Lt. Comdr. Richard E. Johnson. The LST rammed its nose into the sandy beach and men and equipment poured ashore to establish a base.[37]

However, what early reconnaissance teams had failed to note was the constant wind that buffeted Amsterdam, an island with no natural harbor or bay. As a result, during the two months the base was in operation, the men constantly waged a struggle to prevent boats and barges from being blown on the offshore reefs.

While the hunting there was not like it had been at other bases, the two squadrons managed to account for eleven barges, two 100-foot luggers, and a 200-foot minelayer sunk. The minelayer, torpedoed on the night of September 21 by *PT 342,* was one of the two largest surface ships sunk by the PTs during the New Guinea campaign. It also provided a PT with a rare opportunity to use torpedoes rather than guns against the enemy.

With the action dropping off in September, in October the two squadrons returned to Mios Woendi. By now, additional squadrons were based at Mios Woendi—Squadrons 9,10,12,18 and 21; these were soon joined by part of Squadron 36, led by Lt. Comdr. Francis D. Tappaan and the first two Higgins squadrons to operate in New Guinea, Squadron 13 commanded by Lt. Comdr. Alvin W. Fargo, Jr., and 16 under the command of Lt. Comdr. Almer P. Colvin. In the end Mios Woendi had the distinction of being the largest PT base in New Guinea.[38]

PTs at Mios Woendi continued to carry out combat patrols until November 16. By then MacArthur's spearhead had landed at Morotai Island, roughly midway between New Guinea and

Mindanao, as a preliminary to the major offensive to liberate the Philippines.

By then the PTs in New Guinea had been operating for twenty-three months, building up from the original six boats and one small tender to a force of fourteen squadrons and eight tenders, virtually MacArthur's only naval support. They had been in nightly action along 1500 miles of the New Guinea coastline, as well as the coastal waters of New Britain and the Admiralties. Against fierce enemy resistance whose opposition at no time let up, the PTs, combined with MacArthur's air force in daylight sweeps, had taken a terrible toll of the enemy. Not only was the entire coastline littered with the wrecks of hundreds of sunken and burned-out barges, but in the enemy's former encampments were the bodies of thousands of soldiers who had refused to surrender, and who had died from lack of supplies.[39] Left behind were an estimated two hundred thousand of the Emperor's troops, scattered mainly in small bands, on New Guinea, New Britain and in the Admiralties doomed to starvation. The cost to the PTs was twenty-nine boats, mainly lost due to running aground.

Although the U.S. Navy, as in the Guadalcanal campaign, makes little reference to the role played by PT boats in the New Guinea campaign, this was more than compensated for by officers like Major General F.H. Berryman, commanding the 2nd Australian Corps, who wrote the New Guinea PT commander:

> The following evidence emerging from recent operations will illustrate the cumulative effect of the activities of your command:
>
> A. The small degree to which the enemy has used artillery indicates a shortage of ammunition.
>
> B. The enemy, in an endeavor to protect his barges, has been forced to dispose his normal field artillery over miles of the coast when those guns might well have been used in the coastal sector against our land troops.
>
> C. Many Japanese diary entries describe the shortage of rations and the regular fatigues of foraging parties to collect native food, which is beginning to be increasingly difficult to obtain.

D. A Japanese prisoner of war stated that three days' rice food, now has to last nine days. This is supported by the absence of food and the presence of native roots on the enemy dead.

E. There is definite evidence that the enemy has slaughtered and eaten his pack-carrying animals.

From the above you will see how effective has been the work of your squadrons and how it has contributed to the recent defeat of the enemy.[40]

After the war, top-ranking Japanese officers concluded the New Guinea campaign contributed a good deal to Japan losing the war. During the period 1942-44, the Japanese poured tremendous amounts of troops, weapons, equipment, and planes onto MacArthur's Southwest Pacific area. To quote one general, "It can be said without exaggeration, that on this front the war machine not only received its first definite setback...but bled itself white continuously thereafter. Of the masses of troops and materials committed to that area—the critical area upon which Japan pinned its hopes of an integrated Asiatic Empire—none were ever successfully evacuated or withdrawn to fight elsewhere than in the defeated or bypassed sectors of their initial historical advance."

The long-fought campaign for the "green hell" that was New Guinea was finally over, but the Allies were still a long way from Tokyo.

Mios Woendi, largest PT base in New Guinea, near island of Biak, near the end of the campaign for New Guinea. *Courtesy of WWII PT Boats Museum and Archives, Germantown, Tennessee, USA.*

PT boats in the South Pacific always seemed to attract natives. They provided PT crews with intelligence on Japanese positions and conditions on the islands, information the PT crews put to good use, strafing the Japanese if their camps were situated close to the island shores. *Courtesy of WWII PT Boats Museum and Archives, Germantown, Tennessee, USA.*

PT 104 refueling underway. PT boats making the passage to the Philippines routinely were forced to refuel underway. *Courtesy of WWII PT Boats Museum and Archives, Germantown, Tennessee, USA.*

Japanese survivors of sunken ships tended to prefer death to capture and if captured, frequently opted for suicide, trying to take an American with them. But on occasion, PT crews were ordered to take captives for intelligence purposes. In such cases, PT crews had to use drastic measures: note the photo shows the use of a boat hook to haul the individual aboard. The boat hook usually was used to stun the swimmer, then hook him and haul him aboard. Note the armed crewman standing ready, just in case. *Courtesy of WWII PT Boats Museum and Archives, Germantown, Tennessee, USA.*

CHAPTER EIGHTEEN

PTS VERSUS F-LIGHTERS AND E-BOATS

While the number of PT squadrons engaging the Japanese was increasing dramatically in the Pacific, a single PT squadron was earning a reputation for bold exploits in combat against German and Italian naval forces in the Mediterranean. Commissioned in New Orleans in early 1943, Motor Torpedo Boat Squadron 15 consisted of twelve boats numbered *201-212* Commanded by Lt. Comdr. Stanley M. Barnes,[1] for most of its eighteen-month service in the Mediterranean, the squadron would operate under British control alongside the Royal Navy's motor torpedo boats, called MTBs, Britain's equivalent of American PT boats.[2]

As aggressive as any PT commander in the Pacific, Commander Barnes early on demonstrated an inclination toward direct action. Initially, the squadron was slated for assignment to the warm and peaceful waters off Midway, 3,500 miles behind combat in the Pacific, but Barnes assured his eager squadron that somehow he would see that they saw some action. Not that this convinced his men; nor, as he admitted later, was he certain he could cause there to be any change in the orders.

Once commissioned, the squadron proceeded to Norfolk under its own power where the boats were to be loaded on cargo ships for passage through the Panama Canal to the Pacific. At the giant Norfolk naval base, however, following a conference with base commanding officers, Barnes received new orders: they would go to the Mediterranean, the first American PT squadron to cross the Atlantic to fight in Europe. Initial shipment of the boats would be in two sections of four boats each; the third section, consisting of PTs

209-212 and crews, would remain behind pending available transport under the command of squadron executive officer, Lt. J.B. Mutty.

Shortly, PTs *201-204* were loaded on the Navy oiler *Enoree,* accompanied by Lieutenant Commander Barnes, and *205-208* on the *Housatonic* along with Lt. Edwin A. DuBose. The *Enoree* reached Gibraltar first, on April 13. The next day, all boats were in the water and Lieutenant DuBose—destined to be an ace combat PT officer in the forthcoming months, led the boats to the British torpedo-boat dock where they received their full load of Mark VIII torpedoes before setting out for Oran in North Africa.[3]

Arriving at Oran, the PT crews were bitterly disappointed to learn they were to proceed to Cherchel, three hundred miles from the closest combat, for an unspecified period of training.

"I decided to take the bull by the horns and bum a ride to Algiers in an Army truck to see Vice Admiral Henry K. Hewitt," recalled Barnes. Barnes hoped to convince the admiral, who was commander of all U.S. naval forces in northwest African waters, that the squadron would be better based at Bone, 265 miles further east within reach of the fighting.

The trip lasting several hours, and much to his chagrin, the squadron commander learned when he got to the admiral's headquarters that the orders had already been changed; and Lt. Richard H. O'Brian, the officer commanding in Barnes's absence, had gotten the boats underway to arrive at Algiers ahead of the squadron commander.

On the following day, April 17, Lieutenant DuBose led the boats the rest of the way to Bone. Bone was the forward base for British MTBs and MGBs, or motor gunboats. These MTBs, with guns substituted for torpedoes, were the Royal Navy's answer to German motorized barges. Called F-lighters, like the Japanese *daihatsus,* such vessels were employed by the enemy to transport troops and supplies, and were even more heavily armed than their Japanese counterparts in the Pacific. As in the Southwest Pacific, the barges would prove to be the major target for American PTs.

Since Squadron 15 lacked battle experience, and the British had been fighting in the Mediterranean for months, Commander Barnes welcomed the assistance offered by the local MTB commander, Lt.

Comdr. R.A. Allan, RN. Thus began a congenial relationship that would last until Squadron 15 was disbanded eighteen months later.[4]

By this time, Gen. Erwin Rommel's famed Africa Korps was in Tunisia, and Britain's MTBs and MGBs were patrolling the coast nightly to prevent Axis troops escaping across the ninety-mile-wide strait to Sicily from Tunisia's Cape Bon.

Like the South Pacific Islands, European coastal waters were ideal for motor torpedo operations. From the opening days of the war in Europe, German E-boats, the Allied short term for "Enemy motor torpedo boat," had prowled the waters of the English Channel, opposed by British MTBs. Shortly, with the war spreading to North Africa and the Mediterranean the German boats operating with Italian motor torpedo boats faced British and finally U.S. PTs, providing the only occasion in history in which motor torpedo boats of four different nations would be engaged in combat in the same waters.

Since both the German and Italian motor torpedo boat forces were well developed and experienced, their presence made Allied area commanders nervous. The U.S. had rushed Squadron 15 to the Mediterranean to counter the threat and aid the hard-pressed Royal Navy in harrying the Axis powers.

On the night of April 17, the entire Squadron 15 sailed on its first mission. But not until the night of May 8 did they make contact with the enemy. That night, Barnes, on *PT 206,* joined MTBs *316* and *265* under the command of Lt. Dennis Germaine, RN. Their mission was to patrol the coastal areas southward between Cape Bon and Ras el Mirth. At 10:45 p.m., at Ras Idda Bay, Lieutenant Germaine's MTB entered the harbor to search for a possible target. At a time when neither PTs nor the British boats were fitted with radar, operations on moonless nights close to shore were fraught with the unexpected. Recalled Lieutenant Commander Barnes:

"Pretty soon Germaine came up on the radio with the startling statement that there were lots of ships in there, so I took the remaining boat with me and started in. It was as black as the inside of your pocket, but sure enough, right there in front of me was a ship.

"By the time we saw it against the dark background of the land we were inside the torpedo-arming range and had to go all the way around to the other side of it before getting a good shot.

"Thinking there were other targets around, I lined up and fired only one torpedo—our first!

"It ran hot and straight, and after what seemed like an interminable time made a beautiful hit forward. The whole ship blew up in our faces, scattering pieces of debris all around us and on deck. Just like in the movies.

"We immediately started to look for other ships but could find none. Neither could we find a British friend, who, it turned out, was temporarily aground, so we just eased around trying to rendezvous. Pretty soon he found us—and promptly fired two fish at us, one of which passed right under our bow and the other under our stern, much to our alarm and his subsequent embarrassment."[5]

As it so happened, a flight of planes began dropping bombs nearby, and by the light of accompanying flares, Barnes was able to find and rejoin Germaine. The Squadron 15 commander later remarked that he personally thought the ship he torpedoed was aground—noting, "although it certainly made a fine spectacle going up..." Barnes's suspicions proved to be true.

The embarrassment on the part of the British did not end there: "Actually," said Barnes, "Germaine had not seen any ships and had mistaken some peculiar rock formations for a group of enemy vessels."[6]

Nor was the British embarrassment yet ended. That night, *PT 203* under the command of Lt.(jg) Robert B. Reade in company with MTBs *61* and *77* was patrolling in the vicinity of Ras el Mirh when, for the second time that night, an MTB ran aground, this time three hundred yards off the beach beneath the guns of the Axis fort at Kelibia. After the crew set the boat, *MTB 61,* afire so it would not fall into enemy hands, Lieutenant Reade, his boat illuminated by the flames, and under machine-gun fire from the shore, maneuvered his boat alongside the burning MTB, took the crew aboard and withdrew safely. In the meanwhile the now bewildered fort was still blinking challenges. Such were the uncertainties that befell even veterans as they aggressively carried out their patrols.

Two nights later, on May 10, the Royal Navy made another mistake involved Barnes's PTs. To quote the unofficial PT report:

Returning from an uneventful patrol off Cape Bon, the *202, 204,* and *205* were skirting the shore to give wide berth to Allied destroyers stationed in the bay of Tunis and be back along friendly coastline before daylight and possible plane attack. Suddenly they found themselves in an argument between a British destroyer which had wandered south of its designated area, and German E-boats. The destroyers, having heard German voices over the E-boat's radio planning an attack on her, opened up with star shells and 40-mm fire in the direction where the American PTs also found themselves at the time. With all this disturbance, the *202* and *205* lay smoke to clear out, but Ensign E.S.A. Clifford, who was last in the PT formation on the *204,* seeing an excited E-boat reply to the destroyer by opening fire, turned and strafed it going away, leaving it burning. Out of the confusion, another destroyer followed the *205* for an hour, firing star shells. Figuring that he couldn't make it all the way back, Lieutenant (jg) R. H. O'Brian decided to take the *205* into Bizerta, which was supposed to have been evacuated by the Germans on the 7th. Shore batteries doubting his identity as Allied, however, and there were a few tense moments while they shelled him briefly. Still it appeared safer inside than out, so he proceeded in without being hit and picked his way into the shambles of Bizerta harbor where they tied up and rested easy. Two hours later he was disgusted when British landing craft came in and asked him to move out of the way so that photographers could take pictures of them as the first Allied craft to enter the harbor.[7]

The two destroyers engaging the PTs were the *H.M.S. Lamerton* and *Wilton,* both Hunt-class destroyers similar to the U.S. DE-class. Based on subsequent reports, it was the *Lamerton* that pursued O'Brian: according to the *Lamerton's* skipper, his ship chased a suspected E-boat that finally got away after being subjected to "further heavy gunfire."

Only when the ships were back at base did their commanders realize that all the vessels they engaged were not E-boats. According to the report of the Royal Navy's 6th Destroyer Flotilla, "A full discussion between destroyer and coastal craft officers, [the Royal Navy's term for MTBs and MGBs was 'Coastal Forces'] on return to Bone made it clear that both enemy E-boats and American coastal craft were encountered at the same time. The Hunts were engaging the E-boats on one side and did not see the friendly recognition signals on the other." In any event, Capt. J. W. Eaton, RN, commanding the 6th Destroyer Flotilla, stated, "Whatever they were engaging, they were themselves obviously having a riotous time."[8]

In a final touch, for whatever reasons, the C.O. of the Royal Navy's 12th Cruiser Squadron claimed the three PTs were off station, but the destroyer skippers admitted their responsibility, saying they had gone further south in search of excitement and were themselves off station. The recognition signals of star cartridges fired by the PTs had been mistaken for 20-mm fire. Again, the problem was flawed communications.

Ashore, the battle for North Africa continued. Caught between British forces to the east and American and British forces to the west, Axis resistance in Tunisia crumbled. Allied ground forces entered Bizerta on May 7. The way was now open for the next major step in the Allied plan—the invasion of Sicily.

As preparations for the invasion were being undertaken, changes were made concerning Barnes's PTs and the British MTB and MGB flotillas: Bone, under the command of Lieutenant Commander Allan, became the major repair and training base for boats and crews in the western Mediterranean while Bizerta was now solely an operations base for PT Squadron 15, as well as the 18th and 23rd MTB and 19th MGB Flotillas.[9]

For Barnes's PT men, it was a rude reminder of their lowly naval status. Ordered to set up operations in Bizerta, squadron personnel cleaned up a hanger and moved in their equipment. When the main Allied forces arrived, however, they found themselves ousted without ceremony, the space taken over by officers from the heavy warships. "We cleaned up half the buildings in Bizerta," recalled one member of Squadron 15. "As fast as we made it presentable, we were kicked out. We ended up with only a fraction of our original space, and we had to fight tooth and nail for that."[10]

However, at Bizerta, from May 13 to 27, Barnes's squadron enjoyed a period of relative quiet while undergoing additional training. At this time, SO radar sets shipped from the States were installed on the squadron's eight initial boats reaching the Mediterranean, plus an additional ten Higgins PTs added to the squadron. The additions included the last four PT boats originally assigned plus another six boats, number *213* through *218*. With a total of eighteen boats, Squadron 15 was now equal in size to three six-boat British MTB or MGB flotillas.[11]

With the PTs now fitted with radar, equipment still lacking on the British boats, the crews of the two forces devised a system of radio signals to vector the British boats against objectives when British and American boats were involved in simultaneous attacks during operations.

With the Allied invasion of Sicily, the greatest amphibious invasion of war to date, the PTs along with the British boats were back in action once again. With the invasion scheduled for July 10, an attempt to mislead the enemy into expecting the attack would be against Crete and the Aegean Islands, as well as landings in Greece or on Sardinia, the PT boats and British flotillas began extending their patrols along the coast of Sicily; their task was also to seek and destroy the enemy and collect intelligence on enemy movements.[12]

With the sudden defeat of the Axis in North Africa, General Eisenhower was reluctant to exploit the victory by mounting a premature invasion of Sicily. Instead, he chose to capture the Italian Island of Pantelleria. An ideal fixed aircraft carrier, Pantelleria's 42.5 square miles of rocky land lies in the Sicilian Strait not quite halfway toward Cape Bon, Tunisia. Eisenhower meant to deny the enemy's use of Pantelleria's excellent radio direction stations that would prevent a tactical surprise attack on Sicily.

Enemy strength on Pantelleria was correctly estimated by intelligence to be formidable, about ten thousand men, with one hundred gun emplacements and an indeterminate number of aircraft.

Port Pantelleria, on the northwest end of the island, was also a seaplane and motor torpedo base for Italian and German boats.[13]

Occupation of the island in the face of a determined defense was viewed as a major challenge. In an effort to conserve manpower for the upcoming Sicilian invasion, Eisenhower sought to first weaken the enemy garrison's morale by aerial bombardment using the Northwest African Air Force. The naval stage of the invasion would be under Rear Admiral R.R. McGrigor, RN. The only U.S. naval force involved would be PT Squadron 15.[14]

Allied bombers began raids on Pantelleria on May 8; the Royal Navy's heavy ships began throwing shells on the night of May 30. Finally, on the night of June 5, Commander Barnes's Squadron 15 and three MTBs were given the task of sweeping around the island on the lookout for E-boats and attempts by the Axis to either evacuate or reinforce the island. Under the command of Lt. E.C. Arbuckle, PTs *209, 210, 212,* and *218* cruised close to the north shore at eight knots with engines muffled, but all they saw were Allied planes dropping bombs, and smoke and flames rising skyward.

On the morning of June 11, D-Day, the Royal Navy's 15th Cruiser Squadron shelled the island in support of the invading assault troops while Barnes's Squadron 15 in full force, patrolled a line between Pantelleria and Porto Empedocle, Sicily, to prevent any last minute evacuation, or to intercept any E-boats that might attempt to interfere with the landings. For this operation, five MTBs and MGBs were attached to Barnes's squadron. However, no E-boats sought to interfere and very few Italian troops tried to evacuate. The PTs' only casualty occurred at 9:30 p.m. when a Junkers 88 bombed the boats, causing the loss of one man.[15]

On Pantelleria Island, enemy resistance was negligible. Shortly, at 11:55 a.m., a white flag was sighted flying from the garrison's semaphore tower. The Italian commander had surrendered his force of 11,121 Italians and 78 Germans. The only casualty among the British assault force was one soldier bitten by a jackass.[16]

The question as to why the garrison surrendered so easily became a matter of intense debate on both sides and among all branches of the services. However, the answer was never resolved;

but one might ponder how different the results would have been if the garrison had been Japanese, or even German.

With the end of the Pantelleria operation, the invasion of Sicily, code named Operation "Husky," was next on Eisenhower's list of objectives. In preparation for what was to be a massive amphibious operation, the PTs, MTBs and MGBs were employed by Special Services and the Office of Strategic Services for clandestine operations, such as landing agents and supplies on Crete and Sardinia. The Services were to continue to use the boats on such missions, particularly in the lull before Allied invasions, until the end of the war.[17]

It was at this time that British agents devised a wild hoax worthy of a cheap novel. Deemed so important as to rate a code name, Operation "Mincemeat," its purpose was to mislead the Axis into believing the forthcoming invasion was somewhere other than Sicily. With permission of his heirs, the body of a man who had died of pneumonia was given the name "Major William Martin;" dressed in the uniform of a Royal Marine, his pockets stuffed with forged identification papers and important documents, the body was set afloat off the coast of Spain by a submarine in such a manner that when it washed up on the shore near Cadiz, it would be assumed the "major" had been killed in a plane accident. As anticipated, when the body floated ashore, an Axis agent recovered all papers on the "major" and forwarded them to Berlin. The key documents were a letter between members of the Allied high command stating that Sicily was a mere diversion, and the real target was the Peloponnesus. Another document suggested that Sardinia was also to be invaded.[18]

As related after the war in a book entitled *The Man Who Never Was*, the ploy fooled Hitler; on May 21, the German High Command ordered that defense "measures be taken in Sardinia and the Peloponnesus" and to have priority over any others. On July 9, Berlin signaled the German admiral in Italy that, "Sardinia and Corsica are the first targets.... An assault on Greece is most probable." Coastal batteries were installed on the Greek coast, and most of the E-boats then in Sicilian waters were diverted to the coast of Greece.

With the invasion of Sicily, Barnes's PTs and the British MTBs and MGBs found themselves in the thick of the action but in different areas. The British boats would cover the eastern flank of the invasion armada composed of British ships landing British troops; the boats would then conduct nightly patrols of the Straits of Messina and the approaches to Syracuse and Augusta. With the U.S. Navy participating in the Sicily invasion, Squadron 15 would be detached briefly from British control and assigned to the Western Naval Task Force, made up of American forces commanded by Vice Admiral Hewitt. Once again, Barnes's PTs had a task never before considered by the U.S. Navy: in a further attempt to confuse the enemy, Admiral Hewitt organized a "Demonstration Group" under Comdr. Hunter R. Robinson riding on *PT 213,* with ten air-sea rescue "crash" boats. In the early hours of D-Day, they were to operate off Cape Granotola, at the western tip of Sicily as far as possible from the true landing site, emitting false radio transmissions, firing rockets and other pyrotechnics, playing records simulating the rattling of anchor chains and the clanking of landing craft, all for the purpose of creating the false impression that a full-scale assault would occur there in daylight. However, although they did their best, the act failed to impress the enemy ashore.[19]

On the morning of the invasion, the rest of Barnes's PTs were given another assignment, one that would lead to another of those tragic experiences with "friendly" destroyers attacking PT boats. American troops were being landed at Licata, twenty-four miles west of Porto Empedocle, a base for a flotilla of Italian motor torpedo boats, termed MAS boats by the Italian Navy. So concerned were the Allies about the potential threat posed by these boats that the high command ruled Empedocle out as an invasion site. Furthermore, Allied intelligence correctly reported the existence of a minefield in the area. To prevent the MAS boats from attacking the Allied invasion fleet, a special naval screen was formed composed of Barnes's remaining seventeen PTs and the destroyer *Ordronaux,* commanded by Lt. Comdr. Robert Brodie.[20]

The screening group arrived at its assigned position off Empedocle at around 11 p.m. July 9. *Ordronaux* began an offensive sweep outside the minefield while Barnes's PTs patrolled the eastern edge of it. The Brodie-Barnes screening group was under

Admiral Hewitt's direct command, while the destroyers assigned to screen and provide fire support for the ships carrying the U.S. 3rd Infantry Division and two Ranger battalions, were attached to Task Force 86 commanded by Rear Adm. R. L. Conolly: TF 86 had no knowledge of or was even in communication with the Brodie-Barnes force.

Accordingly, Lt. Comdr. E. L. Robertson, as officer in tactical command of destroyers *Roe* and *Swanson,* whose mission was to protect TF 86 from E-boats suspected to be in the area, made the logical deduction. Observing numerous small pips on their radar screens, *Roe* and *Swanson* charged. Lieutenant Commander Barnes flashed the recognition signal at the two ships, but to no avail. At 2:55 a.m., at a range of 1,500 yards, just as Commander Robertson was about to order his ships to open fire on the PTs, the skipper of *Roe* remembered the Porto Empedocle minefield ahead. Swerving hard in an effort to fall in astern of *Swanson, Roe* rammed *Swanson* at right angle on the port side abreast of her forward stack at 25 knots, with *Swanson* making 20 knots, crumbling *Roe's* bow, bringing both ships to a halt.

Miraculously, no one was hurt on either ship; but both destroyers were so seriously damaged that they had to be sent to Malta and Bizerta for repairs.[21] One can imagine the awkward difficulty Commander Robertson and the skipper of the *Roe* experienced in writing their reports on this night's action.

Two nights later, on July 12, Barnes's PTs were again ordered to confuse the enemy with a fraudulent demonstration off Cape Granitola. Splitting his PT boats and joined by twelve crash boats, he conducted the operation, racing along parallel to the beach behind a smoke screen, noisily imitating a major naval fleet. Searchlights blazed on the shore; a shore battery opened fire and shells landed close to the boats. As Barnes reported later, "Apparently the enemy was convinced that a landing was about to take place when it detected the large number of boats in our group approaching the beach, for they opened heavy and accurate fire with radar control.... I immediately reversed course and opened the range. One shell damaged the rudder of a crash boat and another fell ten yards astern of a PT. The demonstration was called a success and we withdrew."

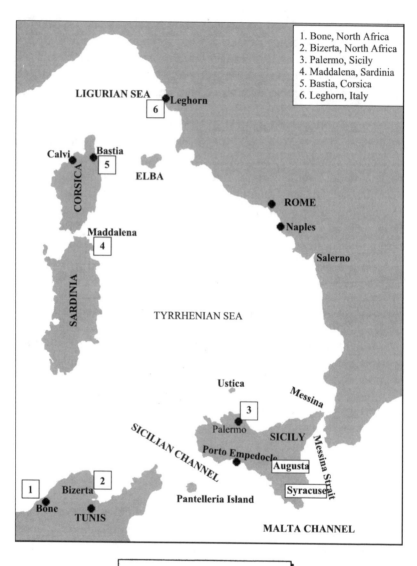

1. Bone, North Africa
2. Bizerta, North Africa
3. Palermo, Sicily
4. Maddalena, Sardinia
5. Bastia, Corsica
6. Leghorn, Italy

LIGURIAN SEA ●Leghorn
6

Calvi ●Bastia
CORSICA 5

ELBA

● ROME

● Naples

Maddalena
4

Salerno

SARDINIA

TYRRHENIAN SEA

Ustica

Messina

3
●
Palermo

SICILY

Porto Empedocle
●
Augusta

Messina Strait

SICILIAN CHANNEL

1 Bizerta 2

● Bone
TUNIS ●

Pantelleria Island

Syracuse

MALTA CHANNEL

Map 7
The Mediterranean Sea:
Tyrrhenian Sea area

Evidently Barnes was right. The next day, Axis newspapers reported an attempted enemy landing on the southwest coast of Sicily had been bloodily repulsed.[22]

By the night of July 12-13, resistance on the beachheads of Sicily had been eliminated and ground troops were starting to advance. On the afternoon of July 22, the U.S. Seventh Army commanded by General Patton began entering Palermo, the metropolis of western Sicily. With no naval support in the area, Admiral Hewitt's cruisers and destroyers having proceeded to Algiers for maintenance, four PTs of Squadron 15 were the first Allied vessels to show the flag in the harbor.[23]

According to Commander Barnes, he departed Bizerta on the evening of July 22 with four PTs to patrol the Tyrrhenian Sea, the waters bordered by Sicily, Italy, Sardinia and Corsica. As Barnes related later:

> At dawn the next day we were off Ústica. The first thing we saw was a fishing boat putt-putting toward Italy. Going over, we saw a handful of very scared individuals crawling out from under the floor plates, hopefully waving white handkerchiefs. This was the staff of the Italian Admiral at Trápani. The only reason we didn't get the Admiral was that he was late getting down to the dock and his staff said to hell with him. In addition to a few souvenir pistols and binoculars we captured a whole fruit crate of thousand-lira notes which we reluctantly turned over to the Army authorities later. While this was going on, one of the other boats spotted a raft with seven Germans on it feebly paddling out to sea. We picked those up too.[24]

The PTs departed Ustica for Palermo about thirty miles to the south with the fishing boat in tow. According to Lt. H. R. Manakee, the squadron intelligence officer, Barnes towed the fishing boat at 25 knots, which opened the seams of the old craft, forcing the Italian staff officers to bail for their lives with their steel helmets.[25]

At 8 a.m. Barnes led the little flotilla into Palermo Harbor, as noted, making the PTs the first U.S. vessels to enter the harbor. They had to pick their way through a harbor littered with some fifty sunken vessels of various sizes and types, and the dockside was in shambles as well, the result of Allied bombing and shelling, and the retreating enemy's efforts to leave nothing of value behind.

Three Squadron 15 boats arrived at Palermo on July 23; they were followed by the balance of the eighteen-boat squadron led by Lieutenant Manakee. With the PTs based at Palermo, their mission was to patrol the northern approaches to the Strait of Messina, the narrow strip of water separating Sicily from the toe of the Italian boot, preventing the enemy supply or evacuation of Sicily. On the night of July 24-25, the three boats arriving at Palermo on June 23 carried out the first patrol: in tactical command of the division was Lt. Arbuckle on *PT 209* skippered by Lt.(jg) W. Knox Eldridge, with *PT 216* under the command of Lt.(jg) Cecil Sanders and *PT 204* commanded by Lt.(jg) Clifford.

In the early hours of July 25 near Palmi, a PT division encountered the 8800-ton Italian merchant ship *Viminale* being towed stern-first toward Naples; at first the PTs took a lead in the wrong direction owing to the enemy's strange posture. But then the *216* scored a torpedo hit on the ship; then, despite being under fire from coastal batteries, the boats strafed the tug until it was dead in the water and smoking. As the PTs withdrew they saw tbe *Viminale* sink stern first. Later the tug went to the bottom.[26] This was the first U.S. Navy victory in the Tyrrhenian Sea, and it served to warn the Italians they could no longer freely supply Sicily except across the Strait of Messina.

Two nights later, it was the PTs' turn to be on the receiving end. That night, three boats with Lieutenant Mutty as officer in tactical command riding on *PT 202* commanded by Lt.(jg) Robert D. McLeod, along with *PT 210* skippered by Lt.(jg) John L. Davis, Jr., and *PT 214* with Lt.(jg) Ernest W. Olson at the helm, clashed with the infamous F-lighters. As noted, such craft were the German equivalent of the *daihatsus* in the South Pacific. Called F-lighters by the Allies, and MFPs (*Marine-fahrprahme,* literally "Naval perambulators") by the Germans, they were by any name formidable craft; 163 feet long, diesel powered with a top speed of 10 knots, capable of carrying up to 100 tons of cargo, so compartmentalized were the F-lighters that it was virtually impossible to sink them with anything less than a torpedo. However, with F-lighters drawing only four and one-half feet, and the PTs' Mark VIII torpedoes, designed for attacks on heavy ships with a minimum running depth of eight feet, getting a hit required a virtual miracle.[27] Moreover, the German craft were armed with automatic weapons, all of which posed a challenge to the vulnerable PTs.

On this night, Mutty's division found seven F-lighters in column near the volcanic island of Stromboli northeast of Messina Strait. Slipping to within five hundred yards undetected, each PT fired two torpedoes, and at three hundred yards started to turn away. In the midst of the turn, the second F-lighter in column sent up a flare, apparently a signal to fire. All the lighters immediately loosed a torrent of machine-gun and cannon fire, which the PTs returned. The three boats then laid smoke and withdrew at high speed. Damage was light. German records show all torpedoes missed and damage to the PTs consisted of a punctured gasoline tank on *PT 202*, along with several holes in the hull with one man wounded. The other boats were not hit.[28]

On the night of July 28-29, three boats under the tactical command of Lieutenant Arbuckle on *PT 218* commanded by Lt.(jg) Donald W. Henry, with Olson's *214* and *PT 203* skippered by Lt.(jg) Reade, attacked what they thought were three F-lighters off Cape Orlando. In fact they were MAS boats, vessels somewhat smaller than the American PT. The PTs' torpedoes were well aimed but passed beneath the shallow-draft Italian motor torpedo boats. As the three boats idled away, Arbuckle decided to attack again, making a strafing pass with the *218,* as the other two boats maneuvered for another torpedo attack. Closing to the point-blank range of one hundred yards, the *218* opened fire: according to the PTs' action report, "This was immediately returned with a heavy volume of fire from all enemy vessels...directed principally at *PT 218.* The boat was hit repeatedly with 20-mm and suffered considerable damage which included the holing of the vessel below the waterline forward, puncturing of both forward gas tanks, and disabling one engine. The engagement was broken off in some confusion."

Lieutenant Arbuckle, plus the skipper of the PT, and Ens. Edmund F. Jacobs, the *218*'s executive officer, were badly wounded; the boat's skipper and Jacobs were flat on the deck.

However, although painfully wounded in the heel, Arbuckle managed to prop himself up and organize the crew's efforts to save the boat. With eighteen inches of water flooding the crew's quarters, and several hundreds of gallons of 100-octane gasoline sloshing about in the bilges, the *218* boat was in a bad way. The crew bailed out the flooded compartments and plugged the biggest holes. Three hours later, Arbuckle brought the riddled PT alongside the destroyer *Wainwright* at Palermo, and then collapsed.[29]

On the night of July 29-30, the PTs out of Palermo again clashed with the enemy. This time, Lt.(jg) Richard O'Brian on Clifford's *PT 204* and Lt. Norman Devol commanding *PT 207,* engaged two F-lighters escorted by four MAS boats, firing six torpedoes and strafing the Italian motor torpedo boats before heavy return fire forced them to retire. However, according to the Italian officer commanding MAS boats in the action, later interviewed in Capri, one F-lighter was sunk and one MAS boat so badly damaged that it was abandoned and sunk by the other MAS boats.

Following the clash on the night of July 28-29, there were repercussions, the report having finally reached Admiral Hewitt's headquarters, Squadron 15 was instructed to avoid further action with the MPFs.[30] In an attempt to cope with the F-lighters, PT boats and destroyers instituted joint patrols. But again, for the PTs, operating in the same waters as "friendly" destroyers proved hazardous. On one occasion, the destroyers fired on the PTs, drenching their foredecks with the first salvo. With Barnes's boats some five knots slower than the destroyers, the PTs were forced to run under the protection of enemy shore batteries on Cape Rasocolmo, which guns obligingly fired on the destroyers, forcing them to retire seaward.

Even as Squadron 15 sought to deal with the MAS boats and F-lighters, the PTs continued to be engaged in special operations for the Office of Strategic Services. One such mission was code named "Operation MacGregor;" it involved an unlikely plot with a secret letter from the Allied high command to the Italian Naval Command, seeking to convince its admirals to turn their fleet over to the Allies. The PTs' role was to land and recover the agent carrying the letter and to bring someone out for further discussion. While waiting for the call, Barnes assigned Lt. O'Brian to the task of training members of the squadron in navigating and handling a rubber boat. The first effort to carry out the plan occurred on August 10 in the Gulf of Gaeta; it failed due to the presence of too many fishing vessels, which made an unobserved landing impossible. The second attempt, on August 12, was a success, at least as far as Barnes's men were concerned. As it turned out, owing to a previous secret agreement, the Italian navy had already sailed from Genoa to surrender to the British at Malta.

Meanwhile naval operations in support of Allied forces in Sicily continued. At the end of July, Admiral Hewitt had organized the few U.S. warships still in Sicilian waters into a Support Force; just as the Seventh Fleet in the Southwest Pacific was General MacArthur's Navy, Task Force 88, as it was designated, was in effect, General Patton's Navy, responsible for providing gunfire support for the Seventh Army as it advanced along the coast, and provided amphibious landing craft for "leapfrog landings" to be carried out behind enemy lines. Commanding was Rear Adm,. Lyal A. Davidson. On the night of August 15-16, six Squadron 15 boats were assigned to screen off these landings at Spadafora from possible E-boat attacks. Commanding the northern PT group was Lieutenant DuBose aboard *PT 205* skippered by Ens. Robert T. Boebel, accompanied by *PT 215* under the command of Lt. George A. Steele, Jr., and *PT 216* commanded by Lt.(jg) Sanders. When the PTs spotted two E-boats off the Italian coast the chase was on.[31]

"The Germans opened a heavy and accurate fire with 40-mm, 20-mm and smaller guns and headed south at high speed," reported Barnes. "The fire was returned with all guns that could bear in the overtaking chase and range closed to 400 yards. The enemy turned away, laid smoke and dropped depth charges, employing every possible evasive maneuver. The PTs were handicapped by their inability to make more than 25 knots, the *216* lagging the other PTs to such an extent that it was unable to take part in the engagement for any length of time.... All PTs were hit repeatedly but miraculously no serious damage was incurred. Four men were wounded on the *PT 216*. Subsequent interview with an Italian E-boat flotilla commander after the capitulation of Italy revealed that in the engagement the German E-boats suffered heavy casualties totaling 14. These included the German flotilla commander who was killed."

Although, owing to their lack of speed, O'Brian's PTs were unable to close with the E-boats, they caused the enemy to retire, thus accomplishing their mission, protecting the task force from an E-boat attack. Due to limited maintenance facilities, the boats being overloaded, and the heat in the Mediterranean during the summer of 1943, much like the PTs in the South Pacific, none of the boats could do better than 27-28 knots, and some, much to their frustrated crews' disgust, were considerably slower.

Under the circumstances, the E-boats powered by modified diesels had a considerable advantage. Furthermore, the E-boats' targets were Allied cargo ships and heavy warships. Consequently E-boat crews made every effort to avoid PT boats' attempting to screen Allied vessels. Here, indeed, was the opportunity for the Germans take full advantage of their boats' superior performance.

On July 13, even before Barnes's squadron began operating from Palermo, British troops advancing on Sicily's south coast captured Syracuse, and on the 16th took Augusta. The latter promptly became the major MTB and MGB base, commanded by Lieutenant Commander Allan. With the Allied invasion of Sicily, the effort to isolate the island from the mainland and prevent supplies and reinforcements from the mainland reaching Sicily became a major objective. As Barnes's PTs endeavored to prevent supplies reaching Sicily by way of Italy's west coast, the British boats sought to do the same on the opposite coast of Sicily. Thus MTBs and MGBs from Augusta began patrolling the Messina Strait.[32] Indeed, the clashes between Barnes's Palermo-based PTs with MAS boats, F-lighters and E-boats, would almost seem tame affairs compared to the ordeal experienced by their British peers in the Messina Strait. During one night, July 14, MTBs on patrol in the Strait encountered two surfaced submarines and sank one, the *U-561,* with a torpedo; then another group of MTBs surprised and sank two E-boats after a furious exchange of gunfire; the British boats were then outrun by seven MAS boats. Finally, an Axis shore battery on the mainland sank *MGB 641* with all hands. Two nights later, on July 16, *MTB 316* was lost with all hands in action against an Italian cruiser, and on the 21st, during a bombing raid on Augusta, *MTB 288* was sunk at her moorings.

For all the Allies' final success on Sicily, the victory would be marred in the end. The efforts of the Allies to prevent the enemy's evacuation from Sicily by way of the three-mile-wide Messina Strait to the mainland has barely been mentioned by historians, doubtless because, as in the case of the Japanese evacuation at Guadalcanal and at Kiska, neither side cared to dwell on the event for obvious reasons.

Commander Barnes was aware of what was occurring, but his PTs were forbidden south of the Cape Rasocolmo latitude;[33] this effectively barred them from entering the Messina Strait. The Allied commander of the Sicily operation, Admiral of the Fleet Cunningham, RN, was aware the evacuation was in progress, but after some thought, decided there was "no effective method" of preventing it, "either by sea or air," This left the matter up to Britain's MTBs and MGBs.

It was an impossible task for the British boats; it was the PTs' good fortune that they were not ordered to join the British boats in this deadly assignment. The evacuation of Axis forces from Sicily began on August 3. By then the three-mile-wide Strait was covered by around 150 German 88-mm and Italian 90-mm dual-purpose guns ranged along both sides of the Strait, along with countless machine guns and lighter-weight cannon. Searchlights made a night attack by Allied vessels hazardous. MAS boats, E-boats and submarines posed a threat for any large Allied vessel that might be tempted to venture into the Strait to interfere. Thus protected, employing various sizes of barges and other craft, the Germans and Italians ferried men and equipment across the Strait to the mainland, men and equipment to add to the defense against the coming Allied attack on the mainland.

The Royal Navy's MTBs and MGBs did their valiant best to interfere: on the night of August 11, three MTBs engaged six small vessels, boldly chasing them into Messina, knocking out an Italian motor raft. This marked the only occasion when the Allies managed to halt the evacuation. On the night of August 15 *MTB 665* was hit by coastal batteries and sunk with all hands. On the night of the

16th, two more British boats were forced to withdraw after being damaged by shellfire.

On August 17, the evacuation was complete: the Germans had taken out no fewer than 39,569 troops, along with 9605 vehicles, 94 guns, 47 tanks, over 2000 tons of ammunition and fuel, plus tons of stores—all in six days and seven nights. The Italian evacuation ended on August 16. According to their commander, 62,000 Italian officers and men, 227 vehicles, 41 artillery pieces—and 12 mules—were ferried to the mainland.[34]

Thus the bulk of German forces in Sicily—three divisions—got away in good order with all their weapons and most of their materiel, "completely fit for battle and ready for service,"

On the positive side, the Allied invasion of Sicily was followed by the downfall of Mussolini, on July 29, marking the first crack in the Axis dream of world domination.

With the evacuation in progress, and with Barnes's PTs restricted from the Messina Strait, the squadron was naturally anxious to find another way of engaging the enemy. Again the result was an operation hardly conceived by the U.S. Navy for its PTs. Returning from a night patrol off the north coast of Sicily, Lieutenant Dubose intercepted a small sailboat and captured a German officer and six Italian merchant sailors headed for Italy from the island of Lipari, one of the Eolie group north of Italy. Questioned, the sailors indicated that there were no Germans still in the islands, that all there were Italians who would welcome a chance to surrender to Americans.

Accordingly, under orders from Admiral Davidson to effect the surrender of the Eolie Islands, Dubose set off from Palermo on the morning of August 17 aboard *PT 215* commanded by Lieutenant Steele, along with *PT 216* skippered by Lieutenant (jg) Sanders, and *PT 217* commanded by Lieutenant Devol. The boats carried an unusual assortment of passengers: an American military government representative, another Army officer, seven Army enlisted men, and seventeen extra Squadron 15 enlisted men. The destroyer *Trippe* accompanied the PTs as a support force.

The vessels entered Lipari Harbor without opposition. Indeed, the PTs found the Italian Naval Commandant of the islands waiting for them on the dock. Within minutes he had surrendered unconditionally the islands of Alicudi, Filicudi, Salina, Stromboli, Lipari and Volcano.

While the military government officer negotiated with the mayor over the establishment of a civil government, armed PT men and the Army troops rounded up nineteen prisoners; after the commandant sent a radio message demanding concurrence of the other islands in the surrender, the radio was put out of commission. Only the island of Stromboli balked at surrendering.

The PT boats now rumbled over to Stromboli. There they found an Italian chief petty officer and thirty of his men had destroyed the barracks and confidential papers. Barnes's men "occupied" the island, taking nineteen more prisoners and putting the radio station out of commission. The chief and his men, under guard, were put on the PTs for transport back to Sicily and a prison stockade.

On the way back to Palermo, the boats stopped at Lipari once more where they picked up fifty more prisoners bound for the stockade. Back at Palermo the crews learned that Messina had fallen that same day; the campaign for Sicily had ended.[35] The battle for mainland Italy was yet to begin. There followed a short respite before the PTs, MTBs and MGBs were called upon to take part in the invasion of Italy.

Following an artillery barrage across the Strait on September 3, the day Italy signed the Armistice, the first Allied ground troops were ferried across the Strait. They encountered little resistance; but again it was the quiet before the storm.

The Allies' principal opening gambit in the Italian campaign and the battle for the Mediterranean involved Barnes's PT Squadron, two flotillas of MTBs, and a flotilla of British gunboats. The flagship of this small force of combatants was the U.S. destroyer *Knight*. Termed a "Diversion Group," under the command of Capt. C. L. Andrews, its primary mission was to stop enemy coastal traffic north of Naples and capture islands in that famous gulf. On September 8, the small naval force departed from Palermo for the islands of Ventotene, twenty miles west of Naples, Ischia and Capri, carrying fifty seasoned paratroops. In part, the reason for the troops was the hope to capture Mussolini, believed to be on the island.

At 11:45 p.m., the group of vessels approached Ventotene and a recorded broadcast directed that the Italian garrison on the island surrender. But the presence of German troops on Ventotene prevented Italian compliance. The paratroops were thus landed and *Knight* headed back to Palermo for reinforcements. However, by the time the destroyer returned, the Germans had surrendered. But the Diversionary Group missed Mussolini, who it turned out had fled to Sardinia days earlier. On September 12, Ponza surrendered to Andrews's force. On the following day Capri was taken. Ischia and Procida were occupied on September 14. At noon September 17, Andrews's Group was dissolved.[36]

During this period, the Allied invasion of Salerno, code named Operation "Avalanche," had been carried out, D-Day being September 9, with Naples thirty miles to the northwest of the objective.

With Allied troops ashore at Salerno, Squadron 15 spent the following days in Salerno Bay and patrolled by night. As the tanker scheduled to arrive with their gasoline failed to appear, the PTs were forced to limit their operations. While waiting, their main mission was to guard the ships in the roadstead against attacks by E-boats, which by now had acquired a fearsome reputation. While there, the PTs performed a variety of tasks the crews found boring: carrying passengers between ships and beaches, otherwise acting as taxis, as couriers, disseminating orders to vessels that could not otherwise be contacted, laying smoke during air raids, and supplying island garrisons.[37]

On the 18th, Sardinia fell to a force of two MGBs. Again, Mussolini missed being captured, this time by hours. The island of Corsica, Napoleon's birthplace, quickly followed suit. The Royal Navy immediately put Sardinia to use, establishing an advanced base for its Coastal Forces in the magnificent harbor of La Maddalena, the former Italian naval base. By the end of September, Comdr. Robert Allan had moved his base there from Messina; his 20th MGB Flotilla immediately began patrolling the northwestern waters, especially around Elba.[38]

With the arrival of the tanker and its supply of gasoline, Barnes's PTs, now back under command of the Royal Navy, also headed for Maddalena, arriving on October 4 along with the 7th MTB Flotilla. From this point on, except when temporarily detached for special missions, Squadron 15 would be a part of Britain's Coastal Forces in the Mediterranean war.[39]

Almost immediately, part of Barnes's squadron moved to Bastia, on Corsica, putting the PTs within range of the Ligurian Sea and Genoa, Italy's largest port.

Much like the advanced PT bases in the South Pacific, La Maddalena and Bastia were nothing less than stark. The proper repair and support for Squadron 15 did not begin to arrive from Palermo until mid-November; Barnes's men were thus happy to end up with a windfall of galley equipment, cutlery, and crockery from a mined and abandoned British landing craft, "to the incalculable improvement of their own primitive mess."[40]

On September 8, Italy capitulated. In the forthcoming months it would be the Germans who tenaciously resisted the advancing Allied armies fighting their way up the Italian "boot." As Allied aircraft destroyed rail lines and harassed truck convoys on roads, in order to supply their forces fighting in central Italy, the Germans assembled a fleet of small, coastal vessels, including F-lighters; they also commandeered French and Italian coastal vessels. Formed in small convoys, they traveled down the coast at night from Genoa and ports on the French Riviera. To safeguard these convoys, minefields were laid out to sea forming a lane down which the shallow draft vessels could travel, staying close to the shore without concern for Allied destroyers. Further protection was provided by heavy shore batteries, thus discouraging heavy Allied warships from approaching MAS boats commandeered from the Italians, E-boats, and R-boats (Raumbootes)—German designed diesel-powered coastal escort vessels—were also employed in large numbers. Displacing 110 to 175 tons, with a length of 85 to 134.5 feet, with a speed of 23-225 knots, armed with 40-mm and bigger guns, they provided a challenge to the PTs in themselves. The Germans also used torpedo boats, vessels unique to navies such as Germany and Italy, a vessel largely resembling a scaled-down destroyer in size and capability, along the lines of an American DE.[41]

Arguably, however, the most fearsome vessel the Germans used in defense of the coastal convoys was the infamous flak lighter. With their supply columns harassed by the Allies, the Germans pulled a number of F-lighters out of service; these were then armored as well as armed with as many heavy guns as possible, up to and including the famed German 88-mm cannon. More than any weapon during World War II, the 88-mm was feared for its capability as an anti-aircraft and anti-tank gun. Firing a shell weighing 19.8 pounds with a muzzle velocity of 2,690 feet per second, employed by flak lighters they had a range of 52,500 feet. A single 88-mm was capable of knocking out a cruiser; needless to say, a single shell would simply obliterate a PT boat.

Facing these shallow-draft threats, Squadron 15 torpedomen with the Mark VIII torpedoes, tinkered with their underwater missiles in hopes of getting them to run at a shallower depth than eight feet, but this merely caused the Mark VIII to become more unpredictable, alternately porpoising and diving like a playful seal. But PT skippers set them to run shallow anyway, theorizing that a porpoising torpedo at least had a fifty-fifty chance of getting a hit on the shallow draft enemy.

The first definite enemy encounter involving PTs operating from Sardinia and Bastia occurred south of Giglio Island on the night of October 22-23 when the hard-charging Lieutenant DuBose in tactical command of three PTs made a successful torpedo attack on a small cargo vessel escorted by four R- or E-boats. One of four torpedoes fired by the PTs was a hit and the ship disappeared in a blinding flash. As *PT 212* commanded by Lieutenant (jg) Sinclair was lining up for a shot, an out-of-control Mark VIII torpedo fired by one of the other PTs flashed by under his stern. At that moment, DuBose radioed, asking the *212* skipper how many torpedoes he had fired. "None, yet," Sinclair responded, "I'm too damn busy dodging yours."[42]

On the night of November 2-3, two PTs led by Lieutenant O'Brian torpedoed a converted tanker estimated to be of 4,000 tons; before it disappeared, it managed to put an incendiary bullet through a gasoline tank of *PT 207*. The resultant explosion blew a hatch open, and flames shot as high as the top of the PT's radar mast. A quick-thinking radioman grabbed a fire extinguisher, opened the nozzle, threw it below, and slammed the hatch cover closed; another crewman blanketed the tank compartment with CO_2, smothering the flames.[43]

With November came winter conditions in the Mediterranean. Despite high seas and winds, the PTs sought to maintain their nightly patrols. But on occasion, this bordered on the impossible. One such night was November 29; with the weather especially foul, Lieutenant (jg) Clifford commanding *PT 204* and a second boat were patrolling near Genoa. As the hours dragged by, the wind continued to rise; water smashed over the bow in blinding sheets, drowning out the radar signal. Visibility dropped to less than a hundred yards. The *204* soon became separated from the second boat and plunged on alone.

About three and a half miles from Bastia, from out of the darkness came four R-boats within slingshot distance, laboring and plunging on an opposite course. A fifth R-boat then materialized ahead of *PT 204*; before the PT could alter course the two boats struck one another a glancing blow with their bows. Then, at the unbelievable range of ten yards, the R-boats opened fire on the *204*. For a long fifteen seconds the two sides exchanged fire. With the odds five to one, bullets and cannon shells ripped the PT; torpedo tubes, ammunition lockers, ventilators and gun mounts were all hit, the superstructure was reduced to virtual splinters. But in what was nothing short of a miracle, all the enemy's bullets and shells missed the *204's* gasoline tanks, while the engines continued to run without faltering, and what was an even bigger miracle, not a single PT crewman was scratched in the exchange.[44]

In the fall of 1943, the Germans began to operate an increased number of the small Italian destroyers they had commandeered. With a top speed of 30 knots, armed with four to six torpedoes depending on the class, the main battery consisting of three or four 4-inch guns, these steel-hulled coastal vessels were more than a match for a PT boat. With a draft of barely eight feet, they were largely immune to torpedoes.

Barnes's PTs would have a number of close calls with these vessels. One night two PTs patrolling between Elba and Leghorn encountered a pair of these destroyers and were lucky to escape. To add insult to injury, on a stormy night in December, torpedo boats shelled Bastia for fifteen minutes when the seas were too heavy for the PTs to sortie.

Lt. Edwin DuBose.
Courtesy of WWII PT Boats Museum and Archives, Germantown, Tennessee, USA.

Three PT officers of Squadron 15 based at Bastia, Corsica, left to right: Lt. J.B. Mutty, Lt. Richard O'Brian, and Squadron Commander Lt. Comdr. Stanley M. Barnes. *Courtesy of WWII PT Boats Museum and Archives, Germantown, Tennessee, USA.*

PT 211, a Squadron 15 boat, tied up at Bastia, Corsica in February 1944. One of the first PT boats to operate in the Mediterranean Sea, *PT 211* was one of the squadron boats finally handed over to the British upon departure of the Americans. *Courtesy of WWII PT Boats Museum and Archives, Germantown, Tennessee, USA.*

Anticipating a return call, a few nights later Barnes led four boats to sea as a reception committee. Ten minutes after reaching a position offshore, the PTs' radar picked up two targets heading toward Bastia at 20 knots. But then, the targets, later identified as torpedo boats, reversed course. Barnes pursued, hoping to maneuver them into a battle with the PTs off Elba. That is just what happened. There, PTs clashed with the torpedo boats in a confusing melee that ended with no one wounded or killed, and no damage done. German records showed that on this night, the shelling of Bastia had been cancelled due to "unfavorable weather conditions."[45]

While the action was inconclusive, for what is was worth, it did prevent the enemy from taking full advantage of his control of the Italian coast from Gaeta northward.

On October 1, advancing Allied troops entered Naples. They found it in worse condition than Palermo: retreating German troops had left fires burning along the waterfront, the harbor filled with wrecks, and the city in ruins. Delayed time bombs had been left in locations where they were most likely to cause the most havoc among the civilian population. Indeed, it seemed the Germans were driven more by a sense of revenge against the Italians than in preventing Allied use of the port.

In January 1944, two Squadron 15 PT boats were detached temporarily. They would head south to serve as water-taxis for General Mark Clark, commanding the Fifth Army advancing northward through Italy. As noted, PT crews viewed taxi service as boring duty, as it usually was. But this was to be an exception.

On January 22, 1944, Allied troops had landed at Anzio, thirty-seven miles south of Rome. As an Allied amphibious invasion, the operation would acquire the distinction of being among the least successful, one where Axis forces managed to prevent the exploitation of the landing for a prolonged period.

In January 28, General Clark decided to proceed from Naples to Anzio. With members of his staff, he boarded *PT 201* at the mouth of the Volturno River, fourteen miles north of Naples for the seventy-mile run to Anzio. Commanding *PT 201* was Lt.(jg) George Patterson. Accompanied by *PT 216* the *201* started north.

Forty-five miles to the north, the minesweeper *Sway* was patrolling the southern approaches to Anzio. The *Sway* had been warned to expect an attack on Anzio by enemy planes, and the skipper knew that E-boats usually coordinated their attacks with aircraft. Sighting two high-speed vessels approaching out of the sun, *Sway* challenged with its blinker light. Without reducing speed, Patterson answered with a 6-inch signal lamp, too small to be seen against the sun's rays. When *Sway* opened fire, Patterson fired an emergency recognition flare, but it, too, was lost in the sun's rays. As further evidence of a lack of hostile intent, the PTs reduced speed, but this simply made them a better target.

The *Sway's* next shell hit the *201*'s chartroom, killing one of General Clark's officers and a crewman, and wounding Lieutenant Patterson, as well as the boat's executive officer, Ens. Paul R. Benson.[46]

Despite his wound, Ensign Benson took the wheel, zigzagging the *201* back south at high speed. A few miles further south, the *201*'s dead and wounded were transferred to a British minesweeper.

With General Clark still anxious to reach Anzio, the PTs headed north once more. This time they approached the *Sway* at a slower speed and identified themselves as "friendly" with a bigger signal light. With the sun now higher, the *Sway* had no trouble reading the signal and the PTs passed to continue on their way. Ashore at Anzio, the nightmare for Allied ground forces dragged on.

At sea, the formidable system devised by the Germans for protecting their convoys continued to be a challenge for Allied naval forces. Commenting on operations during January and February 1944, Captain J. F. Stevens, RN, commanding Coastal Forces, Mediterranean, declared:

> "There is no question but that the interruption of the enemy's sea communications off the west coast of Italy presents a difficult problem. He had made extensive use of minefields to cover his shipping route, and while Coastal Forces are the most suitable forces to operate in mined areas, the enemy has so strengthened his escorts and armed his 'shipping' that our coastal craft find themselves up against considerably heavier metal. Furthermore, the enemy's use of F-lighters of shallow draft does not provide good torpedo targets. Everything that can be done to improve our chances

of successful attack is being done. Plans for diversionary attacks in the hope of breaking up an enemy convoy and cutting off stragglers have been made. Torpedoes will, if possible, be fired at even shallower settings. Meanwhile, if they cannot achieve destruction, Coastal Forces will harry the enemy and endeavor to cause him the utmost possible alarm, damage and casualties."[47]

Indeed, for the PTs, MTBs and MGBs, the challenge of dealing with the enemy's coastal defensive system was proving costly. It was the Messina Strait all over again, and this time the PTs were involved along with the British. By now, some of Barnes's PTs had been fitted with rocket launchers. The major difficulty with rockets was their lack of accuracy. Nevertheless, Barnes decided, under the circumstances, they were worth a try. On the night of February 18, he departed Bastia on *PT 211* commanded by Lt.(jg) Page H. Tullock, accompanied by *PT 203* under the command of Lt. Robert B. Reader and *PT 202* commanded by Lt.(jg) Robert D. McLeod. Recalled Barnes:

"I saw a small radar target come out from behind the peninsula and head over to one of the small islands south of Giglio. Thinking it might be an F-lighter, I ordered rocket racks loaded. He must have seen us, because whatever it was—probably an E-boat—[it]speeded up and ducked into the island before we could make contact. That presented the first difficulty of a rocket installation. There we were with the racks all loaded and the safety pins out. The weather had picked up a little, and getting those pins back in the rockets and the racks unloaded was going to be a touchy job in the pitch dark on wet, tossing decks. I decided to leave them there for a while to see what would happen. At about midnight it started to kick up a great deal more. I had just about decided that whatever it was we were looking for wasn't going to show up, and I was getting pretty worried about the rockets heaving out of the racks and rolling around in a semi-armed condition on deck. I decided to take one last turn around our patrol area and head for the barn."[48]

In the end, thanks to the PT's radar and Barnes's persistence, the rockets would be put to use.

"On our last southerly leg we picked up a target coming north at about 8 knots, and I closed right away, thinking to spend all our rockets on whatever it was. As we got closer, it appeared to be two small targets in column—a conclusion which I later used as an outstanding example of 'Don't trust your interpretation of radar too blindly.'

"Just about the time we got to the 1,000-yard line firing range the lookouts started reporting vessels everywhere, all the way from our port back around to our starboard bow. I had arranged the other two boats on either side in line abreast and ordered them to stand by to fire on my order over the radio. I gave the order and we all let go together. During the eleven seconds the rockets were in flight nobody fired a shot, but a couple of seconds after the rockets landed what seemed like a dozen enemy craft opened up. The formation was probably three or four F-lighters escorted by two groups of E-boats. We had passed through the two groups of escorts on our way to our firing position. Now it was time to turn away, and as my boat turned to the right we found that the *202* was steaming right into the convoy. To avoid collision we had to turn back and parallel the *202*. Just at that time the engines on my boat started to labor and unbelievably coughed and died—all three of them. We were smack dab in the center of the whole outfit, with the enemy shooting from all sides...The volume was terrific."

Barnes learned later that the *202*'s rudder had temporarily jammed and she was unable to turn. Meanwhile, the *203* lost all electrical power, including the radar and compass lights. When the *203* saw the other two PTs were maintaining their course, she made a wide circle at high speed laying smoke. Confusion now reigned on both sides. Eventually both the *202* and *203* got away by ducking through the enemy formation, while leaving the helpless *211* behind in the midst of the enemy.

"This business lasted for four or five minutes," said Barnes; "even the shore batteries came in to illuminate with starshells. Fortunately, there was enough smoke in the air to keep the issue confused. That confusion was the only thing that saved us."

Since the PTs were not firing guns, the Squadron 15 commander noted, "it was obvious that the enemy was frightfully confused with us weaving through the formation. They were hard at work shooting each other up, I am sure they sank at least one of the E-boats, because several minutes later they started firing again off to the north, and there was a large gasoline fire in the channel which burned for a long time.

"We got clear by the simple process of just sitting still and letting the enemy pass around us and continue north," said Barnes.

After finally getting one engine started, Barnes's PT made its way to the rendezvous point only a couple of miles distant; he arrived just in time to see the other two boats, on the radar screen, leaving. Apparently the two skippers had given the *211* up for lost. Barnes tried to reach them by radio, but got no response.

Forced to return to base alone, the squadron commander expected to find the other two boats badly shot up. To his utter surprise, he found both unscathed. Strangely enough, all three boats had emerged undamaged; equally amazing was the fact that all three PTs were disabled to some degree during the operation. For the two skippers who had failed to rendezvous following the engagement, Barnes had a few well-chosen words which he imparted in private.

As for the rockets, there was no evidence they had inflicted any damage on the enemy; following this experience, Barnes firmly decided there would be no further use of rockets by the squadron's PTs.

Earlier, in November, Barnes proposed another solution to the problem posed by flak lighters. Noting the PTs possessed radar, the MTBs had reliable torpedoes which the American boats lacked, and the MGBs were armed with a six-pounder cannon, a weapon heavier than any gun on a PT boat, Barnes's idea was to form a combined force, with the PTs scouting and coordinating attacks by the British boats. The idea was implemented with some success; however, even the MGBs' guns were no match for the heavy weaponry of the flak lighters.

The solution to the problem came from Comdr. Robert A. Allan at Sardinia. In operational command of the western area, with one flotilla of MTBs and of MGBs along with Barnes's PTs, Allan proposed to form a Coastal Forces Battle Squadron centered on three LCGs (landing craft gun) borrowed from the nearby British amphibious unit. Manned by crack Royal Marine Artillery gunners, each craft mounted two 4.7-inch and two 40-mm cannon; the slow LCGs would be screened against E-boats or destroyer attacks by MTBs and MGBs; as scouts, Barnes's PTs would again provide target data using radar. This would be the most successful small boat unit of the war.[49]

By March 27, the new squadron was assembled and ready for the first operation. The battle line included LCGs *14, 19* and *20* escorted by *MTB 634* and MGBs *660, 662* and *659*. The scouting force consisted of *PT 212* commanded by Lt.(jg) T. Lowry Sinclair and *PT 214* skippered by Lt.(jg) Robert T. Boebel under the tactical command of Lieutenant DuBose riding on the *212*. In addition to scouting, in the event of an attack, the PTs had the added responsibility of screening the force from enemy destroyers that sometimes accompanied the convoys.

In addition to the battle line and the scouting force, the squadron contained a control group: Commander Allan aboard the *218* commanded by Lt.(jg) Thaddius Grundy accompanied by the *208* with Lt.(jg) John M. Torrance at the helm. Allan would be in overall tactical command of the battle squadron, relaying the bearings and ranges to targets received from DuBose to the LCGs.

When the battle line arrived off San Vincenzo, south of Leghorn, on the evening of March 27, DuBose's scouting PTs were dispatched north to conduct a fast sweep in search of targets. At around 10 p.m. Dubose radioed Allan that he had located what he presumed were six F-lighters headed south off the coast. Allan immediately moved his force into position for an interception.

An hour later, Dubose radioed a warning; the six lighters and a two-destroyer escort to seaward. He added his PTs would attack as soon as they were in position. Ten minutes later, the control group's radar picked up the F-lighters and the two destroyers. Recalled Allan: "It was not possible for us to engage the convoy as our Starshells, being fired inshore over the target, would serve to illuminate us for the escorting destroyers which were to seaward. Fire was therefore held during many anxious minutes."[50]

Although filled with tension, in fact, it took DuBose a mere ten minutes to reach a position to attack: Two of his PTs slipped to within four hundred yards and fired three torpedoes before wheeling about and retiring behind a cloud of smoke. However, they did not escape unscathed. A 37-mm shell from one destroyer exploded in *PT 214's* engine room, damaging the center engine and wounding MoMM2/c Joseph F. Grossman, the duty engineer. In spite of his wounds, the motor mac remained at his post and kept the damaged engine running until the boats were safely out of range.

Typically, the retiring PT crews saw a waterspout shoot skyward and heard a deep explosion, but there is no evidence the enemy ships were damaged. What is certain is that the two destroyers, doubtless to everyone's surprise, turned and fled back north, abandoning their charges to their fate—an unthinkable act on the part of an escort.

Commander Allan immediately maneuvered his battle line into position and ordered the LCGs to open fire. The LCGs first fired starshells, which lit the beach brilliantly. Surprised, the confused F-lighter gunners began firing into the sky in the belief they were being attacked by aircraft. The LCGs now opened fire on the targets: the first F-lighter exploded with a tremendous force. Within ten minutes, three more F-lighters were ablaze. The two remaining lighters attempted to escape but were cornered with their backs to the beach and pounded to pieces by the LCGs' 4.7-inch shells. "Of the six [F-lighters] destroyed," commented Allan, "two, judging by the impressive explosions, were carrying petrol, two ammunition, and one a mixed cargo of both." He added with a hint of sorrow, "The sixth sank without exploding."

In commenting on the night's operation, Allan noted a key factor in its success was the attack on the escorts by the PTs, thus allowing the LCGs to fire undisturbed on the convoy of lighters; but for this the action could have developed differently. It was, said Commander Allan, "the crucial point of the whole engagement, and Lt. E. A. Dubose, USNR, and Lt.(jg) R. T. Boebel, USNR, are to be commended for their skill and courage in carrying out this attack.

Also to be commended is Lt.(jg) T. Grundy, USNR, who commanded the controlling PT with coolness and skill.[51]

With the waters around the Tuscan Archipelago teeming with enemy traffic, another raid, termed "Operation Gun," was carried out on the night of April 24. Once again the three LCGs provided the battle line and Allan rode on *PT 218,* one of the boats making up the control unit; this time the *218* was joined by *PT 209.* Again Dubose led the scouting force on *PT 212* accompanied by the *202* and *203.* MTBs *633, 640* and *655* with MGBs *657, 660,* and *662* rounded out the escort group tied directly to the LCGs.

Departing Bastia, the force was in position off Vada Rocks by 10 p.m. Within five minutes of their arrival, both the scouting and control PTs had numerous contacts on their radar screens, converging on Allan's force from both north and south. With targets approaching from both directions Allan wondered if both were supply convoys—one loaded headed south, the other empty returning to Genoa or the French Riviera, or was the group from the south about twenty-five miles from the battle group an escort force intent on meeting and screening the lighters headed south? Allan decided prudence was called for. He would wait and see.

After a considerable wait while the battle group remained undetected, the two convoys were observed passing one another and continuing on their respective courses. With that, Allan ordered an attack on the southbound convoy, a group of eight F-lighters and a tug en route from Leghorn with supplies for San Stefano further down the coast.

The F-lighters were close inshore when the LCGs opened fire; initial starshells illuminated the F-lighters. Within three minutes, two were vaporized, hit by the LCGs' 4.7-inch shells. Burning debris blown skyward landed on the nearby shore starting brush fires, providing a brilliant spectacle visible as far away as Bastia some fifty miles away.[52] Two more F-lighters quickly hit were sent to the bottom, along with the tug. Allan sent the MGBs to close the beach in search of any further targets while he maneuvered the battle group into position to intercept more radar contacts to seaward. The MGBs found one F-lighter beached, undamaged and abandoned by most of its crew. They shelled the vessel, setting it afire before picking up survivors. Allan then ordered the MGBs involved back to Bastia.

Meanwhile, the LCGs had fired on three more targets. These turned out to be flak lighters. Fortunately, two of these lethal vessels were hit with the first salvo before they could return fire. Exploding ammunition now provided another spectacular display. The third flak lighter poured a torrent of fire at the LCGs; 20-, 40- and 88-mm shells churned the sea near the unarmored British landing craft.

In response, Allan ordered *PT 218* to charge the lighter and draw its fire. Before the *218* could close, the flak lighter was hit and withdrew behind the smoke created by the first two exploding flak lighters. Allan now ordered the accompanying control boat, *PT 209,* to pursue the damaged flak lighter. The *209* raced forward into the smoke accompanied by several MGBs. Charging through the darkness, Lieutenant Eldridge soon found the crippled lighter. Although the PT and MGBs inflicted further damage, the flak lighter crew managed to beach their vessel south of San Vincenzo.

Meanwhile, DuBose had decided to overtake the northbound convoy which had been carefully avoided earlier. Slipping undetected to within firing range, the PTs fired three torpedoes and turned to idle quietly away. However, DuBose's boats were immediately taken under fire by the enemy. The PTs opened their throttles wide and withdrew at high speed behind a protective smoke screen. Neither side suffered damages in the encounter. It was after midnight when the Battle Squadron finally regrouped. It seemed the hunting was over for the night. However, at 4 a.m. April 25, the radio station at Bastia warned Allan of a radar contact three miles due west of Capraia. Suspecting this was an E-boat lying in wait for his return, Allan sent DuBose's scouting group ahead to investigate.

In fact, the enemy force consisted of three German torpedo boats; as near as can be determined, the vessels were engaged in unrelated minelaying operations off Capraia.[53]

As DuBose's PTs closed to about 2,500 yards, too far away for a likely torpedo hit, a sharp-eyed German lookout spotted the American boats. Enemy starshells illuminated the intruders. In response, a quick-thinking crewman on the *202* fired a captured five-star recognition flare; this caused the Germans to hesitate allowing DuBose's PTs to continue their approach. At 1,700 yards, DuBose decided he had pushed his luck far enough. Four Mark VIII torpedoes hit the water for the run toward the enemy as the PTs turned retire. Shortly, one torpedo hit the *TA 23*; now the enemy opened fire on the withdrawing PTs but all escaped unscathed. The *TA 23* was so badly damaged in the action that she had to be abandoned and sunk by one of the other vessels.

This finally ended the night's action for the Battle Squadron. This model of Allied cooperation, without damage or loss to itself, had sunk five F-lighters, four formidable flak lighters and a tug, scored a torpedo hit on a destroyer, and captured a dozen German prisoners.

As the end of April drew near, two additional PT squadrons began to arrive in the Mediterranean. Both were newly commissioned, Squadron 29 with new 80-foot Elcos, numbered *552-563*, and Squadron 22 fitted with new 78-foot Higgins PTs, numbered *302-313*. Both would be based at Sardinia and Corsica. Notably, both were armed with the new Mark XIII aerial torpedoes with roll-off racks as described earlier. As a result of their experience with the flawed Mark VIII torpedoes, the veterans of Squadron 15 were overjoyed to receive their Mark XIII torpedoes. On the night of May 18, it fell to the veteran Lieutenant Clifford on the *204* boat, accompanied by two other PTs, to make the first attack with the new torpedoes. It proved to be a near-fatal experience. Patrolling in the Tuscan Archipelago the PTs' radar detected what turned out to be two flak lighters. Under a hail of bullets and cannon fire the PTs closed and launched their torpedoes. However, one of the Mark XIII torpedoes managed to do what the old torpedo had never been quite able to do; circling back the missile hit the *204* in the stern, punching its warhead into the lazaret, leaving its body dangling outside in the PT's wake.

Climbing down into the small compartment at the PT's stern, TM2/c Lewis H. Riggsby stuffed towels in the warhead's impeller vanes preventing it from becoming armed. This experience foresaw the Mark XIII torpedoes' poor performance rivaling that of the old Mark VIII torpedo. Sadly, the U.S. Navy's PTs had yet to be armed with a reliable torpedo.[54]

Nonetheless, the action continued in the Mediterranean, with additional operations carried out by Allan's Battle Squadron. In May, bolstering his operations, Allan received additional forces in the form of the 7th MTB Flotilla, an unusual mixture of American-built Higgins PTs and new Vosper MTBs.[55]

In an effort to increase pressure on the enemy, Squadron 29 began operating from Calvi, a new base established on the west coast of Corsica, closer to the French and Italian coast west of Genoa. Squadron 15 was now split between Calvi and Bastia. Barnes, who by now had received the Navy Cross for leadership and heroism in the Tunisian and Sicilian campaigns, was now in operational command of all three PT squadrons.[56]

About this time, Allan's MTBs received a new and improved British torpedo, the British Mark VIII Two-Star equipped with a magnetic exploder. Rather than requiring a hit, the torpedo exploded as it passed beneath the keel of the target ship, detonated by the vessel's own magnetic field. This was the ideal weapon for coping with the shallow-draft lighters. Again, the plan was to combine radar-equipped PTs with MTBs and their weaponry. The results were nothing short of dramatic. On the night of May 9, three MTBs of the 7th Flotilla sailed with *PT 203*. The MTBs' new torpedoes blew up two F-lighters. The following night was another success; two MTBs accompanied by *PT 214* attacked a merchant vessel escorted by five R-boats off Vada Rocks. The MTBs' torpedoes scored one positive and one probable hit on the merchant vessel and one probable hit on one of the escorts. On May 27, off Spezia, three MTBs accompanied by *PT 218* intercepted five F-lighters escorted by an E-boat. The MTBs blew up three lighters with their new torpedoes, and forced a fourth lighter to beach. Resuming patrol, an hour later the MTBs and PT sighted a 1,500-ton merchant ship escorted by a destroyer or a small sloop. With only one torpedo among the MTBs, the shot proved to be a hit. The merchant ship broke in half and sank. Having fired its four Mark XIII torpedoes, all misses, the disgusted *PT 214* crew, other than providing radar data, had failed to contribute to the total night's score of three F-lighters and one merchant ships sunk.

But the American Mark XIII torpedoes were not a complete failure. From May to July, operating alone, PTs claimed two corvettes, eleven F-lighters, one cargo ship and several small craft sunk, and one motor torpedo boat, *MAS 562,* captured.

With the 7th MTB Flotilla continuing to patrol the waters in search of enemy vessels, the PTs joined the British 56th MTB/MGB Flotilla as part of an amphibious invasion force, code named Operation "Brassard," the invasion of the island of Elba. Dominating the Tuscan Archipelago, Elba, famous in history as the first home of Napoleon on exile, is a rugged little island some thirty miles long; it was garrisoned by about three thousand Germans, a figure many times the Allied intelligence estimate. D-Day was planned for June 17, thirteen days after General Clark's Fifth Army entered Rome, following some nine months of bitter fighting against the German army as the Allies advanced north from Salerno. As a point of national pride, the French Army of Liberation was insistent on being the force to take Elba back from the Germans.

One problem the invasion faced was the large number of mines in the waters off the island. Deep-draft ships could not be risked there. On the other hand, for nine months the PTs and boats of Coastal Forces had operated in these waters with immunity. Thus the decision was made that PT and MTBs and MGBs would support the landings.

On the night of June 16-17, thirty-seven of Barnes's PTs joined the British boats providing naval support in landing twelve thousand French, North African and Senegalese troops. Again Barnes's PT were the only U.S. Navy combat vessels engaged.

Again the PTs made use of their sound gear: five PTs approached the northern coast of the island at midnight; about a half-mile offshore, they put eighty-seven French raiders over the side in rubber life rafts. Then the five boats joined five other PTs at the side of Elba closest to the mainland. At 2 a.m. the PTs began racing along off the coast of the island, laying smoke and dropping smoke generators. With the shoreline blanketed behind the 16,000-yard-long towering wall of smoke, four PTs moved to the seaward side of the smoke and began blaring the recorded sound of an invasion fleet over loud-speakers. To add to the illusion, the PTs fired rockets toward the shore simulating a pre-invasion shore bombardment. The remaining PTs in the group also carried out an imitation of radio conversations as if being made between vessels involved in landing operations.

Their efforts seemed a success: enemy searchlights in Elba probed the smoke, and shore batteries sent a stream of shells hurtling seaward, thus disclosing their positions for use of air strikes to be carried out at dawn.

Meanwhile, at the actual landing site on the island's south coast, Lt.(jg) Eads Poitevent, Jr., commanding *PT 211,* was serving as radar picket to guide the landing craft ashore. To his intense alarm, he observed a radar pip emerge out of the harbor at Marina de Campo. He could not make an attack without alarming the enemy ashore; but somehow he had to divert the enemy and lure him away from the landing barges.[57]

Poitevent chose to sail the *211* boldly toward what turned out to be an E-boat; easing closer Poitevent made friendly blinker signals then began moving away from the landing craft. It required fifteen minutes of effort to lure the E-boat into harmless waters and he was able to return to his post.

But the wandering E-boat would not stay away. It finally blundered into the path of a PT laden with a deck load of British commandos heading for a pre-invasion site. The PT was forced to put the commandos over the side three-quarters of a mile further from shore than planned. Another PT saw the meandering E-boat, and believing it was a friendly vessel, tried to join it in a formation. Lt.(jg) Harold J. Nugent commanding *PT 210* having observed the E-boat's wanderings, issued a subtle warning to the PT by the radio. The E-boat finally faded off the radar and ceased to be a problem.

With the waters finally clear, the PT crews breathed easier, but only temporarily. Radar showed a big target approaching. Preparations were made to launch torpedoes, but the PTs held their fire until a positive identification could be made: the target on radar could be friendly invasion vessels slightly off course.

Lieutenant Nugent challenged with his blinker light. The closest vessel answered, flashing the correct signal as specified. Recalled Nugent:

"...convinced that the ships were part of the invasion convoy which had probably become lost, I called to my

executive officer, Lt.(jg) Joel W. Bloom, to be ready to look
up the ship's correct position in our copy of the invasion plan,
I brought the *210* up to the starboard side of the nearest ship,
took off my helmet, put the megaphone to my mouth, and
called over, 'What ship are you?' I shall never forget the
answer. First there was a string of guttural words, followed
by a broadside from the ship's 88-mm and five or six 20-mm
guns. The first blast carried the megaphone away and tore the
right side off a pair of binoculars that I was wearing around
my neck. It also tore through the bridge of the boat, jamming
the helm, knocking out the bridge controls, and scoring a
direct hit on the three engine emergency cutout switches
which stopped the engines.

"I immediately gave the order to open fire, and though
we were dead in the water and had no way of controlling the
boat, she was in a position to deliver a full broadside.

"After a few minutes of heavy fire, we had reduced the
firepower of the closest ship to one wildly wavering 20-mm
and one 88-mm cannon which continued to fire over our
heads throughout the engagement.

"It was easy to identify the ships, as the scene was well
lighted with tracers. They were three ships traveling in a close
V, an E-boat in the center with an F-lighter on either flank.

"We were engaging the F-lighter on the starboard flank
of the formation. As the ships started to move toward our
stern the injured F-lighter screened us from the fire of the
other two ships, so I gave the order to cease fire.

"In the ensuing silence we clearly heard screams and
cries from the F-lighter.

"Two members of our engine-room crew, who were
topside as gun loaders during battle, were sent to the engine
room to take over the chief engineer's duties, for I was sure
he was dead or wounded. However, he had been working on
the engines throughout the battle and had already found the
trouble. We immediately got underway.

"We found out, however, that our rudder was jammed in
a dead-ahead position, but by a great good fortune we were
headed directly away from the enemy, so I dropped a couple

of smoke pots over the side and we moved off. The enemy shifted his fire to the smoke pots, and we lay to and started repairs.[58]

To Nugent's astonishment not a single *210* crewman was wounded. But the boat had taken a massive beating: one burst of 20-mm shells had ripped through the chartroom, reduced the chart table to splinters, knocked out the lighting system, detuned the radio and scarred the radar. Another burst had torn though the engine room, damaged the control panels and the hull. Fortunately, all hits were above the waterline. Also holed were the turrets, turret lockers and ventilators.

"We called the *209* alongside and sent off a radio report to the flagship on the action and the direction in which the ships retired," said the *210* skipper.

The commander of the *209* told Nugent that his boat had been hit only twice, but with deadly effect. One of the shells had hit the boat's 40-mm gun loader, killing him instantly.

Allied troops had overrun Elba within two days. The subsequent mounting of heavy guns on Elba by the Allies denied Germans the use of nearby coastal waters and the road running along the Italian coast.

Even before the Allied landings on Elba, there were changes: Many of the MTB and MGB flotillas were being transferred to the Adriatic to join others already there. With the landings on Elba complete, more followed. Finally, on August 1, the PTs were withdrawn from operations to prepare for the invasion of southern France, scheduled for August 15.[59] The final phase of the naval war in the Mediterranean was about to start.

CHAPTER NINETEEN

ACTION IN
THE ENGLISH CHANNEL

Even as the Mediterranean campaign progressed with all its attendant drama and uncertainty the main event, the Allied invasion of France, code named Operation "Overlord," was now the focus of the war in Europe. As in previous naval operations in waters close to enemy-held coasts, PT boats were to play a significant role.

As usual, what was needed at the start was accurate intelligence. In April 1944, in response to an OSS request, PT Squadron 2, having ceased operations at the end of 1943 at the conclusion of the Guadalcanal campaign, was recommissioned with three Higgins PTs, the *71, 72* and *199*. Commanded by Lt. Comdr. John Bulkeley, the squadron was specifically formed to carry out cloak-and-dagger operations, landing and picking up intelligence agents along the enemy-occupied coast of France. For this mission the PTs were fitted with special navigational equipment to aid in locating points on the French coast. In addition, crews were trained in launching and rowing special four-oared boats with padded sides and muffled oarlocks, allowing men and equipment to be landed on beaches swiftly and silently on the blackest of nights.[1]

Squadron 2 arrived at Dartmouth in April, making it the first American PT squadron to operate in the English Channel. Not surprisingly, as PT men, the assignment was viewed with less than enthusiasm. An example of a mission likely to prompt the most grumbling was the order to land on the Normandy shore and scoop up buckets of sand to be returned to England. The men could not have known that a scientist who claimed to know the Normandy beachhead declared the point where the landings were scheduled to take place consisted of spongy peat covered with a thin layer of sand, and Allied tanks, trucks and other mobile equipment would bog down helplessly on these beaches. In any event, the samples of sand returned by the PTs proved the scientist was wrong, and that the invasion plans need not be changed.

The Squadron's first cloak-and-dagger mission occurred on May 19; that night, *PT 71* landed agents and their equipment on a beach within five hundred yards of German sentries without being detected. By the time the operation ended in November, the Squadron had completed nineteen secret missions for the OSS. The crews never knew the identities of their charges, and never made enemy contact, which was the whole idea.[2]

With the Allied invasion of Europe scheduled for the first week in June, three new PT squadrons were shipped across the Atlantic for operations in the English Channel, Squadron 34 commanded by Lt. Allen H. Harris fitted with twelve new 80-foot Elco boats, numbered *498-509*; Squadron 35 led by Lt. Comdr. N. Richard Davis, Jr., also with twelve new Elco boats, numbered *510-521*; and Squadron 30 under the command of Lt. Robert L. Searles, a veteran of the Guadalcanal campaign and the clashes with the Tokyo Express, with twelve Higgins PTs, numbered *450-461*. Appointed commander of all PT operations was Lt. Comdr. John Bulkeley.[3]

The primary role of the PTs and British MTBs based on the English Channel during the invasion would be to defend the flanks of the Allied spearhead landing on the French coast and to maintain guard over the subsequent flow of cross-Channel traffic of supplies, equipment and added troops. It was anticipated that the main threat would come from enemy destroyers and other small combat vessels, of which the Germans were well equipped. Of special concern were German E-boats based along the enemy-held coast Cherbourg to Holland under the command of Fregattenkapitan (Commander) Rudolph Peterson, with headquarters at Scheveningen. In the Mediterranean, the E-boats had had considerable success, at least during the earlier part of the war. With increased signs of a pending invasion of France, the Germans had increased the number of E-boats stationed along the English Channel.

The Allied fear of E-boats was well founded. Although PT boats in the Mediterranean were likely to encounter F-lighters and flak lighters, or even Italian MAS boats, in the English Channel it was the E-boats that were a source of concern. The German boats' light gray color, with their low silhouette and evasive tactics made them a force to be reckoned with. At 6 knots, the German boats with their diesel engines were difficult to detect at night. In calm seas, their top speed of 40 knots or more provided a tremendous advantage over the Allied boats, and in the typically rough waters of the North Sea and the Channel, the German boats' round-bilge hull translated into a clear advantage over the American and British boats with their hard-chine hulls, hulls that tended to slam heavily in rough seas.[4] However, like the Japanese destroyers in the Pacific, the E-boats lacked radar, thus providing the PTs with some operational advantage. Aware an invasion of France was imminent, although not certain of the date or location, the German defenders mounted their own preparations. In keeping with basic military doctrine, the commander of the E-boats was soon engaged in a battle of wits with the Allies. One of the most telling E-boat blows involved the 5th and 9th Flotillas based at Cherbourg. In the early hours of April 28 the German boats boldly crossed the Channel and attacked a convoy of American LSTs engaged in an invasion rehearsal in Lyme Bay, off England's south coast. Through the use of torpedoes, the E-boats sank two LSTs and damaged a third; the E-boats escaped to return to base without loss or damage. The American loss numbered 749 U.S. soldiers and sailors.

An alarmed Rear Admiral Alan G. Kirk, commanding the Western Naval Task Force, the American portion of the planned invasion, perceived the E-boats at Cherbourg as a threat that had to be dealt with. Kirk's proposed solution was PT boats. This created a crisis when Commander Bulkeley told the admiral that the .50-caliber guns in the PTs' turrets were insufficient armament to deal with the more heavily armed E-boats. For some reason, possibly because there were no enemy barges to be dealt with in the English Channel, or possibly because of the rush to get the new PT squadrons shipped across the Atlantic to the Channel for the invasion of Europe, the PTs lacked the 37-mm on the bow that was part of the regular armament on boats headed for the South Pacific.

Kirk's reaction was straightforward and immediate. On May 28, he cabled his immediate superior, Admiral Sir Bertram Ramsey, RN, Supreme Naval Commander: "Am most desirous of obtaining for American PT boats under Lt. Comdr. Bulkeley suitable semi-automatic gun for mounting on forecastle. This weapon needed to counter German stern gun on E-boats when chasing them. U.S. Mark IV 37-mm cannon is most suitable type known in this theater."[5]

Since none of these guns were available in Europe, the request sparked an extraordinary response among the top Allied commanders: Admiral Ramsey forwarded Kirk's request to General Eisenhower, Supreme Commander, who promptly forwarded it to Generals Marshal and Arnold in Washington for immediate action. By the evening of June 2, U.S. Navy aircraft were en route to Europe with the first 37-mm cannons destined for Bulkeley's PTs at the Royal Navy base at Portland, England: crews immediately set to work installing the weapons. Additional 37-mm cannons followed for installation in the days ahead.

In brief, Operation "Neptune," the naval part of "Overlord," called for two massive task forces to land troops on the French coast, one on either side of the line represented by Seine Bay. The east side was the British area, the west, the American, the latter under the command of Admiral Kirk; units of the U.S. First Army would land at "Omaha" and "Utah," an area extending over a twenty-mile front. The American PTs would screen the west flank from enemy naval forces, the MTBs and MGBs the British, or opposite flank.[6]

With D-Day originally scheduled for June 5, a group of three PT boats were to be part of the spearhead forces. As such, they departed England on the fourth to rendezvous with minesweepers off the coast of the Isle of Wight and began to cross the Channel towards the Seine Bay. Only after they were on their way did General Eisenhower decide that, in view of the bad weather forecast, that D-Day be postponed until the sixth. As it was, the three PTs were all set to make a landing on their own, a day ahead of time, possibly disclosing the location of the forthcoming invasion, the consequences of which hardly bear contemplating. Luckily they were intercepted by a patrolling destroyer when they were only halfway across the Channel and sent back to Portland.

Although both invasion flanks were targeted by Fuhrer der Schnellboote Petersen, thanks to Allied vigilance, the E-boats were kept at bay on the first day. But this changed. During the period of June 8 to June 12, of the sixty-eight Allied invasion vessels lost, notwithstanding the presence of PT boats, only mines sank or damaged more vessels than E-boats.[7]

While the PTs had little contact with E-boats on the west flank, their ability to operate with impunity in mined waters proved an asset. Rather than battling E-boats, the PT crews would spend much of their time rescuing survivors of mined ships. On June 8, the destroyer *Glennon* was maneuvering off the Saint Marcouf Islands, north of Utah Beach preparatory to bombard a shore battery. While going astern, the ship struck a mine. A minesweeper took the crippled ship in tow while a second minesweeper went ahead, sweeping a path. The destroyer-escort *Rich* approached and her skipper asked if he could be of assistance.

"Negative," the *Glennon's* captain answered, "clear area cautiously, live mines." The words came too late. An explosion shook the *Rich* from stem to stern; immediately a second explosion tore fifty feet of the aft end of the DE away; then a third mine exploded forward. Her keel broken, the *Rich* was reduced to a mass of wreckage, decks littered with the bodies and body parts of crewmen.

Nearby PTs rapidly closed on the DE to take survivors off the ship or from the mine-filled waters. A crewman on *PT 508* spotted a survivor bobbing in the water and heaved him a rescue line. The sailor calmly refused the offer: "Never mind the line," he said, "I have no arms to catch it."[8]

The skipper of the *508*, Lt. Calvin R. Whorton, dove in the sea to rescue the armless sailor. But it was too late: by then the man had gone under. Fifteen minutes later, the *Rich* followed, along with 79 of her crew: seventy-three wounded survived.

Nor were the PTs completely safe from mines. On the evening of June 7, *PT 505* closed on what the crew thought was the periscope of a U-boat. As the *505* was preparing to drop its depth charges she hit a mine. The explosion injured two crewmen; one of the *505's* depth charges was blown off its mount, the Packard engines were shifted off their mounts and the boat began to sink by the stern.

In an effort to save the vessel, the crew jettisoned the torpedoes and the other depth charge, transferring the radar and radio to *PT 507*. The *507* then took the crippled PT in tow, towing it to Saint Marcouf Island. On the following morning, the landing craft hauled the *505* up on the beach.

Later, when the tide went out, leaving the *505* high and dry for six hours, the determined crew used the time to patch the hole in the hull. On June 11, *PT 500* took the *505* in tow for the long voyage back to Portland, England, a trip made even longer by the fact that the tow line broke four times during the passage.[9]

Ashore, the ground war continued, with Allied successes falling far short of projected gains: on Omaha Beach American troops had a precarious hold. By the end of the first day, the Germans had recovered a copy of the Allied plan indicating Cherbourg was an American objective. Despite the threat of entrapment, Hitler refused to allow the troops in Cherbourg to pull back. On the eighteenth, American troops closed on the port, and Hitler personally charged the commandant of the Cherbourg garrison "to defend to the last bunker and leave the enemy not a harbor but a field of ruins." The garrison defended Cherbourg until June 27; as part of the defense, a number of coastal batteries continued to hold out on the outer breakwater.

To silence the batteries, the Navy sent an oddly composed group of six PTs and the destroyer *Shubrick*. Just what the PTs were expected to accomplish against heavy guns shielded by concrete casemates is not clear. Perhaps the reputation of the PTs for accomplishing the near-impossible had misled the high command. But a daylight attack on shore batteries by PT boats defies logic.

Not too surprisingly, Lieutenant Commander Bulkeley led the PTs. Leaving four boats posted offshore with the destroyer, Bulkeley, aboard the *510,* led the *521* as they closed on the forts. At a range of 150 yards, the PTs futilely raked the forts with machine gun and cannon shells. The enemy's return fire was intense and accurate, hitting and disabling the *521*. For five long minutes the *PT 521* lay dead in the water while her motor macs worked feverishly to restart the engines and Bulkeley's PT raced in circles around the stalled vessel.

With near-misses falling close to the *Shubrick,* the destroyer's skipper recalled the PTs and moved out of range; the *510* and *521* followed, having accomplished little other than to expend ammunition and draw enemy fire. Fortunately, none of the crewmen were wounded or killed.[10]

With the fall of Cherbourg came more changes; Britain's Coastal Forces, previously responsible for operations off the Cherbourg Peninsula, were switched from Plymouth to the eastern flank to work with MTBs covering the British assault area. In the western area assigned to PTs, a flotilla of gunboats and MTBs were added, providing further support. As was the case since the first days of the invasion, there were few encounters with the elusive E-boats; but much effort was involved in rescuing survivors of mined ships, as well as delivering messages and ferrying passengers. In one case, *PT 71* commanded by Lt. William N. Snelling cruised close to the invasion beaches with Generals Eisenhower, Marshall, Arnold, Hodges and Bradley, plus Admirals Kirk, King, Stark, Wilkes and Moon, almost certainly a record for the amount of gold brass to be carried on one PT boat.

Following reduced enemy activity in the American zone, the PTs of Squadrons 30 and 35 were transferred to Portsmouth, while the rest of the PTs joined the British boats operating from Dartmouth and Plymouth off the coast of Brittany and among the Channel Islands. And there were other changes; after lengthy service with PT boats, Bulkeley was given command of a destroyer, the *Endicott.* His position as commander of PT squadrons in the area was assumed by Lieutenant Harris.[11]

As the ground battles along the Normandy coast increased in intensity, possession of the Channel Islands, Jersey, Alderney, Guernsey and Sark, by the Germans became a source of concern: with a naval base on Jersey, it was the practice of the Germans to carry out nightly sorties against Allied vessels. The mission of PT Squadrons 30 and 35 was to seal off the Channel Islands.

For the Americans, the operation began on a grim note: on the night of August 8, five Squadron 35 boats supported by the destroyer *Maloy* were patrolling off Jersey. The weather had been good during the night, but as dawn approached, a thick fog rolled in. At 5:30 a.m. the *Maloy's* more efficient radar detected six targets. Aboard the destroyer in tactical command of the PTs, Lt. H. J. Sherertz, dispatched three boats from the northern end of the scouting line to launch an attack. Blinded by the fog the PTs fired their torpedoes by use of radar; all were misses.

Thirty minutes later, Lieutenant Sherertz vectored *PTs 508* and *509* to an attack position. The two boats, using their own radar, charged through the swirling fog at full speed. At five hundred yards the commander of *PT 509*, Lt. Harry M. Crist, a veteran of action in the South Pacific, fired a single torpedo. Lieutenant Whorton, the skipper of *PT 508*, the captain who had earlier tried to save the armless sailor, was unable to launch his torpedoes as his radar chose that moment to break down. To assist the *508* in lining up for a shot, Lieutenant Crist conned Whorton's boat by radio as the two PTs circled back for a second attack. This time, both boats launched torpedoes using Crist's radar; again all were misses.[12]

Circling back after completing the attack, Whorton lost sight of the *508* in the fog but heard gunfire somewhere in the fog. When he completed the circle, Whorton found only swirling fog. Whorton's hour-long search for the *509*, hampered by his defective radar, proved unsuccessful.

Lieutenant Sherertz finally ordered Whorton to return to the *Maloy* with his defective radar and the search was continued by *PTs 503* and *505*: At 8 a.m. the PTs' radar detected a target in the St. Helier roadstead. At two hundred yards, the fog lifted briefly to reveal an enemy minesweeper dead ahead on a collision course. The quick firing *503* unleashed a torpedo which missed as both PTs opened fire on the German vessel. In the brief but violent exchange of gunfire at point-blank range, two PT sailors were killed and four wounded on *PT 503*, and one crewman was wounded on the *505*.[13]

On the following day, a search plane sighted the body of a crewman from the missing *509*; ten days later a bullet-riddled portion of the *509*'s hull was discovered floating in the Channel. Not until Germany surrendered was the mystery surrounding the fate of the *509* and her crew revealed. The source of the revelations was its sole survivor, RM2/c John L. Page, following his liberation from a prison camp the following year. His story is noteworthy in that it provides a rare view of the sudden and violent end to which a PT and crew could be lost in combat. It also offers an illustration of the different conditions PT crewmen experienced when taken captive by the Germans rather than by the Japanese. Recalled Page:

> "After firing one torpedo by radar, the *509* circled and came in for a gunnery run. I was in the charthouse on the radar. Lt.(jg) John K. Pavlis was at the wheel. I remember we were moving fast and got pretty close before receiving return fire. When it came it was heavy and accurate.
>
> "One shell burst in the chartroom, knocking me out. When I came to, I was trying to beat out flames with my hands. I was wounded and the boat was on fire, but I pulled the detonator switch to destroy the radar and then crawled on deck.
>
> "The bow of our boat was hung up on the side of a 180-foot minesweeper. From the deck of the enemy sweeper, Germans were pouring in small-arms fire and grenades. Every thing aft of the cockpit was burning. I struggled forward through the bullets and bursting grenades to the bow—I have no idea how long that journey took—and the Germans tossed me a line. I had just enough strength to take it and they hauled me aboard."[14]

According to Page, the Germans stretched him out on the sweeper's deck while they struggled to pry the burning PT boat free of their vessel. They barely succeeded: Just as the *508* broke clear, it exploded with a massive roar. "I couldn't see it," said Page, "but I felt the heat and the blast."

As the minesweeper headed back to St. Helier, German crewmen carried the wounded Page to the crew's quarters for emergency medical treatment: Page was in a bad way; he had a broken right arm and leg, a bullet was lodged in his right lung, and his body had 37 bullet and shrapnel wounds. It was incredible that he was alive. But many of the German crew were not.

> "I managed to count the dead," said Page. "There were fifteen of them and a good number wounded. It's difficult to

estimate how many, because they kept milling around. I guess
I conked out for a while. The first thing I remember is a first-
aid man putting a pack on my back and arm. Then I could
hear the noise of a ship docking.

"After they removed the dead and wounded, they took me
ashore at St. Helier. They laid me out on the dock for quite a
while, and a couple of civilians—I found out later they were
Gestapo agents—tried to question me, but they saw I was
badly shot up, so they didn't try to question me further."[15]

The critically wounded Page was taken to the former English
hospital in St. Helier; there skilled German surgeons performed a
series of operations—he could not recall how many—removing
bullets and shrapnel from his body. The operations would continue
for four months, the final operation to be performed on December
27, 1944. Page was liberated on May 8, 1945, when Germany
surrendered.

While Page was in the hospital, three bodies of the PT crew were
recovered, washed ashore on Jersey. The British Red Cross took
over the bodies and they were buried with full military honors.[16]

In the meantime, the battles off the Normandy coast increased in
intensity. Nevertheless, by September 1, all German vessels had
been driven from the Dover Straits. For the first time in four years
the Channel was cleared of the enemy. During the final week, Allied
naval forces, including PTs and MTBs, sank nine armed landing
craft, five coastal vessels, two trawlers, two R-boats and one E-boat,
and damaged several more E-boats to the point they were no longer
serviceable.

With the Allied armies ashore advancing, most of the Channel
ports were liberated by the end of the month. With the main phase
of the invasion of Normandy complete and the Channel cleared of
the enemy, supplies could be landed anywhere along the coast
without naval support. At this point, with the exception of Squadron
35, now based at Cherbourg, the PT squadrons operating in the
Channel were disbanded, the boats transferred to Russia under lend-
lease.

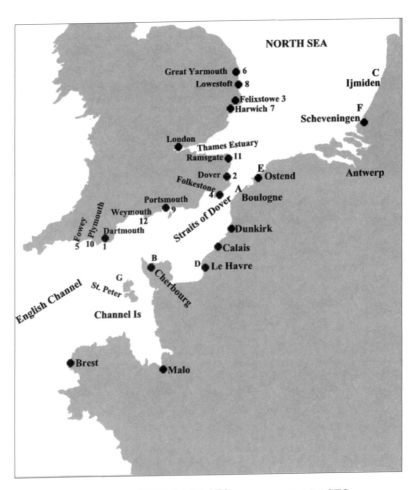

NORTH SEA

Great Yarmouth ● 6
Lowestoft ● 8
Felixstowe 3
Harwich 7

C
Ijmiden

F
Scheveningen ●

London ●
Thames Estuary
Ramsgate ● 11
Dover ● 2
Folkestone 4
A
Portsmouth ● E ● Ostend
Weymouth 9 Straits of Dover Boulogne
12
Fowey Plymouth
Dartmouth Dunkirk ●
5 10 1 Calais ●
D ● Le Havre
B ●
G Cherbourg
St. Peter
English Channel
Channel Is

Antwerp

Brest ●
Malo ●

MTB BASES

Dartmouth (1)
Dover (2)
Felixstowe (3)
Folkstone (4)
Fowey (5)
Great Yarmouth (6)
Harwich (7)
Lowestoft (8)
Portsmouth (9)
Plymouth (10)
Ramsgate (11)
Weymouth (12)

S-BOAT BASES

Boulogne (A)
Cherbourg (B)
Ijmiden (Holland) (C)
Le Havre (D)
Ostend (Belgium) (E)
Scheveningen (Holland) (F)
St Peter (Guernsey) (G)

PT BASES

Dartmouth (1)
Plymouth (10)
Portsmouth (9)

CHAPTER TWENTY

THE RIVIERA WAR

Even as Allied armies landed at Normandy and began their advance, a second Allied invasion was brewing in southern France. Owing to the immense demand for supplies, the Allies found the available Channel ports incapable of handling the need. Another port was necessary. The result was Operation "Anvil," as it was originally called; "Dragoon," as Churchill called it, since he claimed he was "dragooned" into it by Eisenhower and Roosevelt.[1]

Since the Allies lacked the shipping to carry out the Normandy and southern invasion simultaneously, the latter was postponed until August 15. H-Hour was 8 a.m., Marseilles was the main objective, with the French naval port of Toulon the second target. With both well protected by 240-mm coast defense batteries, rather than make a direct assault Allied troops would land on nearby beaches.

On August 1, PT Squadrons 15, 22 and 29 commanded by Commander Barnes were withdrawn from operations in the Ligurian Sea in preparation for the invasion. Again most were to be employed in the pre-invasion role of simulating invasions at different places in an effort to confuse the enemy as to the actual landing site. However, a number of PTs would land U.S. Army Rangers on Cape Negre and the offshore islands of Levant and Port Cros: the Rangers' goal was the capture of enemy coastal batteries that might endanger the left flank of the main assault force. British MTBs of the 7th Flotilla would help guard the right flank of the assault force from possible attacks by German vessels from Genoa and Spezia, although few were expected due to the limited naval forces now possessed by the enemy.[2]

Prior to the invasion, Allied naval forces assembled in nearby Italian ports; among these were destroyers whose task was to provide shore-support fire, including Free Greek and Free Polish ships. Recalling past encounters with friendly destroyers, Barnes made it a point to parade his PTs past the ships in daylight so they could get a good look at what a PT boat looked like.[3]

On August 14, D-Day minus one, Squadron 22 accompanied by two British gunboats, a fighter direction ship and three slow but heavily armed motor launches sailed from Corsica toward Genoa trailing balloons as radar targets intended to confuse the Germans. Off Genoa, the force turned west toward Cannes and Nice. Commanding the force was the Hollywood film star, Lt. Comdr. Douglas Fairbanks, Jr.[4]

Off the Antibes, the PTs and launches maneuvered creating as much noise as possible with their recordings while the gunboats bombarded the shore. The enemy responded with several salvoes by coastal batteries that passed harmlessly over the PTs. Commander Fairbanks now led the force west. Between Marseilles and the Port of Toulon, the Fairbanks-led group joined a second group of vessels made up of eight Squadron 29 PTs, eleven crash boats and four motor launches under the command of Lieutenant Commander Bulkeley on the destroyer *Endicott*. Concealed by a smoke screen, the motor launches and destroyer bombarded the beach, the crash boats trailed balloons and the PTs played recordings of an invasion in progress. For two nights, the deception continued; meanwhile the Germans talked of imminent invasions at Marseilles and Toulon and of an Allied naval force including five battleships they intended to defeat.

Before the last demonstration, Lieutenant Commander Bulkeley radioed a message saying, "because of the furious resistance on the beach," the landings at La Ciotat would be postponed a few days. The deception worked. Concluding the landings were merely delayed, the Germans pulled mobile artillery and infantry from other points to defend a site at which no landings would be made.[5]

Ultimately, the enemy's naval response to the actual invasion was slight; however, few vessels appeared. One of the crash boats slow to retire after the final demonstration encountered two such vessels, a converted Egyptian yacht heavily armed, and a corvette, the *Capriolo,* a 565-ton warship taken over from the Italian Navy by the Germans. When the lightly armed crash boat radioed for help, the *Endicott* was nearly out of sight on the horizon. Commander Bulkeley immediately turned and steamed back at flank speed; at a distance of seven-and-a-half miles the destroyer opened fire, but its efforts were hampered by the fact that earlier the previous night, while trying to simulate a large bombardment force, all but one of its 5-inch guns had been fused by the heat. Nevertheless, the one operative gun alternated firing on the two enemy vessels.

Two PT boats accompanying the *Endicott* closed and fired torpedoes at a range of three hundred yards, but the alert enemy skippers with their small, maneuverable craft, managed to comb the tracks, causing the torpedoes to miss. Meanwhile, the *Endicott,* having closed to 1,500 yards, raked the decks of the enemy ships with 20- and 40-mm cannon. With that the British gunboats and the *Endicott* used their guns to pound the two vessels until they sank. The PTs and the *Endicott* picked up 211 survivors who became prisoners of war.

The weather on D-Day was fair and calm. Rocket-equipped LCTs and destroyers bombarded the beaches as landing craft with troops headed for shore. By nightfall, some sixteen thousand men and their equipment were ashore. Only the landings on the northeastern site near the Golfe de la Napoule, facing Cannes, encountered opposition. On its west flank, the shores of the Golfe de Frejus were badly wanted by the Army. Prior to the war, the French had built a seaplane base and a small airfield there. The Germans, anticipating this would be an objective, had prepared a strong defense.

As the land battle continued, in accord with standard PT practice, following the successful invasion by the main force, Barnes moved his squadrons forward closer to the fighting, establishing a base near Saint Tropez. But again PT operations were slowed by a gasoline tanker that failed to arrive.

By late August 16, there were still only rumors of a tanker arriving. One such rumor had a tanker anchored in the Golfe de Frejus, fifteen miles to the northeast. Lt.(jg) Wesley Gallagher commanding *PT 202,* and Lt. Robert Dearth commanding *PT 218,* set out together to run the rumor down. As noted, prior to now the

PTs in the Mediterranean had experienced few setbacks. But this was about to change.

It was 11 p.m. as the two PTs were rounding the point at St. Aygulf prior to entering the gulf when the *202* boat struck a mine, blasting the stern off the boat, and hurling four crewmen into the sea. Immediately, four *202* men jumped into the water as rescuers. As Lieutenant Dearth sought to maneuver his boat to pick up the swimmers, a second mine blew the stern off the *218* boat. With both boats abandoned and the crews in life rafts, a muster showed one man was missing, and six wounded. The dazed survivors paddled ashore, arriving shortly after midnight. There they hid in an abandoned, partially destroyed fisherman's hut. Venturing out after daylight, to their immense relief they found they were in Allied territory. A short ride provided by a Navy beachmaster soon had them back at their base.[6]

To the PT veterans of the Mediterranean campaign, the loss of two boats and men was no less disturbing than the cause: after months of operations, in one night Squadron 15 had lost two boats to a weapon that until now the PTs had been immune.

A week later, disaster struck again: On August 24, the commander of Task Force 86, Rear Adm. L. A. Davidson, heard that the Port-de-Bouc, west of Marseilles in the Gulf of Fos, had been captured by the French Underground. He ordered minesweepers to clear the gulf and for a PT boat to confirm the report. *PT 555* commanded by Lt. Bayard Walker drew the assignment. Admiral Davidson sent Captain de Frigate M. J. B. Bataille, a French naval liaison officer attached to his staff, along with Lt. Walker on the *555* boat.

Approaching the Gulf of Fos, *PT 555* passed a number of minesweepers; Lt. Walker was warned that shore batteries were active near the mouth of the Gulf. "It was decided," said Walker, "that we could enter the Gulf of Fos, despite fire from coastal batteries, since we presented such a small target. Nonetheless," Walker added, "we entered the Bay cautiously."

Inside the Bay, *PT 555* was greeted by a cheering crowd on the shore waving little French flags. At the dock, Captain Bataille was met by a fellow French naval officer, Lieutenant Grantry, who had parachuted into the area several weeks earlier in civilian clothes to organize a resistance group and prevent demolition of the port by the withdrawing Germans.

After about thirty minutes, during which the necessary information was obtained, *PT 555* headed out to sea at 29 knots. "A few minutes later," reported Walker, "a terrific blast exploded beneath our stern, carrying away the 40-mm gun and the gun crew and almost everything else up to the forward bulkhead of the engine room.... The four torpedoes were immediately jettisoned and we anchored with two anchors from separate lines."

Crewmen manned the life raft to rescue the men in the water. The raft returned with one body, one man with a broken leg, and one uninjured sailor. Four crewmen were never found.

Shortly, a fisherman's boat came out from shore to assist. The dead man and the crewman with the broken leg were put aboard along with a pharmacist's mate. Lieutenant Walker, who spoke French, went along as interpreter and the boat started for Port-de-Bouc.

They had gone only a hundred yards when Lieutenant Walker spotted a suspicious green line with green floats spaced about a foot apart. His cry of warning came too late: a massive explosion tossed the boat in the air, throwing its occupants into the sea.

The PT skipper came to the surface under the capsized boat. Once in the clear, he found the dead sailor had disappeared forever. The injured man was pulled from the water and placed on the bottom of the overturned boat. In view of the disaster, Lieutenant Walker considered things could have been worse: at that moment, just as the fisherman's boat sank, a French pilot boat arrived and took the survivors aboard and returned them to the shattered PT boat.

By this time, the PT's crew had jettisoned all topside weight except one twin .50-caliber mount, as protection in the event of an air attack. As there was an urgent need to get the information to Admiral Davidson that Port-de-Bouc was in French hands, Captain Bataille and Lt. Stanley Livingston, the *555* boat's executive officer, set out to paddle a rubber raft to the town of Carro, five miles distant at the entrance to the Gulf of Fos. If they were lucky, they might find an Army message center to relay their report.

By now, despite the efforts of two teams of bucket brigades, *PT 555* was sinking. At midnight, the radar was jettisoned and the confidential documents were brought on deck in a lead-weighted sack. But help was on the way.

Shortly after sunrise, Lieutenant Livingston and Captain Bataille returned from Carro with a small flotilla made up of two pilot boats, and two fishing boats. The two officers had been disappointed: they found no Army message center, but they did bring back help.

Two boats took the battered PT in tow; with the other two boats leading and Lieutenant Livingston and Captain Bataille in the bows on the lookout for mines, they started toward shore. But there were so many mines that the boats turned and headed for Carro.

Once at the Carro dock, on Cape Couronne, *PT 555* settled to the bottom. With the crew now without a home, the town turned an abandoned house by the dock over to the Americans. The French Underground helped by bringing a group of Italian prisoners of war over to make it livable. Best of all, the U.S. cruiser *Philadelphia* sent an officer ashore with a radio to report possible targets; Lieutenant Walker managed to make contact with the officer who sent the long-awaited message to Admiral Davidson saying Port-de-Bouc was in friendly hands, but that the harbor was no place for Allied ships.[7]

Walker included information that some three thousand enemy troops were a short distance from Carro and the Resistance fighters had hopes the Allies would launch an air strike coupled with an infantry attack to destroy the Germans, Walker concluded his message, saying:

"I had asked the pastor of the Catholic church at La Couronne, a village slightly more than a mile from Carro, to say a Mass on Sunday morning for the five we had lost. A High Mass was celebrated in the church, crowded to the doors at 10:30.

"The pastor and the local people had gone to considerable trouble to decorate the church with French and American flags and flowers. The choir sang, despite the broken organ, and the curé gave a moving sermon in French. Four FFI [Underground] men, gotten up in a uniform of French helmets, blue shirts and white trousers, stood as a guard of honor before symbolical coffins draped with American flags.

"After Mass our men fell in ranks behind a platoon of FFI, and followed by the whole town, we marched to the World War I monument. There a little ceremony was held and a wreath was placed in honor of the five American sailors.

"We were told that a collection was in the progress of being taken up amongst the local people, in order to have a plaque made for the monument planned for their own dead in the war. The plaque will bear the names of the five Americans who gave their lives here for the liberation of France."[8]

Indeed, the people of La Couronne did not forget. On the lonely coast at the mouth of the Rhone River, a plaque would be affixed to a monument reading:

TO OUR ALLIES, RALPH W. BANGERT, THOMAS F. DEVANEY, JOHN J. DUNLEAVY, HAROLD R. GUEST, VICTOR SIPPIN.[9]

With the Germans in retreat ahead of advancing Allied armies, members of the Resistance increasingly harried the enemy. At sea the battle continued to favor the Allies as well. On August 24, one of the most effective Anglo-American teams consisting of two motor torpedo boats, *PT 559* commanded by Lt. R. A. Nagle and *MTB 423*, under the command of Lt. A. C. Blomfield, RN, slipped inside the harbor of Genoa. About five miles from the city, they sighted what they thought was a destroyer and hit it with a single torpedo. In fact, it was a mere harbor-defense craft, but this was just the start. Two nights later, the pair of boats attacked a group of three armed barges, and sank two of them. Over the last nine days the two managed to sink four F-lighters, eight armed barges, capping the eleven-day spree with the sinking of the German corvette *UJ 2216*, formerly the French *L'Incomprise*.[10]

On August 28, Marseilles and Toulon surrendered. Operation Dragoon had achieved its objective in less than half the time predicted. By now, the PT bases at Calvi and Bastia had been abandoned. For the balance of the war in Europe, the PTs and British boats of Coastal Forces would be based at Leghorn on the Italian mainland. From there they resumed their patrols in the Gulf of Genoa, stalking enemy convoys between Genoa and Spezia. Their September score included seven F-lighters, one corvette, four barges and one merchant ship, plus more probables claimed.[11]

But the hunting was becoming more difficult. Such losses prompted the Germans to increase convoy escorts, install heavier guns on the F-lighters, and increase the number of coastal batteries overlooking the convoy routes as a counter against marauding MTBs and PT boats, a response similar to that employed by the Japanese in the South Pacific against PT boats. Furthermore, weather conditions, worsening with the approach of winter, also caused a decline in enemy contacts.

In October, due to reduced enemy resistance, Squadron 15 was disbanded, its remaining sixteen boats transferred to the Royal Navy under lend-lease, thus ending eighteen months of Mediterranean operations. Most of the other PT squadrons in the Mediterranean would also be shortly withdrawn, some boats sent back to Melville, others turned over to Russia. After the war, the boats sent to Russia would become part of the Soviet development of missile boats.

Now, only Squadron 22 remained in the Mediterranean, patrolling from St. Maxime and, from October to the end of the war, from Leghorn. With the hunting now less productive, Squadron 22's boats had to range farther afield and closer to shore in search of the enemy. As usual, such tactics had their hazards. On November 17, *PT 311* commanded by Lt. B. W. Creelman hit a mine and went down with the skipper, the executive officer, and eight of its thirteen-man crew. As the last PT lost in the Mediterranean, it shared the fate of the previous three PTs, all sunk by mines.[12]

The last big fight in the Mediterranean theater involving a PT boat against enemy surface craft occurred on the night of November 19 when *PT 308* skippered by Lt.(jg) Charles H. Murphy and two MTBs sank the 1,000-ton German corvette, *UJ-2207,* formerly the French *Cap Nord*.[13]

With the reduction in enemy naval forces, the Western Naval Task Force commanded by Vice Admiral Hewitt was disbanded and redistributed. Many PTs were assigned to the Flank Force,

Mediterranean. As this was largely made up of French vessels, command went to French Contre-Admiral Jaujard.

By now, the new Mark XIII torpedoes were arriving in increasing numbers. Consequently Admiral Jaujard authorized the PTs to fire their old Mark VIII torpedoes into enemy-held harbors. The first such firings occurred on the night of March 21; at a range of two miles PTs *310* and *312* fired four Mark VIII torpedoes into the harbor at Savona, Italy. Three exploded on the beach.

On April 4, the same two PT boats fired four torpedoes from offshore aimed at the resort town of San Remo. Two exploded. On the eleventh, PTs *305* and *313* launched four Mark VIII torpedoes into Vado. On April 19, with Lt. Comdr. R. J. Dressling, commanding Squadron 22 in tactical command, PTs *302* and *305,* fired the final three Mark VIII torpedoes into Imperia and were rewarded by a single explosion. On April 27, members of the Italian Underground took over all the Italian ports.[14]

On the following night, Admiral Jaujard, with a flare for the dramatic as much as a victory parade, led the entire Flank Force, including Squadron 22, in a ceremonial sweep of the Riviera Coast. It was the final PT operation in the Mediterranean. Ten days later, on May 8, Germany surrendered—the war in Europe was over.

By then, American PTs had been operating in the Mediterranean for two years. Four out of a total of forty-two boats from three squadrons had been lost. Five PT officers and nineteen men had been killed in action, seven officers and twenty-eight men wounded in action.[15]

For Squadron 15, operating continually in the Mediterranean theater from April 1943 until October 1944, as much as any PT squadron, the record is deserving of special note: this eighteen-boat squadron, based successively in North Africa; Sicily; La Maddalena, Sardinia; Bastia, Corsica; and southern France, operating mostly with British Coastal Forces had conducted a multiple role: operating to prevent the enemy's evacuation of troops from North Africa, screened Allied fleet landings during the invasions of Sicily, Anzio, Elba and southern France. In doing so, squadron boats had successfully been engaged in seventy-three actions destroying thirty enemy vessels with nine probably destroyed, damaged twenty-four vessels with eight probably damaged, amounting to 56,300 tons all told, the equivalent of fifty times each PT boat's own tonnage. Along with these achievements, the squadron carried out fifty-five OSS missions, transported, landed and retrieved OSS personnel from enemy shores. The cost to the squadron: two boats lost to enemy mines, with sixteen boats damaged due to enemy action, one officer and three enlisted men killed in action, and seven officers and twenty-four enlisted men wounded in action.[16]

However, the fighting was still not over. On the other side of the world other PTs were still locked in battle with an unyielding foe. For some of the PT crewmembers who served in the Mediterranean, there was still more fighting to be done.

CHAPTER TWENTY-ONE

RETURN TO
THE PHILIPPINES

Having leapfrogged his way through New Guinea, General MacArthur was ready to turn his attention to the Philippines. As PT boats had been among the last vessels to oppose the enemy in the final days of April 1942, they would be in the van in the battle for the liberation of the islands. But first there was a problem. The distance from New Guinea to the Philippines was too great even for MacArthur to reach in one leap. In part, this was because the big enemy-held island of Halmahara lay in the path and would first have to be neutralized, and partly because MacArthur needed one more air base within range of his fighter planes to provide initial support during the first phase of the invasion.

The solution was simple: in another demonstration of leapfrog tactics, MacArthur would bypass the 170-mile-long Halmahara and seize the nearby smaller, lightly defended island of Morotai. Separated from Halmahara by a twelve-mile-wide strip of water, possession of the forty-five-mile-long, egg-shaped Morotai would put MacArthur within three hundred miles of the Philippines. PT boats based at Morotai would patrol the twelve-mile-wide strait, preventing the thirty-seven thousand Japanese on Halmahara from retaking Morotai while MacArthur continued his advance to the Philippines.

On September 15, a task force under the command of Rear Admiral Daniel Barbey appeared off Morotai. MacArthur accompanied the invasion force on the cruiser *Nashville*. With no enemy resistance offered, Morotai was quickly in Allied hands. On the following day, Commander Bowling, commanding PT boats in

Rear Adm. Thomas Kinkaid's Seventh Fleet, arrived from New Guinea with Squadrons 10, 12, 18 and 33, a total of forty-one boats, accompanied by the tenders *Oyster Bay* and *Bobjack.*[1]

Immediately Bowling received an order to report to Rear Adm. Barbey aboard his flagship. Commander Bowling, along with his intelligence officer, Lt. Donald Seaman, as well as Lieutenants Swift and Arthur M. Preston, commanding Squadrons 18 and 33 respectively, jumped on a PT and raced to the flagship where they were shown to the admiral's cabin. The admiral told them of a crisis: planes from the six U.S. escort carriers had been bombing and strafing Halmahara in support of the invasion of Morotai; the admiral told the PT officers how that morning, one of the aircraft from the carrier *Santee* had been shot down in Wasile Bay, sixty miles south of Morotai. Although wounded, the pilot, Ens. Harold A. Thompson, had bailed out and parachuted into the water a few hundred yards from the shore.

A PBY had dropped a rubber raft to the pilot who had inflated it and climbed aboard. Now the raft was lodged against an abandoned Japanese cargo vessel, tied to its anchor chain, 150 yards from shore. Efforts by the PBY to land and rescue the pilot had failed because of heavy enemy fire from shore. Planes from the carriers were flying in relays over the downed pilot, keeping the Japanese at bay by occasional strafing passes, but there was no doubt the enemy was closing in and meant to take the pilot captive. Was there anything the PTs could do?[2] That the admiral had considered the PTs as an answer to the problem was a reflection of their record of success against the enemy during the New Guinea campaign.

Bowling and his officers, veterans as they were of the New Guinea campaign, had no illusions. The bay had a narrow entrance, was mined and defended by numerous shore batteries. A daylight rescue effort by PT boats under these conditions was a virtual suicide mission.

"I'd hate to have to order my PTs to go after the pilot," said Bowling. Admiral Barbey answered that he had no such intention.

In any event, there would be no need to issue such an order: "I feel confident," Bowling told the admiral, "that with air cover I can find two volunteer boat crews to try it, provided the officer in charge will have complete discretion in the matter and could turn back, breaking off the attempt without fear of censure or criticism if at any time it appears necessary to avoid losing his men and boats."[3]

With the admiral's agreement to the conditions, Both Lieutenants Swift and Preston volunteered to take two boats and make the rescue effort. Since Lieutenant Swift's squadron was scheduled to start patrolling off the island that night, Bowling assigned the mission to Preston. Then Bowling's intelligence officer spoke up, pointing out that as one who had studied the strait leading to the bay, he could be of great assistance in the rescue.

Begrudgingly, since he was reluctant to lose his intelligence officer, the man who knew so much about the area, Bowling agreed. Immediately Lieutenant Preston hurried back to Morotai. The commander of *PT 489*, Lt. Wilfred B. Tatro, and the skipper of *PT 363*, Lt. Hershel F. Boyd, along with their crews were quickly assembled. When Preston explained the mission along with the risks, all volunteered.

Quickly, with Preston in tactical command riding on the *489* followed by the *363*, the two boats headed south at full speed. Approaching the entrance to Wasile Bay, the experienced eyes of the PT crews were quick to note the mountainous terrain on both sides of the entrance. No doubt the Japanese had shore batteries positioned able to command the entrance. And there was another concern: the sky was empty. There were no aircraft from the *Santee* waiting to cover the rescue effort as agreed. With time running out for the pilot, the PTs headed toward the bay. At a distance of four miles from the entrance, coastal batteries opened fire; with shells falling nearby, Preston ordered a high-speed withdrawal.

Then the aircraft from the *Santee* arrived; with that, Preston headed back toward the bay's entrance at top speed. The noise increased until it was deafening; the roar of diving aircraft engines and machine fire blended with the boom of coastal batteries and exploding shells, and the wide-open PT engines.

As if by a miracle, the boats finally reached the cargo vessel; the *489* crewmen could see the pilot crouched in the raft still tied to the vessel's anchor chain. Quickly Lieutenant Tatro maneuvered his boat close to the pilot as *PT 363* provided covering fire. Overhead, the *Santee* aircraft continued strafing the nearby Japanese positions.

Lt., later Lt. Commander
M.S. "Swifty" Swift, commander of
PT Squadron 18. *Courtesy of WWII
PT Boats Museum and Archives,
Germantown, Tennessee, USA.*

Hollywood film star, Lt. Commander Douglas Fairbanks, Jr. aboard a PT
boat while commanding operations in support of Allied invasion forces.
*Courtesy of WWII PT Boats Museum and Archives, Germantown,
Tennessee, USA.*

Ensign Dudley J. Johnson, commanding *PT 127* in action in the Suriago Strait during the Battle of Leyte Gulf. *Courtesy of WWII PT Boats Museum and Archives, Germantown, Tennessee, USA.*

Four New Guinea PT officers on the PT tender *Hilo* examining captured Japanese weapons; from left to right: Lt. Donald F. Seaman, intelligence officer for PT squadrons, 7th Fleet; Lt. Comdr Robert Leeson, commander PT Squadron 7; Comdr. Selman "Biff" Bowling, former commander PT Squadron 21, now commanding PT squadrons, 7th Fleet; and Lt. Comdr. John Harllee, former commander Squadron 12, now Bowling's Chief of Staff. *Courtesy of WWII PT Boats Museum and Archives, Germantown, Tennessee, USA.*

To the anxious crew of the *489* boat, it was apparent the wounded Thompson was having difficulty getting the raft free of the anchor chain. Moments earlier, one of the aircraft had swept by laying a smoke screen. But now the smoke was starting to clear. At any time, the Japanese on the nearby shore would be able to see and shoot at the PTs.

At this point, Lieutenant Seaman and MoMM1/c Charles D. Day plunged into the sea, swam to the raft and towed it back to the PT. Eager hands quickly hauled the exhausted pilot aboard and soon the two PTs were racing back toward safety. This time the planes did not fly as close as they had previously. Later Preston learned that by then the aircraft were critically low on fuel and some were out of ammunition. Nevertheless they remained overhead until the PTs were safely out of the bay.

By then the boats had been under fire for over two-and-a-half hours; the rescued pilot had been down for seven hours. Remarkably, neither PT boat had been hit by enemy fire, and not a man had been wounded. As a result of this rescue, Lieutenant Preston received the Medal of Honor; the second of only two such medals awarded a PT officer during the war, the first going to John Bulkeley as commander of Squadron 3 in the days before the fall of the Philippines. In recognition for their efforts, the two men who dove into the sea to rescue Thompson were each awarded a Silver Star.[4]

Even before MacArthur landed at Morotai, there were major changes afoot affecting the Pacific war. Ever since departing from the Philippines in 1942, the general had dreamed of returning, of landing on Mindanao. But by now, U.S. carrier planes launched by Admiral Halsey's Task Force 38, had so devastated the southern Philippines that the JCS decided to cancel the Allied landings on Mindanao and to allocate the forces to landings at Leyte with MacArthur in command. The general eagerly approved.[5]

The Leyte invasion was set for October 20, with MacArthur's Seventh Fleet landing the 6th Army, the entire operation supported by Halsey's Third Fleet. On October 10, MacArthur's armada started toward the Philippines with the general aboard the *Nashville* in his capacity as Supreme Commander of the Southwest Pacific

Area. At 6:30 a.m. October 17, a minesweeper arrived off Leyte Gulf. By noon the waters had been cleared for the invasion force.

As it so happened, the landings at Leyte were easy. A calm sea, no mines, and only slight enemy resistance, mostly mortar fire, greeted the Americans. The liberation of the Philippines was off to a good start.

With the invasion a mere four hours old and the American beachhead expanding, MacArthur left the *Nashville* ten miles offshore, boarding an LCM and accompanied by his staff and war correspondents, headed for shore. An hour and half later, the LCM's ramp was lowered as the craft edged slowly forward to ground on the sand bottom still fifty yards from shore. MacArthur had expected the landing craft to tie up at a nearby pier so he could step ashore, flawlessly dressed and dry. However, with few docks standing, the Navy beachmaster did not have the time to direct the LCM to one of them. Typically, the naval officer-beachmaster was not impressed, in particular by an LCM carrying an Army officer. An impatient MacArthur had no choice but to step off the ramp into knee-deep brine and splash angrily ashore, destroying the neat crease in his trousers and the shine on his shoes.

It was then that a newspaper photographer snapped that famous picture of the Pacific war showing the scowling general, which millions of readers saw as an illustration of MacArthur's steely determination rather than anger aimed at an impertinent naval officer. When MacArthur saw the photograph, he was quick to see its image value, so the following day he repeated the action, wading ashore for Army cameramen in sight of puzzled assault troops. Later upon seeing the first photograph, they declared it a phony, and another touch was added to the troops' anti-hero image of the general.[6]

For Commander Bowling, the problem was getting the PT boats the twelve hundred miles from New Guinea to the Philippines. Due to the urgency of the invasion, no cargo ships were available to transport the boats. The PTs would have to make the trip on their own bottoms.

A week before the invasion, with Bowling aboard, the tender *Oyster Bay* departed from Mios Woendi with two other tenders, two Army vessels, and the seaplane tender *Half Moon* bound for Leyte

Gulf. Accompanying them were three PT squadrons, Squadron 7 commanded by Lt. Comdr. Robert Leeson, Squadron 21 led by Lt. Comdr. T. Gleason, and Squadron 36 skippered by Lt. Comdr. Francis D. Tappaan. Joining them at Morotai were Squadrons 12 commanded by Lt. Weston C. Pullem, Jr. and 33 commanded by Lt. Murray Preston, making a total of forty-five PTs. During the voyage the PTs were under the tactical command of Commander Leeson. They would refuel as needed en route from escorting tenders, making a brief stop in Palau so as to arrive with enough fuel to begin operations immediately on October 21, the day following the invasion.[7]

For Commander Bowling, this was a time of anxiety, made no less so due to the date of the scheduled departure, Friday the thirteenth. Left behind at Morotai to patrol the waters off Hamahara were Squadrons 10 and 18, later to be joined by Squadron 11. In what was an amazing example of a small number of thirty-odd PTs neutralizing a major force, the Morotai PTs making nightly patrols in two or three-boat sections, would keep the thirty-seven thousand armed Japanese bottled up on Hamahara until the end of the war.[8]

As Bowling had feared, by the time the PTs reached Leyte their crews were exhausted. Nevertheless, that night, the boats began patrolling Leyte Gulf, the first to be carried out by PTs in the Philippines since John Bulkeley's Squadron 3 had faced the Japanese at the start of the Pacific war.

Enemy contacts were not long in coming. During the first three nights, PTs sank seven *daihatsus* and a small freighter. But this paled when compared to what lay ahead. The easy landing by Allied forces at Leyte was part of the enemy's Philippine defense strategy. Aware of the deadly effect of Allied pre-invasion naval bombardment, Major General Makino, commander of the 16th Division defending Leyte Island, had placed his main defensive line well inland. As for the Imperial Navy, following a series of setbacks in the Central Pacific, the main body had been held back from combat against U.S. ships in strength. But the Japanese Navy planned to fully resist the Allied invasion of the Philippines.

During late July and nearly August 1944, the Japanese devised a plan called "Sho-Go," meaning "Operation Victory." Typically, the plan was complex. In fact, there were four separate plans, one for each potential landing site, "Sho-1," the defense of the Philippines, was naturally the most important, and with the Allies invading the Philippines, would be the plan employed.

Thus, with the Allied invasion fleet approaching Leyte, the stage was set for the greatest naval battle of all times, the Battle of Leyte Gulf. Even before the first American soldier stepped on the beach at Leyte the Sho-1 plan was being put into effect. As simplified, Sho-1 employed three separate fleets aimed at repulsing the invasions: a Northern Decoy Force comprised of four carriers and two battleship carriers, escorted by one light cruiser and eight destroyers. Its role was to lure Halsey's supporting Third Fleet north away from the beaches at Leyte. Since the carriers lacked aircraft, and were therefore no real threat, the Japanese were willing to sacrifice them as part of the plan.

A second, five battleships, ten heavy cruisers, two light cruisers and fifteen destroyers, or Central Striking Force, was to slip through the San Bernardino Straits at the northern tip of Samar, entering Leyte Gulf north of Leyte at dawn October 25, and descend on MacArthur's now defenseless transports, ships that carried the supplies critical the success of the 6th Army in the Philippines, "like a wolf on the fold" while Halsey was hundreds of miles to the north chasing the useless carriers. Commanding the Central Force was Vice Adm.l Takeo Kurita, a veteran of Midway and a commander who had on occasion led the Tokyo Express during the Guadalcanal campaign.

A Southern Striking Force, divided into two sections, the first under the command of Vice Adm. Shoji Nishimura with two battleships, one heavy cruiser and four destroyers; the second commanded by Vice Adm. Kiyohide Shima with two heavy cruisers, one light cruiser and four destroyers. The two fleets were to pass through Surigao Straits, the narrow passage south of Leyte; entering Leyte Gulf from the south it would join Kurita's Central Striking Force, destroying MacArthur's transports.

Initially October 22 was the date for execution, as the transports were unloading. However, Vice Admiral Kurita declared it was impossible for his force to steam that distance in time for the attack; thus "X-Day," the day for what was to be Japan's Decisive Battle, was postponed until the 25th.

Although Admiral Halsey's Third Fleet, a massive naval force, was the major American fleet at Leyte Gulf, MacArthur's Seventh Fleet, a slow but powerful fleet centered on six old battleships, played the role of providing close support for the American troop landings at Leyte.

On October 24, search planes from the carriers of the Third Fleet sighted Admiral Kurita's ships in the China Sea rounding the southern tip of Mindoro. At 8:20 a.m. Admiral Halsey received the report. To proceed through the San Bernardino Straits to engage Kurita was impossible; it was presumed the waters were mined, and only the Japanese knew their location. Furthermore, Nimitz had specifically issued an order that no ships pass through the straits without his express permission.

At about 9 a.m., carrier planes sighted the "Southern Strike Force," now well across the Sulu Sea, some fifty miles southwest of Negros and northeast of Mindanao. Sixty miles behind the first section of the Southern Strike Force steamed the second part commanded by Admiral Shima.

With a major naval battle in the offing, a likelihood of a disaster arose on the American side. Owing to the U.S. Navy's command system, while the Seventh Fleet commanded by Admiral Kinkaid was directly under MacArthur, Admiral Halsey owed its allegiance to Admiral Nimitz in Hawaii. Thus the two fleets engaged in the same landing operation had no common superior nearer than ten thousand miles away in the form of the Joint Chiefs of Staff.

Misled by the exaggerated claims of his carrier pilots attacking the Central Striking Force in San Bernardino Strait, and believing Kurita had turned back, Halsey headed the Third Fleet north at top speed in pursuit of the decoy carriers. But Kurita, having lost a few ships, soon turned back and resumed his advance. Admiral Kinkaid, alone at Leyte Gulf with his Seventh Fleet, misinterpreting Halsey's message as he departed, assumed that part of the Third Fleet was still on station in Leyte Gulf; he turned his full attention to intercepting the Southern Strike Force coming through Surigao Strait. The cargo ships and the various vessels forming the invasion fleet were now virtually at the mercy of the approaching Central Striking Force.

MacArthur returning to the Philippines. Disembarking from a cruiser earlier, he stands on the bow of *PT 525*, an 80-foot Elco. Left to right: Lt. Alexander W. Wells, PT skipper; Gen. MacArthur; Comdr. Selman S. "Biff" Bowling; Lt. Gen Walter Kruger. *Courtesy of WWII PT Boats Museum and Archives, Germantown, Tennessee, USA.*

On October 23, ten PTs of Squadron 10 under the command of Lieutenant Pullen along with five boats of Squadron 7 led by Lieutenant Commander Leeson, were ordered to Liloan, on Panaon Island, off southern Leyte. The Army had secured Panaon as a base for the PTs. To the PT crews it looked like a routine assignment. Their mission was to guard the thirty-five-mile-long Surigao Strait. They had no idea that within the next twenty-four hours they would be embroiled in one of the most crucial naval battles of the Pacific war.[9]

Although Admiral Kinkaid knew an enemy surface force was coming through Surigao Strait, determining exactly where the enemy was and his precise composition was urgent. He had only four radar-equipped Black Cats for night searches. Two went out after dark to reconnoiter the Mindanao Sea but found nothing, and one was accidentally shot down by a PT. Fortunately, the PT made up for it by rescuing its crew.[10]

At 2:43 p.m., October 24, Kinkaid ordered Rear Adm. Jesse Oldendorf, commanding his bombardment and Support Group, to station his ships across the narrow twelve-mile-wide stretch of water between Leyte and Hibuson, where Surigao Strait enters Leyte Gulf, adding that he was to prepare for a night action. These included his six old battleships, plus four heavy cruisers, four light cruisers and twenty-one destroyers as well as a number of cruisers and destroyers borrowed from other units of the Seventh Fleet.

One of Oldendorf's problems was that all of his battleships except one had been at Pearl Harbor. Indeed, the *California,* and *West Virginia* had been sunk and later salvaged. Since they were intended for shore bombardment rather than ship-to-ship battles, only *West Virginia, California* and *Tennessee* were fitted with the latest gunnery radar sets; the others had older radar equipment which made it difficult to locate targets. Oldendorf thus ordered the battleships to hold their fire until they were sure of getting hits.

An noon, Kinkaid ordered Commander Bowling to send all PT boats into Surigao Strait and the Mindanao Sea. Without night-flying radar equipped aircraft, Kinkaid would use the PTs as the "eyes of the fleet." Their orders were to first, report all contacts, surface or air, radar or visual; that done, they were to attack independently.[11]

Of the forty-five PT boats originally making the voyage to Leyte, six were inoperative due to problems following the recent long passage. For the upcoming night's operation, Bowling formed the remaining thirty-nine boats in thirteen three-boat sections and dispatched them to positions along the shores of Surigao Strait, Mindanao and the Bohil Islands, into the Mindanao Sea beyond the end of the Strait. The farthest boats would be one hundred miles from Oldendorf's waiting battle line. By darkness all boats were in their assigned positions.

On this night, the waters of the Strait were smooth, if not glassy; visibility was good until a few minutes after midnight when the moon set, leaving a pitch-black sky. A few rain squalls soon drifted through while occasional flashes of sheet lightning were seen as thunder rumbled in the distance.

The PT action this night in Surigao Strait is not easy to reconstruct. As has been noted, attacks involving multiple numbers of PT boats against warships were prone to be more in the nature of barroom brawls. Also, unlike larger warships, PTs kept sketchy logs, and actions recalled based on memory are likely to be less accurate. As can best be determined, however, here is what happened.

For the PTs, the element of surprise was quickly lost. At 10:36, Ens. Peter Gadd's radar on *PT 131,* the first boat to detect the approaching Japanese, picked up two large targets. Accompanied by PTs *130* and *152,* the *131* headed for the targets at 24 knots. As a result of radar, the Americans knew where to look, permitting them to spot the Japanese before they were sighted by the enemy. At 10:50 the mammoth bulk of two battleships loomed out of the night: The two radar targets shortly broke into five separate targets, the two battleships, two cruisers and a destroyer led by Admiral Shima. Aboard *PT 152,* Lieutenant Pullen, in tactical command of the PT boat section, attempted to radio the sighting as ordered, but got no response.

As had been shown many times earlier in the war, aided by exceptionally powerful night binoculars, the Japanese had few of any equals in the area of night vision. At 10:52 the lookouts on the destroyer, *Shigure,* sighted the approaching PTs. With the range still three miles, Nishimura's battleships fired starshells. With the sea illuminated, *Shigure* closed at high speed and opened fire with her 5-inch guns; red and yellow tracers mixed with high-explosive shells screamed by the PTs to explode close by while the beam of the destroyer's searchlight briefly illuminated the PTs.

The *152* was hit by a 5-inch shell; the explosion tore away the bow-mounted 37-mm cannon, killed the gunner, stunned the loader, wounded three crewmen, and set the boat afire. Knocked down along with others on deck, Lt. Joseph A. Eddins, *PT 152's* skipper, scrambled to his feet and helped extinguish the fire.[12]

Also hit was *PT 130* commanded by Lt.(jg) Ian D. Malcolm. A shell struck a torpedo warhead before tearing through the bow. Neither the torpedo nor the enemy shell exploded; and no one on the boat was injured. The undamaged *PT 131* maneuvered between the enemy and the two damaged boats, laying smoke while firing torpedoes without effect. The *131* was then hit by a 5-inch shell that passed through the boat without exploding, knocking out the radio. All three PTs then retired behind a smoke screen, still pursued by enemy fire. As the three boats fled, Vice Adm. Shoji Nishimura, on battleship *Yamashiro,* recalled the *Shigure,* and radioed Admiral Kurita:

> "Advancing as scheduled while destroying enemy torpedo boats."[13]

Frantic to radio the contact report to Admiral Oldendorf, Lieutenant(jg) Malcolm on *PT 130,* who Admiral Kinkaid later noted was "using his head," ran south until he encountered Lt.(jg) John A. Cady's PT section near Camiguin Island. There, the *130* skipper boarded Ens. Dudley J. Johnson's *PT 127* and used its radio; at ten minutes after midnight Macolm's report was picked up by the PT tender *Wachapreague,* at 12:26 a.m. Oldendorf received the message on the cruiser *Louisville.* It was the first word the admiral had had on the Southern Striking Force in 14 hours.[14]

Aboard *PT 152,* having extinguished the fire and determined that despite damage to the bow his boat was still capable of 24 knots, Lieutenant Eddins began a stern chase of the enemy, but with Nishimura's ships making an estimated 22 knots, Lieutenant Pullen finally gave up.

Following this engagement, the rest of the PT encounters in and near Surigao Strait occurred after midnight, on October 25. The first occurred at 12:15 a.m. involving PTs *146, 151,* and *190.* In tactical command of the three boats, Lt.(jg) Dwight H. Owen noted the distant flashes of gunfire and starshells and the far-off sweep of searchlights.

Then followed a period of quiet. At about this time, the moon set and the night became pitch black. Squalls swept by, then Lieutenant Owen's radar began picking up targets. In accord with orders, Owen tried to radio the sighting, but Nishimura's radio operators were jamming the frequency. Owen did the next best thing; he attacked. In the darkness the three PTs closed on what they thought was a battleship; in fact, it was Nishimura's heavy cruiser, the 12,000-ton *Mogami,* veteran of the Battle of Midway as well as a number of other clashes with U.S. forces

Again, the enemy's lookouts were quick to spot the attackers. At 1,800 yards, *Mogami's* searchlight snapped on, the beam probing the darkness. Ensign B. M. Grosscup at the helm of *PT 146,* and Ens. J. M. Ladd commanding *PT 150* fired one torpedo each. Then the destroyer *Yamagumo* opened fire and the PTs retired at high speed under a smoke screen. In the midst of the action, the *150*'s port engine failed for three minutes, but although shells repeatedly landed nearby, not one was a hit. Nor did the PTs' torpedoes find their targets.[15]

At 1 a.m., having brushed by two PT sections, with the Southern Striking Force nearing the entrance to the Surigao Strait, Nishimura ordered "approach formation"; with destroyer *Miohishio* leading, followed by destroyer *Asagumo,* next came destroyers *Shigure* and *Yamagumo* flanking the flagship battleship *Yamashiro.* Following at a distance of four kilometers came the second battleship, *Fuso.* Both huge vessels displaced 37,000 tons and mounted twelve 14-inch guns. *Mogami* trailed the *Fuso* at a distance of one kilometer.

The van of Nishimura's force reached the narrow entrance to Surigao Strait about an hour later and began passing between Panaon and Sumilon Islands. Lurking off the southern tip of Panaon were PTs *132, 134* and *137.* In tactical command aboard the *134* was Lieutenant Commander Leeson. Leeson proceeded to make a textbook attack, to a point. Racing in to close range despite being illuminated by searchlights and starshells, braving heavy but inaccurate shellfire, at 2:05 a.m. the *134* fired three torpedoes, then turned hard and evaded the searchlights. In spite of the daring attack, however, all the *134*'s torpedoes missed, as did those of the other two PTs.[16]

Even as Leeson's boats withdrew, another three boats, all from Squadron 33, were closing on Nishimura. All were 80-foot Elcos: *PT 490* commanded by Lt. (jg) John McElfresh, *PT 491* skippered by Lt.(jg) Harley Thronson, and *PT 493* under the command of Lt.(jg) Richard Brown. In tactical command of the section was Lieutenant Brown. Picking up Nishimura's ships at a range of eight miles on his radar, Brown led in the attack. Along the way the PTs were engulfed in a lucky rain squall that concealed them until they were within seven hundred yards of the enemy. The three PT skippers concentrated on Nishimura's destroyers. At 2:07 a.m., Lieutenant McElresh fired two torpedoes at the lead destroyer. Lieutenant Thronson launched two more torpedoes at the second destroyer. All were misses.

Nishimura's ships immediately turned their attention to this new threat. The inevitable searchlights illuminated the PTs and a torrent of shells followed. As PT gunners returned fire, Thronson withdrew at top speed, but McElfresh, his boat brightly illuminated, continued to close. At the point-blank range of 350 yards, as his gunners were firing a withering stream of bullets and shells at the destroyers and enemy shells were churning the sea around the PT, McElfresh fired his last two torpedoes, again without results. However, the *490* skipper reported his gunners shot out a searchlight; but to no avail; another immediately found the boat. With his supply of torpedoes exhausted, the *490* skipper turned to withdraw. But the enemy finally had the range: a shell smashed into *PT 490,* shattering its searchlight; a second ripped through the hull above the waterline. Struck by shrapnel, TM3/c Arthur G. Peterson was knocked to the deck. Staggering to his feet he managed to reach the smoke generator and turn it on before collapsing.

As the wounded *490* withdrew, *PT 493*, which had not yet launched its torpedoes, still unobserved by the enemy, closed to a range of about five hundred yards and fired two torpedoes, then opened fire with guns. The enemy's searchlights now switched to the *493*.[17] Recalled Lt. Brown:

> "At this close range we could see Japanese sailors scrambling about the ship, and we poured it into them, but the concussion of their exploding shells was steadily closer, so I ordered my executive officer, Nick Carter, to come hard left, open the throttles and *GET OUT!*
>
> "I went aft to release smoke for a screen so we could return to fire our remaining torpedoes, but we had penetrated an outer destroyer screen without knowing it and had Japs all around us. Eight searchlights pinned us down like a bug on a needle."[18]

A shell tore through *PT 493* from side to side, above the waterline; a second shell ripped through the engine room below the waterline, shattering the auxiliary generator and damaging the engines. With water pouring in through the hole the boat seemed doomed. But a quick-thinking motor mac, MoMM2/c Albert W. Brunelle, slipped his life jacket off, stuffed it in the hole, and then turned his attention back to the engines.

Abovedecks, another shell tore away the boat's canopy covering the chartroom, killing two crewmen, severely wounding Brown, his executive officer and three crewmen. Despite his wounds, Carter, who was thrown to the deck by the explosion, made his way across the blood-covered deck and steered the PT away from the danger. With motor mac Brunelle keeping the engines running, Carter, although weak from loss of blood and suffering from shock, continued steering the boat for Panaon Island.

By the time he beached the PT on the island, the Packard engines, although still running, were almost underwater. At daybreak, the tide rose, lifting the shattered PT allowing it to slip into deep water and sink. The survivors would be rescued shortly after sunrise by Thronson's *PT 491*.[19]

Immediately after the clash with Lieutenant Brown's section, Nishimura's force was sighted by *PT 523*, *PT 524* and *PT 526*, silhouetted by its own starshells. Each boat fired two torpedoes at a target they identified as a cruiser. If correct, this would have to be the *Mogami,* an incredibly difficult ship to deal with, as events were about to prove. Again the PTs made no torpedo hits, nor were any damages or injuries suffered as the boats retreated covered by a smoke screen under heavy fire.

After beating off the latest PT attacks, Nishimura steamed on at 20 knots for three quarters of an hour. Ahead, stationed south and east of Leyte Island's Amagusan Point lay the final two sections of PTs, the *320, 330,* and *331* led by Lt. G. W. Hogan, and the *323, 328,* and *329* under the tactical command of Lt. H. G. Young.

However, at 2:45 a.m. the radar on the waiting U.S. destroyers stationed near Oldendorf's battleships picked up Nishimura's approaching force. The PTs had done what they were ordered to do. Throughout their engagements, the various PTs were either sending or attempting to send contact messages to Admiral Oldendorf. Although not all got through, and some of those that did were delayed, enough were received to provide a fairly accurate record of the enemy's progress. In doing so, one PT boat had been lost, ten boats damaged by enemy fire, three crewmen killed, and an additional number wounded.[20]

The last two PT sections were now ordered to stand clear. In the end, Oldendorf's heavy ships would annihilate Nishimura's force: Nishimura's flagship *Yamashiro* sank at 4:19 a.m., taking the admiral down with it, along with all but a handful of the battleship's thirteen-hundred-man crew. Only *Shigure* and *Mogami,* although damaged in the battle, survived.

For the PTs in the strait, the action was not yet over. Sixty miles to the rear of Nishimura was the second half of the Southern Strike Force commanded by Admiral Shima, centered on the heavy cruisers *Nachi* and *Ashigara,* each fitted with ten 8-inch guns, escorted by the light cruiser *Abukuma,* another veteran of the Pearl Harbor attack. The three big ships were screened by four destroyers. Shima's force had been spotted well out in the Mindanao Sea: Admiral Oldendorf first received word of Shima's force at 12:38 a.m. October 25.[21]

Due to the earlier engagements with Nishimura's ships, the PTs were now scattered, and unable to attack Shima as he entered the strait. Moreover, the PTs had fired the bulk of their torpedoes against Nishimura's ships. And as a result of Nishimura's earlier radioed warnings, the PT boats would not have the advantage of the element of surprise.

It was 3:15 a.m. when the radar of Leeson's *PT 134* detected Shima off Panaon Island's Binit Point. Using a convenient rain squall as cover, Leeson fired his last torpedo undetected, but again it was a miss.

At 3:55 a.m., *PT 137* commanded by Lt.(jg) Michael Kovar, one of the three boats attached to Leeson's section, was still guarding the strait. Prior to the earlier attack on Nishimura's ships, the *137*'s auxiliary generator had failed along with the radio and radar. Nonetheless, although separated from the other PTs, Kovar continued to patrol. At the moment Leeson made his unsuccessful attack, Shima's ships were in column formation, two destroyers leading, with two destroyers following the cruisers. Approaching Binit Point, Shima increased speed to 26 knots, swinging the column to clear the point before turning north to enter the strait, simultaneously ordering the lead destroyers to fall in astern.

As this order was being executed, lookouts on *PT 137* spotted one of Shima's destroyers: at a range of nine hundred yards, Kovar fired one torpedo; it ran hot and straight but "was observed to pass under the beam of the destroyer." The destroyer opened fire on the *137*; simultaneously, the PT crew heard a deep explosion. Unknown to Kovar and his crew, the torpedo passing beneath the targeted destroyer, had struck one of Shima's deeper draft cruisers, the *Abukuma,* killing thirty crewmen. The damage caused by the explosion forced the ship to reduce speed to 10 knots.[22] This caused the cruiser to fall out of the column as Shima continued to hurry northward.

Two days later, the crippled *Abukuma* would be sunk by Allied aircraft. Since, as noted, Kovar had not been aware of the cruiser's presence when he fired the torpedo, the hit was pure luck. Nevertheless, for his act, Kovar received the Navy Cross.[23]

By 4 a.m., minus *Abukuma,* and still unaware of Oldendorf's victory over Nishimura, with speed increased to 28 knots, Shima raced up the strait intent on joining Nishimura in Leyte Gulf. One can imagine his sense of dismay in finding, that as a result of an engagement with an enemy naval force, with the exception of two battle-damaged ships, Nishimura and his force were no more.

Sometime after 5 a.m., having reached the scene of the battle, Admiral Shima realized he was alone, two cruisers with a destroyer escort against a more powerful enemy. With that, Shima began a retreat down the strait toward the safety of the Mindanao Sea; this time he was accompanied by Nishimura's only surviving ships. But the Japanese again had to run the PT gauntlet.

It had been a long night for the PT crews as well. At 6:20 a.m., the three-boat section consisting of PTs *150, 194* and *196,* sighted Shima's retreating force. The *150* attacked the flagship *Nachi,* firing one torpedo without success.

The PT crews quickly discovered the *Nachi's* gunners were as skilled as those on the enemy destroyers. Return fire hit *PT 194,* seriously wounding three of the crew. Ten minutes later, *PT 190* sighted Shima's ships. Two escorting destroyers immediately charged the PTs with guns blazing, causing the *190* to retreat at full speed behind a smoke screen.

Admiral Shima then detached one of his destroyers to locate and assist the *Abukuma,* and a second to accompany the damaged *Mogami* whose speed had been reduced due to the earlier battle damage. Shima also moved the balance of his ships closer to the shore of Mindanao as he continued his retreat, reducing the threat from further attacks.

By 6:45 a.m., thanks to a hard-working crew, the *Mogami* was able to increase speed. With the coming of daylight the cruiser and her escorting destroyer were sighted by *PT 137.* Both the *Mogami* and the destroyer opened fire, forcing Kovar to retreat. Five minutes later, the cruiser and destroyer were sighted by *PTs 489, 492* and *495,* three Squadron 33 boats. However, the three were unable to make an attack as by then, the two ships were headed away "at speed." This was the final PT contact with the enemy in the strait.

By this time, the smoldering floating debris from sunken ships along with the inevitable patches of fuel oil littered the waters of the strait. Among the wreckage, large numbers of Japanese could be found, some injured and most covered with oil. PT boats and U.S. destroyers picked their way through the wreckage in hopes of rescuing the men and giving aid, but as in the past, few survivors chose to be rescued by the Americans.

As for the *Mogami,* although the veteran cruiser was able to evade the PTs in the strait and survive the clash with Oldendorf's battleships, her luck ended the following day when she was sunk by U.S. carrier planes in their search for fleeing survivors of the recent sea battles. Of Nishimura's force, only *Shigure* survived to reach home.

The Battle of Surigao Strait was thus a smashing American victory, the culmination of timely PT contact reports, U.S. destroyer torpedo attacks, and a bombardment by battleships of the waiting Seventh Fleet, all at the cost of a handful of American lives, one PT boat and one destroyer lost. How many Japanese died is unknown, but estimates place the number in the range of five thousand.

Following the battle, critics were quick to point out that despite the number of PT boats involved, only one torpedo hit was made. But in a radio message from Hawaii, Admiral Nimitz made clear his view:

THE SKILL, DETERMINATION AND COURAGE DISPLAYED BY THE PERSONNEL OF THESE SMALL BOATS IS WORTHY OF THE HIGHEST PRAISE.... THE PT ACTION VERY PROBABLY THREW THE JAPANESE COMMAND OFF BALANCE AND CONTRIBUTED TO THE COMPLETENESS OF THEIR SUBSEQUENT DEFEAT.[24]

Further north, in stark contrast to the American victory in Surigao Strait, Admiral Kurita's Central Striking Force emerging from San Bernadino Strait caused a near panic. When American naval commanders learned that Admiral Halsey had taken the entire Third Fleet north in pursuit of an enemy carrier force, leaving Leyte Gulf and MacArthur's transports unprotected, they feared the worse. If Kurita's powerful surface force were to reach Leyte Gulf, the American invasion of the Philippines faced potential disaster.

In what was something in the nature of a miracle, the cautious Kurita, when nearing Leyte Gulf, reversed course and retreated, after sinking five small warships, thus ending the threat. Still further north, Admiral Halsey's carrier-borne aircraft annihilated the enemy's carrier decoy force. The Japanese plan to destroy

MacArthur's transports had failed. And in the three days of naval conflict, the Imperial Navy had been eliminated as an effective fighting force: in what is known as the Battle of Leyte Gulf, the Japanese had lost four carriers, three battleships, plus seventeen other heavy warships. By comparison, U.S. losses were light: one light carrier, two escort carriers and three destroyers, and one PT boat. Thus ended one of the largest naval battles in recorded history.

Despite such losses, however, as the U.S. Navy would quickly learn, the Japanese Navy was far from prepared to admit defeat. And the new weapon that appeared would be one more feared than anything previously encountered by the Allies on any front.

CHAPTER TWENTY-TWO

PT BOATS VERSUS
THE *KAMIKAZES*

Following the Battle of Leyte Gulf, with the virtual elimination of the Japanese naval fleet as a threat, an understandable atmosphere of victory prevailed aboard the ships of Admiral Kinkaid's Seventh Fleet in Leyte Gulf. However, it was really the quiet before the storm. Indeed, the U.S. Navy was about to face the unbelievable, the *kamikazes*; pilots bent on committing suicide by smashing their aircraft against Allied ships, with aircraft carriers and PT boats a priority; "The only weapon I feared in the war," Admiral Halsey said later.

On October 15, a Japanese naval pilot deliberately attempted to crash his aircraft into a Third Fleet carrier. The effort failed when the plane was shot down a short distance from the target. At dawn, October 21, the day the PTs arrived at Leyte Gulf after their voyage from Morotai, an enemy bomber crashed headlong into the Australian heavy cruiser *Australia,* one of the many Allied ships supporting the landings on Leyte Gulf. Thirty men including her skipper were killed, with another sixty-four wounded, twenty-six seriously.[1] That night, the wounded *Australia* with her battered crew was ordered back to Manus, an island north of New Guinea.

On October 25, following the Allied victory in the Battle of Leyte Gulf, the nightmare of the Seventh Fleet began. At 10:00 a.m., nine Zeros approached the gulf. Five peeled off and began to dive. Two minutes later, "General Quarters" sounded on the escort carrier *St Lo* as antiaircraft guns opened fire among ships in the gulf. In spite of the hail of bullets, the first Zero crashed on the *St Lo's* flight deck and exploded. Soon the ship was ablaze; thirty minutes

later, the blackened twisted wreckage that was the *St Lo* capsized
and sank. Destroyers picked up 784 survivors, about half of whom
were wounded; 114 of the ship's company had been killed.[2]

Moments before the first Zero smashed into the *St Lo,* a second
Zero took aim at the escort carrier *Kalinin Bay.* Hit by antiaircraft
fire, the plane began smoking. Striking the carrier at an angle, the
Zero skidded off the carrier's port bow, its bomb failing to explode.
Shocked crewmen quickly extinguished the flames left in its wake.

The pilot of the third Zero tried to finish the job, but with his
plane also hit by antiaircraft fire, he only managed a glancing blow
before his aircraft plunged into the sea. The plane's bomb detonated,
causing numerous casualties among the crew of the *Kalinin Bay* as
well as putting some holes in the carrier's hull.

The fourth pilot chose the escort carrier *Kitkun Bay* as his target,
aiming his aircraft at the ship's bridge, strafing as he approached.
When the plane missed the bridge, the pilot dropped the nose of his
aircraft intending to crash on the flight deck, but struck the port
catwalk and crashed into the sea some thirty-five yards from the
ship. Bomb and aircraft now exploded, starting fires aboard the
carrier but inflicting only minor damage.

The fifth and last of the suicide planes headed for the escort
carrier *White Plains.* Hit repeatedly by antiaircraft fire, the plane
missed the ship's port catwalk by inches before exploding in a ball
of fire and slamming into the sea, showering the flight deck with
burning debris, cutting off the ship's electric power and denting its
armor plating. Thus began a new round in Japan's defense of the
Philippines, one Zero, one pilot, one ship.[3]

Among the ships with guns blazing away at the Zeros during
their attacks were those of the PT tender *Willoughby.* Like the crews
of other ships in Leyte Gulf, the actions of the five Japanese pilots
shocked the tender's crew. At the moment, the Americans had yet to
grasp the idea that sensible men could be committing organized
suicide: initially they were prone to dismiss the acts as isolated
incidents on that part of a few fanatics. But they would soon learn
the terrible truth.

That night, Tokyo announced the formation of the Kamikaze
Special Attack Corps—named after the "divine wind" that saved
Japan from the Mongol invasion centuries before. On the following

day, four Zeros carrying three-hundred-pound bombs, attacked four more escort carriers on Leyte Gulf, with nearly similar results. For Allied ship crews, the knowledge the Japanese air force had adopted suicide as a tactic was, to say the least, unnerving. The sight of a *kamikaze* coldly and intentionally starting an attack with the intent of destroying himself as well as his victim shook the resolution of antiaircraft gunners, creating something akin to panic among Allied crews. "A countermeasure must be found soon," one captain wrote in his diary.[4] Another officer observed how historically, when one nation acquired a weapon, the other side soon devised a similar one. But, here, he noted, the Japanese had come up with a weapon upon which they had the undisputed monopoly, one that was most certainly all theirs.

Concern on the part of the Allied command was quickly apparent: for the first few days after October 25, the commander of amphibious forces forbade hospital ships to enter Leyte Gulf. Afterwards they were limited to three hours, just long enough to pick up casualties and get out. In the United States, Britain and Australia, newspapers were asked to refrain from mentioning "enemy suicide attacks." All American naval personnel visiting Australia or returning to the U.S. were not under any circumstances to mention such attacks. And Admiral Nimitz clamped on the heaviest censorship of the war on the subject: suicide planes "fell" on ships when correspondents actually knew better. In Japan, the chancellor of a university, speaking of suicide on the part of Japanese pilots, declared, "One thing is now clear: America has lost the war."[5]

Thus far, the *kamikazes* had focused on carriers. The PTs soon learned they were also targets. The PT tender, *Wachapreague,* had just arrived at Leyte Gulf from the battle in Surigao Strait with a group of PT boats when, suddenly, five Japanese aircraft dove out of the clouds. Gunners on the ship and the nearby PTs opened fire on the attackers, downing one, then two more, the aircraft plunging into the sea.

But the enemy also scored. Hardest hit was *PT 134*; having successfully survived the battles in Suriagao Strait, its luck finally ran out: one crewman was dead, and four wounded by bomb fragments. Perceptively, following the attack, Lt. Comdr. H. A.

Stewart, skipper of the tender, remarked dryly to his staff, "Apparently the enemy is somewhat hostile to anything connected with PT operations."[6]

Indeed, the statement would shortly prove prophetic. That same night, *PT 132* commanded by Ens. Paul Jones accompanied by *PT 326,* slipped into a nearby cove and attacked two barges loaded with ammunition and fuel, setting them afire and sinking them. At dawn, the two PTs started back to the tender. No one saw the lone Zero that dropped a bomb that exploded barely ten yards from the *132,* killing two men and wounding Ensign Jones, his executive officer and eight men.

On the following night, two 80-foot Elcos from Squadron 36, PTs *523,* and *525,* in tactical command of Lieutenant Commander Tappaan, were patrolling off Leyte when four Zeros dropped out of the night sky, strafing and bombing. The *523* took the brunt of the assault; eight men were killed: Commander Tappaan and two officers, plus six enlisted men and an Australian news correspondent were wounded in the attack.[7]

By now, the ground battle for Leyte Island had become a bloody yard-by-yard slugfest. One small portion of the Combined Fleet had been a success with its Transport Unit commanded by Vice Adm. Naomasa Sakonju. In defense of Leyte, Japan had planned on bringing in reinforcements to drive the Americans into the sea once Admirals Kurita, Nishimura and Shima wiped out their supplies and support vessels. Admiral Sakonju, although no Tanaka, on the opening day of the big naval battle, embarked two thousand troops in destroyer-transports at Cagayan, Mindanao and landed them the next morning on the back side of Leyte at Ormoc. This marked the beginning of a little-known series of dashes providing reinforcements similar to what had occurred during the campaign for Guadalcanal with the Tokyo Express. Until October 30, the Japanese reinforcement operation ran without interruption when B-24s sank an empty *Maru* in Ormoc Bay.

With Ormoc Bay the principal point for landing enemy reinforcements on Leyte Island, the PTs once again were employed in the role of busting barges and intercepting another Tokyo Express.[8] Indeed, the key to the defense of Leyte was not Tacloban, the regional capital, but, rather the island's largest port on the western shore of the island, thirty miles from where the Sixth Army made its assault. Numerous clashes followed: as the Americans advanced, fighting their way across Leyte against stubborn resistance, PTs began to encounter enemy destroyers more frequently around Ormoc.

On the night of November 9-10, Lieutenant Preston, leader of the earlier rescue effort to recover the downed pilot in Wasile Bay, led two Squadron 33 boats, PTs *492* and *497*, around the tip of Leyte and up the west coast of the island to Ormoc Bay; Preston's was one of several PT sections off Leyte's west coast. Shortly after 1:15 a.m., off the southern entrance to Ormoc Bay, Preston's lookouts sighted the silhouettes of three destroyers slipping around the north side of Ponson Island in the middle of the bay. Lieutenant Preston ordered a torpedo attack; the two boats closed and fired all eight of their torpedoes. Following a brief pause, a violent explosion shattered the night as flames leaped skyward from the last destroyer in the column. The two other destroyers immediately turned to pursue the PTs, lobbing 5-inch shells, sheering away only when Preston's PTs ran dangerously close to the shore of Ponson Island.

As the two PTs withdrew, Preston observed there were now only two images on his radar where before there had been three. Back at base the following morning he jubilantly described how the explosion of the destroyer when torpedoed was like a fireworks show back home. However, once again Japanese records failed to confirm the sinking.[9]

The next engagement of note in Ormoc Bay occurred on the night of November 28-29. That night Lt. Roger H. Hallowell in tactical command of four PTs left Leyte for Ormoc. Off the bay's entrance, he left PTs *128* and *191* on patrol and entered with PTs *127* and *131*. By the light of the moon, Hallowell saw a subchaser; slipping to within eight hundred yards the two PTs launched all eight of their torpedoes and emptied their rocket tubes. Withdrawing under fire, the crews reported hearing a loud explosion, which was what PT skippers and crews almost always said. However, this time they were right. The Japanese later admitted the loss of the subchaser *SC 53*.

Once outside the bay, Hallowell transferred to the *128* and returned with the second pair of PTs and their full load of torpedoes for yet another attack, accompanied by the first two PTs, the latter to provide covering fire. However, a search for the subchaser proved fruitless, and with good reason, as the vessel had been sunk in his first attack.

But Hallowell believed he saw a freighter moored to a dock; although under fire from the aroused enemy, the two PTs with torpedoes fired all eight missiles. All four boats then withdrew without damage. Ten days later, when the Army took Ormoc, they found Lieutenant Hallowell's "freighter" was the Japanese *PC 105,* sitting on the bottom of the harbor alongside the dock with a massive hole in its hull.[10]

During November and the ground battles for Leyte, Imperial Headquarters continued to push reinforcement convoys to Ormoc. By mid-November, the Japanese had managed to land forty thousand reinforcements at Ormoc. But to no avail. On Pearl Harbor Day, the U.S. 77th Infantry Division landed a few miles from Ormoc, catching the Japanese by surprise. Three days later Ormoc fell. During this tense period, the PT boats fired a number of torpedoes with uncertain results.

Reluctant as they were to risk more destroyers near Leyte, the Japanese dispatched two destroyers to evacuate naval personnel still on the island. They arrived on the night of December 11-12; the waiting naval personnel were quickly embarked and the ships were soon in their way. However, off the west coast of Leyte, one of the destroyers was picked up by the radars of *PT 490* commanded by Lt. John McElfresh, and *PT 492* commanded by Lt. Melvin W. Haines. At a range of one thousand yards, Haines fired four torpedoes; McElfresh fired two torpedoes. A tremendous explosion followed and the destroyer, later identified as the 1,315-ton *Uzuki,* sank immediately, along with recently evacuated personnel.[11] This was the last reported action between PT boats and enemy destroyers near Leyte.

As the battle for Leyte dragged on through December, Japanese attempts to supply and reinforce its troops continued, but with barges and small vessels, thus providing the PT boats with continued action west of the island.

In mid-December, however, the PTs were reminded that the *kamikazes* considered them fair game when the *323* was crashed by two suicide planes in Surigao Strait and completely destroyed. It was the first PT to suffer such a fate. But it would not be the last.

With the Allied advances on Leyte, a PT base was established at Ormoc Bay with Squadron 7 led by Lieutenant Hallowell and Squadron 12 commanded by Lieutenant Pullen operating. Later, Squadron 12 would be replaced by Squadon 25 commanded by Lt. Comdr. Theodore R. Stansberry with Pullen's squadron ordered to accompany MacArthur's advance toward Luzon.

Ranging amongst the islands west of Leyte, the Ormoc-based PTs continued to engage enemy vessels until March 1945, when the Eighth Army captured Cebu City and resistance in the area virtually ceased. In that three-month period, the Ormoc PTs racked up an impressive score of over 140 barges and over sixty miscellaneous vessels loaded with supplies, reinforcements and equipment sunk or damaged, and six aircraft downed.[12]

For MacArthur, although the landings at Leyte were a strategic victory, the slow advance of his troops against the stubborn Japanese defense on Leyte was frustrating. Even as the troops under MacArthur's command continued their battle to overwhelm the enemy defenders on Leyte, an impatient MacArthur planned to land four divisions on Luzon in Lingayen Gulf, some one hundred miles north of Manila on December 20. But with fighter cover needed over the invasion fleet, this meant another island, still closer to Luzon had to be taken for use as an air base. His choice was the primitive island of Mindoro, 290 miles northwest of Leyte Gulf.[13]

On the bright afternoon of December 12, an Allied invasion convoy sailed from Leyte Gulf bound for Mindoro's Mangarin Bay. As it transited Surigao Strait on December 13, Japanese reconnaissance planes reported the flotilla numbering eighty vessels. The convoy, in fact, carried some twenty-seven thousand men of the so-called Western Visayas Task Force. In addition to destroyers, the escorts included PT Squadrons 13 and 16, plus PTs *227* and *230*, all Higgins boats under the tactical command of Lt. Comdr. N. Burt Davis. No PT tender accompanied the squadrons since the ponderous vessels were considered too vulnerable to *kamikaze* attacks. For assistance and support, the PTs would rely on the Seabees; they were to set up a base of sorts at Mangarin Bay using an LST.[14]

From the moment it departed Leyte, all eyes in the convoy were on the sky, alert for *kamakazes.* It was not long before what was expected happened: on the second day, a *kamikaze* slipped through the convoy's defense and crashed into the portside of the invasion fleet's flagship, the cruiser *Nashville,* striking the vessel within a few feet of the cabin MacArthur had recently occupied during the passage to the Philippines. The explosion of the aircraft's bombs touched off the 5-inch and 40-mm ammunition in the ready lockers topside, killing 133 officers and men, including both the Army and Navy chiefs of staff and colonel commanding the bombardment wing. As a result, the *Nashville* turned back to Leyte. Two hours later, ten more *kamikazes* appeared. This time, the target was the destroyer *Haraden;* fourteen men died. The *Haraden* was also forced to return to Leyte.

At 7 a.m. December 15, Allied troops landed on the beach at Mangarin Bay. Thirty minutes later, Lieutenant Commander Davis led five PTs into the bay where *LST-605* was to be positioned as the PTs' tender and base for operations.

Minutes later, the *kamikazes* appeared: three dove on the destroyers in the bay and were downed by the combined fire of the PTs and ships. A fourth *kamikaze* passed over the stern of *PT 221* skippered by Ens. J. P. Rafferty and was hit by the full force of the PT's guns; the aircraft spectacularly cartwheeled along the surface, spraying flames and water before disappearing beneath the water.

A final seven planes attacked a group of approaching LSTs whose escort included eighteen PTs commanded by Lt. Comdr. Alvin W. Fargo, Jr. Sighting the aircraft, Commander Fargo ordered PTs to positions between the slow-moving LSTs and the *kamikazes.* The order had barely been executed when the planes swept in. The PTs' guns downed three *kamikazes* but four of the planes penetrated the defense screen; two were downed by the combined antiaircraft fire of the LSTs and PTs. Two *kamikazes* broke through, however. One slammed into *LST-738,* laden with troops, explosives and high octane gasoline, the other struck *LST-472,* loaded with supplies: both vessels quickly sank. PTs and destroyers rescued more than two hundred survivors from the water.

On the following morning, as *LST-605* was in the process of unloading supplies on the beach in Mangarin Bay and most of the

PTs were in the bay, a lone *kamikaze* dove on the LST. The PT and LST gunners opened fire, shooting the tail off the aircraft; the *kamikaze* crashed on the beach fifty yards from the LST, killing five men and wounding eleven.[15]

But there was more trouble coming. Thirty minutes later, eight aircraft appeared. *PT 230* commanded by Lt. Byron F. Kent was heading seaward when it was attacked by three of the pilots. The fate of the fifteen-man crew and the PT depended on a guessing game between the *kamikazes* and Lieutenant Kent. The diving pilots would try to anticipate where the PT boat would be; the PT skipper's tactic was to wait until the final moment before swerving hard to avoid the diving aircraft and its bomb and being blown to pieces.

With the PT running at full speed, Kent watched the first aircraft as it steepened its dive to about 70 degrees. When it was apparent the *kamikaze* was committed, Kent threw his helm hard right: he guessed correctly—the *kamikaze* hit the water thirty feet off the starboard bow.

Immediately the second plane began its dive. When the pilot was at a point where he was unable to pull out his dive or change direction, Kent applied hard left rudder: The *kamikaze* smashed into the water forty-five feet from the racing PT.

In spite of the failure of his two fellow pilots, even as the *230*'s gunners continued to fill the air with bullets and cannon shells, the third *kamikaze* screamed down. Recalled Lieutenant Kent, after first zigzagging, "I swung suddenly at right angles." The aircraft slammed into the bay just astern, raising the boat's stern out of the water and showering the 40-mm gun crew with flame, smoke, debris and water. All the crewmen were slightly dazed but none was injured and the boat was undamaged.[16]

Other PTs in the bay were undergoing similar experiences. Like Lieutenant Kent, their skippers were pushing their boats to top speed as they dodged, feinted, changed speed and swerved to evade plunging enemy aircraft: A *kamikaze* dove on *PT 77* skippered by Lt. Frank A. Tredinnick. Like Kent, Tredinnick maintained course and speed until the last minute, then chopped his throttles: the plane, whose pilot had correctly estimated the proper lead, crashed into the sea ten yards ahead of the boat. Lt.(jg) Harry Griffin, Jr., commander of a third boat, *PT 223*, turned hard right just before a *kamikaze* crashed close by, showering his boat with water but inflicting no injuries to crewmen or damaging the boat. Lt.(jg) J. E. Erickson with *PT 298* had an even narrower escape. Pursued by two *kamikazes,* he maneuvered at top speed. As Erickson recalled:

"The gunners fired a steady stream of shells into one plane as it came down in a steep dive and crashed fifteen feet off the port bow. The second plane circled until he saw his partner had missed, and he dived on our stern, strafing as he came. The gunners fired on him until he crashed three feet off the starboard bow, spraying the deck with debris and water. One man was blown over the side by the concussion but was rescued uninjured."[17]

The combined fire of the PTs brought the last *kamikaze* down before it could pick a target.

Later that day, as the *224* and *297* were departing for the night patrol, two planes dropped three bombs and missed. The ships in the bay shot one of the aircraft down; the other was last seen trailing smoke as it disappeared over the trees. Japanese records indicate that on the 16th, fourteen Navy aircraft and four Army aircraft attacked the vessels in Mangarin Bay.[18]

However, the PTs' good fortune could not last. On the afternoon of the 17th, three *kamikazes* appeared over Mangarin Bay. One went into a steep dive aimed at Lt. Comdr. Almer P. Colvin's *PT 300.* It is logical to assume that the *kamikaze* pilots had been studying the previous failures of their brother pilots in attacking PT boats: Waiting until the final moment, Commander Colvin turned hard right, but this time the *kamikaze* pilot guessed right; the plane crashed into the *300*'s engine room, splitting the boat in half. The stern, weighed down by the engines, sank immediately; the burning bow remained afloat for eight hours, a grim reminder of the results when a *kamikaze* guessed right. Commander Colvin was seriously wounded, four crewmen were killed, four reported missing, one officer and four men wounded. Only one *PT 300* crewmember escaped uninjured.

The *kamikazes'* final score at Mindoro during the days following the landings was four LSTs and one PT boat sunk and one cargo ship damaged.[19]

But the enemy was far from defeated. Just before darkness, on December 26, a PB4Y search plane eighty miles northwest of Mindoro sighted the giant battleship *Yamato,* along with one cruiser and six destroyers steaming hard toward Mindoro. After radioing the alarming report, to be sure someone got the message, the pilot landed at San Jose Airfield on Mindoro to report to the local commander. In addition, word of a second force of cargo ships and troop transports departing from Subic Bay in southern Luzon was received.

The two reports caused alarm on the Allied side. It was clear the enemy was planning a coordinated amphibious operation aimed at driving the invading Americans out of Mindoro. Estimates placed zero hour at sometime late on December 26.

With every Allied capital ship at Leyte, too far away to reach Mindoro Island in time, it would be up to the PTs at Mangarin Bay to confront the enemy.

"Recall all patrols to assist in the defense of Mindoro," Admiral Kinkaid ordered Lieutenant Commander Davis. After days of playing Russian roulette with pilots intent on suicide, the PT crews were about to face a group of capital ships escorting a landing force.

Commander Davis concluded the best tactic was to attack the thin-skinned enemy transports with torpedoes as they closed the Mindoro beach, then to machine-gun any landing barges trying to reach the shore. With all his PT boats in poor condition after the recent twelve days of operations, Davis chose to position the best nine boats on a patrol line three miles from shore. Two PTs under the command of Lt. P. A. Swart on their way to contact Mindoro guerrillas were called back and vectored in the direction of the approaching Japanese task force with orders to attack as soon as contact was made.

The commander of U.S. ground troops on Mindoro, Brig. Gen. William C. Dunckel, one of the officers painfully wounded when the *kamikaze* crashed into the *Nashville,* hastily deployed elements of the 503rd Parachute Regiment to counter the enemy landings. The commander of Fifth Air Force fighters operating from the captured air strip on Mindoro ordered his planes in the air to launch an attack on the approaching Japanese.

Shortly after 8:30 that night, north of Mangarin Bay, Lieutenant Commander Fargo, skipper of Squadron 13 in tactical command of four boats, sighted antiaircraft tracers on the horizon, an estimated forty-five miles away. Fargo concluded the Mindoro-based fighters had found the Japanese and were attacking. At 9:15 p.m., the PT radars picked up several blips. Soon lookouts discerned the silhouettes of six ships at a range four miles.

Almost immediately, the enemy spotted the PTs. Gun flashes on the ships were followed by screaming shells. However, Fargo's orders were to scout and report, not attack the ships until they approached the beach.

As ordered, Fargo radioed his contact report. But then, to the dismay of the PT crews, the Mindoro fighters attacked the PTs. A bomb dropped near *PT 77,* did what the *kamikazes* had been unable to do, wounding every man in the crew and seriously damaging the 77-foot Elco. A second bomb exploded close to *PT 84,* blowing one crewman overboard.[20]

When the distressing news was radioed back to Commander Davis by an enraged Commander Fargo, Davis ordered *PT 77* back to Mangarin Bay escorted by *PT 84,* and for Fargo to take the two remaining PTs through the strait between Ilin Island and Mindoro and attack the enemy's transports if they should appear off Mindoro's southern beaches.

In any event, no transports appeared. Indeed, the sighting report was in error. The enemy force, commanded by Rear Adm. Masatome Kimura, rather than including a battleship, consisted of two cruisers and five destroyers. Encountering the PT boats and attacks from the air, Admiral Kimura bombarded San Jose and the nearby area for twenty minutes, doing little damage and causing no casualties before withdrawing.

But he did not escape unscathed. Racing to his assigned position, Lieutenant Swart's two PTs, the *221* and *223,* sighted the retreating ships. Japanese searchlights illuminated the two PTs and fired salvos that landed dangerously close. Lt.(jg) Harry Griffin, Jr. commanding *PT 223* launched two torpedoes at a range of four thousand yards. Three minutes passed, then flames shot high in the air from the third ship in line. A deep-sounding explosion was heard by the PT crew. Later, when the PT men hauled a reluctant Japanese survivor from the water, they learned the ship sunk was the 2,000-ton *Kiyoshima,* one of the Imperial Navy's newest and most powerful destroyers.

In the Mindoro bombardment, which the Japanese call the REI operation, Admiral Kimura claimed the sinking of two medium transports, two small cargo ships, and a PT boat. The U.S. Fleet intelligence officer marked it as one tanker sunk. The effort did nothing to hamper the Mindoro operation, however.

During this time, the bitter battle for Leyte continued. Nevertheless, on the day after Christmas, MacArthur announced the Leyte campaign "can now be regarded as closed except for minor mopping up.... General Yamashita has sustained perhaps the greatest defeat in the military annals of the Japanese." When General Krueger, commanding MacArthur's Sixth Army, handed Leyte over to General Eichelberger and the Eighth Army, he repeated MacArthur's claim that all that remained on Leyte was some mopping up, adding only about five thousand Japanese remained to deal with. A month later, a disgusted Eichelberger commented: "Mopping up, hell; we have already killed twenty-seven thousand." And Leyte was yet to be secured.

Indeed, the fighting on Leyte dragged on into 1945, keeping four U.S. divisions tied down along with two PT squadrons at Ormoc Bay until spring. The final cost of Leyte was 3,500 Americans killed and twelve thousand wounded. For the Japanese, Leyte was a disaster. By the time the struggle ended, losses numbered some fifty thousand troops on the island, including some of their elite infantry divisions, plus an estimated forty thousand lost on ships sunk en route to the island. Gone also was much of their fleet, and virtually their entire air force, with the exception of the *kamikazes.*[21]

On December 27, the day following MacArthur's announcement on Leyte, a large supply convoy began shaping up in Leyte Gulf. All told, it numbered sixty-one vessels: LSTs, LCIs, Liberty ships, eight Army tankers, two loaded with aviation gasoline, a Navy tanker and the PT tender *Orestes.* Nine destroyers provided an outer defense; twenty-nine PT boats would give close support. Again, the objective was Mindoro's Mangarin Bay; this was the first phase of

MacArthur's invasion plan to land troops on Luzon. Conspicuously absent were heavy warships such as aircraft carriers, battleships, or cruisers.

Aboard the *Orestes* was Captain George F. Mentz, commander of a diversionary group. The role of this force was to launch attacks against southern Luzon prior to the main assaults mounted by MacArthur scheduled for January 9, 1945.

Navy expectations were that the *kamikazes* would be active, and the voyage would be rough. The expectations were correct: the convoy departed December 12 had been relatively fortunate; however, this second convoy would suffer, in part because poor flying weather over Leyte kept Allied fighters slated to provide air cover grounded while the skies were clear over Japanese fields.

The first *kamikaze* attack came in mid-morning the first day when three aircraft approached. The first sought to crash-dive an LCI but was shot down by *LCI-1076*. The second overshot the aviation tanker *Porcupine* and crashed into the sea. However, the third struck a merchant ship, the *John Burke,* loaded with ammunition; ship, crew, pilot and plane disappeared in one brilliant flash. A small Army freighter nearby sank as a result of the massive concussion. *PT 332,* five hundred yards away, was jarred by the concussion.[22]

The LCI flagship, *LCI-624,* hurried to the scene to rescue crewmen, but found only two survivors, both from the Army ship, and one died shortly after being rescued. Sixty-eight merchant sailors had vanished with the two ships.

Even darkness brought no relief: about 7 p.m. a torpedo bomber dropped its lethal missile and sent *LST 750* to the bottom.

For four days and nights, the lumbering convoy endured the reign of terror as Japanese fighters and bombers attempted to crash the ships with varying success. Three LCIs each shot down a plane. On the 30th, three planes were shot down before noon, one by a PT boat whose gunners downed the aircraft as it dove on an escorting destroyer. Fortunately, some LCIs had surgical teams aboard; many wounded on the ships were thus transferred to these vessels for treatment. By the time the convoy reached the harbor at San Jose, its gunners had shot down eighteen *kamikazes.*[23]

Inside Mangarin Bay, crews hurried to unload the cargoes, but not quick enough. At 3:05 the *kamikazes* struck. Five bombers diving from high altitude sliced through the air defenses. One crashed into the destroyer *Pringle,* a glancing blow before smashing into the sea. The aim of the second pilot was better: the diving aircraft struck the tanker *Porcupine* with such force the plane's engine crashed through the deck to emerge from the ship's bottom; seven men were killed and eight wounded. The stern of the tanker was quickly enveloped in flames, a dangerous condition for a tanker.

The third plane hit the destroyer *Gansevoort* amidships, cutting power lines, starting fires, and opening a massive hole in the main deck. The destroyer *Wilson* came alongside and its crew helped extinguish the flames. The crippled destroyer was then towed to the PT base.

In an effort to prevent the tanker from exploding, a destroyer fired a torpedo blowing the burning stern off the tanker; the intent was to blow the burning part off before the flames reached the gasoline stored in the ship's tanks; but the effort failed. The blast spread burning gasoline across the water, starting new fires on the *Gansevoort.* The new fires were finally quelled by volunteer PT men. In the end, the *Porcupine* burned to the waterline.[24]

But for the PT boats, the blow closest to the heart occurred when the final plane smashed into the PT tender *Orestes.* Hit by a torrent from the PTs' guns and nearby LCIs, the screaming *kamikaze* first hit the water then bounced upward to slam into the starboard side of the tender, the aircraft's bombs boring through the ship's hull to explode inside, blowing men into the sea. Instantly the tender burst into flames. In this nightmare, ruptured fire mains prevented the crew from battling the flames.

On the bridge, Captain Mentz lay crumbled, seriously wounded, his body covered with blood; next to him lay his fatally wounded chief of staff, Comdr. John Kremer, Jr. Scattered along the deck were the bodies of mutilated officers and men, some burned beyond recognition. Nearby PT boats rushed to pull stunned survivors from the water.[25]

But an even greater calamity threatened ships and men: if the flames reached the 37,000 gallons of 100-octane gasoline and supply of torpedoes and ammunition, the *Orestes* would disappear in a massive explosion, along with all that were aboard. Nevertheless, Lieutenant Commander Davis led the PT crews as they scrambled aboard to rescue the wounded from the flames.

No less daring was Comdr. A. Vernon Jannotta, the LCI flotilla commander, who brought his flagship, *LCI 624,* alongside the burning *Orestes* and led a volunteer fire-fighting and rescue party aboard the tender, by now mass of flames, intense heat, exploding ammunition, and mangled bodies.

After a long ninety minutes, the flames were finally extinguished and the wounded removed. For the *Orestes* it was a disaster: six officers and fourteen enlisted men of her crew were dead; thirty-seven men were missing; seven officers and sixty-eight enlisted men were wounded. To keep the *Orestes* afloat, Commander Jannotta lashed an LCI on either side of the tender and pushed it up on the beach. For his actions, Commander Jannotta was awarded the Navy Cross. With Captain Mentz seriously wounded and his chief of staff dead, Jannotta took command of the task group. For this he would later receive a Silver Star.[26]

For the Americans at Mangarin Bay, it had all been a bad day—the fifth *kamikaze* also found a target. Any weapon that is one hundred percent effective must be deemed a fearsome weapon, noted one perceptive observer. But an enigmatic fate was to deal yet another—twenty-four hours later, on New Year's Day, a Japanese plane flew over Mangarin Bay and dropped a single fragmentation bomb, killing eleven of the *Orestes's* survivors and wounding ten others.

Again, on the afternoon of January 4, PTs *78* and *81* opened fire on four Japanese aircraft overhead, hitting one. Trailing smoke, the pilot glided down to smash into the side of the ammunition ship *Lewis Dyche,* anchored a quarter of a mile from the two PTs. The explosion sent the ship to the bottom taking seventy-one merchant sailors with her; the resultant falling debris damaged the two PTs, killing two crewmen and wounding ten others. This disaster marked the end of the *kamikaze* attacks on Mindoro. However, from October to December, *kamikazes* caused the deaths of 470 American sailors and soldiers, added to the 763 sailors and soldiers killed at Leyte. As Commander Jannotta wrote perceptively in his report:

"This new weapon employed by the enemy—the suicide diver or human torpedo—constitutes a serious threat to naval forces and shipping."[27]

Indeed, this was so recognized by the Navy. For their performance at Mindoro's Mangarin Bay against this threat, the PTs received a Navy Unit Commendation saying:

"As the only naval force present after retirement of the invasion convoy, this task unit served as the major obstruction to enemy counterlandings from nearby Luzon, Panay, and Palawan, and bore the brunt of concentrated hostile air attacks through a five-day period, providing the only antiaircraft protection for persons ashore. The gallant officers and men...maintained a vigilant watch by night and stood out into the open waters close to base by day to fight off repeated Japanese bombing, strafing, and suicide attacks, expending in three days the ammunition which had been expected to last approximately three weeks in the destruction or damaging of a large percentage of attacking planes.[28]

By now, however, the focus of the war had switched to Luzon, the most northerly of the larger islands. Here the invading Allied forces would face the most massive of all *kamakaze* attacks.

In preparation for the invasion, Squadron 24 commanded by Lt. Stanley C. Thomas and Squadron 25 led by Lieutenant Commander Stansberry, were temporarily attached to Task Group 77.11; essentially, their task was similar to the PTs that had operated on the Mediterranean, to escort raiding parties, land scouts on Luzon behind enemy lines, and work closely with local guerrilla forces harassing the enemy. Squadron 28 commanded by Lt. Comdr. George A. Matteson, Jr., and Squadron 36 commanded by Lt. John W. Morrison, Jr., under the tactical command of Lieutenant Commander Tappaan with the tender *Wachapreague* would operate in Lingayen Gulf in support of landings by the U.S. Sixth Army slated for January 9, 1945.[29]

The landings would not be a duplication of the relatively easy landings by MacArthur at Leyte. Gen. Tomoyuki Yamashita, commanding the defense of the Philippines, the general MacArthur had declared to have so thoroughly defeated at Leyte, was well aware of the upcoming battle. Interviewed by reporters from Tokyo, the 6-foot-two-inch, two-hundred-pound, bullet-headed general, known as the "Tiger of Malaya" following his capture of Singapore early in the war, gave the reporters an earful. Speaking boastfully, he declared, "The loss of one or two islands does not matter. The Philippines have an extensive area and we can fight freely to our hearts' content. I shall write a brilliant history of the Greater East Asia Co-Prosperity Sphere in the Philippine Islands." Following the interview, a Radio Tokyo commentator declared: "The battle for Luzon, in which 300,000 American officers and men are doomed to die is about to begin."[30]

Carlos Romulo, the editor and publisher of the *Manila Herald,* the Philippines English-language newspaper, recalled his horror in 1941 on hearing Radio Manila announce the Japanese had come, that "eighty enemy transports had been sighted in Lingayen Gulf." After thirty-seven months of waiting, he wrote; "Now, it is their turn to quake."[31]

But it was not just the Japanese who were quaking, if indeed they were. Three hellish days lay ahead for the Allied invasion convoy departing Leyte. Expecting the worse, the U.S. Navy took extra precautions. Even so, it was worse than expected. In fact, the rain of *kamikazes* would nearly cause the cancellation of the landings on Luzon.[32]

The invasion armada departed Leyte on New Year's Day under the command of Admiral Oldendorf; it was not long before the 164 ships were reeling under attacks. The terror began on January 4 when a lone *kamikaze* slammed into the "Jeep" carrier *Ommaney Bay,* sending her to the bottom with her complement of aircraft. More unnerving to the embattled crews was the attack at noon, January 6, when a burning suicide plane smashed into the bridge of the battleship *New Mexico,* instantly killing the ship's captain and twenty-six other men. Among the dead were Prime Minister Churchill's liaison officer with MacArthur's headquarters, his aide, and a *Time* magazine correspondent; eighty-seven men were also wounded.[33]

As a result of the continued attacks, Admiral Oldendorf sent a message back to Admiral Kinkaid, his superior and commander of the Seventh Fleet: Oldendorf warned Kinkaid that the continuous *kamikaze* attacks on the convoy placed the mission in doubt.[34]

Before the shocked Allied command could respond, fate stepped in: the wave of *kamikazes* ended. The Japanese on Luzon had exhausted their supply of aircraft. Before they could be resupplied, on January 9, S-Day, Admiral Oldendorf's battleships reached Luzon and began bombarding the beaches. Assault elements of four divisions of General Krueger's Sixth Army were soon wading ashore against little opposition. Four days later PT Squadrons 28 and 36 with the tender *Wachapreague* and Lt. Comdr. Francis Tappaan arrived at Lingayen Gulf. Immediately the PTs began patrolling the gulf. On the first night they sank four *daihatsus*. A few nights later, *PT 532* commanded by Lt. B. M. Stevens and *PT 528* with Lt. G. S. Wright at the helm each fired four torpedoes at a 6,000-ton freighter, damaging the ship and forcing her skipper to beach and abandon her.

But the PTs were about to encounter a new foe, the *shinyo:* small Japanese suicide motorboats. In August 1944, the Imperial Army had secretly formed a force of suicide boats: small craft operated by one man, fitted with two 120-kilogram depth charges to be dropped alongside the enemy ship. The Japanese Navy also mobilized a suicide unit in October, however, the Navy's version was loaded with six hundred pounds of high explosives; a firing pin detonated the charge when the craft hit the side of the ship. Like the Army's boat, its operation was by a single crewman.[35]

The Japanese planned to concentrated a large number of suicide boats in large numbers along the coast under strict secrecy where an enemy landing was anticipated; at the appropriate moment, under cover of darkness the boats would slip from their hiding places and attack the anchored Allied ships.

As the boats were built by different companies, they varied somewhat in performance and size. In length, they ranged from about seventeen feet to slightly over twenty-one feet, with a beam of five and a half to six feet. Like PT boats, construction was entirely of wood without armor protection. Powered by gasoline engines, 67-hp Nissans and Toyotas and six-cylinder Chrysler automobile engines, they had a maximum speed of 15 to 18 knots, and a range of up to 250 miles.[36]

With the expected Allied landings on the Lingayen beaches, the Army suicide boats lay hidden along the shore. Because their depth charge armament was more effective against thin-skinned transports, the operators were ordered to concentrate on those vessels.

Shortly after 2 a.m on January 10, a force of forty suicide boats emerged from their hiding places and headed silently for the anchored American transports. All reached the Lingayen anchorage without being detected. At 3:37 a.m., the first LST spotted two small boats approaching and opened fire, destroying one boat.

The firing alerted the rest of the ships. In what was to become a case of mass chaos among the Americans with jittery ships' gunners firing wildly, sometimes hitting other nearby ships, suicide boats damaged one LST, forcing it to beach, and sank an LCI. A suicide boat's depth charges also damaged a transport, killing twenty troops and three sailors, blowing a twelve-foot hole in the vessel's side; another suicide boat's depth charges jarred a destroyer severely before the boat escaped.

With the appearance of the suicide boats, the PTs were assigned a new task: to seek and destroy these small vessels, if possible, in their hiding places along the shore before they had a chance to attack.[37]

It was in conducting such a search that the last two PTs of World War II would be lost; ironically it would be to "friendly fire." On January 29, American troops stormed ashore on western Luzon. On the night of January 31, ships screening the landings had been attacked by twenty or more midget submarines, one of which sank the *PC 1129*. Immediately following the sinking, a flotilla of suicide boats unsuccessfully attacked the DE *Lough*. On the following night Lt. John H. Stillman, a PT veteran of the Solomons campaign, set out with PTs *77* and *79* to hunt down the troublesome suicide boats. During the mission, Lieutenant Stillman's orders were to remain south of Talim Point; U.S. destroyers and DEs would operate north of that point in search of the suicide boats. But as on earlier such occasions, the plan went awry with disastrous results.

That night, three miles south of Talim Point, the two PTs encountered the U.S. destroyer *Conyngham* accompanied by the *Lough*. The *Lough* first fired starshells and the two PT boats retreated southward at top speed while attempting to communicate with the two ships by radio and blinker light. Their efforts failed.

The two PTs might still have escaped, but *PT 77* ran aground. A shell from the *Lough* hit, blowing the crew into the water. *Lough's* next shell struck *PT 79*: the boat exploded; it disappeared beneath the surface along with her skipper, Lt.(jg) Michael A. Haughian, MoMM1/c Joseph E. Klesh, and QM3/c Vincent A. Berra.[38]

Aided by the light from the burning *77* boat, the swimming PT men gathered. The count showed there were thirty survivors. In addition to the three dead on *PT 79*, Lieutenant Stillman, the officer in tactical command, was missing. He was never seen again.

The survivors managed to swim to shore two miles away where guerrillas sheltered them until February 3 when they were rescued by PTs *227* and *230*.

Meanwhile, the battle for Luzon continued. With 275,000 men to defend the island, General Yamachita deliberately refrained from defending the beaches at Lingayen Gulf, having no intention of seeing them blasted to pieces by the guns of Oldendorf's battleships. He had no intention of defending Manila either: instead, he positioned his troops on the high ground so that MacArthur's men would have to come to him.[39]

For MacArthur, who had promised the Joint Chiefs of Staff he would have his men in Manila within four weeks of the landings, time was crucial. Urged on by MacArthur, on Saturday, February 3, patrols of the 1st Calvary raced ahead to cross the city limits into Manila, the first U.S. troops to enter the capital since December 1942. Their first act was to release prisoners held at Santo Thomas.

By now, with the end of the Solomons and New Guinea campaigns, twenty PT squadrons had been moved forward to operate in the Philippines. Late on the night of February 3, two PTs under the tactical command of veteran Lt. Henry S. Taylor slipped into Manila Bay. The two boats were the first American surface vessels to enter the bay since the surrender of Corregidor in May 1943. According to intelligence, the bay was "lousy with Japs." The two PTs crept by enemy-held Corregidor with engines muffled and continued on undetected to Manila, twenty-three miles away.

They found the city in flames. MacArthur hoped to make a formal entrance into Manila. However, this was impossible: General Yamashita had declared Manila an open city, evacuating his men to the hills, leaving thirty thousand sailors and marines behind to

destroy port facilities and supplies, before following. But Rear
Adm. Sanji Iwabuchi, commanding the marines and sailors, failed
to follow orders. Admiral Iwabuchi having decided to defend
Manila, the atrocities followed. Soon the Japanese marines' and
sailors' uniforms were soaked in Filipine blood and the flames of
the burning city were visible fifty miles away. Not until February 27
were the Americans able to gain control of Manila. By then the city
was a vast pile of rubble. True to their code, virtually all thirty
thousand of the Japanese defenders had fought to the death. Before
dying, they would round up and murder most of the city's 100,000
Filipine civilians.[40]

Even as the battle for Manila raged, MacArthur ordered that
Corregidor be attacked and retaken. At 8:30 a.m. February 16, PT
boats were in position near Corregidor to support the attack. Aboard
PT 376, Lt. Raymond P. Shafer eyed the massive array of warships
whose guns were pounding the island fortress. For the Americans,
Corregidor stood as a symbol of heroism in defeat, a place where
General Wainwright held out for a month before surrendering,
where Japanese soldiers hauled down the American flag and ground
it into the dirt beneath their feet.

According to Allied intelligence, Corregidor was held by 850
Japanese. In fact, the island garrison was manned by five thousand
typically dedicated soldiers and sailors. Furthermore, during the
period of occupation, the enemy had done all he could to make the
position impregnable.

MacArthur's plan called for a combined air and sea assault on
the island. As the PT boats hovered close by, a flight of U.S. cargo
planes approached carrying some 2,200 troopers of the 503rd
Parachute Infantry Regiment commanded by Col. George M. Jones.
The troopers were to parachute from the aircraft at low altitude,
between 350 and 400 feet for maximum accuracy, in hopes of
landing on the two-and-one-half-mile-long and narrow highest level
point of Corregidor, aptly named Topside. Towering 550 feet in the
air, its sheer cliffs above the water made it a tricky drop zone. The
slightest wind could prove disastrous, resulting in men in parachutes
missing their target and landing in the bay. Weighed down with as
much as ninety pounds of gear, entangled in parachute risers, the

unfortunate troopers could easily drown unless quickly rescued. This was the role of the waiting PTs.

In fact, many troopers missed the drop zone. And PTs as a result braved intense small arms fire from Japanese on the island as the boats raced in close to Corregidor's shore to pull troopers from the water. Other jumpers missed the flat surface that was Topside only to find themselves stranded on the cliff-sides. Spotting twelve or fourteen of these men working their way down the side of the cliff to a narrow strip of sand, Lt. John A. Mapp, commanding the *376,* sent the PT racing toward the shore to drop a rubber raft over the side just fifty yards from the beach. Lieutenants Charles Adams and Ray Shafer quickly clambered into the raft and paddled rapidly to shore to return the stranded men to the boat as Japanese sniper bullets snapped around them. Moments later, another group of stranded troopers were observed frantically waving their arms from the shore. Adams and Shafer repeated the rescue operation, returning the stranded men to the PT boat. Meanwhile, other PTs were performing similar rescue operations. Later, Colonel Jones declared that were it not for the presence of the PTs, many paratroopers who missed the drop zone would have died.[41]

Later that morning, a regiment of the 24th Infantry Division stormed ashore from landing craft. The battle for Corregidor would last twelve bloody days. By the time it ended, an estimated 4,500 Japanese were dead, the remainder having managed to escape from the island. The American toll numbered 1,200 casualties, more than a quarter of their original assault force. Shortly after dawn March 2, just two weeks short of three years since boarding *PT 41* with Lieutenant Bulkeley, MacArthur and his staff walked down to the Manila dock where four PT boats waited. He had left Corregidor aboard a PT and he was returning the same way—aboard *PT 373* commanded by Lt. Joseph Roberts.

At 10 a.m. the PT boats carrying the general and his staff eased up to Corregidor's North Dock on Bottomside. Eyeing the recent damage done by bombs and shells, MacArthur remarked that the island had been smashed beyond recognition.

As he stepped from the PT to the rickety dock, the Supreme Commander was greeted by Colonel Jones who saluted smartly, saying, "Sir, I present to you—Fortress Corregidor."

Congratulating the colonel on a brilliant operation, MacArthur pinned a Distinguished Service Cross on the officer, declaring: "I see that the old flagpole still stands. Have your troops hoist the colors to its peak, and let no enemy ever haul them down."[42]

By now, with some 212 PTs operating in the Philippines, and more PT bases established, Mindoro had become a principal staging and repair base as well as a base for operations—in fact, patrols from there would continue until April.

Pending the invasion of the Japanese home islands, PT boats carried out more mop-up operations of the type that had become their major role during the last three years of the war. An example was the island of Morotai where as few as two PT squadrons had continued to patrol, keeping the thirty-seven thousand men of the Japanese garrison on the larger island of Halmahara isolated for nearly a year while MacArthur occupied the Philippines. On August 14, 1945, when the war ended, the PT men learned just how large and potent the garrison was: 37,000 troops, 19,000 rifles, 900 cannon, 600 machine guns, and a massive amount of miscellaneous supplies were surrendered to the American commanders on Morotai by the garrison.

With the Philippines largely secure, it was expected that PT boats would participate in the invasion of Okinawa. But such was not to be. Kelly Turner, now a Vice Admiral, evidently still had memories of how a PT boat sank his flagship during the New Georgia campaign. Now possessing sweeping authority as Commander Amphibious Forces in the drive across the Central Pacific, Admiral Turner was in the midst of preparations for the invasion of Okinawa. According to the Rear Admiral John Hall, the overall commander of PTs reported to Hall at Leyte inquiring as to the training of PT boats for the upcoming Okinawa landings. Admiral Hall in turn contacted Turner by dispatch asking what part PT boats would play in the landings so he could arrange for appropriate training. According to Hall, Turner answered that PT boats would not be allowed to enter the Okinawa area until four days after the landings or later. Admiral Hall then added:

"He evidently had no use for them, and I had no use for them. When I was doing my part of the Normandy landing…they were of no use whatever."[43]

According to Vice Admiral (ret.) George C. Dyer, in his book, *The Amphibians Came to Conquer, The Story of Richmond Kelly Turner*, many U.S. naval officers who served in the Guadalcanal and New Georgia campaigns thought PT boats to be "anywhere from somewhat to vastly overrated by the public and the press."[44]

In any event, as the A-bombs were dropped on Japan, which ended the war shortly thereafter, the views of Turner, Hall and officers who shared their view on PT boats were soon irrelevant. At least for the moment.

PT base 17, Bobon Point, Samar, the Philippines, where, following WWII, many PT boats were destroyed. *Courtesy of WWII PT Boats Museum and Archives, Germantown, Tennessee, USA.*

An S-boat, or *Schnellbooten*, Germany's motor torpedo boats, a frequent PT foe in both the Mediterranean and in the English Channel. *Courtesy of WWII PT Boats Museum and Archives, Germantown, Tennessee, USA.*

At the end of the Pacific war; the Japanese command of by-passed Halmahara Island surrendered formally to Allied commanders on nearby Morotai Island. For eleven months, two Morotai-based PT squadrons had prevented some 37,000 enemy soldiers from escaping from Halmahara to join the defense of Japan. *Courtesy of WWII PT Boats Museum and Archives, Germantown, Tennessee, USA.*

EPILOGUE

By the time World War Two ended, the U.S. Navy had over five hundred PT boats in forty-two commissioned squadrons in operations, twenty-five squadrons in the Pacific. The PT base in the Philippines at Bobon Point, Samar, would be the largest ever established.[1] Three more squadrons of new Higgins PTs scheduled to be commissioned, were turned over to the Soviet Union. With peace, virtually overnight, the U.S. squadrons were disbanded. Men received individual orders authorizing their return to the states by "available transportation," men who had faced death and carried out countless patrols together as crews, stepped ashore to return home, never to see one another again.

Left behind were the boats. By now, most were too battered and worn to be worth salvaging. Of more than two hundred PTs in the Philippines, inspection revealed 118 were defective: Most of the older boats had dry rot, fractured frames and keels, burned out engines and other assorted defects. These were stripped of usable equipment and burned without fanfare off the Samar beach. Those worth saving were disposed of by the Foreign Liquidation Commission,[2] the boats turned over to such countries as South Korea and Norway. Initially, a few boats were retained by the Navy, including those attached to Melville as part of the training squadron; eventually, however, they would be sold by the War Shipping Administration, some for as little as five thousand dollars. By the end of 1945, all but three of the Navy's PT squadrons had ceased to exist. Soon, they too, would be gone.

Although the PT boats were gone, the same was not true of the men who had made the term "PT" synonymous with boldly winning. The most famous, of those of course, would be President John F. Kennedy. One might suspect the tragedy involving *PT 109* and his resultant image as a war hero after the war was a political advantage. Nor did Kennedy forget his comrades: seated in the VIP box in Washington, D.C., at the 1961 inaugural parade as one of the invited guests was William F. Liebenow, skipper of the PT boat that rescued Kennedy and his stranded crew after the *109* disaster. Earlier, Kennedy interrupted his campaign for Representative of Massachusetts to rush to the side of Leonard Thom, his former executive officer on the *109*. Returning to Ohio after the war, Thom married his college sweetheart and began working on his master's degree at Ohio State while selling insurance. In October 1946, while driving from Columbus to the home of his wife's parents in Youngstown, his car struck a train near Ravenna. He died the following day.

Rising to the rank of Rear Admiral, John Harllee took his retirement; in 1961 Kennedy appointed him to serve on the Federal Maritime Commission. In 1962, Kennedy appointed Byron White as justice of the Supreme Court; Kennedy also appointed former PT skipper Paul B. Fay, Jr., Under Secretary of the Navy.[3]

Other PT men acquired political prominence as well; Lieutenant Shafer who helped save the paratroopers at Corregidor returned home to be elected governor of Pennsylvania. And former PT officer Howard Baker would serve for many years with distinction as a senator from Tennessee.

Captain Bowling returned home still disturbed by the Navy's handling of the Medal of Honor award to Lieutenant Preston and the awards to the other men who participated in the rescue of the pilot at Wasile Bay. Bowling, who by any standards was qualified to make the judgment, considered this to be one of the most perilous rescues of the war. He had recommended that Preston be awarded the Medal of Honor, and the other men involved, the Navy Cross. When Seventh Fleet downgraded the awards, an outraged Bowling caused such an uproar that it carried all the way to Washington, and the original decorations were finally approved. However, such behavior in the bureaucratic Navy virtually assured there would be career-damaging repercussions. Apparently this was true for Bowling. In 1957, still holding the rank of captain, Bowling took an early retirement and joined Texas Industries in Corpus Christi, Texas.

Former PT men also proved successful in the world of sports: Lt. Michael Burke was instrumental in the CBS takeover of the world famous New York Yankee baseball team in 1964, going on from there to become president of the New York Knicks basketball team, as well as the New York Ranger hockey team. Walter Lemm, "Wally" to legions of sports fans, back from duty with the PTs in the South Pacific, became a successful coach of the St. Louis Cardinals and later, of the Houston Oilers, crowning it all by being named the National Football League's Coach of the Year for 1964.

In Hollywood, film star Robert Montgomery returned from the war with the rank of lieutenant commander after seeing PT action in the Solomons. One of his most memorable roles after returning to Hollywood would be that of John Bulkeley in the film "They Were Expendable" also starring John Wayne as Lieutenant Kelly, Bulkeley's squadron executive officer. Montgomery would pass on in 1981, but the movie remains a favorite, viewed regularly on the TV screen along with "PT 109" depicting the disaster that befell John Kennedy and his crew.

Indeed, no name is more associated with American PT boats during the war that that of John Bulkeley. Hailed as the star in MacArthur's escape from Corregidor, the basis for the book, and previously referred to Hollywood film "They Were Expendable." Once can imagine, given the subsequent course of the war in the Pacific, what might have happened if Bulkeley had failed and MacArthur had been killed or captured by the Japanese, this at a time when the world was witnessing a series of Allied defeats in both Europe and the Pacific. MacArthur's successful escape to Australia provided a boost to the sagging morale of the American public at a critical moment in the war. Furthermore, MacArthur's desperate decision to defend Australia by landing his troops in New Guinea, at a time when it was generally accepted that Australia was all but lost, was a move that shocked his staff as much as the Japanese, one that proved crucial in halting an advancing enemy that until that time had seemed unstoppable.

It is thus inarguable that MacArthur's New Guinea success along with the Allied victory at Guadalcanal was instrumental in reversing the tide in the Pacific war. Notably, as recalled, in both, PT boats played a key role.

As to the question of whether the PTs were worth the expenditure, it is interesting to find that following the war, opponents as well as supporters of PT boats each argued that the results confirmed their positions.[4] Judged in the traditional manner, that is total tonnage sunk, the foes of PT boats had a case. As sinkers of ships, their record was undistinguished. Indeed, on the whole, motor torpedo boats during World War Two played a relatively minor part. Germany's S boats, or E-boats, as termed by the Allies, the most successful in attacking ships, sank a mere 1.1 percent of Allied merchant shipping as compared to 68.1 percent by submarines.[5] However, unlike Germany's S-boats, American PTs performed multiple assignments in close support of Allied troops; tasks requiring guns rather than torpedoes. That the PTs were a success in these roles was aptly confirmed by frontline Allied commanders as well as by the Japanese, no small accomplishment in itself. Doubtless the Allies would have won the war without the use of PT boats, but it would have taken longer and more lives would have been lost along the way.

As an aside, immediately after MacArthur's troops occupied Tokyo, accompanying Allied newsmen quickly located the notorious Tokyo Rose whose sultry voice and popular records for so many months had been the source of Allied entertainment as well as unease. On September 1, 1945, a diminutive Iva Ikuko Toguri met two correspondents at Tokyo's Imperial Hotel accompanied by a Japanese newsman and her Portuguese-Japanese husband, Philip d' Aquino.[6]

Asked if she was Tokyo Rose, she answered with a smile, "The one and only." Questioned further by the reporters, she explained how an intelligent woman with a degree from UCLA who loved America, became a traitor serving the country she hated for $6.60 a month, making daily radio broadcasts for the "benefit of Allied forces in the Pacific," because the only other option was compulsory work in a munitions factory. She told the newsmen how she had gone to Japan under protest before the war at her mother's insistence to visit family relatives, and was unable to leave with the sudden outbreak of war.

Despite her explanations, Iva was later arrested, tried and convicted for the crime of treason. Sentenced to ten years in prison and fined $10,000, she would be released after serving six years. Some thirty years later, when memories of that war had grown dim,

Iva successfully argued she was innocent of the crime since she was coerced into making the broadcasts: she was pardoned by President Gerald Ford on his last day in office.[7]

But the U.S. Navy was not quite ready to turn its back on PT boats. In 1945, the Navy authorized construction of four new experimental PT boats incorporating lessons learned in four years of combat; all had aluminum instead of wooden hulls, and all were powered by four 2,500-hp, 16-cylinder Packard V-type gasoline engines. The boats were larger than the World War Two boats, ranging from 89.5 to 105 feet in length, displacing between 89 and 102 tons, with a draft of five feet. Armament included racks for four torpedoes, two 40-mm cannon, two 20-mm dual Oerlikon cannon, one 81-mm mortar and one smoke generator. All were fitted with radar. One boat, *PT 809*, was built by Elco; missing as a builder was Andrew Higgins. Disgusted with the problems of dealing with the War Labor Board, the National Labor Relations Board and problems with unions, he closed all twenty-one of his plants. He would die on August 1, 1952.

In 1951 the four boats, PTs *809* through *812*, were delivered to the Navy and designated Squadron 1. Tests were conducted until 1956: the fastest of the four, PT *811* built by John Trumphy & Sons, was capable of a top speed of 55 knots "under ideal conditions." For the others, 40 knots-plus was the maximum.

In 1957, PT *812* was converted to gas turbine power, making it the first small craft to be so powered in the United States. In 1958, with tests completed, the squadron was decommissioned. Reverting to its pre-World War Two views, the Navy again decided it had no need for such vessels. PT *809* was renamed *Guardian* and assigned to the Secret Service as a guard boat for the President's yacht. PTs *810* and *811* were struck from the Naval Register in 1960. PT *812*, was also struck from the Naval Register that same year, and transferred to Korea in April. There she served until 1967 when her turbines were removed. She was finally scrapped in 1968.[8]

As before, the U.S. Navy was alone among nations in making this decision. And no nation chose to invest more heavily in the effort to design and improve the capabilities of motor torpedo boats than the Soviet Union. By the close of the war, the United States had delivered about one hundred Higgins and 80-foot Elco PTs to

Russia. Based on the 80-foot Elco, the Soviets built a motor torpedo boat designated the P-6-class. With a length of 85 feet, displacing 65 tons, like the U.S. Navy's four experimental boats received for testing in 1951, the Soviet product was powered by four engines, in this case, 4,800 b.h.p. diesels providing a reported top speed of 45 knots. Armament included two 21-inch torpedo tubes, two turrets mounting twin 20-mm AA cannon and depth charges or mines.

Early models even had the thimble-shaped radar dome similar to that of the U.S. SO-13 type radar used on American PTs at the end of World War Two. The all-wooden hulled P-6 entered service in 1954 with the USSR building some five hundred boats. The Soviet Navy kept between 200 and 250 P-6s, in what became a standard Soviet practice, distributed the rest of the P-6s widely abroad, twelve to Cuba, six to Algeria, thirty-six to Egypt, six to North Vietnam, as well as additional P-6s to a host of other nations friendly to the Soviet Union, notably China, this last nation further declaring its interest in motor torpedo boats by constructing eighty duplicate P-6s, some of which were exported to another nation hostile to the West, namely North Korea, with a version, now called the *Swatow,* being supplied to North Vietnam.[9]

For the Soviet Union, such interest in motor torpedo boats was understandable in light of the battles with the German Navy during World War Two. With the war over, the basic mission of the Soviet Navy was to combat the Soviet's new enemy. In 1946, in a carefully phrased statement, Soviet Admiral Alafuzov, hinting that that "enemy" was the United States, declared the enemy "is virtually dependent on its sea lines of communication." In the period that followed, nothing changed.

Not prepared to rest on its laurels, during the 1960s, while attention of the West was elsewhere, the Soviet Navy introduced more advanced boats. For the first time the Soviets used steel hulls and employed more powerful diesels to propel the new boats, including the *Shershen*-class motor torpedo boat. With a length of 110 feet, displacing 150 tons, she was twice the size of the P-6. Armament included four 21-inch torpedo tubes, two depth charges racks and mine rails.

Although the Warsaw Pact navies received considerable numbers of the Soviet-built craft, Poland and East Germany now undertook to design their own motor torpedo boats. Yugoslavia, having enjoyed the benefits of both Russia and the West, found its navy included craft supplied and paid for by both sides. Some one hundred duplicates of the 78-foot Higgins PTs were built in Yugoslavia after World War Two, armed with two 17.7-inch torpedoes plus one 40-mm cannon and two .50-caliber machine guns, powered by either Packard engines or German diesels. During the 1960s, these elderly craft were augmented by the more modern Soviet *Shershen* motor torpedo boats.

With continued improved motor torpedo boats in a number of the world's navies, the Vietnam War would serve, once more, to remind the U.S. Navy that PT boats had their uses. When Seal teams were assigned the task of entering the Gulf of Tonkin to destroy a number of *Swatows,* Chinese motor torpedo boats that bore a remarkable resemblance to the U.S. 80-foot Elco PTs handed over to the Soviet Union at the end of World War Two were encountered. Ironically, the same U.S. Navy that saw no value in PT boats considered Vietnamese PTs a potential threat to its heavy warships offshore. To deal with the *Swatows,* in a scenario straight out of World War Two, the Commander, U.S. Military Assistance Command Vietnam, proposed the use of American PTs in conjunction with Seals in covert operations against North Vietnam. On October 6, the Chief of Naval Operations, Adm. David McDonald, ordered the Chief, Bureau of Ships, to prepare *PT 810* and *PT 811* to be reactivated by January 1963 for operations, including quieting the engines, an essential necessity, as recalled, for boats conducting covert operations near hostile shores.

The boats' operators were unenthusiastic. They pointed out the two PTs had been used hard in earlier tests and believed they were unserviceable. On the basis of World War Two experience, they also thought the gasoline engines were too dangerous for such operations. Despite such reluctance, PTs *810* and *811* were eventually deployed to Da Nang.[10]

With the sudden need for PT boats and no domestic capability to build such vessels, for the second time in its history, the U.S. Navy turned to a foreign power, this time to Norway, where the U.S. was financing a five-year naval building program. Prior to 1951, Norway's experience with motor torpedo boats was limited to operating a number of captured German S-boats. That year, however, the German boats were replaced by U.S. 80-foot Elco PTs. That same year, the keel of the first Norwegian-designed motor torpedo boat was laid. With a length of 87-feet, displacing 75 tons and powered by four Packard engines, the wooden hulled boats were essentially enlarged Elcos. Top speed remained 41 knots; and armament consisted of the familiar four 21-inch torpedo tubes, plus a 40-mm cannon and two 20-mm cannon for use in anti-aircraft defense.

In October 1962, Secretary of Defense Robert McNamara requested the Navy obtain "two foreign-made craft of the PT boat category from Norway." The result was two fast boats, called the *Nasty*-class; later, production of additional boats was handed over to John Trumpy & Sons, Annapolis, Maryland, the builder of *PT 811*. Eventually fourteen *Nasty*s would join the two initial PTs in Vietnam. With the U.S. not yet officially at war with North Vietnam, to preclude future embarrassment to the U.S. Navy and the government, the newly appointed CinCPacFlt, [Commander-in-Chief, Pacific fleet] Adm. U. S. G. Sharp, strongly recommended that the "boats" be stricken from U.S. Navy records for record purposes.

With limited boats on hand, as was the case in the early days of World War Two, PT operations off the north coast of Vietnam were necessarily short of World War Two accomplishments. But in successfully landing spies and raiders on enemy shores, participating in kidnappings and assassination operations, once again the PTs demonstrated the same capabilities so useful in that earlier war. For example, in May 1964, PT boats captured a North Vietnamese junk with six passengers; these were handed over to the CIA for intense interrogation.

Moreover, as a consequence of the activities of these boats, as in the campaign for New Guinea during World War Two, the enemy was forced to divert precious resources to strengthen his coastal defenses. One result was the historic confrontation between two U.S. destroyers, the *Maddox* and *Turner Joy,* and North Vietnamese motor torpedo boats in the Gulf of Tonkin. On that occasion, the U.S. Navy sought intelligence on Viet Cong supply routes, the location of enemy radar sites and other such items.

According to American intelligence, ten newly arrived *Swatows* had been added to four North Vietnamese motor torpedo boats in the area. On the night of August 4, as the two U.S. destroyers were carrying out their mission in the gulf, reports were received indicating they were being stalked by two North Vietnamese *Swatows,* the *T-142* and *T-146.*

At 8:01 p.m., the *Maddox* radar detected a surface contact forty-two miles to the northeast. Both *Maddox* and *Turney Joy* established radar contact showing three vessels closing at 30 knots.[11]

In the action that followed, the two destroyers narrowly escaped being hit by the *Swatows'* torpedoes. Given the fact that the enemy's boats were of an early model lacking sophisticated electronic gear common to newer boats, and that the *Swatows'* attacks were poorly coordinated, plus that there were no more than three attacking enemy craft, the two destroyers could consider themselves lucky to have escaped unscathed: Soviet doctrine required that multiple attacks to be made "simultaneously" on a target.

In August 1965, PTs *810* and *811* were disposed of, sunk as targets. Once again the U.S. Navy was without PT boats or a domestic builder of such vessels, and the Navy's conviction was that it had no need for such small vessels.

In a related field, one closely related to motor torpedo boats, the U.S. Navy continued improvements in torpedo performance, as did other naval powers. In fact, by the end of World War Two the electric torpedo eliminating the telltale wake of the steam-powered torpedo, was being employed by both sides. And by the end of the war the magnetic exploder, as shown by the Royal Navy with its MTBs, was being employed successfully. Two decades after the World War Two, acoustic torpedoes, homing on a ship's sound, were common; wire-guided torpedoes followed, all weapons that in themselves made motor torpedo boats a threat to any heavy vessel. One of the latest and no less lethal in this collection was the Soviet "wake-chaser," a torpedo designed to follow a wake and hit a large warship aft, its most vulnerable point. In particular, its target would be the U.S. aircraft carriers, the centerpiece of American naval power.

Moreover, no longer would the small naval combatants' lethal sting be confined to torpedoes, as sophisticated as they might be. As predicted by that PT commander during World War Two who proposed replacing PTs' torpedoes with rockets; less than two decades later, theory turned into reality. On October 21, 1967, the navies of the West were rudely shocked. While patrolling just over twelve miles offshore from Egypt's Port Said, the Israeli destroyer *Eilat* was sunk by surface-to-surface cruise missiles fired from a small vessel that was a descendant of the American PT boats handed over to the Soviet Union following World War Two.[12] As the first ship to be sunk by a missile, it was an historic event that changed naval warfare as dramatically as appearance of the torpedo in the nineteenth century. Like a torpedo, the cruise missile could be launched from a platform as small as a modified torpedo boat, in this case a Russian SS-N-2, code named "Styx" by NATO. Similar in size to a torpedo with a length of 23.3 feet, weighing over 2000 pounds with an 880-pound warhead, it differs from a torpedo in that it has small wings and travels at a speed of Mach 0.8. with a range of over eighteen nautical miles. In the case of the *Eilat,* the Soviet-built missile boat supplied to Egypt was armed with four cruise missiles rather than torpedoes.

Five years earlier, missiles were given slight attention by the navies of the West. But not so the Soviet Union. As part of its continued effort to counter the power of the post-World War Two U.S. Navy, between 1959 and 1961 the Soviet navy fitted its P-6 boats with two Styx guided missiles. This was followed by a boat designed to carry cruise missiles: a small high-speed boat known to the West as the Komar (Mosquito). The Soviets followed their practice of providing other nations with a number of the boats— nations like Algeria, Cuba, and Syria—with two hundred retained in the Soviet Union's inventory.[13]

During the early 1960s the Soviet introduced another, larger version, the Osa (Bee), a missile boat capable of 35 knots, armed with four Styx missiles. Like the Komar, the Osa was heavily exported, appearing in at least eight foreign navies, such as East Germany, Poland, Egypt, Cuba and Communist China.

During February and March 1971, eight Osas were delivered to India as deck cargo aboard a Soviet merchant ship. In the 1971

Indo-Pakistani War, three Indian Osas fired nine Styx missiles at Pakistani ships, sinking one destroyer and putting a second out of action. Note should be made that the missiles were fired beyond range of the destroyers' guns, the sinkings thus demonstrating the over-the-horizon hitting accuracy of the radar-guided Styx.

Initial missile boats of the decade of the 1960s, the type that sank the Israeli destroyer, lacked "over-the-horizon" capability. But that was no longer true. The revolution in computers and communications has made a capable fire-control system standard on the new boats. To put it bluntly, the age the computer married to the PT naval tradition has opened up a new world: by the end of the twentieth century, eighty percent of the world's warships were patrol-sized vessels armed with cruise missiles capable, all for sale to anyone with the money to buy. Patrol craft in the tradition of earlier PT boats, now possessed the destructive power that rivaled many destroyers and frigates around the world.

For navies dependant on large warships, absorbing the first hit by a surface-to-surface missile cannot be an option. A single missile can disable, if not sink, anything smaller than an aircraft carrier. And a carrier would in all probability be unable to carry out its mission. All would result in a massive loss of life. It would also provide an enormous psychological-political victory for an enemy, even if in subsequent action his entire force were lost.

As was true in World War Two, when faced with a potential disaster, there are two options: pull back, as the U.S. Navy did at Guadalcanal and New Guinea, or attack the potential threat platforms before they can attack.

Remarkably, the appearance of the Styx did not disturb the U.S. Navy's high command. The service, dominated by naval aviators with their carriers, argued that carrier-borne aircraft could strike Soviet targets from 750 miles at sea. Soviet missile boats coming out that far would have to run a gauntlet of air attacks all the way.[14]

Nevertheless, with the appearance of Komars in Cuba in 1962, the same year they reached Egypt, the U.S. Navy began experimenting with converting existing air-to-air missiles for use as ship-to-ship missiles. With the results proving a disappointment, and lacking a sense of urgency, the U.S. Navy discontinued the program. This would be the Navy's position for another decade.

But in this, the U.S. Navy would be virtually alone. Following the success of the Styx missiles launched from missile boats and the sinking of the Israeli destroyer, other navies of the West began to either develop or acquire their own missile boats as well as missiles. In most cases, the programs paralleled motor torpedo boat advances. By the 1970s, "wave-hugging" antiship missiles, either homing on infrared emissions or guided by sophisticated, virtually unjammable radar seekers were available for purchase in the West on the open market. Mounted on small, high-speed, difficult-to-detect seagoing platforms, the missiles with ranges of twenty-five to fifty miles, meant that that for navies with large warships, the only warning of imminent disaster might be a brief alarm by a passive electronic detection system; if the sea skimmer happened to be a "heat-seeker," there might be no warning at all.[15]

In March 1970, a youthful Admiral Elmo R. Zumwalt, Jr., an officer with strong ideas, became the U.S. Navy's Chief of Naval Operations. Among the first programs to be adopted was one to develop a surface-to-surface antiship cruise missile for the U.S. Navy. A second program provided for the development of a small, high-speed missile boat as a platform. Like the discarded PT boat, the missile boat's role would be to strike against enemy surface vessels. Like the PTs of World War II, the proposed missile boats would patrol narrow coastal waters like the Mediterranean. Another use as envisaged by Zumwalt would be to free the U.S. Navy's larger and more expensive warships from operations inside the range of a surprise cruise-missile attack, especially in waters close to hostile shores.

In a radical departure from the conventional, Zumwalt's choice was a 170-ton hydrofoil armed with cruise missiles, the latter yet to be developed by the U.S. Navy. Plans called for six hydrofoils, or PHMs, for Patrol Hydrofoil Missile, to be built by Boeing Aircraft of Seattle, Washington.

Displacing 218 tons, somewhat heavier than planned, the keel of the first boat, *Pegasus,* was laid on November 5, 1973. On June 29, 1974, the controversial Zumwalt's tour as CNO ended. Following Zumwalt's departure, the Navy cancelled the PHM program. In the end, only four of the initially planned six PHMs would be completed. After two years of operations, despite positive reports, the unit would be decommissioned. While visiting the PHM patrol division during its period of operations,[16] the then-Secretary of the Navy J. William Middendorf, asked the commander of the Sixth Fleet, Admiral Frederick Turner, why the U.S. Navy didn't have more fast, missile-armed patrol craft. Not withstanding Admiral Zumwalt's earlier projection for the use of such vessels, Admiral Turner answered that it was a question of [a lack of] a mission.[17] This had been the Navy's standard view for decades, despite the success of the PTs in World War Two.

Although the PHM was based on the concept of the PTs—expendable craft capable of destroying larger vessels with missiles—the PHMs' high silhouette, its deep draft, complexity, and hydrofoil instead a planing hull, were negative factors. The PHMs' draft while foilborne was a mere eight feet, but it is difficult to imagine a PHM patrolling in shallow water near a hostile shore with her high silhouette, a plume of water spewing out behind her, not to mention the sound of her gas turbine engine drawing attention to its presence. In the event the PHM chose to retract its foils and operate on the hull using its auxiliary diesel at a speed of 11 knots and a draft of six feet, to increase speed, the PHM would have to switch back to foils, and in the process, the draft would increase to twenty-three feet. Worse, the PHM with its foils was even more fragile than the planing PT. The two after foils supported 68 percent of the PHM's weight when foilborne, the forward foil supported the rest. If one or more of the struts takes a hit, the boat would settle down with a "swooch" with speed reduced to 12 knots. As recalled, PTs were able to take a considerable number of hits to the hull and maintain speed, the speed of the planing hull sometimes preventing water from entering the boat until speed was reduced, if the boat had been holed below waterline.

On the other hand, certainly the fire-control system and missile armament on the PHM was a vast improvement over that of the PT. But in guns, the PHM with its one remote-controlled 76-mm cannon, left much to be desired: for air defense, the PHM skipper, in the event his one cannon suffered battle damage, would doubtless give a lot to have a number of other guns to shoot with.

Overall, one is inclined to believe the Navy would be best served by the use of a combination of PHMs and PT types, the latter able to operate in shallow waters close to coastal areas, the former to operate in deep water.

In response to the potential threat posed by hostile nations possessing their own small craft with missiles, after years of avoiding the issue, the U.S. appears to once again considering building small surface combatants, currently referred to as littoral combat ships, or LCSs.

As in earlier times, voices within the U.S. Navy have suggested there is a role for a small, high-speed warship; two of the more recent were those of Vice Adm. Arthur K. Cebrowski, at the time president of the Naval War College, and retired Navy Captain Wayne P. Hughes, at the Navy's Post Graduate School. More recently, the concept has had the support of the Chief of Naval Operations, Adm. Vern Clark. He has called for some sixty LCS vessels. But such a program would have to overcome certain major obstacles, one of those being the U.S. Navy's long entrenched aversion to small combatants. It is possible that with the passage of time, Admiral Clark will succeed where Admiral Zumwalt failed. For while the Russian navy is no longer deemed a threat, there is ample historic reason to believe that other enemies exist, namely Communist China with a major fleet of missile and torpedo boats, and any other nation with the ability to purchase such small combatants.

NOTES

INTRODUCTION

1. Cooper, 36
2. Johnson, 19
3. ibid
4. ibid, 23
5. ibid, 25-26
6. ibid, 26; Cooper, 50
7. Johnson, 32; Cooper, 51
8. Connelly, 22
9. ibid, 16
10. Johnson, 15
11. Morison, Vol. II, 262-263
12. Johnson, 46; Gray, 270
13. Johnson, 46-47
14. ibid, 52; Connelly, 32
15. Cooper, 81

ONE: FIRST BLOOD

1. Toland, 211
2. Breuer, 8
3. Connelly, 41
4. ibid
5. Time-Life, *The Rising Sun*, 57
6. Breuer, 14-15
7. ibid, 12
8. Morison, Vol. III, 151
9. Breuer, 13
10. ibid
11. Manchester 212
12. Breuer, 20
13. ibid, 23

14. Manchester 222-223
15. Manchester, 225
16. Breuer, 26
17. Whitman, 122
18. Breuer, 26
19. ibid, 27
20. ibid, 30
21. ibid, 30-31
22. ibid, 32-33
23. Whitman, 253
24. ibid, 267-268

TWO: A GENERAL'S ESCAPE

1. Manchester, 254-255
2. ibid, 254
3. ibid
4. ibid
5. Breuer, 42
6. Breuer, 41
7. ibid
8. Johnson, 43
9. Manchester, 255
10. Breuer, 43-44; Manchester, 255
11. Manchester, 256
12. Breuer, 44
13. Manchester, 257
14. ibid, 256
15. ibid, 257
16. ibid, 255
17. Breuer, 44
18. ibid, 46
19. Manchester, 259
20. Breuer, 46
21. Manchester, 262
22. ibid, 262
23. ibid, 263; Breuer, 49

THREE: TO KIDNAP A PRESIDENT

1. Breuer, 52
2. ibid, 53
3. ibid
4. ibid
5. Perret, 269
6. Breuer, 53; Manchester, 265
7. Breuer, 54
8. ibid
9. ibid, 56
10. ibid
11. ibid, 57
12. ibid
13. ibid
14. ibid, 58
15. ibid, 61; Cooper, 87
16. ibid, 61; ibid, 87
17. ibid, 61; ibid, 87
18. Cooper, 88
19 Breuer, 62; Johnson, 36; Cooper, 88
20. Cooper, 88
21. Breuer, 63
22. Breuer, 64; Cooper, 88
23. Johnson, 46
24. Cooper, 64-65
25. ibid, 65
26. Breuer, 65; Chun, 16; Connelly, 46
27. Breuer, 66; Cooper, 88, 146-147
28. Breuer, 66
29. Bergamini, 1234-1235
30. Breuer, 67; Perret, 299
31. Breuer, 68
32. Breuer, 68; Perret, 299
33. Perret, 219

FOUR: LONG VOYAGES

1. Morison, *The Two Ocean War*, 148
2. Cooper, 147
3. ibid
4. Morison, Vol. VII, 4
5. ibid, 16
6. ibid. 16
7. Johnson, 64
8. ibid, 59
9. ibid
10. ibid, 59
11. ibid, 37
13. Morison, Vol. II, 263; Breuer, 71

FIVE: GUADALCANAL

1. Johnson, 82
2. ibid
3. ibid, 86
4. Dull, 192
5. Johnson, 86
6. Lord, 1, 3; Morison, Vol. V, 10
7. Breuer, 76; Frank, 309
8. Johnson, 86
9. ibid
10. Frank, 316
11. Johnson, 86
12. ibid
13. ibid, 88
14. ibid, 91
15. Frank, 318; Johnson, 95
16. Johnson, 92
17. Frqnk, 318
18. Johnson, 92
19. Frank, 318; Morison, Vol. V, 174
20. Wilmott, 72
21. Morison, Vol. V, 175; Frank, 320-321
22. Morison, Vol. V, 176

23. Frank, 322
24. Morison, Vol. V, 176; Johnson, 95
25. Morison, Vol. V, 178
26. ibid; Frank, 333
27. Morison, Vol. V, 183
28. ibid, 189; Coggins, 99

SIX: PTS VERSUS THE TOKYO EXPRESS

1. Morison, Vol. V, 194; Johnson, 99; Frank, 358
2. Johnson, 99
3. Morison, Vol. V, 224
4. Johnson, 99-100
5. ibid, 101
6. Frank, 407
7. ibid, 421
8. Johnson, 101
9. ibid
10. Frank, 422
11. Johnson, 101
12. Frank, 423
13. Johnson, 104
14. Frank, 461
15. Morison, Vol. V, 262
16. Johnson, 105
17. ibid, 105-06
18. Morison, Vol. V, 262-263; Frank, 464
19. Morison, Vol. V, 263
20. Johnson, 106
21. ibid, 106-107
22. ibid, 107
23. ibid
24. Frank, 490
25. ibid, 498

SEVEN: STARVATION ISLAND

1. Morison, Vol. V, 290
2. Connelly, 46
3. Johnson, 107

4. Orita/Harrington, 130
5. Frank, 527
6. Frank, 500; Orita/Harrington, 131
7. ibid; Orita/ Harrington, 133
8. Frank, 523; Johnson, 108
9. Frank, 523
10. Frank, 499-500; Toland, 418-419
11. Frank, 502; Orita/Harrington, 167
12. Frank, 502
13. Frank, 146; Morison, Vol. V, 81
14. Morison, Vol. V, 313-314
15. Morison, Vol. V, 313
16. ibid, 318
17. O'Conner, 71
18. ibid
19. Frank, 520-521
20. Morison, Vol. V, 319; Johnson, 108; Frank, 520-521
21. ibid; ibid; Frank, 521
22. Johnson, 108
23. Toland, 418
24. O'Conner, 71-72
25. Frank, 523
26. Frank, 523; Johnson, 108
27. Johnson, 108
28. Johnson, 110; Frank, 523-524; Keating, 52
29. Keating, 49-50
30. ibid, 50-51
31. ibid, Frank, 524
32. Keating, 51; Frank, 524
33. Keating, 52
34. O'Conner, 71
35. Toland, 421; Frank, 527
36. ibid; ibid
37. Frank, 493; Morison, Vol. V, 288
38. Smith, 354-355 (USMC)
39. Morison, Vol. V, 330-331
40 Toland, 425
41. Toland, 425; Frank, 538
42. Toland, 426; Frank, 539
43. Frank, 547
44. ibid, 547-548

45. ibid, 548
46. Frank, 549; Johnson, 111
47. Johnson, 111
48. Johnson, 111; Frank, 549; Breuer, 94
49. Frank, 549; Breuer, 95
50. Morison, Vol. V, 339
51. ibid
52. Frank, 582
53. Johnson, 112
54. Frank, 587
55. ibid,
56. ibid, 588
57. ibid
58. Johnson, 112
59. Frank, 595
60. Morison, Vol. V, 371
61. Johnson, 112
62. Morison, Vol. V, 369

EIGHT: THE FORGOTTEN WAR

1. Cooper, 160; Morison, Vol. VI, 47; Keating, 61
2. Cooper, 170; Breuer, 92
3. Morison, Vol. VI, 32
4. Perret, 272
5. Morison, Vol. VI, 47-48
6. ibid, 48; Keating, 63
7. ibid, 49
8. Orita/Harrington, 132
9. Jane's Fighting Ships, 1944-5, 611
10. Mayo, 175
11. ibid, 176
12. Morison, Vol. VI, 53
13. Mayo, 164
14. Keating, 60
15. Morison, Vol. VI, 53; Cooper, 161
16. Ibid; Cooper, 161
17. Breuer, 105-06
18. Morison, Vol. VI, 57-58
19. ibid, 61; Cooper, 162

20. Keating, 67-68
21. Cooper, 163
22. Breuer, 120
23. Keating, 72; Morison, Vol. VI, 137
24. Cooper, 163

NINE: GUADALCANAL NORTH

1. Dyer, 458
2. ibid, 460
3. ibid, 463
4. Donovan, 58
5. Steinberg, 80-81; Morison, Vol. VI, 145
6. Steinberg, 81
7. Orita/ Harrington, 156
8. ibid
10. ibid, 157
11. Morison, Vol. VI, 151; Dyer, 560
12. Morison, Vol. VI, 151; Dyer, 560-61
13. Dyer, 561
14. Morison, Vol. VI, 151
15. ibid, 155
16. ibid, 209; Cooper, 155-56
17. Morison, Vol. VI, 209
18. ibid
19. Keating, 77-78

TEN: *PT 109*

1. Donovan, 36
2. ibid, 38; Johnson, 30
3. Donovan, 42
4. ibid, 44
5. ibid, 45
6. ibid, 72
7. ibid, 73
8. ibid, 76
9. ibid, 77
10. ibid, 79
11. ibid, 84

12. ibid, 90
13. Morison, Vol. VI, 210
14. Donovan, 98
15. ibid, 99
16. ibid, 100
17. ibid, 103
18. ibid, 106
19. Watts, 126-127
20. Breuer, 110; Keating, 81
21. Donovan, 121-212; Morison, Vol. VI, 210
22. Donovan, 127
23. ibid, 132
24. Morison, Vol. I, 211
25. Donovan, 122; Cooper, 151

ELEVEN: ORDEAL

1. Cooper, 152
2. Donovan, 140; Morison, Vol. VI, 211
3. Donovan, 115, 143; Lord, 218-219
4. Donovan, 143
5. Donovan, 143; Lord, 222
6. Lord, 245
7. Donovan, 117; Lord, 7
8. Lord, 7
9. Donovan, 117; Lord, 219-220
10. Lord, 222
11. Donovan, 145
12. ibid, 146
13. ibid, 148
14. ibid, 151-152
16. ibid, 156-57
16. ibid, 149
17. ibid, 155
18. ibid, 157
19. ibid, 159
20. ibid, 163
21. ibid, 162
22. ibid, 165
23. ibid, 166

24. Donovan, 166; Lord, 223
25. ibid; ibid
26. ibid; ibid
27. ibid, 171
28. ibid
29. ibid
30. ibid, 17
31. ibid, 176
32. ibid, 177
33. ibid, 183; Lord, 226
34. Donovan, 183-184
35. Donovan, 184-185 Lord, 228
36. Donovan, 18
37. ibid
38. ibid, 185, 186
39. ibid, 189
40. ibid, 190
41. ibid, 191; Lord, 229

TWELVE: TARGET: VELLA LAVELLA

1. Morison, Vol. VI, 213
2. ibid, 219
3. ibid, 220
4. ibid, 221
5. ibid
6, Connelly, 47
7. ibid
8. ibid
9. Steinberg, 86
10. Morison, Vol. VI, 224
11. Steinberg, 83
12. ibid, 87
13. ibid, ; Morison, Vol. VI, 227
14. ibid; ibid
15. Morison, Vol. VI, 229
16. ibid, 233
17. ibid, 236
18. Breuer, 116
19. Morison, Vol. VI, 242-243

20. Breuer, 122-123
21. Donovan, 197
22. ibid, 197-98

THIRTEEN:
THE RETURN OF JOHN F. KENNEDY

1. Donovan, 196
2. ibid, 198
3. ibid
4. Cooper, 157
5. ibid, 201
6. ibid, 202
7. ibid, 203
8. Morison, Vol. VI, 281; Steinberg, 89
9. Morison, Vol. VI, 293
10. Donovan, 205
11. ibid, 204
12. ibid, 206
13. ibid, 208
14. ibid, 210
15. ibid, 214
16. ibid, 217
17. ibid, 218

FOURTEEN: PTS VERSUS *DAIHATSUS*

1. Morison, Vol. VI, 255
2. ibid, 257
3. Morison, Vol. VI, 257; Johnson, 129
4. Morison, Vol. VI, 257
5. Breuer, 115
6. Morison, Vol. VI, 259
7. ibid, 260
8. Breuer, 119
9. ibid
10. Johnson, 52
11. Breuer, 120
12. ibid, 122
13. ibid, 126

14. Breuer, 130-131; Keating, 97
15. Orita/Harrington, 171
16. ibid, 174
17. ibid, 157, 162
18. Morison, Vol. VI, 268
19. ibid, 273
20. ibid
21. ibid, 273-74
22. Cooper, 164
23. Morison, Vol. VI, 372
24. Breuer, 133
25. ibid, 137
26. Morison, Vol. VI, 379
27. ibid, 372
28. Cooper, 164
29. Breuer, 139; Prados, 300
30. Breuer, 139
31. Tanaka, 112-14
32. Breuer, 140-41
33. ibid, 141
34. ibid. 142; Cooper, 165
35. Breuer, 143; Johnson, 132; Cooper, 165-66
36. Breuer, 145
37. ibid, 146
38. ibid
39. Cooper, 166

FIFTEEN: A BATTLE BETWEEN GENERALS

1. Morison, Vol. VI, 389
2. ibid, 390
3. Orita/Harrington, 192
4. ibid
5. ibid
6. ibid, 192-93
7. Johnson, 132-35
8. Perret, 355
9. Morison, Vol. VI, 435
10. Breuer, 150
11. ibid

12. ibid, 151
13. Morison, Vol. 435
14. ibid, 438
15. ibid, 446
16. ibid, 447; Keating, 93
17. Cooper, 164-65
18. ibid, 162-63
19. Breuer, 152
20. ibid
21. ibid, 153
22. ibid, 153-54
23. ibid, 154
24. Johnson, 135
25. ibid
26. Breuer, 156
27. ibid, 157

SIXTEEN: CHRISTMAS AT BOUGAINVILLE

1. Steinberg, 89
2. ibid, 90
3. Morison, Vol. VI, 303; Steinberg, 89
4. Morison, Vol. VI, 341
5. ibid, 329; Breuer, 132-33
6. Morison, Vol. VI, 329; Keating, 87
7. Morison, Vol. VI, 342-43; Keating, 87-88
8. Breuer, 131-32
9. Morison, Vol. VI, 353
10. ibid, 354
11. ibid, 362
12. ibid, 413
13. ibid, 416
14. ibid, 428
15. ibid, 430
16. ibid, 431

SEVENTEEN: TARGET: DUTCH NEW GUINEA

1. Cooper, 168

2. Keating, 104
3. ibid
4. ibid
5. ibid, 105
6. ibid, 107
7. ibid
8. Morison, Vol. VIII, 66
9. ibid, 67
10. ibid, 70
11. Cooper, 169
12. Breuer, 160
13. Breuer, 162
14. Johnson, 52-54
15. Morison, Vol. VIII, 72
16. Johnson, 137; Keating, 108-109
17. Johnson, 137; Keating, 109-110
18. Morison, Vol. VIII, 73
19. ibid, 74
20. Johnson, 137
21. Morison, Vol. VIII, 74
22. Cooper, 169
23. Morison, Vol. VIII, 91-92
24. Breuer, 165
25. ibid, 169
26. ibid
27. ibid, 169-70
28. ibid, 170; Morison, Vol. VIII, 132
29. Breuer, 170
30. ibid, 172
31. ibid, 173
32. ibid, 174
33. ibid, 171
34. Breuer, 174-175; Keating, 110-111
35. Keating, 110
36. Breuer, 171
37. Morison, Vol. VIII, 143; Johnson, 137
38. Cooper, 170
39. ibid
40. Keating, 122-23

EIGHTEEN: PTS VERSUS F-LIGHTERS AND E-BOATS

1. Morison, Vol. II, 263
2. Johnson, 114
3. Keating, 127
4. Morison, Vol. II, 264
5. Keating, 130
6. ibid
7. Morison, Vol. II, 265
8. ibid
9. Cooper, 179
10. Keating, 133
11. Morison, Vol. II, 266
12. ibid
13. ibid, 276
14. ibid, 277
15. ibid, 278
16 ibid
17. Cooper, 180
18. Morison, Vol. IX, 46
19. ibid, 20-21; Keating, 134-135
20. Morison, Vol. IX, 78; Keating. 135
21. Morison, Vol. IX, 78-79; Keating. 135-136
22. Keating, 136-137
23. Morison, Vol. IX, 187
24. Morison, Vol. IX, 188; Keating, 137-138
25. Morison, Vol. IX, 188
26. Morison, Vol. IX, 189; Connelly, 48; Cooper, 182; Smith, 230-231 (US Navy)
27. Morison, Vol. IX, 189-90; Smith, 531 (US Navy)
28. Smith, 531 (US Navy)
29. ibid, 531-532
30. Morison, Vol. IX, 190
31. Smith, 533
32. Cooper, 181
33. Morison, Vol. IX, 213
34. ibid, 215-16
35. Keating, 142-143
36. Morison, Vol. IX, 301

37. ibid
38. Keating 145; Cooper, 198
39. Cooper, 198
40. Morison, Vol. IX, 308
41. Johnson, 114
42. Keating, 145
43. Morison, IX, 309; Keating, 145-46
44. Keating, 147
45. Morison, IX, 310
46. Keating , 148-49
47. Johnson, 114
48. Keating, 150
49. Johnson, 114
50. ibid, 118
51. ibid
52. ibid; Cooper, 201
53. Ibid, 131; ibid, 202; Keating, 158
54. Keating, 159; Knott, 52-53; Gannon, 177
55. Cooper, 202
56. ibid
57. Keating, 161
58. ibid, 164
59. Cooper, 204

NINETEEN:
ACTION IN THE ENGLISH CHANNEL

1. Cooper, 237
2. ibid
3. ibid
4. Tent, 37
5. ibid, 66
6. Cooper, 239
7. Tent, 144
8. Keating, 169-70
9. Connelly, 49
10. Keating, 171
11. Cooper, 247
12. Keating, 172
13. ibid, 173

14. ibid, 173-74
15. ibid, 174-175
16. Keating, 175; Cooper, 248

TWENTY: THE RIVIERA WAR

1. MacDonald, 321
2. Cooper, 260
3. Keating, 178
4. ibid
5. ibid, 181
6. ibid, 182-84
7. ibid, 188
8. ibid, 190
9. ibid
10. ibid
11. Cooper, 260
12. ibid, 260 -61
13. Keating, 191
14. ibid, 192
15. ibid, 193
16. Rosen, *Proceedings*. April 1985, p.33

TWENTY-ONE: RETURN TO THE PHILIPPINES

1. Johnson, 138; Breuer, 180
2. Breuer, 181
3. ibid, 182
4. Cooper, 268
5. Manchester, 387
6. Johnson, 138
7. ibid; Breuer, 186; Cooper, 268; Keating, 201
8. Keating, 236
9. Breuer, 190
10. Stewart, 95; Morison, *The Two-Ocean War*, 478
11. Stewart, 99; Cooper, 270; Keating, 207; Breuer, 191
12. Stewart, 102; Cooper, 270; Keating, 208-209; Breuer, 192
13 Toland, 559
14. Stewart, 102; Breuer, 193

15. Stewart, 103; Keating, 210
16. Stewart, 103; Breuer, 193
17. Keating, 214
18. ibid
19. ibid, 217
20. Cooper, 270
21. Johnson, 142
22. Cooper, 271
23. Cooper, 271; Keating, 211-212; Stewart, 105
24. Keating, 218

TWENTY-TWO: PTS VERSUS *KAMIKAZES*

1. Warner, 92
2. ibid, 106-08
3. ibid, 108
4. ibid 113
5. ibid, 114
6. Breuer, 200
7. ibid, 200-01
8. Johnson, 144
9. Breuer, 202
10. Keating, 220
11. Cooper, 272; Prados, 693; Breuer, 202; Johnson, 144
12; Cooper, 272-273; Johnson, 144
13. Prados, 694
14. Keating, 222; Breuer, 205
15. Keating, 224
16. Keating, 225; Breuer, 206-207
17. Keating, 225
18. Prados, 695
19. ibid
20. Keating, 227; Breuer, 210
21. Manchester, 405
23. Breuer, 211
24. Keating, 231
25. Breuer, 212; Keating, 232
26. Keating, 232
27. ibid, 233
28. ibid, 233-234

29. Cooper, 273
30. Manchester, 406
31. ibid, 407
32. Warner, 151
33. Morison, *Two-Ocean War*, 482; Warner, 156
34. ibid, 483; ibid, 157
35. Johnson, 144
36. Cooper, 53-54; Warner, 162-163
37. Keating, 234
38. ibid, 235
39. Perret, 438
40. ibid, 450-451
41. Keating, 217
42. Perret, 453
43. Dyer, 1083
44. ibid

EPILOGUE

1. Johnson, 154
2. ibid
3. Breuer, 227
4. Johnson, 5
5. Cooper, 288
6. Toland, 865-866
7. Wheal, Pope and Taylor, 475
8. Chun, 154
9. Baker III, *Proceedings*, May 1972, 244-45
10. Edwards, 56-57
11. ibid, 60-61
12. Rabinovich, 3-10
13. Baker, *Proceedings,* May 1972, 244-245
14. Zumwalt, 76-77
15. Baker III, *Proceedings*, May 1973, 240
16. Kelly, 81
17. ibid, 79

APPENDIX A

U.S. NAVY
ENLISTED RATING ABBREVIATIONS

BM   Boatswain's Mate
EM   Electrician's Mate
FN   Fireman
GM   Gunner's Mate
MM   Machinist's Mate (or MoMM)
PO   Petty Officer
QM   Quartermaster
RM   Radioman's Mate
SC   Ship's Cook
SF   Shipfitter
SM   Seaman
TM   Torpedoman's Mate
SN   Signalman

APPENDIX B

PT Loss Record (Numerically)

22 Foundered in heavy weather	June 11, '43	North Pacific
28 Grounding	Jan. 12, '43	Dora Harbor, Alaska
31 Grounding	Jan. 20, '42	Subic Bay, Philippines
32 Scuttled to avoid capture	Mar. 30, '42	Sula Sea
33 Grounding	Dec. 15, '41	Off Pt. Santiago (Philippines)
34 Sunk by aircraft	April 9, '42	Off Cauit Is. (Philippines)
35 Demolished to avoid capture	April 12, '42	Cebu Island
37 Sunk by surface ships	Feb. 1, '43	Guadalcanal
41 Scuttled to avoid capture	April 15, '42	Mindanao, Philippines
43 Sunk by surface ships	Jan. 10, '43	Guadalcanal
44 Sunk by surface ships	Dec. 12, '42	Guadalcanal
63 Explosion of unknown origin	June 18, '44	Off New Ireland
67 Explosion of unknown origin	Mar. 17, '43	Tufi, New Guinea
68 Grounding	Oct. 1, '43	New Guinea
73 Grounding	Jan. 15, '45	Philippines
77 Sunk by (friendly) ships	Feb. 1, '45	Luzon, Philippines
79 Sunk by (friendly) ships	Feb. 1, '45	Luzon, Philippines
107 Explosion of unknown origin	June 18, '44	Off New Ireland
109 Sunk by surface ship	Aug. 2, '43	New Georgia
110 Sunk by collision	Jan. 26, '44	Off New Georgia
111 Sunk by surface ships	Feb. 1, '43	Guadalcanal
112 Sunk by surface ships	Jan. 10, '43	Guadalcanal
113 Grounding	Aug. 8, '43	Buna, New Guinea
117 Sunk by air attack	Aug. 1, '43	Rendova
118 Grounding	Sep. 7, '43	Vella Lavella
119 Explosion unknown origin	Mar. 7, '43	Tufi, New Guinea
121 Sunk air (friendly) attack	Mar. 27, '44	New Guinea
123 Sunk by air attack	Feb. 1, '43	Guadalcanal
133 Sunk by shore battery	July 15, '44	New Georgia

135 Grounding	April 12, '44	New Britain
136 Grounding	Sep. 17, '43	New Guinea
145 Grounding	Jan. 4, '44	New Guinea
147 Grounding	Nov. 19, '43	New Guinea
153 Grounding	July 4, '43	Solomons
158 Grounding	July 5, '43	Munda Point, Solomons
164 Sunk by air attack	Aug. 1. '43	Rendova Harbor
165 Sunk by submarine	May 23, '43	South Pacific
166 Sunk air (friendly) attack	July 20, '43	New Georgia
172 Grounding	Sep. 10, '43	Vella Lavella
173 Sunk by submarine	May 23, '43	South Pacific
193 Grounding	June 25, '44	New Guinea
200 Sunk by collision	Feb. 22, '44	Aleutians
202 Mined	Aug. 16, '44	Mediterranean
218 Mined	Aug. 16, '44	Mediterranean
219 Foundered in heavy weather	Sep 1944	Aleutians
239 Destroyed by fire, unknown	Dec. 14, '43	Solomons
247 Sunk by shore battery	May 5, '44	Bougainville
251 Sunk by shore battery	Feb. 26, '44	Bougainville
279 Sunk by collision	Feb. 11, '44	Bougainville
283 Shore battery	Mar. 17, '44	Bougainville
300 *Kamikaze*	Dec. 18, '44	Mindoro, Philippines
301 Fire of undetermined origin	Nov. 7, '44	New Guinea
311 Mined	Nov. 18, '44	Mediterranean
320 *Kamikaze*	Nov. 5, '44	Off Leyte, Philippines
321 Grounding	Nov. 11, '44	Philippines
322 Grounding	Dec. 23, '43	New Guinea
323 Sunk by air attack	Dec. 10, '44	Philippines
327 Shore battery	Mar. 7, '44	New Guinea (Hansa Bay)
338 Grounding	Jan. 28, '45	Sula Sea (Philippines)
339 Grounding	May 27, '44	New Guinea (Biak)
346 Air (friendly) attack	April 29, '44	Off New Britain
347 Air (friendly) attack	April 29, '44	Off New Britain
353 Air (friendly) attack	Mar. 27, '44	New Guinea
363 Shore battery	Nov. 25, '44	Morotai
368 Grounding	Oct. 11, '44	Morotai
371 Grounding	Sep. 19, '44	Philippines
493 Sunk by surface ships	Oct. 25, '44	Philippines (Surigao St)

509 Sunk by surface ships   Aug. 9, '44   English Channel
555 Mined   Aug. 23, '44 Mediterranean

* * *

Losses by Cause/Frequency

Cause	Number	Percentage
1. Grounding	21	30.4
2. Air attack	12	17.0
3. Surface warship	8	11.5
4. Explosion/fire unknown origin	6	8.7
5. Shore battery	6	8.7
6. Mined	4	5.8
7. Collision	3	4.3
8. Scuttled	3	4.3
9. Sunk by submarine	2	3.1
10. Storms	2	3.1
11. Lost when ship sunk in transit	2	3.1
Total = 69		100%

Note: The greatest number of boats lost was the result of grounding while patrolling close to shore in the hunt for the elusive *daihatsus*. Second, minus losses due to attacks by "friendly" aircraft, losses due to air attacks drop to the bottom of the list. Finally, all losses caused by mines occurred in the Mediterranean in the final days of that campaign.

GLOSSARY

Americal: a U.S. Army unit formed in early 1942 comprised of men subsequently designated the Americal Division (for "Americans in New Caledonia" Division)

APA: Attack transport

APD: High speed destroyer transport

B-17: Boeing Flying Fortress; a four-engined heavy bomber, USAAF

B-25: North American Mitchell; a twin-engined medium bomber, USAAF

Beaufighter: Twin-engined fighter, 2-man crew, British

"Betty": Mitsubishi, twin-engined torpedo-bomber, 7-man crew, land-based, IJN

"Black Cat": PBY Catalina, painted black for operations in the Pacific in support of Allied naval operations, USN

Bushido: Literally translated, "the way of the warrior." The deep-rooted Japanese belief in the code that prevented surrender to a foe, with death in battle a privilege.

C-47: Sky troop transport, USAAF

Coastal Forces: In the Royal Navy, a unit formed in November 1940 consisting of MTB and MGB flotillas as well as other such small craft engaged in naval operations against the enemy. In the Mediterranean, U.S. PT forces were generally under the command of and part of such Forces.

Contre-Admiral: In French Navy, the equivalent of a U.S. rear admiral.

Corsair: Single-engine, gull-winged fighters, U.S. Navy and Marine Corps

Cruiser: A large warship common to all major navies, generally displacing 8000 tons, capable of speeds in excess of 30 knots. Also a favorite target for motor torpedo boats.

Daihatsu: Motorized landing barge with a shallow draft employed by Japan's military; the PTs' primary foe during much of the war in the Pacific.

DE: Destroyer escort, antisubmarine ship, generally displacing 1,150 tons or more capable of 18 to 24 knots.

Decisive battle: The concept that the outcome of the war could be decided by one massive engagement, a view primarily held by Japan's naval high command.

Destroyer: Essentially ships displacing 1200 to 1500 tons armed with torpedoes, depth charges, and 4.7 or 5-inch guns. Known as "tin cans" because of their thin skin and "greyhounds of the sea" because of their high speed, they were generally used to screen the battle fleet.

E-boat: The Allies term for "Enemy motor torpedo boat." In this case German motor torpedo boat, Highly effective in the coastal waters of Europe, generally considered to be the best motor torpedo boat in operation during World War II.

Escort carrier: Otherwise known as "Jeep" carriers, the ships were developed to provide antisubmarine aircraft to protect convoys. Unfinished merchant hulls converted to carriers.

F4F: Grumman Wildcat, carrier-borne, single engine fighter, USN

F4U: see Corsair

F6F: Grumman Hellcat, carrier-borne, single engine fighter, USN

F-lighter: A steel motorized barge, 163 feet in length, with a top speed of 10 knots, designed to carry supplies and cargo, the most frequently engaged type vessel by PTs in the Mediterranean. Owing to the shallow draft, the F-lighter was virtually immune to the PTs' torpedoes and had to be attacked with guns.

Flak lighter: With F-lighters intercepted by PT boats, to provide increased protection, the Germans converted a number of F-lighters into the flak lighters, adding numerous guns, up to and including the famed 88-mm cannon, weaponry that posed a challenge for ships as heavily armed as cruisers.

Flotilla: Naval unit, generally six - eight vessels, the basic naval unit of the Royal Navy's MTBs and German E-boats.

GN: German Navy

Greater East Asia Co-Prosperity Sphere: A policy pronounced by Japan in 1938 envisaging an Asia united in spirit, under Japan's domination, along with the defeat of the white colonial powers in the Far East.

Higgins boat: See LCVP

IJA: Imperial Japanese Army

IJN: Imperial Japanese Navy

"Jeep" carrier: see escort carrier

Ju-88: Junkers, twin engined fighter and bomber, German Air Force

"Kate": Nakajima B5N, 3-man single-engine, carrier-borne torpedo bomber, Japanese Navy

LCG: Landing craft, guns

LCI: Landing craft, infantry

LCPR: Landing craft, personnel ramp

LCVP: Landing craft vehicle and personnel

LCVPR: Landing craft, vehicle and personnel, ramp

LST: landing ship, tank

Mark VIII torpedo: U.S. vintage torpedo designed for WWI destroyers arming PT boats during the first years of WWII; however, the weapon possessed numerous flaws.

Mark XIII torpedo: U.S. aerial torpedo, replacing the Mark VIII as armament for U.S. PT boats; it, too, possessed numerous flaws.

MAS boat: Italian motor torpedo boat; (Motoscafo Anti-Sommergibile - motor anti-submarine boat). Vessels between 50 and 70 feet in length, armed with two to four torpedoes, plus light machine guns, capable of speeds in excess of 40 knots.

MTB: Motor torpedo boat

P-38: Lockheed Lightning, twin-engined fighter, USAAF

P-39: Bell Airacobra, single-engined fighter, USAAF

P-40: Curtiss Tomahawk, single engine fighter, USAAF

P-47: Republic Thunderbolt, single-engined fighter, USAAF

PBY: Catalina, twin-engined seaplane/amphibian, USN

PB4Y: Catalina, a late model with increased engine power, USN

"Pete": Mitsubishi F1M, a 2-man single engine, reconnaissance, Japanese Navy

PHM: Patrol hydrofoil, USN

Porpoise: A torpedo that once launched, runs erratically on the surface.

Port: As in port side of vessel; the left side when facing forward

Quarter: On a ship, a 45-degree horizontal arc, on either side from astern.

RAA: Royal Australian Air Force

RAN: Royal Australian Navy

RN: Royal Navy

Savo Island: A small island, four and a half miles wide with a 1700- foot high peak standing sentinel over the northwestern approach to Sealark Channel, separated from Guadalcanal's Cape Esperance to the southwest by 7.5 mile wide passage, and 15 miles distant from Florida Island to the north.

Slot: Allied nickname for the New Georgia Sound, the sea passage extending over 300 miles running between the Solomon Islands.

Squadron: Basic unit for American PT boats, usually 12 in number.

Starboard: The right side of a vessel as one faces forward.

TBF: Grumman Avenger, single engine, carrier-borne torpedo-bomber, USN

Tokyo Express: American nickname for Japanese high-speed destroyers making regular runs down the Slot with supplies and fresh troops for Guadalcanal.

Tokyo Rose: Americans' name for feminine propagandist who made regular broadcast over Radio Tokyo, whose sultry voice and playing of popular records made her popular, her purpose being to demoralize Allied troops. A graduate student of UCLA with a degree in zoology, her true name was Iva Ikuko Toguri. After the war she claimed she was coerced by the Japanese into making the broadcasts.

Val: Aichi 99, single-engine, carrier-borne dive-bomber, 2-man crew, Japanese Navy.

Zeke: Mitdsubishi Zero, carrier-borne single-engine fighter, 1-man crew, Japanese Navy.

CHRONOLOGY

Dec 1936 – Admiral Emory S. Land, Chief of Bureau of Construction and Repair, U.S. Navy, submitted a note to the CNO, Admiral Leahy, urging the Navy consider use of motor torpedo boats in view of recent improvements by certain foreign powers, such boats to be employed to defend the nation's coast, freeing the Navy's heavy ships for offensive operations on the high seaes. The note passed on to Navy's General Board for consideration, the suggestion was approved.

May 1937 – Secretary of the Navy Claud Swanson endorsed Board's approval urging development of a number of such experimental craft.

May 1938 – Congress appropriated a $15,000,000 supplement to 1938 Fiscal Year Naval Program for construction of experimental vessels; this was followed by a Navy sponsored design competition for two sizes of boats, a 54- and 70-footer, armament to be two torpedoes, with alternate machine guns or depth charges. Vessels would be capable of at least 40 knots, weigh no more than 20 tons, enabling them to be transported on cargo ships. A prize of $15,000 to go to the winner in each class.

Sep 1938 – With 37 designs received, the Navy chose three in the 54-foot category and five in the larger size; asked for more detailed plans to be received no later than November 7, 1938.

Jan 1939 – Assistant Sec of the Navy Charles Edison approached Henry Sutphen, executive vice president of the multi-division Electric Boat Company with a naval division in Bayonne, New Jersey. Edison proposed the company, with its experience in designing and building small craft, consider participating in the Navy's motor torpedo boat program. Aware Great Britain with its long experience was ahead of the U.S. in building MTBs, the Royal Navy's term for their boats, Edison hoped to persuade Sutphen to go to England at his own expense to purchase British boat to compare with the American boats.

Feb 1939 – With Navy's approval of Edison's plan, Sutphen sailed for England with only a verbal agreement that Edison would do all he could to convince the Navy to purchase the boat once it was in the U.S.

Mar 1939 – The Navy announced the winner in the two categories of the more detailed designs received as requested.

May 1939 – Navy officials announced the awarding of contracts to three boat yards to build six experimental boats based on winning designs. The Navy also to build two boats of its own design in the Philadelphia Navy Yard: The vessels to be constructed numbered 1 through 8. By then the Navy had chosen the term "Patrol Torpedo Boat" for its boats, each to be given a PT number, formed into 12-boat squadrons.

Sep 1939 – Sutphen returned to New York from England aboard the liner *SS President Roosevelt* with a British-built 70-foot Scott-Paine MTB. Two days earlier, World War II broke out in Europe. *PT 9*, the Scott-Paine MTB, was barged to Groton, Conn. for study by Elco engineers.

Dec 1939 – After viewing the British boat, the Navy used the balance of the appropriated funds on a contract with Elco for 23 boats, the boats patterned on the British MTB, with *PT 9*, number needed to form two 12-boat squadrons.

May 1940 – The U.S. Navy proposed three experimental PT squadrons, Squadron 1 to include the eight boats now being built, Squadron 2 containing *PT 9* through *20*, all Elco boats with torpedoes, and squadron 3, with Elco boats armed with depth charges for anti-submarine use.

June 1940 – Having obtained the needed data to build duplicate boats Elco finally turned *PT 9* over to the Navy.

July 1940 – Squadron 1 was formed consisting of only three boats. But by now Squadron 2 had received most of its new Elco boats.

Jan 1941 – Squadrons 1 and 2 carried out test deployments to Cuba via Miami. But Squadron 1 still had a mere four boats, and those proved to be failures. The tests also revealed flaws in the Elco boats of Squadron 2. With new appropriations, the Navy ordered improved boats: the tested boats were turned over to Britain under the Lend-Lease program. The boats of Squadron 3 equipped as sub chasers, soon followed, leased to Britain as gunboats for use in the war in Europe.

With the decision to arm PTs with four torpedoes rather than two, 7 feet would be added, making the Elco 77 feet long.

July 1941 – The Navy conducted tests comparing a second group of PT boats submitted by builders.

Aug 1941 – Unofficially termed the "Plywood Derby," the tests were repeated when one builder protested his boat did not get a fair evaluation. By now Elco's new 77-footers were available to compete. Also participating in the second test were a 76-foot boat built by Andrew Higgins, a boat builder from New Orleans, and a boat built by the Huckins Yacht Company of Jacksonville, Florida.

Dec 1941 – With the tests concluded, the Navy awarded contracts to three builders; having decided the PTs would carry still more armament, the Navy decided the next boats would be between 75 and 82 feet in length. Studying the resultant designs, the Navy decided Elco was to build 36 of the 80-foot design; Higgins, 24 of its 78-footer; and Huckins eight of its 78-footer. By now the Navy had 29 77-foot Elcos in three squadrons, still in experimental stage,

Squadron 1 with 12 boats at Pear Harbor, Squadron 2, with eleven boats in the New York Navy Yard due to be shipped to Panama for defense, and Squadron 3 commanded by Lt. John Bulkeley with six boats, arriving in the Philippines in September, based at Cavite Navy Yard, Manila By.

The Japanese bombed Pearl Harbor.

Mar 1942 – After losing two boats in defense of the island of Luzon, Squadron 3, with the four remaining boats, used by Gen. MacArthur to escape to Mindanao on the first phase of his escape to Australia, the second to be aboard a B-17

The Navy received the last 20 PTs of the original contract for 77-foot Elcos.

April 1942 – With the loss of the remaining four PTs of Squadron 3 in the waters around Mindanao, Lt. Bulkeley and a few squadron officers, under orders from MacArthur, were flown from the Philippines to Australia.

May 1942 – Corregidor Island, the last American bastion of defense in the Philippines, fell to the Japanese. A few lucky Squadron 3 members escaped by submarine, but most became prisoners of war. Nine would die, but 29 would survive to be released at the end of the war.

June 1942 – With the threat of a Japanese attack on Midway Island, Squadron 1 was ordered from Pearl Harbor to Midway as part of the defense, its primary role as scouts before the attack, and rescue vessels for American pilots downed during the Battle of Midway. And to conduct searches for crippled Japanese warships after the battle.

Sep 1942 – Following the U.S. victory at Midway, four PTs, as Division 1 under the command of Lt. Clinton McKellar, were detached from Squadron 1 at Midway and shipped to Seattle. From there the boats proceeded north through the Alaska Inland Passage under their own power, completing a 2500-mile voyage to arrive at

Dutch Harbor. Continuing from there, the four boats began operations in the Aleutians in support of American ground and air units against invading Japanese. During the campaign, PTs in the Aleutians would operate from bases such as Finger Bay, Adak, Amchitka, and Cosco Cove, Attu. Their main foe was the weather.

Jan 1943 – At Bayonne, New Jersey, Elco laid the keel for the first 80-foot boat.

Feb 1943 – The Navy established a PT training academy at Melville, Rhode Island; the staff included PT veterans back from the Pacific.

Apr 1943 – Eight Higgins boats of the newly commissioned Squadron 15 commanded by Lt. Comdr. Stanley Barnes transported aboard transports arrived in the Mediterranean. The Squadron joined the Royal Navy's MTB and MGB flotillas base at Bone, North Africa, in the war against German and Italian forces.

May 1943 – Squadron 15's boats received radar sets from the States; another 10 Higgins PT boats arrived from the States assigned to the squadron. With the advance of Allied troops in North Africa, Squadron 15 and the British flotillas advanced to Bizerta.

July 1943 – Squadron2, now based on the Panama Sea frontier, was instructed to detach eigh boats to form a new Squadron 3. Commanded by Lt. Comdr. Alan R. Montgomery, the squadron was to prepare for shipment "somewhere in the South Pacific."

Aug 1943 – U.S. Marines, 1st Division, landed on Guadalcanal, marking the first American offensive in the Pacific. Within hours, in the Battle of Savo Island, the U.S. Navy suffered a humiliating defeat at the hands of the Japanese Navy. The battle was merely the first in a series witnessed during the six-month campaign for Guadalcanal.

The first four boats of the newly formed Squadron 3 departed Panama on a ship to Noumea, New Caledonia.

Sep 1943 – From his base in Australia, General MacArthur landed the first U.S. troops in New Guinea, opening his campaign for that island against the advancing Japanese army.

Oct 1943 – The four PTs of Squadron 3 led by Comdr. Montgomery, from New Caledonia, arrived at Tulagi Island, the first advanced PT base in the South Pacific, across Sealark Channel from Guadalcanal. Absent available heavy ships of the U.S. Navy due to severe losses, the PTs would provide the Marines fighting on the larger Guadalcanal with close naval support; operations against the "Tokyo Express" began immediately. The squadron's second four PTs reached Tulagi, shipped directly from Panama.

With the outcome of the campaign for Guadalcanal in doubt, Admiral W. Halsey replaced Admiral Ghormley as commander U.S. Naval forces, South Pacific.

Nov 1943 – PTs from Squadron 2 arrived at Tulagi to augment Squadron 3 as the Japanese made another of their series of massive preparations to retake Guadalcanal.

Dec 1943 – A "Black Cat" squadron (PBY patrol planes, painted black) was assigned to the "Canal." As part of night operations, the aircraft worked closely with PT boats.

Marines departed Guadalcanal, replaced by the U.S. Army Americal Division commanded by Gen. Patch. Before leaving, Marine Gen. Vandergrift, commanding the Marines on the island, while not overly pleased by the Navy's heavy ship support, singled out the Tulagi PTs, commending the crews for their aggressive efforts in opposing the Tokyo Express.

Some 600 miles to the west, six PT boats, towed part way, arrived at New Guinea's Milne Bay as support for Gen. MacArthur. Designated Division 17 under the command of Lt. Daniel S. Baughman, as in the case of Guadalcanal, owing to the lack of available U.S. Navy warships, the PTs were to provide naval support in the ground war against the Japanese.

With the war over 200 miles west of Milne Bay, Divison 17 established an advanced base at Tufi, close to the fighting. The PTs' main opponent were *"Daihatsus,"* Japanese motorized landing barges, the principal craft used by the enemy to supply the New Guinea garrisons, along with a number of submarines.

Jan 1944 – MacArthur's troops inflicted a major defeat against the Japanese at New Guinea's Buna, the first such victory against the Japanese in the war. However, Colonel J. Sladen Bradley, chief of staff, U.S. 32nd Inf. Div., noted by cutting off the enemy's supplies the PTs at Tufi played a significant part in bringing about the victory. Australian General Edmund Herring, commanding Allied forces in New Guinea, also credited the night patrolling PTs and daylight sweeps by MacArthur's planes with weakening the enemy to the point of defeat.

Feb 1944 – Guadalcanal was declared secured following the Japanese evacuation of the island. Army General Patch commended the Tualgi PTs and issued medals to the men for their part in winning the struggle for the island.

In New Guinea, newly formed squadrons, Squadron 7 led by now Lt. Comdr. John Bulkeley, on a second tour, and Squadron 8, led by Lt. Comdr. Barry Atkins, arrived. A main PT rear base, nicknamed "Fall River," was established at Kona Kope, Milne Bay. Commander Morton C. Mumma, former skipper of the U.S. submarine *Sailfish*, was appointed commander of New Guinea PT boats under Gen. MacArthur.

In the Solomons, PT Squadron 2 and destroyers provided naval support for Allied amphibious landings in the Russells, the next group of islands north of Guadalcanal. A new advanced PT base was established in the Russells.

Mar 1944 – In New Guinea, PTs under Comdr. Mumma, were designated Task Group 70.01 (Motor Torpedo Boats Seventh Fleet), responsible to Gen. Macarthur. In the Battle of the Bismarck Sea, the Japanese suffered a major defeat while attempting to reinforce New Guinea with ships from Rabaul laden with troops and equipment. In attacks by MacArthur's air force and New Guinea PTs, the enemy lost all transport ships and many escorting destroyers as well as some 3000 of the 6900 crack troops. After the battle, Tokyo Rose referred to the PTs as "the Butchers of the Bismarck Sea," threatening dire treatment if captured.

Although starvation now threatened their troops in New Guinea, the Japanese would rely on the less effective *Daihatsus* and submarines to supply their garrisons, a method, due to the aggressive patrolling PTs, that failed.

April 1944 – MacArthur was appointed commander of the Southwest Pacific Area. Adm. Halsey prepared to advance north through the Solomons, target Rabaul.

Lt. John F. Kennedy arrived at Tulagi, now a rear base, and was given command of *PT 109*, replacing the departing skipper returning home.

May 1944 – Tufi-based PTs, keeping pace with MacArthur's advancing ground forces, moved forward to a new base at Morobe.

Lt. John F. Kennedy, commanding *PT 109* with a new crew, arrived at the Russells and began operations.

June 1944 – PT boats in the Solomons joined in support of amphibious landings on the islands of New Georgia and Rendova.

Simultaneously, MacArthur's PT boats, part of an amphibious operation, with PTs carrying troops, landed men at New Guinea's Nassau Bay.

July 1944 – At Rendova, Captain E. J. Moran, former skipper of the cruiser *Boise*, assumed command of four PT squadrons supporting the New Georgia campaign, Squadrons 5, 9, 10, and 11, all told some 52 boats, operating from Rendova Island, across six-mile-wide Blanche Channel from New Georgia Island, and a second base at Lever Harbor on New Georgia Island facing the Slot.

Lt. Kennedy arrived at Rendova with *PT 109* and jined other PTs engaged in the campaign for New Georgia. PT boats from Lever Harbor landed Army and Marine scouts on the island of Vella Lavella, north of the island of Kolombangara and returned them to base.

Aug 1944 – *PT 109* commanded by John Kennedy was run down by a destroyer, one of four Japanese ships making a supply run to Kolombangara from Rabaul: two *109* crewmen were lost. Aided by an Australian Coastwatcher, almost a week later, Kennedy and his surviving crew returned to Rendova.

New Georgia fell to Allied troops as Japanese troops finally evacuated the island to Kolombangara.

U.S. troops in the Solomons, led by PT boats, bypassed Kolombangara to land of Vella Lavella. A new advanced PT base was established at Vella Lavella's Lambu Lambu cove facing the Slot.

In New Guinea, new 80-foot Elco boats from Squadron 12, the first squadron was shipped from the States equipped with the new Mark XIII torpedo with new roll-off racks, plus 40-mm cannon mounted aft for use against barges. The squadron skipper was veteran PT officer, Lt. Comdr. John Harllee.

Sep 1944 – At Tulagi, Lt. Kennedy recovered from his ordeal with the loss of *PT 109*, rather than going home, volunteered to command *PT 59*, and older 77-foot Elco being converted to a gunboat to cope with enemy barges.

With the enemy's evacuation of Vella Lavella, Admiral Halsey prepared to land troops on Bougainville to establish a PT base and build an airstrip. Allied aircraft based at Bougainville would be in range of the major enemy base, Rabaul.

Oct 1944 – Lt. John Kennedy with *PT 59* arrived at Lambu Lambu to join a small force of PTs patrolling Choiseul Island, the enemy's last stronghold in the Central Solomons.

PTs, by order of Adm. Wilkinson, commanding the advance in the Solomons, landed a reconnaissance party in the Treasuries just south of the big island of Bougainville and the Shortlands.

Nov 1943 – To support American troops landed on Bougainville at Empress Augusta Bay, PT boats in the Solomons moved forward and began operations from Capt Torokina, Empress Augusta Bay and the Treasuries.

Lieutenant Kennedy, weak from malaria and a painful back, aggravated by the impact on *PT 109* by the enemy destroyer, left *PT 59* and departed for the States.

Squadron 21, commanded by Comdr. Selman Bowling, a newly commissioned Elco squadron, arrived at Morobe. Like Squadron 12, all boats were radar equipped and similarly armed with new torpedoes and 40-mm cannon.

Dec 1944 – With MacArthur's troops continuing to advance, the PTs abandoned Morobe for a new advance base at Dreger Harbor. They were joined by Squadrons 18 led by Lt. Henry Swift, 24 commanded by Lt. Comdr. N Burt Davis, Jr., and 25 skippered by Lt. James R. Thompson.

Tokyo sent a message to its New Guinea field commanders ordering the destruction of PTs as a preliminary to further operations.

In the Solomons, Allied troops on Bougainville completed an airstrip and bombers began attacking Rabaul.

Jan 1945 – Following MacArthur's advances, PTs at Dreger Harbor extended their patrols still further west. Having advanced a mere 240 miles in six months, with over 2000 miles still separating him from Manila, MacArthur decided to lengthen his leaps.

Anxious to maintain the speed of his drive, Admiral Halsey dispatched two PT boats from Bougainille to scout the Green Islands. He meant to establish another PT base and construct an airfield as a further link in the chain around Rabaul. The PTs with positive information, returned from the mission.

Feb 1945 – As ordered by Admiral Halsey, an amphibious invasion force accompanied by destroyers and 18PTs, including boats from Squadron 10, landed the 4th Marine Regiment in the Green Islands encountering no opposition. PT boats began operation from the new base.

In New Guinea, troops under the command of Gen. MacArthur, supported by PT Squadron 18 and 21 plus destroyers, landed troops of the U.S. 1st Cav. led by Maj. Gen. Innis P. "Bull" Swift in the Admiralty Islands.

April 1945 – U.S. troops supported by PT boats and destroyers, secured a victory on the Admiralties. General Swift took pains to declare the victory was in no small way the result of close naval support. PTs immediately began operating from a new advanced base at the Admiralties Seeadler Harbor. With an added base at Talasea, MacArthur's PTs now patrolled four areas: the northern New Guinea coast, the Admiralties, and northern and southern New Britain – Squadron 24 based at Saidor was reinforced by Squadron 10, the first transferred to New Guinea from the Solomons.

MacArthur's troops leap-frogged to Hollandia, in Dutch New Guina; Dreger Harbor PTs moved forward in support, Squadrons 12 and 18 to Hollandia, Squadrons 7 and 8 to Aitape.

Squadron 2, recommissioned with four Higgins boats, shipped to the English Channel under Lt. Comdr. John Bulkeley to support cloak-and-dagger operations preceding the Allied invasion of France.

May 1945 – Three newly commissioned squadrons, Squadron 34 commanded by Lt. A. Harris; Squadron 35 led by Lt. Comdr. N. Richard Davis, Jr.; and Squadron 30 commanded by Guadalcanal veteran Lt. Robert Searles were shipped from the States to the English Channel in anticipation of the Allied invasion of Europe. PTs in the Channel were placed under the command of John Bulkeley.

In the Solomons, following fierce fighting, Japanese on Bougainville were isolated. U.S. airstrip at Empress Augusta Bay began launching bombing raids on Rabaul: Army General Griswold, commanding Allied ground forces at Bougainville, paid the PTs, destroyers and gun-armed LCIs credit for the Bougainville victory.

In New Guinea, the U.S. 41st Div. under General MacArthur landed on the island of Biak at the western tip of New Guinea. As ground troops battled for Biak, PT Squadron 12 arrived at Mios Woendi, a small island 10 miles south of Biak as naval support, whereupon the startled squadron was warned by Tokyo Rose during a radio broadcast that they should expect an immediate air attack.

June 1945 – PTs based at Aitape, joined by Allied cruisers and destroyers from Seeadler Harbor, supported U.S. Army forces defending Aitape against attacks by bypassed Japanese troops.

In the Mediterranean, Squadron 15, as part of the Royal Navy, supported Allied amphibious landings on Pantelleria Island off the coast of Sicily.

In the English Channel, three PT boats spearheaded the Allied invasion of France.

July 1945 – Mediterranean based Squdaron 15, temporarily detached from British command, joined forces with the U.S. Navy in the invasion of Sicily – Squadron 15 moved forward from North Africa and began operations from Palermo, Sicily.

Aug 1945 – Axis troops retreated en masse from Sicily to the Italian mainland: Two new PT squadrons, 22 and 29, arrived in the Mediterranean and began operations under the overall command of Lt. Comdr. Barnes. The PTs supported the Allied invasion of southern France.

In New Guinea, PT Squadrons 24 and 25 advanced from Mios Woendi to the island of Sansapor.

Sep 1945 – Italy surrendered to the Allies. Only German forces defend Italy.

In New Guinea, General MacArthur landed forces on the small island of Morotai, slightly less than half way to the Philippines. PT squadrons 10, 12, 18 and 33, some 41 boats, with PT tenders *Oyster Bay* and *Mobjack* arrived at Morotai and began operations.

Oct 1945 – Following the Normandy invasion and reduced enemy resistance, with the exception of Squadron 35, PT squadrons in the English Channel were disbanded; some boats turned over to the British, some to Russia under Lend-Lease agreements, others sent back to the Melville training squadron.

In the Mediterranean, Barnes's PTs, once more under British command, joined MTB and MGB flotillas, based at Sardinia, La Maddalena, then Bastia and Calvi, on the island of Corsica.

With enemy resistance finally on the wane, Squadron 15, after 18 months service in the Mediterranean, was disbanded, its boats turned over to the Royal Navy, the crews shipped back to the States. Soon, all other Mediterranean-based PT squadrons followed, with one exception, their boats handed over to the British, or sent to Russia under Lend-Lease. Only Squadron 22 remained, based at Leghorn, Italy.

In New Guinea, Squadrons 24 and 25 returned to Mios Woendi from Sansapor, as few enemy vessels were encountered at the forward island. By now, Squadrons 9, 10, 12, 18 and 21 were based at Mios Woendi, to be joined by Squadrons 13, 16 and 36, making this the biggest PT base thus far established.

MacArthur's forces landed in the Philippines, on Leyte Island. Squadrons 7, 12, 21, 33 and 36, a total of 45 boats under their own power accompanied by the PT tender *Oyster Bay* and the seaplane tender *Half Moon*, completed the voyage to Leyte and began immediate operations against Japanese forces.

Remaining behind at Morotai were Squadrons 10 and 18, later joined by Squadron 11, as assurance the 37,000 enemy troops on Halmahara Island remained isolated, preventing the enemy retaking Morotai.

Nov 1945 – Following the defeat of the Japanese Navy in the Battle of Leyte Gulf, the enemy resorted to *kamikaze* attacks on U.S. ships, including PT boats and their tenders. As the battle for Leyte dragged on, MacArthur continued his advance: an 80-ship amphibious force departed Leyte Gulf for Mindoro Island. The escort included PT Squadrons 13 and 16.

Owing to the continuous threat of kamikazes, no PT tenders accompanied the force – as anticipated, *kamikazes* launched attacks throughout the voyage, inflicting losses.

Dec 1945 – On Leyte, in an effort to disrupt theenemy's supply lines to the island, PT Squadrons 7 and 12 began operations from Ormoc Bay, located n the opposite side of the island.

A second convoy, the first phase of the Allied invasion of Luzon, 61 vessels, departed Leyte Gulf. The convoy included the PT tender *Orestes*, and an escort of 29 PT boats as close escort; destroyers provided additional support. Due to the *kamikaze* threat, no Allied cruisers, battleships or carriers accompanied the invasion fleet.

Jan 1946 – MacArthur's invasion fleet reached Luzon. Following the invasion by U.S. troops, Japanese suicide boats slipped from shore and attacked anchored American ships in the harbor, creating panic and chaos. PT boats were assigned to ferret out the suicide boats.

Feb 1946 – Additional PT squadrons moved from New Guinea to the Philippines.

Mar 1946 – The U.S. 8th Army captured Cebu. By now, PTs based at Ormoc Bay had sunk over 140 *daihatsus* and 60 other small craft carrying supplies to the Japanese on Leyte.

Following the defeat of the Japanese on Corregidor, General MacArthur boarded a PT boat for the return trip from Manila t Corregidor. The Japanese in the Philippines were defeated.

May 1946 – Germany surrendered, ending the war in Europe.

Aug 1946 – Japan surrendered. U.S. Navy disposed of its World War II PTs.

1951 – Four new experimental PT boats designated Squadron 1, were delivered to U.S. Navy for tests.

The Soviet Union continued development of motor torpedo boats based on 80-foot Elco PTs received frm U.S. Navy in World War II

1957 – Navy completed tests on PTs, deciding PT boats lacked a mission in the U.S. Navy.

1960s – Soviets continued advances resulted in a motor torpedo boat armed with a cruise missile, introducing a new naval weapon in the field of naval warfare.

BIBLIOGRAPHY

Baker, III, Arthur Davidson. "Small Combatants." *Proceedings, United States Naval Institute* (May 1972): pp. 240-263
———. "Small Combatants." *Proceedings, United States Naval Institute* (May, 1973): pp. 239-269

Bergamini, David. *Japan's Imperial Conspiracy.* New York: William Morrow & Co., Inc., 1971.

Blair, Clay, Jr. *Silent Victory.* Philadelphia & New York: J.B. Lippincott Co., 1975.

Breuer, William. *Devil Boats.* Novato, Ca.: Presidio, 1987.

Breyer, Siegfried. *Guide to the Soviet Navy.* Annapolis: U.S. Naval Institute, 1971.

Chun, Victor. *American PT Boats in World War II.* Atglen, Pa: Schiffer Military/Aviation History, 1997.

Coggins, Jack. *The Campaign for Guadalcanal.* Garden City, New York: Doubleday & Co., 1972.

Connelly, T. Garth. *PT Boats in Action.* Carrollton, Texas: Squadron/Signal Publications, Inc., 1994.

Cooper, Bryan. *The Battle of the Torpedo Boats.* New York: Stein and Day, 1970.

Couhat, Jean Labayle and A.D. Baker, III. *Combat Fleets of the World 1982/1983.* Annapolis: U.S. Naval Institute, 1982.

Donovan, Robert J., *PT-109: John F. Kennedy in World War II.* New York: McGraw-Hill, Inc., 1961.

Dull, Paul S. *The Imperial Japanese Navy (1941-1945).* Annapolis: U.S. Naval Institute Press, 1978.

Dyer, George C. *The Amphibians Came to Conquer.* Vol. I and Vol. II, Washington D.C.: US Printing Office.

Edwards, Steve. "Stalking the Enemy's Coast." *Proceedings, United States Naval Institute* (February, 1992): pp. 56-62

Frank, Richard B. *Guadalcanal.* New York: Random House, 1990.

Gannon, Robert. *Hellions of the Deep.* University Park, Pennsylvania: Penn State Press, University Park, Pennsylvania, 1996.

Gravett, Brent L. "Peter Tare and the PHM." *Proceedings, United States Naval Institute* (August 1984): pp. 129-131

Gray, Edwyn. *The Devil's Device: Robert Whitehead and the History of the Torpedo.* Annapolis: US Naval Institute, 1975, updated 1991.

Inoguchi, Captain Rikihei, IJN, and Tadashi, Commander Nakajima, IJN. *The Divine Wind.* New York: Bantam Books, 1950.

Jane's Fighting Ships, 1939. New York: Arco, 1939.

Jane's Fighting Ships, 1944-1945. Great Britain: Marston, 1944.

Johnson, Frank D. *United States PT Boats of World War II.* Dorset, England: Blanford, 1980.

Keating, Bern. *The Mosquito Fleet: History of the PT Boat in World War II.* New York: G.P. Putnam's, 1963.

Kelly, John P. "Requiem for the PHM Program." *Proceedings, United States Naval Institute* (August 1977): pp. 79-81

Knott, Richard C. *Black Cats of WWII.* Annapolis: Nautical and Aviation Publishing Co. of America, 1981.

Lord, Walter. *Coastwatcher of the Solomons.* New York: Viking Press, 1977.

MacDonald, Charles B. *The Mighty Endeavor.* New York: Oxford University Press, 1969.

Macintyre, Donald. *The Naval War Against Hitler.* New York: Charles Scribner's Sons, 1971.

Manchester, William. *American Caesar.* Boston and Toronto: Little, Brown and Company, 1978.

Mayo, Lida. *Bloody Buna.* New York: Doubleday and Company, 1974.

Morison, Samuel. *The Two Ocean War.* Boston and Toronto: Little, Brown and & Company, 1963.

Morison, Samuel. *History of the United States Naval Operations in World War II.* Boston: Little, Brown and Co. Vol I, 1984; Vol II, 1984; Vol III, 1982; Vol IV, 1975; Vol V, 1989; Vol VI, 1988; Vol VII, 1984; Vol VIII, 1989; Vol IX, 1990; Vol X, 1956.

O'Conner, Raymond. *The Japanese Navy in World War II.* Annapolis, MD: U. S. Naval Institute, 1969.

Orita, Zenji and Joseph D. Harrington. *I-Boat Captain.* Canoga Park, Ca.: Major Books, 1976.

Perret, Geoffrey. *Old Soldiers Never Die.* New York: Random House, 1996.

Prados, John. *Combined Fleet Decoded.* New York: Random House, 1995.

Prefer, Nathan. *MacArthur's New Guinea Campaign.* Conshohocken, Pa.: Combined Books, 1995.

Rabinovich, Abraham. *The Boats of Cherbourg.* New York: Seaver Books/ Henry and Comp., Inc. 1988.

Rosen, Lt. Comdr Fred W., USN Retired. "Peter Tare and the PHM." *U.S. Naval Proceedings*, p. 33, April 1995

Smith, S.E. *The United States Navy in World War II.* New York: William Morrow & Co. Inc. 1966.

Smith, S.E. *The United States Navy in World War II.* New York: Random House, 1969.

Steinberg, Rafael. *Island Fighting.* Alexandria, Va.: Time-Life, 1978.

Stewart, Adrian. *The Battle of Leyte Gulf.* Scribner's Sons, New York, 1979.

Tanaka, Yiki. *Hidden Horrors, Japanese War Crimes in World War II.* Boulder: Westview Press, A Division of Harper Collins, 1996.

Taylor, John W.R. *Combat Aircraft of the World.* New York: G.P. Putnam's Sons, 1969.

Tent, James Foster. *E-Boat Alert.* Annapolis: Naval Institute Press, 1996.

Toland, John. *The Rising Sun.* New York: Random House, 1970.

Watts, A.J. *Japanese Warships of World War II*, Garden City, New York: Doubleday & Company, Inc., 1966 (reprinted 1970).

Vego, Milan. "Their Torpedo Tactics." *Proceedings, United States Naval Institute,* (June 1984): 58-63.

Vego, Milan. "Their Torpedo Tactics." *Proceedings, United States Naval Institute,* (July, 1984): 139-41.

Warner, Dennis and Peggy. *The Sacred Warriors.* New York – London: Van Nostrand Reinhold Co., 1982.

Wheal, Elizabeth-Anne. *Encyclopedia of the Second World War.* Secaucus, N.J.: Castle Books, 1989.

Whitman, John. *Bataan: Our Last Ditch.* New York: Hippocrene, 1990.

Zich, Arthur. *The Rising Sun.* Alexandria, Va.: Time-Life, 1977.

Zumwalt, Elmo R. Jr. *On Watch.* New York: Quadrangle, 1976.

Wilmott, H.P. *The Barrier and the Javelin.* Annapolis: Naval Institute Press, 1983

INDEX

A

A-BOMB, 387

ABE, Rear Adm. Hiroaki, IJN, 69

Abukuma, light cruiser, IJN, 357-359

  Sunk, Oct. 26, 1944, 358

ADACHI, Gen. Hatazo, IJA, 209, 234, 252-263, 268-271, 279

ADAK (Alaska), 44-46

ADAMS, Lt. Charles, USN, 385

ADMIRALTIES, The, 237-241, 247-248, 256, 262, 270, 281

ADRIATIC SEA, 321

AEGEAN ISLANDS, 289

AFRIKA KORPS, 285

AH CHEU, 22, 25

AINSWORTH, Rear Adm. W. L. "Pug," USN, 131-132, 183

AITAPE (New Guinea), 263-265, 268-271, 273, 276-277, 279

Akebono, dd, IJN, 151

AKERS, Ens. Anthony, USN, 4, 10, 20, 23, 25, 31-33, 39

ALAFUZOV, Adm., SN, 394

ALASKA, xx, 44-45

  Inland Passage, 44

ALBERT, SM2/c Raymond, USN, 147, 170, 193, 196

ALGIERS (North Africa), 284, 294

ALGERIA (North Africa), 394, 398

ALICUDI ISLAND, 302

ALLAN, Lt. Comdr, Robert A., RN, 285, 288, 299, 303, 312-315, 317

ALLIED INTELLIGENCE BUREAU (AIB), 227

Amagiri, dd, IJN, 151-152, 154-157, 159-160

AMCHITKA (Alaska), 44-46

AMSDEN, Jr., Lt. Ralph, USN, 91

AMSTERDAM ISLAND (New Guinea), 280

ANAMI, Gen. K., IJA, 263

ANNAPOLIS, MARYLAND, 396

ANNAPOLIS NAVAL ACADEMY, 141, 150-151, 212

ANDREWS, Capt. C. L., USN, 302-303

Anthony, dd, US, 252

ANTIBES, The, 334

ANZIO (North Africa), 307-308, 341

Arashi, dd, IJN, 85, 152

ARAWE (New Britain), 226-227, 229-230, 233

ARBUCKLE, Lt. E. C., USN, 290, 295-297

Ariake, dd, IJN, 66

Arizona, bb, US, 2

Asanagi, dd, IJN, 151

ASTROLABE BAY, 233

ATKINS, Lt. Comdr. Barry K., USN, 114, 117, 120-121, 223-224

Atlanta, light cruiser, US, 69

  Sunk, Nov. 13, 1942, 69

ATLANTIC OCEAN, 283, 324-325

ARNOLD, Gen. Hap, USAAF, 326, 329

Asagumo, dd, IJN, 354

Ashigara, heavy cruiser, IJN, 357

ATTU (Alaska), 44-46

AUGUSTA (Sicily), 292, 299-300

MTB (British) (cont.)
  MTB 61, 286
    Lost, May 9, 1943, 286
  MTB 77, 286
  MTB 265, 285
  MTB 288, 300
    Sunk, July 21, 1943, 300
  MTB 316, 285, 299
    Sunk, July 17, 1943, 299
  MTB 423, 339
  MTB 633, 314
  MTB 634, 312
  MTB 640, 314
  MTB 655, 314
  MTB 665, 300
    Sunk, August 15, 1943
  Flotilla, 288-289, 312, 321
    7th, 303, 317-318, 333
    18th, 288
    20th, 303
    23rd, 288
  MTB/MGB Flotilla
  56th, 318
MUNDA (New Georgia), 113, 131,
    133, 141-142, 146, 162, 183,
    186, 191, 200
  Airstrip, 141, 186
  Point, 125
MUMMA, Jr., Comdr. Morton C.,
    USN, 114, 117, 120, 226
MUNROE, Lt. Pat, USN, 138
MURPHY, Lt. (jg) Charles H.,
    USN, 340
MURRAY, Lt., USN, 189-190
Murasame, dd, IJN, 67
MUSSOLINI, 301-303
MUTTY, Lt. J. B. USN, 284, 295-
    296

N

Nachi, heavy cruiser, IJN, 357, 359
NAGLE, Lt. R. A., USN, 339

Naganami, dd, IJN, 57, 85, 88
NAGATA, Lt. Comdr., IJN, 274
Nagatsuki, dd, IJN, 100
NAGUMO, Vice Adm. C., IJN, 3
NANKING, CHINA, 200
NAPIER-LION ENGINE, xvi
NAPLES (Italy), 295, 302-303, 307
NAPOLEON, 303, 318
NARU ISLAND, 174-179
NASH, Cpl. Benjamin Franklin,
    USA, 161, 163
Nashville, light cruiser, US, 239,
    343, 346-347, 380, 373
NASSAU BAY, 120-121, 125-126,
    209
Nasty-class gunboat, US, 396
NAVAL BATTLE OF
    GUADALCANAL, 69, 73, 76,
    82, 88, 96
NAVAL WAR COLLEGE, 402
NAVY CROSS, 232, 317, 358,
    378, 390
NAVY AND MARINE CORPS
    MEDAL, 195-196
NATO, 398
NEALE, Comdr. Edgar T., USN,
    109
NEGROS ISLAND, 26, 30-32, 41,
    237, 248
NELSON, MoMM2/c Clarence L.,
    USN, 266
NEW BRITAIN, Island Of, 106,
    116, 119, 151, 209-210, 221,
    223-227, 229, 232, 240-241,
    246-247, 260, 281
  Described, 223
NEW GEORGIA, Island Of, 120,
    124-127, 129-131, 133-135,
    138-152, 145, 148, 161, 163,
    185-187, 189, 200, 250, 386-
    387
NEW GEORGIA SOUND
  See, THE SLOT

INDEX continued.

WESTERN NAVAL TASK FORCE, 292, 325, 240
WESTINGHOUSE, 147
WEWAK (New Guinea), 82, 262-265, 268, 270
White Plains, escort carrier, US, 364
WHITE, Ens. A. E. "Whitey," USN, 99
WHITE, Lt. (jg) Byron R. "Whizzer," USN, 198, 390
WHORTON, Lt. Calvin R., USN, 327, 330
WIGHT, Isle Of, 326
"WILDCAT" See F4F
WILKINSON, Rear Adm. Theodore S., USN, 127-128, 183, 185, 187-188, 190, 192, 251, 256
WILKS, Adm. USN, 329
WILLIAMS, Lt. John B., USN, 218
WILLIAMS, Lt. (jg) Robert J., USN, 260
Wilson, dd, US, 185, 377
Wilton, dd, British, 287
WOOD, Garfield "Gar," xv-xvi
WOOD, Lt. Leighton C., USN, 189
WOODLARK ISLAND, 119, 121
WORLD WAR I, x-xi, 339
WORLD WAR II, ix, xii-xvi, xx, 35, 73, 93, 207, 236, 305, 382, 400
WRIGHT, Rear Adm. Carleton, USN, 78-79
WRIGHT, Lt. G. S., USN, 381

X

Y

YALE UNIVERSITY, 274
YAMAGATA, Gen. IJA, 113
Yamagumo, dd, IJN, 354
YAMAMOTO, Adm. IJN, 43, 59-61, 64, 69, 83, 94-95, 218
Yamashiro, bb, IJN, 353-354, 357
Sunk, Oct. 25, 1944, 357
YAMASHIRO, Capt. Katsumori, IJN, 151-152, 155, 157
YAMAZAKI, PO Yoshitake, IJN, 157
YOKOSUKA NAVAL BASE, 152
YOSHIKAWA, PO *Shigeo, IJN,* 157
YOUNG, Lt. H. G., USN, 357
Yubari, light cruiser, IJN, 129
Yugiri, dd, IJN, 254
YUGOSLAVIA, 395
Yugumo, dd, IJN, 101, 192
Sunk, Oct. 6, 1943, 192

Z

Zane, dd-minesweeper, US, 63
"ZEKE" (Allied code-name for Japanese fighter [Mitsubishi]) See ZERO
ZELL DE JONG, GM1/c Gerard E., USN, 2
"ZERO" (Allied code-name for Japanese fighter [Mitsubishi]), 6, 231, 273, 363-364, 366
ZINZER, MoMM1/c Gerard E., USN, 147, 155
ZUMWALT, Jr., Adm. Elmo, USN, 400-402

Howard F. West, back row, fourth from left, with the rest of the PT crew

ABOUT THE AUTHOR

Howard F. West enlisted in the Navy in 1942. Following boot camp at Great Lakes and torpedo school at Keyport, Washington, he volunteered for service on PT boats and completed the course at the Motor Torpedo Boat training center at Melville, Rhode Island. Shipped to the Southwest Pacific, he arrived at the advanced PT base at Rendova Island in the Solomons where he was assigned to Motor Torpedo Squadron 11, PT-185. In the months that followed, Squadron 11 continued to patrol, moving forward to other island bases in support of advancing Allied ground forces. At the time the war in the Pacific ended, Squadron 11 was based at Morotai Island, midway between New Guinea and the Philippines.

Discharged at the end of the war, the author used his extensive collection of books and articles acquired over following years, along with his own experiences during the war, to write his book. He is currently researching a book concerning the Imperial Japanese Navy in World War Two. He lives in Tacoma, Washington.